The Thirty Years War
A Documentary History

The Thirty Years War
A Documentary History

Edited and Translated, with an Introduction, by
Tryntje Helfferich

Hackett Publishing Company, Inc.
Indianapolis/Cambridge

14 13 12 11 10 09   1 2 3 4 5 6 7

For further information, please address:

Hackett Publishing Company, Inc.
P.O. Box 44937
Indianapolis, IN 46244-0937

www.hackettpublishing.com

Cover design by Deirdre Helfferich
Composition by Agnew's, Inc.
Map by David E. Chandler
Printed at Versa Press, Inc.

Library of Congress Cataloging-in-Publication Data

The Thirty Years War : a documentary history / edited and translated, with
    an introduction, by Tryntje Helfferich.
      p. cm.
    Documents in English; translated from Early New High German, French,
      Swedish, and Latin.
    Includes bibliographical references and index.
    ISBN 978-0-87220-940-4 (cloth)—ISBN 978-0-87220-939-8 (pbk.)
      1. Thirty Years' War, 1618–1648—Sources.   I. Helfferich, Tryntje,
    1969–
    D251.T457   2009
    940.2'4—dc22

                                                     2008048354

CONTENTS

Map: The Holy Roman Empire, 1618–1648   vii

General Introduction   ix

I. Outbreak of the Thirty Years War (1618–1623)   1

  1. The Defenestration of Prague (May 23, 1618)   14

  2. *Apology* of the Bohemian Estates (May 25, 1618)   20

  3. Declaration of Elector Frederick V of the Palatinate
(November 7, 1619)   31

  4. Edict of Ferdinand II Annulling the Bohemian Election
(January 29, 1620)   39

  5. The Treaty of Ulm (July 3, 1620)   46

  6. The Battle of White Mountain (November 8, 1620)   49

  7. Terrifying and Piteous News from Bohemia (1621)   56

  8. Kipper and Wipper Time (1621)   58

  9. Letter of Archbishop Ferdinand of Cologne (July 6, 1622)   60

  10. Letter of Elector John George of Saxony (February 23, 1623)   63

II. The Intervention of Denmark and Sweden (1623–1635)   67

  11. Letter of King Christian IV of Denmark (February 21, 1626)   77

  12. The Austrian Peasants' Rebellion (1626)   82

  13. General Wallenstein on Two Fronts (August–November 1627)   86

  14. The Edict of Restitution (March 6, 1629)   91

  15. Gustavus Adolphus' Invasion of the Empire
(July and October 1630)   98

  16. The Sack of Magdeburg (May 20, 1631)   107

  17. The Battle of Breitenfeld (September 17, 1631)   113

  18. Protestants Triumphant (March 5, 1632)   118

  19. The Swedish Discipline (1632)   124

  20. Memorandum of Hoë von Hoënegg (January 30, 1634)   137

21. The Assassination of General Wallenstein
(February 25, 1634) 144

22. The Battle of Nördlingen and Its Aftermath
(September 6, 1634) 148

23. Advice of Cardinal Richelieu of France
(after September 6, 1634) 151

III. The Long War (1635–1648) 153

24. The Peace of Prague (June 12, 1635) 165

25. Complaint of Elector John George of Saxony
(March 15, 1636) 176

26. Voyage of William Crowne (April–June 1636) 180

27. The Trial of Ludwig Schmalhausen (February 1638) 190

28. Religious Security and War (November 1638–January 1639) 198

29. Diary of Abbot Maurus Friesenegger (1641–1643) 204

30. Preparations for a General Peace Congress (January 6, 1644) 212

31. Military Contributions and French Subsidies (Early 1644) 216

32. Declaration of György Rákóczi, Prince of Transylvania
(February 17, 1644) 227

33. Imperial Instructions for the Peace Congress
(October 16, 1645) 233

34. Letter of Cardinal Mazarin to the French Plenipotentiaries
at Münster (January 20, 1646) 241

35. Diary of Clara Staiger (Spring 1648) 249

36. The Peace of Westphalia (October 24, 1648) 252

IV. Two Wartime Lives (1618–1648) 274

37. A Soldier's Life in the Thirty Years War 276

38. Hans Heberle's *Zeytregister* 302

For Further Reading 325

Index 327

The Holy Roman Empire, 1618–1648

GENERAL INTRODUCTION

> That which has given me cause and occasion to write this little book is as follows. In the year of our Lord 1618, a great comet appeared during the autumn month of November. To see this was terrible and amazing, and moved me such that I began to write, for I thought that it would signify and usher in something great, which has indeed occurred, as the reader will herein find sufficient record.[1]

These words, written sometime after 1618 by a shoemaker living outside the German city of Ulm, began his diary of his experiences during the great Thirty Years War that followed. These words also began my own interest in writing a little book about the war, which was indeed both great and terrible, as our diarist learned to his sorrow. Rather than address this war in the usual way, however, I hope to allow those who experienced it to tell their own stories. Thus the following pages contain thirty-eight different documents, including diaries, diplomatic correspondence, personal letters, broadsheets, treaties, poems, trial proceedings, news reports, and more. Together, they provide a full history of the war and offer a rich and vivid perspective of the period, and of the lives and experiences of the men and women who had the misfortune to live through it. For this was one of the most momentous and destructive wars in European history. Millions died and millions more were displaced, their lives forever changed. When it was over, there was little left to do but pick up the pieces. "May God come to our aid like a father," a woman from Bavaria pleaded, "and send us some means so we can begin to build again."[2]

The Thirty Years War and the Holy Roman Empire

The principal battleground of the Thirty Years War was the Holy Roman Empire of the German Nation. The Holy Roman Empire was a multiethnic, multilingual, and multiconfessional state centered on what is now modern Germany, but also including the modern Netherlands, Belgium, Luxembourg, eastern France, Switzerland, northern Italy, Austria, Slovenia, Hungary, the Czech Republic, and western Poland. It was at the same time a loose federal republic and an elective imperial monarchy, though one family, the Habsburgs, had so long served as emperors that they had almost begun to see the position as hereditary. In some ways the empire was strangely similar to the modern European Union, and the issues involved in the Thirty

1. Document 38.
2. Document 35.

Comet over Heidelberg, 1618 (*Theatrum Europaeum,* I, p. 101, Universitätsbibliothek Augsburg Sign. 02/IV.13.2.26-1)

Years War are ones that still beleaguer us today, such as the proper extent of
the constitutional liberty of states within a larger political federation, the vi-
ability and advisability of religious toleration, and how to justify and pay for
military intervention in another state's civil war.

The Thirty Years War was extraordinarily violent, and was the first war in
European history to involve most European powers in one way or another.
Indeed, some scholars have seen the war as merely a part of one or more
much larger and longer international conflicts involving especially the
French Bourbons, the Spanish and Austrian Habsburgs, the Dutch, the
Scandinavian powers, Poland-Lithuania, and England.[3] This view is bol-
stered by the numerous peripheral but connected conflicts that occurred
simultaneously with the Thirty Years War. For example, the Thirty Years
War influenced and was influenced by the already long-standing French–
Habsburg rivalry, the Polish–Swedish wars, and the Danish–Swedish wars,

3. For example, see Geoffrey Parker, ed., *The Thirty Years' War,* 2nd ed. (London &
New York: Routledge, 1997); S. H. Steinberg, *The Thirty Years War and the Conflict
for European Hegemony, 1600–1660* (New York: Norton, 1967).

along with revolts and wars in the Netherlands, Portugal, Catalonia, Transylvania, and France. The Ottoman Turks were also extremely interested in the progress of the war, as were the English, though neither were direct combatants. Given such international connections, the very name "Thirty Years War" could be misleading, since it suggests an artificial time limit for a much broader series of struggles over control of Europe itself.

Yet the Thirty Years War, while clearly and strongly connected to the broader international scene, was also very much a distinct and inwardly focused civil war. This is the view supported by contemporary residents of the empire, who saw their war as different from the other international conflicts of the time, and who began calling it "the Thirty Years War" as soon as it was over.[4] This interpretation also makes more sense of the last half of the war, for even after the 1635 Peace of Prague, a point at which some scholars have argued that the war threw off its domestic character entirely, a number of powerful imperial princes continued to fight the emperor, and a number of key problems were still unresolved.[5] In this volume I pursue this narrower understanding of the war, focusing on the empire itself and its residents, and explaining the meaning, progress, and outcome of this central European conflagration through the words of contemporaries themselves. I address the interests and actions of the foreign powers, but only to the extent that these directly influenced the civil war in the empire; the many important peripheral wars raging around Europe are left for another volume or another scholar.

The empire's political structure was hierarchical and regional, and although it worked surprisingly well, tension among its various parts became a major contributing factor to the war. Under the Holy Roman Emperor, and choosing him, were the seven greatest princes of the empire, the electors. Three were ecclesiastical princes: the archbishops of Mainz, Cologne, and Trier. Four were secular princes: the king of Bohemia, the duke of Saxony, the margrave of Brandenburg, and the count Palatine of the Rhine. They, along with their rights and duties, had been specified in the so-called Golden Bull of 1356, an imperial edict that was central to the imperial constitution, and they were fiercely jealous of their privileges. Thus when, in the words of the elector of Saxony, they saw their status "afflicted by a not inconsiderable assault" from the emperor, they began to reconsider their loyalty.[6]

---

4. For more on this issue, see K. Repgen, "Seit wann gibt es den Begriff 'Dreissigjähriger Krieg'?" in *Weltpolitik, Europagedanke, Regionalismus: Festschrift für Heinz Gollwitzer,* ed. H. Dollinger (Münster, 1982), 59–70; K. Repgen, "Noch eimal zum Begriff 'Dreissigjähriger Krieg'," *Zeitschrift für historische Forschung* IX (1982): 347–52.

5. See Documents 24 and 25.

6. Document 10.

Below the electors were the remaining imperial princes. These ruled territories of varying sizes and were ranked as imperial estates, meaning they were largely sovereign and answerable to no one but the emperor—a status described as being immediate to the empire. Along with their rank they enjoyed seats in the imperial legislature, known as the diet, and they also belonged to one of ten imperial circles, or regions, each of which held its own circle diet and controlled its own defense and taxation. The imperial diet was divided into three voting bodies, or colleges, one each for the electors, the princes, and the free imperial cities, whose legal status was similar to that of imperial princes. The princes' college was the largest, and included both secular and ecclesiastical princes, but because of complexities caused by the division or conglomeration of various territories over time, some princes had multiple votes within their college, while others had only partial votes.

Within the territories of the individual imperial princes were further secular and ecclesiastical nobles, knights, and burghers (city-dwellers) who were subject to their respective princes' authority rather than being directly subject to the emperor—a status described as being mediate to the empire. These were each termed estates of their local territory (such as the estates of Austria or the estates of Saxony), and they met in their own local diets, where they were usually divided into three groups, one each for the nobles, the clergy, and the burghers. Unlike the emperor, most imperial princes were not elected by members of their estates, but were hereditary lords of their territories (with the notable exception being the kingdom of Bohemia, where the estates claimed the right to elect their king). Yet princes' powers over their hereditary lands were limited by the right of territorial estates to grant all taxation; and, in some places, estates also claimed the right to oversee regency governments, negotiate with other estates or princes, fire princely advisers, appeal to the emperor for redress of perceived wrongs, or even revolt in defense of their fatherland. In the seventeenth century and especially during the Thirty Years War, local estates pressed their claims against their princes with enthusiasm, and backed them up by reference to political philosophers such as Johannes Althusius, who argued that sovereignty belonged to the entire community. This caused a great deal of political tension within territories, a situation that the war exacerbated, for each side tried to use the larger conflict to strengthen its hand against the other.[7]

At the same time that local estates wished for greater liberty from their princes, imperial estates wished for greater liberty from the emperor, and they found the concept of popular sovereignty just as useful. After 1640, princes also had the writings of Bogislav Philipp von Chemnitz, who echoed the sixteenth-century political philosopher Jean Bodin by vigorously argu-

---

7. Document 27.

ing that the empire was an aristocracy rather than a monarchy. The emperor and his supporters, in turn, pointed to the work of such scholars as Henning Arnisaeus and Theodor Reinkingk, who advocated the opposite view. All parties, however, couched their claims not as innovations, but as conservative reactions. The rights and privileges they sought, they argued, were only those they had long held, but were now being denied by the overreaching and tyranny of their rulers or the impertinence and treason of their subjects. The Bohemian rebels, for example, justified their rebellion publicly with the claim that the king's ministers were proceeding "without gaining the proper legal authority from the diet,"[8] while the king argued that the rebels were the ones who had acted illegally, and had thus "forced the duly established and natural authority to wield authorized counterviolence to defend what belongs to it."[9]

At the imperial level, the traditional rights of the princes were termed the German Liberties, and they became the rallying cry for all those princes and estates who rose up to oppose the emperor. They were also among the leading reasons given by those foreign princes and potentates who decided to intervene in the imperial war. The kings of Denmark and Sweden, the prince of Transylvania, and the king of France all agreed that one of their primary goals was, in the words of Christian IV of Denmark, "to save German liberty, which is everywhere suffering."[10] Such expressions of fellow feeling for the constitutional freedoms of the German princes masked other, more concrete aims by the foreign powers, but this does not mean that such liberties, at both the imperial and local levels, were not indeed being infringed by the efforts of rulers to increase their control over those below them. There was a constant shove and push between emperor and princes, and between princes and their estates, during the seventeenth century, and historians casting a dispassionate eye over their disagreements have seen some legal precedent and argument for each side.

An additional grievance among some imperial princes was the great elevation of the electors. It rankled that where a prince's voice was but one (or a fraction of one) among many in his college, an elector's voice meant something more, and his influence and status in the empire were so much greater. Some princes, such as Duke Maximilian of Bavaria, fixed upon entry into the electoral college as a central, and ultimately successful, war aim. Others, such as Landgravine Amalia Elisabeth of Hesse-Cassel, argued in favor of equal treatment for all imperial estates. Her vigorous advocacy of the rights of each prince to be involved in decisions about war and peace helped

8. Document 2.

9. Document 4.

10. Document 11.

ensure both the inclusion of all imperial estates at the final Congress of Westphalia and their status as fellow guarantors of the peace.[11]

The constitutional grievances of the princes and estates were complicated even further by the matter of religion. In the sixteenth century, followers of the church reformer Martin Luther had broken away from the Catholic Church, and when leading princes of the empire had joined this Reformation, the empire had become divided between those who remained loyal to the old Church and those who rejected its authority in favor of the new teachings. The new Lutheran princes also began to reform religious practice and doctrine in their own territories, seizing lands and properties belonging to the Catholic Church and ignoring the protests of displaced monks, nuns, and priests. Catholics, appalled by the rapid spread of what they saw as a new heresy, voted at the 1529 imperial diet at Speyer to bar further reformation and secularization of Church property, which prompted Lutheran princes to issue the protest from which they gained their name as Protestants. At the diet at Augsburg in the following year, Lutheran princes presented to Emperor Charles V their statement of faith, from then on known as the Confession of Augsburg.

The division between the Lutheran princes and the emperor soon worsened, disintegrating into a civil war. The emperor was victorious at first, but his many international obligations pulled him in too many different directions to concentrate sufficiently on any one. For as the product of generations of brilliant marriage alliances by the house of Habsburg, Charles V was not only Holy Roman Emperor, but also king of Spain, ruler of the Netherlands, duke of Milan, archduke of Austria, ruler of Spain's New World conquests, and more. His enormous holdings led many to accuse him of seeking absolute dominion over all Christendom, and he spent his entire life fighting one neighbor or another. Worn down by such challenges, at the 1552 Peace of Passau he finally agreed to grant toleration to princes belonging to the Confession of Augsburg. This concession was then expanded in the 1555 Peace of Augsburg, which granted Lutherans full legal recognition, just treatment in the imperial courts, and the right to reform their territories as they saw fit. Ordinary people were not granted religious liberty, but were allowed the right of emigration. To resolve the issue of confiscated Catholic bishoprics, abbeys, and so on, the peace stated that all Church property seized up to the time of the Peace of Passau would remain in the hands of its current possessors. One further point, hotly contested by the Lutherans, was the so-called Ecclesiastical Reservation, which stated that no further ecclesiastical property could be reformed. Any Catholic bishop or abbot who subsequently converted to the Augsburg Confession must renounce his offices and ecclesiastical privileges.

11. See Document 30.

The Peace of Augsburg allowed the empire to avoid for decades any major confessional conflict, but it was marred by two major problems. First, by specifying legal rights only for "adherents of the Augsburg Confession," or Lutherans, it left out the many followers of other reform movements. Few concerned themselves over the fate of smaller religious minorities, who were regularly persecuted by all sides, but over the years, Calvinists became increasingly powerful in the empire, especially after the 1561 conversion of the elector Palatine, the 1604 conversion of the landgrave of Hesse, and the 1613 conversion of the elector of Brandenburg. Some Calvinist lawyers argued that Calvinism was simply a variation of the Augsburg Confession and so was included equally in the Peace of Augsburg, but both Lutherans and Catholics disputed this.[12] Second, the Ecclesiastical Reservation was never accepted by most Protestants as binding, and it was not fully enforced by the emperors until 1629, by which time many ecclesiastical properties had been long secularized and claimed by Protestant princes for generations. Some who accepted its legality, furthermore, argued that it applied only to immediate ecclesiastical territories. There was nothing structurally prohibiting the members of the empire from resolving these two problems through diplomatic means, but instead they resolved them through the Thirty Years War.

Religious differences were a strong indicator of how parties responded to constitutional disagreements within the empire. Catholic princes, in general, were more supportive of imperial institutions and of the power of the emperor, both of which tended to favor Catholicism. Protestant princes, in general, were more supportive of territorial rights and the power of the imperial estates, and were more likely to join an alliance against the emperor. Yet this generalization breaks down quickly. Catholics did not always agree with the emperor's policies or with each other, and Protestants were often bitterly divided between Lutherans, who had already fought for and won legal recognition and the right to reform their territories as they saw fit, and Calvinists, who had no such clear legal protections and rights, especially after the emperor's 1629 Edict of Restitution, which declared Calvinism illegal.[13]

Furthermore, the political, religious, dynastic, and financial goals each prince had for his own territories often eclipsed any solidarity he might have for his co-religionists in general. Thus alliances during the war were frequently multiconfessional, and princes of the empire were willing to ally with almost anyone who might help them achieve their goals. The Lutheran elector of Saxony, for example, joined the Catholic duke of Bavaria and the Catholic Spanish Habsburgs to aid Emperor Ferdinand II's suppression of

---

12. See Document 28 for an example of how worried Calvinists were about their legal status in the empire.

13. See Document 14.

the Calvinist Bohemian rebellion. He later joined other Protestants and the Lutheran Swedes to defeat the emperor, and, later still, joined again with the emperor to defeat the Swedes. Yet despite these shifts, he always strongly identified as a Lutheran and saw the defense of Lutheranism as a fundamental goal.[14] The fervently Calvinist Landgrave Wilhelm of Hesse-Cassel, in another example, happily entered into an alliance with Lutheran Sweden and Catholic France in order to combat both the emperor and his own Lutheran cousin, the landgrave of Hesse-Darmstadt, who threatened to usurp Wilhelm's control over his lands, his territorial church, and his estates. The foreign powers were similarly willing to cross confessional divides if this would further future gains or prevent future dangers. Cardinal Richelieu of France, for example, warned his king that aggressive intervention in the empire was necessary, for "if the [Protestant] party is entirely ruined, the brunt of the power of the House of Austria [the Habsburgs] will fall on France."[15]

An additional aim of the warring parties, both the foreign powers and the imperial princes, was land. The Swedes and Danes, for example, saw the imperial war as a golden chance to gain territories on their southern borders, while the French hoped to benefit both along the Rhine and in the Spanish Netherlands.[16] Within the empire, the age-old struggle to gain territories— and the honors, titles, and wealth that went with them—intensified during the chaos and opportunity of the war years. Territorial squabbles were then further exacerbated by the failure of many imperial princes to embrace the rule of primogeniture, or inheritance by the eldest son, which meant many more possible claimants and greater room for conflict within families. Furthermore, wide-scale intermarriage among imperial princes meant that dynastic territorial claims were frighteningly complex and difficult to resolve, even by impartial judges. Unfortunately, such judges were sorely lacking in the empire, for of the empire's two supreme courts, one, the Imperial Chamber Court, had ceased to function under the stresses of the Reformation; and the other, the Aulic Council, was entirely under the control of the emperor.

In addition to the structural problems of the empire and the common motivation of acquisitiveness, the war aims of the participants were shaped too by individual character. Personal experiences, beliefs, cherished grievances, family situations, alcoholism, and so on, led the men and women living through this war to respond in different ways, even when faced with the same problems as their neighbors. Local circumstances too, such as poor relationships between princes and their estates, crop failures, looting armies, dynastic squabbles, or any number of other unique circumstances, could cause

14. See, for example, Document 25.

15. Document 23.

16. See Document 34.

local changes that might influence the empire as a whole. These elements of human agency and chance cannot be underestimated in explaining the war, since there were many moments when things might easily have gone differently: errors in judgment, greed, hubris, fear, illness, lost battles, missed rendezvous, failed uprisings, mislaid letters, collapsed negotiations, lost horseshoes. Alliances were created and fell apart; princes changed sides, dropped out, died; new foreign powers were spurred to intervene; strategies shifted with the loss or win of a battle or territory; and on and on. The war was not inevitable, and it was certainly not inevitable in the form that it took.

The Form and Prosecution of the War

The Thirty Years War began, contemporaries agreed, on May 23, 1618, with the so-called Defenestration of Prague, the forcible and unceremonious dumping of three representatives of the king of Bohemia out the window of Prague Castle. The war ended thirty years and five months later, on October 24, 1648, with the Peace of Westphalia, a complicated international agreement that resolved most (but not all) of the original conflicts, and tried to resolve (but did not entirely succeed) the new disputes that had arisen over the intervening decades. Between these two events the war was fought year after year, campaign season after campaign season, with armies numbering as many as seventy thousand men ranging back and forth from Alsace to Bohemia and from the Baltic to the Alps. The soldier Peter Hagendorf alone marched more than fifteen thousand miles over the course of his service in the war, traveling with his family and suffering such hardships as gunshot wounds, the deaths of his first wife and children, lack of food, no pay, robbers, and treacherous weather.[17]

An important factor shaping the form and prosecution of the war was the so-called contribution system.[18] This system, which quickly became the primary method of military financing, depended on "contributions" extracted through force, or the threat of force, from civilian populations. By supporting their armies from occupied lands, rulers were able both to field larger forces for longer than would have been possible otherwise, and to bypass interference from their local estates, whose consent was required for any regular taxation at home. These contributions took a number of different forms and, at one end, equaled nothing more than rough extortion or ransom, a

---

17. See Document 37.

18. Much has been written about the contribution system. See, for example, F. Redlich, "Contributions in the Thirty Years' War," *Economic History Review* 12, no. 2, New Series (1959): 247–54; F. Redlich, *The German Military Enterpriser and His Workforce: A Study in European Economic and Social History*, vol. 47. Vierteljahrschrift für Sozial- und Wirtschaftsgeschichte (Wiesbaden: F. Steiner, 1964).

demand for payment in money or kind from a town or farmstead by a passing troop under the threat of violence or occupation. Hagendorf described this method plainly, explaining that during the march of his company through Pomerania, "wherever we camped overnight, the head of the household had to give each of us a half *thaler,* but it was for the best, since then we were satisfied with him and let him keep his livestock in peace."[19]

At the other end of the contribution system was a more formalized, systematic, and often extended system of war taxation imposed by the commander of an army on an entire region or state.[20] This more regularized method of extraction was less destructive to local infrastructure, but it too came with the overt or implied threat of force. Monies, food, and supplies were collected and then distributed to the officers and troops, or troops were directly supplied by the local residents with whom they were lodged. Locals were, of course, also unhappy with this arrangement, which could be tremendously oppressive. "We have to buy for the soldiers whatever they want to have," the Ulm shoemaker complained elsewhere in his diary, "including meat, wine, beer, and many other things, whatever they can think of."[21]

The contribution system was the most important method of military financing during the war, but it was not the sole method. Regular taxation levied with the consent of willing estates also played a role, as did the personal wealth of princes such as Maximilian of Bavaria. Foreign funding too was extremely important, especially in the latter years of the war, when economic disruption and war damages severely limited the ability of some imperial regions to pay regular contributions. France, in particular, pumped enormous sums into the war, granting large, regular subsidies to the Swedes and numerous imperial estates, beginning years before the French actually entered the war.[22]

The constantly shifting alliances and the sheer volume of participants in the Thirty Years War led to another peculiarity about its form and prosecution: it was marked by almost constant peace negotiations.[23] Held in one town or another between one party or another, these negotiations continuously rehashed the major issues driving the entire war: control of property, territory, and trade; religious liberty; and power—the power of imperial princes over their subjects and estates, the power of the emperor over the princes, and even the power of the various kingdoms of Europe relative to

19. Document 37.
20. See Document 13.
21. Document 38.
22. See Document 31.
23. See Documents 5, 20, 24, 28, 30, 33, 34, and 36.

each other. It was difficult, if not impossible, to separate out these different issues, since contemporaries saw them as fully interrelated. A prince could not protect the religious liberty of his territory, he might argue, without being free of imperial meddling or the limitations placed on him by his estates.

The ongoing results of battles and campaigns confused even more these many attempts at diplomacy, since any new military result might bolster or totally upend the negotiating position of one party or another.[24] Even during the great general peace conference, the Congress of Westphalia, which lasted from 1644 to 1648, the war's fluctuations continued to complicate the negotiations. When the peace finally came it was a compromise.[25] Numerous territories and titles shifted hands, with some princes reaping great rewards and others losing out, and the foreign powers were satisfied with land and money. Constitutional and religious conflicts, while not resolved to everyone's satisfaction, were at least resolved to such an extent that they never again sparked a war within the empire. It was not until 1650 that all the peace terms were implemented and all the troops ordered disbanded.

The War and Daily Life

The war severely damaged the infrastructure of the empire and devastated the lives of millions. While evidence is unreliable, as much as a quarter of the empire's population may have perished, either as a direct result of the war or as a consequence of the disease, famine, economic disturbance, and demographic disruption to which it contributed. "In sum," wrote our Ulm shoemaker,

> it was such a miserable business that even a stone would have been moved to pity, not to mention a human heart. For we were hunted like wild animals in the forests. One was caught and beaten badly, a second clobbered and stabbed, a third even shot dead, and from another were stripped and taken his little piece of bread and clothing.[26]

The war ebbed and flowed, with some areas of the empire emerging completely unscathed; some suffering only from bouts of plague or heavy war taxes; some hit once, twice, or repeatedly by invading armies and looting troops; and some burned to the ground and never rebuilt.[27] Civilians were not usually seen as actual military targets, but were nonetheless exploited, either haphazardly or systematically, to support occupying or traveling

24. See Document 13.
25. For full details of the terms of the peace, see Document 36.
26. Document 38.
27. See Document 26.

armies.[28] Soldiers would be housed with ordinary people, who would be required to supply them with food, drink, and other necessities, and the soldiers' pay would be supplied or supplemented by direct taxation of local residents.[29] Peasants, who had no say in the empire, suffered the most. They carried the brunt of all taxation and lived in the unprotected countryside, so their farms and homes were easy targets for soldiers and robbers, and peasant women were subject to rape and forced concubinage.[30] Some peasants rose up in rebellions, but these were brutally suppressed.[31]

Those people who lived in fortified cities were better protected from casual acts of military brutality and looting, and residents in the countryside would come streaming into such strongholds at the first sight of troops, staggering under the burden of whatever possessions they could carry. Here both burghers and refugees faced horrific overcrowding, disease, and starvation, and even then an army might still somehow break in.[32] One of the most shocking incidents of the war, for example, was the siege and subsequent destruction of the great city of Magdeburg. City resident Otto von Guericke described the horrors of the sack and its aftermath, explaining that, although no one could know exactly the number who had died,

> one could say that, including the two suburbs and those imperial troops who had died and were burned up there . . . it was about twenty thousand people, young and old, whose lives were ended in such cruel conditions or who otherwise had to suffer from bodily injury. The dead corpses, which had been carried out to the Elbe in front of the Water Gate, were not soon able or willing to flow away, for in that place all the water forms a ripple or eddy, such that many of them floated around for a long time, some with their heads out of the water, others reaching out their hands as if toward heaven, giving onlookers quite a horrible spectacle. Many blatherers suggested that it was just as if these dead people still prayed, sang out, and cried to God for vengeance. . . .[33]

Such devastation was hard to understand: both the violence and the capriciousness of it. Many, not just those in Magdeburg, began to see the events

---

28. See Documents 9, 17, 19, 29, 35, 37, and 38.

29. See Documents 37 and 38.

30. Forced prostitution or concubinage was a danger for both peasant women and women of the cities, who might be taken as "booty" by conquering troops. See, for example, Document 37.

31. See Document 12.

32. See Documents 35 and 38.

33. Document 16.

of the war as divine punishment for the sins of the world.[34] Some preachers, poets, and writers suggested the imminent end of the world. One commentator, for example, who was particularly concerned by the effects of the runaway inflation of the 1620s, explained to his readers that "the Last Days of which Christ prophesized have arrived. There shall be great tribulation, with agony and misery on this earth, and great fear and concern for those things that have not come to pass since the beginning of the world."[35] Such fears were only exacerbated by the strange and unsettled climate in Europe in this period, which scientists and historians have identified as the so-called Little Ice Age, with colder and longer winters, heavier rains and hailstorms, increased flooding, and storms.[36]

The princes of the empire were often no less imbued than the common people with a sense of the omnipresence of the divine. They carried a heavier burden, however, since they were constantly reminded by their theologians and court preachers that both God and posterity would judge how they proceeded in the war, and they would be blamed by both for defeat or dishonor. The Saxon court preacher Hoë von Hoënegg, for example, warned the elector that should he "act precipitously and let himself have a peace that was distasteful to God, he not only would gain discord in his heart and conscience over it, but would also have to fear and expect greater discord from God."[37] With such concerns in mind, the landgravine of Hesse-Cassel hesitated to make a peace that would free her people of the burdens of war but would not guarantee the security of her church. "We also had to consider carefully and endeavor zealously," she wrote,

> with a fervent prayer to God, how we might then not only save our conscience and rescue so many thousand souls, but also free ourselves from such an enormously heavy responsibility and from the critical judgment that we must be prepared to withstand from God, all the world, and dear posterity, both during our life and after our death.[38]

The suffering of the common people was decried by their rulers, and many took whatever steps they could to limit the damage caused by the war.[39] Yet for most rulers, larger religious and political goals usually outweighed the tragedy of civilian deaths.

34. See Document 7.
35. Document 8.
36. See Documents 29 and 38.
37. Document 20.
38. Document 28.
39. See Documents 9, 25, 29, and 37.

A Note on the Documents and Translations

The documents, all given here in English, come from libraries and archives across the United States and Europe, and include both original archival sources and those that have been previously published in their original languages. Scholars who wish to refer to the original texts can find citations with each translation. Most of the documents were written in Early New High German (*Frühneuhochdeutsch*), which, especially when written by bureaucrats and lawyers, is notoriously horrible to translate. Spelling was not standardized and regional variations were enormous. I have stayed as true to the original texts as possible, so when documents are gripping and simply written in the original, they appear so also in translation; and where they are boring and pedantic in the original, they appear so also in translation. All translation errors, however, are mine. Those documents that were originally in English retain here their original seventeenth-century spelling, capitalization, and punctuation, which makes them more difficult to read, but also more useful and more historically interesting. To allow readers to read the documents in any order, I provide notes for some of the most obscure terms within each document. This has resulted in some repetition, but it is surely easier to ignore a superfluous footnote than it is to search for missing information.

The documents are divided into four major sections, each with its own section introduction. The first three sections proceed chronologically, tracing the war from beginning to end, while the last section offers the comparison of two long diary excerpts, one from a soldier and the other from a civilian. The documents include a wide variety of types of sources and balance social, political, religious, diplomatic, economic, and military interests and concerns. Since my scholarship centers on the imperial state of Hesse-Cassel, I include a relatively larger number of documents from this area of the empire, but also provide documents from many different geographical regions and from Catholics, Lutherans, and Calvinists alike.

I hope that you find this little book useful, and that it provides you with a better understanding of the long years of the war and of the people who lived through such terrible times.

Acknowledgments

My great thanks to Carla Helfferich, Grant Weyburne, Paul Sonnino, Amy Caldwell, Janet McFall, and Erik Thomson for their invaluable assistance in this project. Thanks also to my editor, Rick Todhunter, for his patience.

I

OUTBREAK OF THE THIRTY YEARS
WAR (1618–1623)

The kingdom of Bohemia, on the far-eastern border of the Holy Roman Empire, was an old state, proud of its distinctive language and traditions.[1] It had also long been a haven for political troublemakers and religious non-conformists, a tendency that exploded in the early fifteenth century, when supporters of the religious reformer Jan Hus (c. 1369–1415) engaged in a series of wars for religious liberty after his death. Hussites, as they were called, rejected Church authority and differed with it on key points of doctrine. They also believed that both the laity and the clergy should receive the Eucharist in both kinds (*sub utraque specie*)—that is, receive both the bread and the wine during the sacrament of communion. Unable to crush these rebels, the Catholic Church and the emperor compromised instead; moderate Hussites, who were also known as Utraquists, were granted the special right to receive communion in both kinds and still remain within the Church. The less moderate followers of Hus, known as the Brethren, refused such compromise with the Catholics. Over the course of the sixteenth century, many Hussites converted to or were influenced by the ideas of reformers Martin Luther and John Calvin, who agreed with Hus on many points of doctrine, including the issue of communion in both kinds. Thus by 1618 the majority of residents of Bohemia had embraced Protestant or Protestant-like ideas in one form or another, and doctrinaire Catholicism had become a distinctly minority religion both in Bohemia and in the surrounding territories of Silesia, Lusatia, and Moravia,[2] which were subsumed under the Bohemian crown.

Added to such religious conflict was the long-standing independent spirit of the Bohemian estates,[3] which constantly pushed to strengthen local autonomy and weaken the influence of their king, whom they claimed they had the traditional right to elect. Beginning in 1526 this elected monarch was Charles V Habsburg, the head of a family that was not only the largest landholder in Europe, but had also maintained a virtual lock on the elective

---

1. Bohemia is now the modern Czech Republic.

2. Today, these territories are split among modern Germany, Poland, and the Czech Republic.

3. The estates of Bohemia were the territorial nobles, knights, and burghers (city-dwellers) who met in the local Bohemian diet (legislature).

position of Holy Roman Emperor since the fifteenth century. The Habsburgs seemed on the verge of European hegemony under Charles V, but on his abdication in 1556, he divided his territories into an Austrian branch (which controlled the Habsburg lands in Central Europe and the imperial seat) and a Spanish branch (which controlled Spain, Naples, the Netherlands, and much of the New World).

Both Habsburg branches were staunch defenders of Catholicism and advocates of strong central monarchical control, and this led to years of conflict between them and their feistier subjects. While the Austrian Habsburgs struggled to control their lands in Central Europe, the Spanish Habsburgs faced similar problems in the Netherlands. There local nobles led a revolt over the efforts of their ruler, Charles V's son Philip II, to crack down on religious nonconformity, increase taxes, and limit local rule. The war in the Netherlands dragged on for decades, until finally, in 1609, the Spanish Habsburgs and the breakaway northern provinces of the Netherlands, which had proclaimed themselves the Dutch Republic, agreed to a twelve-year truce. The year 1609 also marked a painful setback for the Austrian Habsburgs, for in that year the Bohemian estates took advantage of political infighting among the leading members of the family in order to extract the so-called Letter of Majesty from their king, Emperor Rudolph II. This royal document granted Bohemian Protestants significant religious and political independence. In particular, it affirmed the Protestant Bohemian Confession,[4] guaranteed religious freedom in the kingdom, established a unified Protestant consistory for church government, gave Protestants control of the university of Prague, allowed the appointment of twenty-four Defenders (chosen by the estates) to protect the rights of the adherents of the Bohemian Confession, and allowed Protestants to keep their existing churches and build new ones on crown lands.

The Letter of Majesty was grudgingly confirmed by Rudolph's successor as king and emperor, Matthias,[5] and by Matthias' heir and cousin, Ferdinand.[6] Ferdinand's rise had been an uncertain thing, for the question of who would succeed the childless Matthias had bitterly divided the extended Habsburg family. The matter had only been resolved in March 1617 by the secret Oñate Treaty, by which Philip III of Spain released his claims to Bohemia

---

4. The Bohemian Confession was a statement of faith made at the 1575 Diet of Prague. It was generally based on the Lutheran Augsburg Confession (1530), but was vague enough eventually to represent a basic point of agreement for all non-Catholics in Bohemia, including Hussites, Lutherans, and Calvinists.

5. Matthias von Habsburg (1557–1619), Holy Roman Emperor.

6. Ferdinand von Habsburg (1578–1637), later Ferdinand II, Holy Roman Emperor.

and Hungary in return for a promise from Ferdinand to cede to him Alsace, Tyrol, and imperial fiefs in Italy once (and assuming) Ferdinand was elected emperor. The agreement signed, Matthias then attempted to avoid later conflict by having the estates of Bohemia and Hungary predesignate Ferdinand as king. Yet unlike Matthias and his close advisor Cardinal Khlesl (1552–1630), who favored a more accommodating policy toward the Bohemian nobles and Protestants in general, Ferdinand was a Jesuit-trained doctrinaire Catholic who found such religious permissiveness outrageous. He was determined to reverse years of Protestant advances throughout Bohemia, Austria, and surrounding Habsburg territories, and also hoped ultimately to re-Catholicize the entire empire. It was an open secret that Ferdinand agreed to uphold the Bohemian Letter of Majesty only in order to gain the Bohemian crown, and once named as king-designate, he immediately began a systematic attempt to suppress both Protestantism and the local estates in his territories. He was supported in this strategy by many of Matthias' regents, who ruled Bohemia in the name of the king.

Europeans fully expected some sort of war in the year 1621, when the Twelve Years' Truce in the Netherlands was set to expire. But it was in the year 1618 that cosmic indications of trouble began to appear. Chroniclers reported mysterious portents and signs appearing everywhere throughout the Holy Roman Empire, such as earthquakes, poisonous rivers of blood, peculiarly terrifying lights and divine symbols in the sky, and rains of sulfur and blood. Frequent prayer was recommended or even required by some local magistrates as a means of possibly averting God's certain wrath.[7] The *Theatrum Europaeum,* a series of volumes that give a near-contemporary account of the war, described the greatest warning of all: "a terrible comet with a very long, burning tail appeared in the heavens and was seen with particular terror across most of Europe." God Himself, many thought, was foreshadowing horrors to come, giving them a sign so that they "might see that He would punish them because of their sins, and that He had decided to let loose the rod of His wrath. And so this comet has become a true indication of the future punishment of God."[8]

---

7. See, for example, Guenther Bentele, *Protokolle einer Katastrophe: zwei Bietigheimer Chroniken aus dem Dreissigjährigen Krieg* (Bietigheim-Bissingen: Stadtarchiv Bietigheim-Bissingen, 1984), 179–81.

8. Johann Philipp Abilenus and Matthaeus Merian, *Theatrum Europaeum, Oder, Aufführliche und Warhafftige Beschreibung aller und jeder denckwürdiger Geschichten, so sich hin und wieder in der Welt fürnemblich aber in Europa, und Teutschlanden, so wol im Religion- als Prophan-Wesen, vom Jahr Christi 1617. biß auff das Jahr 1629,* Bd. 1 (Frankfurt am Main: Daniel Fievet, 1662), 100–1. For another account of the comet sighting, see Document 38.

And it was in 1618 that the Thirty Years War began, sparked by events in Bohemia. In March, Protestant members of the Bohemian estates met in Prague at a diet to discuss what they saw as Ferdinand's gross interference with their religious and political liberties. Matthias responded to this action with a letter of outrage, threatening the ringleaders with arrest and demanding that no further assemblies take place. The Protestants defied the emperor, however, and reconvened in a diet on May 21, 1618. Then, on May 23, the leaders of the estates came to Hradčany Castle, where the Bohemian chancellery was located, to present to the regents their response to the emperor's demands. This meeting began badly and then quickly got out of hand, most probably as part of a secret plot orchestrated by a leading Protestant nobleman, Heinrich Matthias, count von Thurn,[9] who had decided to seize the moment in order to create a decisive and irrevocable statement of revolution. Rather than only a few members of the estates, therefore, which is what the regents had expected, a huge mass of armed men arrived at the chancellery and then pushed their way into the small council chamber that was reserved for the regents' use. Once inside they singled out two of the leading Catholic regents, Wilhelm Slawata and Jaroslav Borsita von Martinitz,[10] whom they blamed for leading the push against religious and political freedom in Bohemia. Ignoring the men's pleas, the rebels then threw them (and their secretary) out the window, in conscious imitation of a similar act that had taken place during the Hussite Wars (see Document 1).

Soon after the so-called Defenestration of Prague, the Bohemian estates (now entirely controlled by the Protestant rebels) created a provisional government of thirty-six directors. Almost their first order of business was to win allies for their cause. Their *Apology*, or defense, was a large part of this attempt, for they had it published across Europe in order to explain and justify their actions to the larger European community and, they hoped, to gain the support of possibly sympathetic Protestant princes (see Document 2). The Bohemian rebels also quickly moved to seize control of Prague and raise a new citizen militia, which was under the command of one of the leading defenestrators, Count von Thurn, and which easily defeated the few surrounding towns that remained loyal to the Habsburg king. Meanwhile, the estates reversed Ferdinand's attempted re-Catholicization of Bohemia by expelling all Jesuits, crushing the ineffective opposition of minority Catholic residents, and seizing Catholic Church properties.

9. Jindrich Matyas ze Thurn-Valsassina (1567–1640), usually referred to simply as Count von Thurn.

10. Vilém Slavata z Chlumu a Košumberka (1572–1652) and Jaroslav Bořita z Martinic (1582–1649).

Defenestration of Prague, May 23, 1618 (*Theatrum Europaeum,* I, p. 16, Universitätsbibliothek Augsburg Sign. 02/IV.13.2.26-1)

During 1618 and early 1619 the rebellion continued, and the Bohemians gained the support of the neighboring Habsburg hereditary territory of Silesia, along with some secret military assistance from Elector Frederick V of the Palatinate[11] and a regiment of troops sent by the duke of Savoy, which was under the command of the German Count Ernst von Mansfeld.[12] Then, in May 1619, Emperor Matthias died, and Ferdinand, as Matthias' heir, became ruler of all of his territories. Yet not only did the rebels in Bohemia refuse to recognize him as king, they were now joined in their rebellion by the estates of Austria and Moravia. Twice the Bohemian army managed to advance far into Austria and even bombard the emperor's residence at Vienna. But Ferdinand fought back by sending his army, under Lieutenant General Bucquoy,[13] into southern Bohemia. He also insisted on his right, as king of

11. Frederick V, elector Palatine (1596–1632), ruled the territories of the Rhenish (Lower) Palatinate and the Upper Palatinate, and was a leading Calvinist prince of the empire.

12. Ernst, count von Mansfeld (1580–1626), was in the employ of Charles Emmanuel, the duke of Savoy.

13. Lieutenant General Charles Bonaventure de Longueval, count of Bucquoy (1571–1621), was the French-born military commander of the imperial armies in Bohemia.

Bohemia, to attend and vote at the upcoming meeting of the imperial electoral college,[14] which would choose Matthias' replacement as emperor. In Frankfurt on August 28, 1619, by unanimous vote, the seven electors chose Ferdinand, now Ferdinand II, Holy Roman Emperor.

Two days earlier, on August 26, 1619, the Bohemian estates had offered their kingship to Frederick V of the Palatinate.[15] Frederick was a leader of the Protestant Union (a military alliance of Protestant princes), the son-in-law of the king of England and Scotland, and an ally of numerous other powerful princes and states. The rebels expected that these relationships would yield military assistance for their cause, or at least prevent interference. Others, however, such as the elector of Cologne, were incredulous. "If it should be true, that the Bohemians have in mind to set aside Ferdinand and to choose instead a counter-king," he wrote, "then one would have to make oneself ready for a twenty-, thirty-, and forty-year war, for the Spaniards and the House of Austria would rather put into play everything that they possess in this world than to give up Bohemia."[16] Despite the pleas and warnings of numerous observers and heads of state, however, Frederick accepted the crown; on October 25, 1619, in the city of Prague, he was crowned king of Bohemia with great pomp and ceremony.

By taking up the crown offered to him by the Bohemian rebels and thus supplanting Ferdinand, who had strong legal claims to be the true ruler, Frederick transformed a purely local rebellion into an event with empirewide political and religious implications. Knowing that his interference in another ruler's internal affairs might offend the princes of the empire (even the Protestant ones), yet needing military support to defend himself against the Habsburgs, Frederick issued a public defense of his actions on November 7, 1619. In this proclamation, which he mailed to his fellow imperial princes and had published across Europe, he explained both his understanding of the problem in Bohemia and his reasons for accepting the Bohemian crown (see Document 3). Yet such arguments did little to convince other princes of the rightness of

---

14. The electoral college was one of three bodies constituting the imperial diet. The seven electors, who were the princes who chose the emperor, included the three prince-archbishops of Mainz, Trier, and Cologne, and the four secular princes: the duke of Saxony, the count Palatine, the margrave of Brandenburg, and the king of Bohemia. At this time, the first three of these secular princes were Protestant.

15. The estates of Bohemia considered five men as Ferdinand's possible replacement: the king of Denmark, the elector of Saxony, the duke of Savoy, the prince of Transylvania, and Frederick.

16. *Zeitung aus Böhmen, Mähren, Österreich und anderen Ländern mehr,* 1619, nr. 42. Cited in Hans Jessen, *Der Dreissigjährige Krieg in Augenzeugenberichten* (Düsseldorf: K. Rauch, 1963), 70.

Frederick's cause. Catholic princes, in particular, were greatly concerned with how all this might affect the delicate balance of Protestants and Catholics in the empire. The Catholic Duke Maximilian I of Bavaria[17] put this fear most succinctly: "The Bohemian disorders obviously aim at the extermination of the Catholic religion," he wrote, for "the heretical electors and princes in the empire now work to remove the Bohemian crown completely from the House of Austria in order to turn it over to a heretic and thereby gain the majority in the electoral college, so they can then choose a heretical emperor."[18] Protestant princes were also concerned by the specter of war. Among these was the Lutheran Elector John George of Saxony,[19] who was horrified at Frederick's blatant disregard for continued peace in the empire, and warned him that he had no hope of military victory against the Habsburgs.

In addition to sparking a possible empirewide war, however, Frederick's actions also tacitly supported the idea that local estates had the right to pick and choose who was to lead them. Though the crown of Bohemia had its own unique traditions of elective monarchy, over the course of the fifteenth and sixteenth centuries, many local estates throughout the Holy Roman Empire had begun to push the boundaries of their power. They did this by such methods as meeting without being called by their prince, interfering in their prince's choice of ministers, and involving themselves in princely successions and regency governments. In most territories, furthermore, princes were very much dependent on grants of money from their estates. Thus by the time of the Thirty Years War, princes, many of whom were already locked in power struggles within their own territories, did not wish to see their power diminished any further.

The Bohemian rebellion was an extreme example of this growing tension, and Emperor Ferdinand used it to try to drum up support for his cause. And he did need support. By the end of 1619 he had suffered humiliating defeats at the hands of the Bohemian confederate army under the Counts von Thurn and von Mansfeld, and at the hands of Frederick's ally Prince Bethlen Gábor of Translyvania,[20] who had also taken the opportunity offered by the Bohemian revolt to help himself to Habsburg Royal Hungary.[21]

17. Duke Maximilian I of Bavaria (1573–1651), leader of the Catholic League.

18. Kurt Pfister, *Kurfürst Maximilian von Bayern und sein Jahrhundert* (München: F. Ehrenwirth, 1948), 180. Cited in Jessen 71.

19. John George, elector of Saxony (1585–1656).

20. Bethlen Gábor (1580–1629), prince of Transylvania.

21. The Habsburgs held only the northwestern portion of Hungary, which they ruled as a kingdom and which was called Royal Hungary. The majority of Hungary was under control of the Ottoman empire.

But slowly, Ferdinand had begun to gather his resources to fight back. In October 1619, after considerable negotiations, he entered into the Treaty of Munich with Duke Maximilian of Bavaria. By this treaty, Maximilian agreed to use his enormous financial resources and influence in the empire to raise an army in the name of the entire Catholic League (the counterpart of the Protestant Union), and to use it to defeat the rebels. In return, Ferdinand openly promised fully to indemnify Maximilian for all military expenses, and secretly promised to give him Frederick's electoral dignity and lands in the Palatinate, both of which Maximilian had long coveted.

In January 1620 Ferdinand won some additional military support from his cousin, the Spanish King Philip III, and in that same month the emperor convinced Bethlen Gábor to abandon Frederick in return for control over much of Royal Hungary. Even the Lutheran elector of Saxony, John George, decided to come to the aid of the emperor in return for a promise of the lands of Upper and Lower Lusatia and the protection of Lutherans in Habsburg lands.[22] Now considerably better positioned, Ferdinand issued an open letter, dated January 29, 1620, in which he laid out to the entire empire and the rest of the world his understanding of the conflict and his reasons for rising to the defense of what he saw to be his imperiled sovereign rights (see Document 4).

Frederick, unlike the emperor, gained almost nothing from his pleas for assistance. His father-in-law, King James I of England, provided only a loan, and the other Protestant powers of Europe followed his lead and did even less. Still, the religious implications of this matter had raised tensions between the Catholic League and the Protestant Union; both had raised armies, and the possibility of civil war loomed. By May 1620 the emperor's many allies had advanced their plans to such an extent that Frederick's Bohemian adventure seemed likely to collapse. Given the reluctance of almost all Protestant princes to become entangled in a general war, the members of the Protestant Union finally decided to let Frederick fight his own losing battles. With the aid of a diplomatic mediation by the French, led by the duke d'Angoulême,[23] the Protestant Union (represented by Joachim Ernst of Brandenburg-Ansbach)[24] reached an agreement with the Catholic League

---

22. The terms of the agreement were that Saxony would aid the emperor in return for assurances that the elector could keep conquered territories until he was reimbursed for his expenses or until Frederick was defeated, that Lutherans in Habsburg hereditary lands would not be punished, and that lands previously taken by Lutherans from the Catholic Church in the Lower Saxon Circle would remain in Lutheran hands.

23. Charles de Valois, duke d'Angoulême (1573–1650).

24. Joachim Ernst of Brandenburg-Ansbach (1583–1625). Frederick had previously

(represented by Maximilian of Bavaria) on July 3, 1620. This agreement, the Treaty of Ulm, was an attempt to keep the Bohemian matter isolated from the rest of the empire. The Union would remain neutral in exchange for the purely theoretical protection of Frederick's hereditary lands in the Palatinate. In practice, this left Frederick entirely at the mercy of the emperor and his allies (see Document 5).

Once the Protestant Union agreed to step aside, Frederick and the rebels stood virtually alone. Between June and September 1620, the armies of the Catholic League under General Tilly[25] crushed the rebels in Austria; John George of Saxony seized Lusatia and Silesia; and the Spanish army of Flanders, under Ambrogio Spinola,[26] advanced into and overwhelmed most of Frederick's lands in the Rhenish Palatinate—quickly violating the terms of the Treaty of Ulm. The Spanish had long desired this territory, since by controlling the Rhine River they could ensure the smooth transfer of new troops to their war in the Netherlands. In September Tilly's army combined with the imperial army, under Bucquoy, and together they pushed over the Bohemian border and headed for the capital city of Prague. The army of the Bohemians and their confederates, led by Frederick's close advisor, Christian of Anhalt,[27] followed the combined imperial-League army and managed to cut them off right before Prague. There, on November 8, on a hill known as White Mountain, the Bohemian army was quickly and decisively routed, and the imperialists reclaimed Prague (see Document 6).

Only hours after the defeat at White Mountain, Frederick, scoffingly referred to from then on as "the Winter King,"[28] fled with his family and eventually ended up in the Dutch Republic, where he was taken in by his relative, the prince of Orange. The Bohemian rebels were quickly overwhelmed and forced to submit unconditionally to the emperor. He was not merciful. Those whom he deemed responsible for the defenestration were publicly executed, their property confiscated. Elective monarchy was abolished, the Letter of Majesty shredded. Catholicism was reintroduced throughout the Habsburg hereditary lands, Protestantism brutally suppressed, and ministers

---

been lieutenant general of the Union, but had been stripped of this post as punishment for his reckless actions in Bohemia.

25. Johann Tserclaes, count of Tilly (1559–1632).

26. Ambrogio Spinola (1569–1630) was an Italian serving as general of the Spanish army of Flanders.

27. Christian von Anhalt-Bernburg (1568–1630) was a Calvinist prince who had long served Frederick as an advisor and who had strongly supported his decision to take the Bohemian throne in the first place.

28. He had been king only for the single winter of 1619 to 1620.

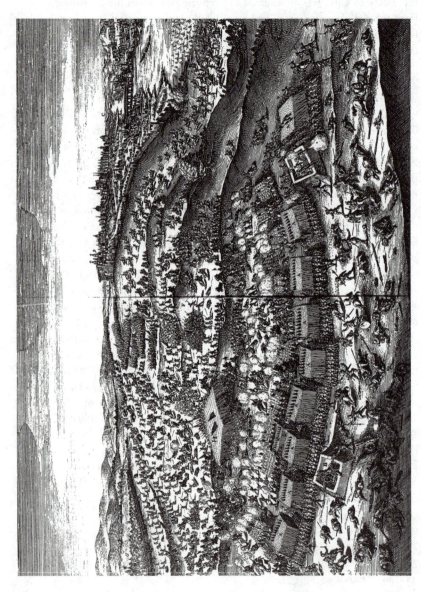

Battle of White Mountain, November 8, 1620 (*Theatrum Europaeum*, I, p. 410+, Universitätsbibliothek Augsburg, Sign. 02/IV.13.2.26-1)

exiled. Tens of thousands of others fled to neighboring Protestant lands in the face of religious persecution and the plundering of uncontrolled imperial soldiers. "O Christian man, behold the distress," wrote a resident of western Bohemia.

> The people have to abandon their own goods along with many supplies. Some simply run away, forced to abandon wife and child. The troops seize children from the breast, murdering them unjustly, and their parents likewise. They murder them terrifyingly, causing great misery and lamentations. Some hope to hide themselves under the hay or straw, in sheds and in barns, and they stay lying there and starving and finally even being burned."[29]

Similar scenes of looting and religious violence were repeated in all areas conquered by the imperialists, both within the confines of Habsburg hereditary lands and in Frederick's Rhenish Palatinate.

After clearing all opposition from Bohemia and its surrounding territories, the emperor's new governor, Karl von Liechtenstein, and his military officer, Albrecht von Wallenstein, set about trying to recoup the funds the emperor had spent in the process of restoring his rule. They did this by massively increasing taxes, confiscating vast tracts of land from Protestant nobles, and manipulating the currency. In 1559 the imperial diet had passed a law regulating the silver content of imperial coins, but by 1618 inflation in the value of silver (spurred on by a decline in silver imports from the New World) had led to the peculiar problem that, while the value of large coins such as the *reichsthaler* remained constant, the amount of silver contained in the smaller, more commonly used coins was worth more than their nominal face value. This fact had been exploited by the cash-strapped Bohemian rebels, who had begun to collect existing coins with high silver content. These were then melted down with quantities of cheap copper, re-minted at the same face value, and then used to buy even more good silver coins, thereby continuing the profit cycle. After the battle of White Mountain and the fall of Bohemia to the imperialists, Liechtenstein and Wallenstein enthusiastically continued and enlarged upon this practice, and their currency manipulation and wholesale debasement of silver coins turned them into extraordinarily wealthy landowners.

The practice of debasing silver coins with copper quickly spread into neighboring Austria, Bavaria, and Saxony, and then throughout the rest of the empire. Hyperinflation set in, and many people, including those who never saw a single soldier, were ruined, especially the poor, who were dependent on fixed wages. The money economy completely broke down in

29. Document 7.

some areas, and in others prices for food and services reached impossible levels, forcing mass dislocation and despair. Commerce in the empire was crippled, and governments found that their economic policy of currency devaluation had backfired, since runaway inflation overwhelmed whatever profits they might have made at the beginning.

Ordinary people blamed their woes on such ready targets as the Jews, greedy elites, and the Devil himself. The traveling money changers who brought the debased coins "are, without doubt, bound to their father, the wretched Devil," a pamphlet declared in 1621, "for he keeps all of them together captive within his kingdom. As they are his bondsmen, performing what he suggests to them, he will also powerfully strengthen them, so that, with words and deeds, they are tied so deeply to these sins that he leaves none of these godless people behind. In these difficult times, they are the reason that such debased money is introduced throughout the world" (Document 8). This time became known in the empire as the Kipper and Wipper period, for the scales (*wippen*) used by money changers to weigh (*kippen*) the amount of silver in coins. After a few years, governments began to take steps to recall debased coins and the currency system slowly stabilized.

Meanwhile, Frederick's remaining troops, led by the count of Mansfeld, retreated before their victorious enemies. They fell back first into the Upper Palatinate, but were too weak to prevent it falling easily into the hands of Tilly. Mansfeld then withdrew into the Rhenish Palatinate, where he battled the Spanish briefly before falling upon the Habsburg territory of Alsace, which he occupied throughout the winter of 1620 to 1621, allowing his troops to pillage at will. The Protestant Union, which had drawn a line in the sands of the Palatinate at the Treaty of Ulm, had done nothing when that line was crossed by Spinola and Tilly. In May 1621, cowed by imperial successes, the Union quietly disbanded. Some in Europe, particularly the English and Spanish, thought diplomacy, not war, was the solution to these current problems, and so tried to convince Frederick that the only way he could ever regain some of his lands in the Palatinate was to renounce the Bohemian throne. Frederick refused. Instead of accepting a humiliating defeat, he made use of financial support from the Dutch to expand Mansfeld's army and to raise two further armies under the command of Georg Friedrich of Baden-Durlach[30] and Christian of Brunswick,[31] whose troops spent the winter in Baden and Westphalia, respectively (see Document 9).

30. Georg Friedrich, margrave of Baden-Durlach (1573–1638).

31. Christian, duke of Brunswick-Lüneburg and administrator of the bishopric of Halberstadt (1599–1626). He was sometimes called "the mad Halberstadter" for his reputation of violent excesses and cruelty.

In the spring of 1622, the armies of Frederick reengaged his enemies. On July 13, 1622, however, Frederick once again dismissed his generals, since they had been unable to work in concert and had thus accomplished little. They marched west to offer their services to the Dutch, whose long truce with Spain had finally expired on April 9, 1621. In September, with no relief in sight, Frederick's capital of Heidelberg finally succumbed to Tilly, whose troops brutally plundered the populace and stripped this great city bare of all of its treasures. The papacy, which had supported the emperor from the beginning, received the famous Heidelberg library as a gift.[32] The emperor was now fully victorious. The rebels had been crushed and Frederick defeated, his lands occupied by the Spanish and Bavarian armies. The only remaining question was how to punish Frederick for his insolence. Many princes of the empire, along with the Spanish and the English, advised the emperor to behave judiciously for the good of all, but his hands were tied by his earlier promises to Maximilian of Bavaria. In 1623, therefore, Ferdinand called a meeting of all leading imperial princes at Regensburg and pushed through the transference of Frederick's title and lands to Maximilian. His only concession to the strenuous opposition of the assembled princes was to promise that the transference would merely be for Maximilian's lifetime, and that Frederick's children and heirs would not be permanently dispossessed.

The emperor's actions deeply concerned both Protestant and Catholic princes on constitutional grounds, since they seemed fundamentally to violate the so-called German Liberties, the traditional rights and privileges of the imperial estates.[33] They considered that if the emperor were allowed to dismiss and appoint electors at will (which seemed to them to violate existing imperial law), then this would represent both an enormous expansion of his power and an extraordinary threat to theirs (see Document 10). Protestants were also angered and frightened by the replacement of a Protestant elector Palatine by a Catholic one, which cemented for the Catholics a strong majority vote in the electoral college. The Regensburg diet thus revived existing political opposition to the emperor and heightened religious tensions, and Frederick used this outrage to revive his sagging fortunes and re-form the armies of Mansfeld and Christian of Brunswick. This move was countered by Tilly, however, who chased Christian out of the Lower Saxon Circle,[34]

32. C. V. Wedgwood, *The Thirty Years War* (Garden City, NY: Anchor Books, Doubleday & Company, Inc., 1961), 156.

33. The imperial estates included the electors, imperial princes, and free imperial cities. See the General Introduction for more information.

34. Circles were the empire's administrative regions.

where he had been recruiting, and defeated him at the battle of Stadtlohn on August 6, 1623.

1. The Defenestration of Prague (May 23, 1618)[35]

[Furious over what they saw to be a flagrant disregard for both their guaranteed religious rights (for example, the right to build churches and oversee their own internal religious communities) and political rights (for example, the right to hold assemblies and see to some degree of self-rule), Protestant members of the Bohemian estates[36] gathered in May 1618 in Prague for an extraordinary assembly. Such a meeting had been specifically forbidden by the emperor, whose regents thus called the leaders of the estates to Hradčany Castle to discuss the matter. Instead, the men stormed the palace and threw two of the emperor's regents and their secretary out the window, an act that became known as the Defenestration of Prague (from the Latin for "out a window").[37] Luckily, these men, who fell more than fifty feet to the courtyard below, escaped with their lives, if not their dignity. Protestant writers later argued that the men had survived only by landing on a dung heap. Catholics put forth a slightly different explanation, which appears at the end of the following description of the incident written (in the third person) by one of the three men defenestrated, Jaroslav Martinitz.[38]]

35. Jaroslav Martinitz, "Beschreibung der Böhmischen Rebellion in anno 1618," Knihovna Národního muzea, Praha, Sign. VI G. 2, p. 24 ff., in Miroslav Toegel, ed., *Documenta Bohemica Bellum tricennale illustrantia*, T. 2, *Der Beginn des Dreissigjährigen Krieges: der Kampf um Böhmen: Quellen zur Geschichte des bömischen Krieges (1618–1621)* (Prague: Academia, 1972), 42–9. A different version of this event also appears in Henry Frederick Schwartz, *The Imperial Privy Council in the Seventeenth Century* (Cambridge, MA: Harvard University Press, 1943), 344–7.

36. Most European states traditionally recognized three major social groupings or estates: the nobility, the clergy, and the burghers (or city-dwellers). In Bohemia, however, the three estates were the nobles, the knights, and the burghers.

37. Historians sometimes refer to this act as the Second Defenestration of Prague, since it was done in conscious imitation of a similar act performed during the 1419 Hussite revolt, whereby seven city council members were killed.

38. Count Jaroslav Bořita (Smeczensky) z Martinic (1582–1649), burgrave of Karlstein and regent of Bohemia. As Bohemia was under the control of the German-speaking Habsburg monarchy, most of the men mentioned in this document are usually referred to by the German, rather than the Czech, versions of their names.

The 23rd of May, a Wednesday, the eve of Ascension Day,[39] four lord regents[40] came from St, Vitus Cathedral, where the procession had been performed and they had heard the holy Mass, and went to the Bohemian chancellery at 8:30 in the morning. They then quickly and assiduously had all the stools and benches, except for a single chair, carried out of the chancellery so that there would be sufficient room for all the arriving Protestant[41] lords. At around nine o'clock, lords from all three Protestant estates, with a great crowd of their aides and servants, entered the castle of His Imperial Majesty[42] at Prague and then the Bohemian chancellery. Unannounced, quite cheekily, and causing a great deal of importunity, they barged even into the council chamber, where there should have been the greatest security and respect.[43] Thus the chancellery was entirely filled with lords and knights alone, while most of the burghers stood outside in front of the door, which therefore had to remain wide open.

The four lord regents who were present stood together in a windowed corner near the furnace, where there was more room, expecting that the Protestants present would now craft a response to the letter from His Imperial Majesty, a copy of which had been communicated to them that Monday. In this letter they had once again been mildly admonished not to conduct another meeting until His Imperial Majesty's arrival, or until they received further decrees.

Instead of [writing a response], [the members of the estates] at once had Lord Paul Rziczan read aloud, in a clear voice, a letter with the following approximate content:

To avoid confusion, I have retained the traditional German versions in the main text, but have included the Czech names of some of the key figures in the footnotes.

39. Ascension Day is the Christian holiday celebrating the bodily ascension of Jesus Christ into heaven.

40. The four regents present were Martinitz, president of the chamber Count Vilém Slawata z Chlumu a Košumberka (1572–1651/2; also known as Wilhelm Slawata von Chlum und Kosumberg), Adam II von Sternberg (the supreme burgrave), and Matthew Leopold Popel Lobcowitz (grand prior of the Order of the Knights of St. John in Bohemia).

41. Here the author uses the phrase *sub utraque,* which means not only Protestants, but also Utraquists and Brethren (see the section introduction, page 1, for more information on this topic). For ease of reading, however, I have here represented this and all subsequent uses of the phrase as "Protestant."

42. Matthias von Habsburg (1557–1619), Holy Roman Emperor and king of Bohemia.

43. Tradition dictated that no one enter the castle fully armed.

His Imperial Majesty had sent to their graces the lord regents a sharp letter that was, by our request, issued to us as a copy after the original had been read aloud, and in which His Majesty declared all of our lives and honor already forfeit, thereby greatly frightening all three Protestant estates. As they also absolutely intended to proceed with the execution against us, we came to a unanimous agreement among ourselves that, regardless of any loss of life and limb, honor and property, we would stand firm, with all for one and one for all . . . nor would we be subservient, but rather we would loyally help and protect each other to the utmost, against all difficulties. Because, however, it is clear that such a letter came about through the advice of some of our religious enemies, we wish to know, and hereby ask the lord regents present, if all or some of them knew of the letter, recommended it, and approved of it.

After this, the supreme burgrave[44] answered that since the lord regents were only present at the Bohemian chancellery in a limited number, and since one of their members—namely Adam von Waldstein,[45] lord high steward—was at that moment lying sick in his house in Prague, they wished the lords of all three Protestant estates to deliver a copy of the letter that had been read aloud, so that they could notify the high steward of it and consult with him. They then would not fail to provide [the Protestants] with an appropriate answer on the following Friday (because Monday was an important holiday).

At this many—including Lord Heinrich Matthias, count von Thurn;[46] Lord Leonhard Colon von Fels; and Wilhelm Popel von Lobkowitz the elder—said to the regents, one after another: "No, no. . . . We want to have a clear answer now from the four of your graces who are now present. . . ."

At this the four regents came together to the window in the corner and answered that they were bound and obliged by a serious oath . . . and that they were thus certainly not entitled to reveal anything that had occurred

---

44. As the supreme burgrave of the castle of Prague, Adam von Sternberg was the representative of the king in his absence and the highest member of the Bohemian government.

45. Adam von Waldstein, also known as Wallenstein, was the brother of Albrecht von Wallenstein, who was later to be the emperor's supreme general.

46. Jindrich Matyas ze Thurn-Valsassina (1567–1640). Count von Thurn, a Calvinist, spent most of his childhood in Austria and so never fully mastered the Czech language. He was one of the most fervent supporters of the rights of the Bohemian nobility and served as one of the Bohemian Defenders, men chosen by the estates to protect Protestantism.

in the council, nor to reveal what they had advised or not advised be done. . . .

The Protestant lords, however, refused to be satisfied with this—especially Count von Thurn, who stated: "Yet this is a very serious question, and you, and especially the lord supreme burgrave and lord grand prior,[47] can answer it. Until you do, we will not leave the Bohemian chancellery; for once, we wish to know and receive a clear answer." Suddenly Lord Hans Litwin von Rziczan uncovered his pistols, which he had hidden on his belt under his coat, grasped hold of them, and fired in a very threatening manner. He then went right up to Lord von Martinitz, defiantly kicked him down, and straddled him. After a brief discussion, the supreme burgrave said: "Because you will have nothing less and have practically forced us, we all wish, before God the Almighty, to protest most strenuously before you and the entire world, publicly and expressly, and we take all of you lords present as our witnesses . . . that we were forced to give this answer, and this we can say with good conscience: that we did not advise anything that was contrary to the Letter of Majesty. . . ."[48]

At which they—especially Counts von Thurn and von Fels, Wilhelm Popel the elder, Bohuslav Berka, Wenzl Wilhelm von Ruppa, Joachim Andreas Schlick,[49] Hans Litwin von Rziczan, Albrecht Hans Smirzicky, and Lord Ulrich Kinsky—discussed this intensely and then loudly and chaotically cried out: "It is clear to us that the imperial letter goes against our Letter of Majesty! Furthermore," they said, "lord supreme burgrave and lord grand prior, we know well that both of you are pious and would not advise such a thing, nor wish to harm us, but must have been persuaded and led astray by Lords Slawata and Martinitz."[50]

After this they turned to these two lords, that is, to Wilhelm Slawata and Martinitz, and said: "You are enemies of us and of our religion, have desired to deprive us of our Letter of Majesty, have horribly plagued your Protestant subjects . . . and have tried to force them to adopt your religion against their wills or have had them expelled for this reason. . . ."

---

47. Matthew Lobkowitz.

48. The Letter of Majesty was issued by Emperor Rudolph II, who ruled as king of Bohemia from 1575 to 1611. It granted freedom of worship and the right of the Bohemian estates to build churches on crown land.

49. Jáchym Ondřej hrabě Šlik (1569–1621). Schlick, a Lutheran nobleman, was one of the Defenders.

50. Slawata and von Martinitz, along with the Bohemian chancellor Zdenek Adalbert Popel von Lobcowitz (who was in Vienna at this time and so escaped the defenestration), were the three most anti-Protestant regents in the Bohemian government and had openly opposed the Letter of Majesty.

[The two regents attempt to defend themselves from these and further accusations brought by the Protestants.]

Then the above-mentioned nine people were thrown into confusion, and also all others who were present; but Lord Count von Thurn and Lord Wilhelm Popel, in particular, strongly challenged the two lords Slawata and Martinitz with these words: "See, all dear lords, these men are great enemies of us and of our religion. . . . Know for certain, all you lords, that so long as they remain in the country, our Letter of Majesty will never be safe, nor will, indeed, the lives of any of us and of our dear wives and children. And were we to keep these men alive, then we would lose the Letter of Majesty and our religion, and all of us would then be stripped and deprived of our lives, honor, and property, for there can be no justice to be gained from or by them. . . ."

Then Lord Wilhelm Popel and several others turned to the other two regents and said: "Lord supreme burgrave and lord grand prior, please leave now; nothing bad will happen to the both of you by our hands, but with these other two we shall have justice. . . ." Then several of them dragged the supreme burgrave and the lord grand prior by their hands out the door of the Bohemian chancellery and led them away.

Immediately after this, the lords furiously and violently laid hands on the two oft-mentioned regents. I think that Count von Thurn and Joachim Andreas, Count von Schlick, along with several others, forcefully seized Lord Slawata, while Lord Wilhelm Popel, Hans Litwin von Rziczan, Lord Ulrich Kinsky, Lord Albrecht Smirzicky, and Lord Paulus Kepler seized Lord von Martinitz. They strongly pulled them here and there through the entire Bohemian chancellery, starting from the fireplace and ending at the window on the opposite side, crying: "Now we will show justice to those who are enemies of our religion!" At this, Lord von Martinitz said loudly: "Since this concerns the will of God, the Catholic religion, and the will of the emperor, we shall suffer everything gladly and patiently." They both seriously thought that they would be led to the door and then held in arrest for some time, but once they had passed by the door and had seen the window opened immediately before them, they both ceaselessly began to ask for the benefit of a confessor, to whom they wished to confess at once, and to ask most fervently for the final righteousness of God. At this, however, the Protestant members of the estates, without considering this ardent request, answered: "Yes, we will soon usher in the mischievous Jesuits[51] as well."

51. Members of the Society of Jesus, a religious order founded in 1540. The Jesuits were the main arm of the papacy in its efforts to combat the spread of Protestantism, and were actively attempting to re-Catholicize Bohemia at this time.

And with this, the aforementioned people grasped onto Lord von Martinitz, who faithfully commended himself to God the Almighty with these words: "Jesus, son of God, have mercy on me; mother of God, remember me," and who wore only a black canvas coat along with rapier and dagger, but not a hat (for this, which had a beautiful braid decorated with gold and precious stones, had been ripped from his hand). Then, bare headed, he was miserably shoved and thrown head first out of the window and into the castle moat, which was perhaps thirty cubits down and rocky. As he, however, strongly and continuously cried out in turn the holy names "Jesus" and "Mary," this terrifying toss and fall not only did not deprive him of life, it also saw him only slightly injured, due to the mysterious grace and compassion of God, achieved through the intercession of our dear and most distinguished Lady. It was then commonly said and staunchly avowed as certain by many pious, God-fearing people—who claimed to have clearly seen this for themselves—that in the air above Lord von Martinitz, who was the first to fall, appeared the most holy and praiseworthy Virgin Mary, the mother of God, as his sublime patron, and, so to speak, slowed him in his fall with her outstretched coat placed beneath him, such that he might fall to the earth much more softly. Thus she mercifully helped to maintain him in life and health and keep him from certain death. Although Lord von Martinitz had not seen this so clearly, nonetheless it had happened. He could clearly remember that while he called out both holy names during his fall (because he had, without despairing, held out strong hopes of finally and at any moment gaining his long-hoped-for holy martyr's crown), it truly appeared to him as though the highest heaven opened itself up to him, and that he should soon enter there into eternal glory.

Next came Lord Slawata, who also devoutly called out to God the Lord, saying: "God, have mercy on me, a sinner." They first badly smashed the fingers of his right hand, with which he had tried to hold on, until they were bloody, and then threw him through the same window, without his hat and in a black velvet coat with his rapier, and he quickly fell to the earth. He rolled eight cubits farther and deeper into the moat than had Lord Martinitz and badly entangled his head in his heavy coat. Finally came the third, Lord M. Philipus Fabricius, imperial councilor and secretary of the kingdom of Bohemia. [He was chosen] mostly because of the demands of Lord Albrecht Hansen Smirzicky, by whom he had also previously been plagued in his writings in all kinds of ways. He was also brought by them, in his coat and without his hat, to this window, where he also assiduously called out to God—"God have mercy on my soul!"—and was thrown into the moat. . . .

2. *Apology* of the Bohemian Estates (May 25, 1618)[52]

[After the Defenestration of Prague, the rebellious Bohemian estates defended their actions by publishing their Apology *(defense), which they distributed across Europe. Thus from its very beginnings the Thirty Years War would be fought both in the popular press and on the battlefield. One may note in this* Apology *the estates' carefully worded attempt to shift the blame for their oppression onto the king's ministers (not the king himself) and the Jesuits, thereby proclaiming to the world that their act was not a rebellion against their rightful lord, but a defensive, justifiable, and legal response to those who, falsely acting in the king's name, had pursued illegal and unjust policies.]*

Apology, or letter of excuse, concerning the inevitable causes that forced all three estates of the commendable kingdom of Bohemia who receive the body and blood of the Lord Christ in both kinds[53] to act in their own defense

We, the representatives of the lords, knights, and cities of Prague, Kuttenberg,[54] and other places: all three estates of this kingdom of Bohemia who receive the body and blood of our Lord Jesus Christ in both kinds, who confess to the Bohemian Confession,[55] and who are now assembled at the castle of Prague, unanimously make it known, both in the name of those present and also on behalf of all those absent, that:

52. Peter Milner von Milhausen, *Apologia oder Entschuldigungsschrift, auß was für unvermeidlichen Ursachen alle drey Stände deß löblichen Königreichs Böheimb, so unter beyder gestalt den Leib und Blut deß Herrn Christi empfangen, ein Defensionwerck anstellen müssen* (Prague: Sam. Adam von Weleslaw, 1618). Copies can be found at the Universitätsbibliothek Augsburg, Sign. 02/IV.13.4.145angeb.01, and the Thüringer Universitäts- und Landesbibliothek Jena, 4 Sax.VI, 2(14), among other places.

53. As in Document 1, when the estates refer here to "those who receive the body and blood in both kinds" (*sub utraque specie*), they mean not just Protestants, but also Utraquists and Brethren (see the section introduction, pages 1–2, for more information). Once again, for ease of reading I have translated the simple phrase *sub utraque* as "Protestant" but have given a full translation when the estates have been more verbose, as in this instance.

54. This town, modern-day Kutná Hora, is forty-five miles southeast of Prague and is famous for its silver mines.

55. The Bohemian Confession was a statement of faith made at the 1575 Diet of Prague. It was generally based on the Lutheran Augsburg Confession (1530), but was vague enough eventually to represent a basic point of agreement for all non-Catholics in Bohemia, including the Brethren, Lutherans, and Calvinists.

In previous years, all three estates and inhabitants of the kingdom have faced, suffered, and endured many and various kinds of terrible hardships and tribulations in both political and ecclesiastical affairs. These were instigated and provoked by evil and turbulent people, both clergy and laymen, but especially by members of the Jesuit sect, whose impetuses, writings, and endeavors have always been aimed primarily toward fraudulently subjugating not only His Majesty,[56] but also all Protestant residents and estates of this entire kingdom under the lordship of the Roman See,[57] a foreign authority. Hereafter, however, in the years 1609 and [16]10 a perfect peace was erected. The Letter of Majesty[58] of His Imperial Majesty of blessed memory, Emperor Rudolph [II],[59] as well as an accommodation[60] made by both sides (Catholics[61] and Protestants) and a general diet,[62] all forcefully confirmed and approved that no side would molest the other; but rather, according to the accommodation that they had made and erected between them, both Catholics and Protestants might and ought freely and peacefully to serve the Lord God everywhere, in any place, and without any interruption by either ecclesiastic or temporal authority. And all of this and more was contained and indicated by the said Letter of Majesty, the accommodation, and the general diet.

At the assumption of his reign in this kingdom and following the customs of this land, His Imperial Majesty, now our most gracious king and lord,[63]

---

56. The king of Bohemia.

57. The papacy.

58. The Letter of Majesty was signed by Emperor Rudolph II on July 9, 1609. It affirmed the Bohemian Confession, guaranteed religious freedom in the kingdom, established a unified Protestant consistory for church government, gave control of the University of Prague to the Protestants, allowed the estates to appoint twenty-four religious Defenders, and allowed the estates to keep their existing churches and build new ones on crown lands.

59. Emperor Rudolph II (1552–1612) was king of Bohemia from 1575 to 1611. His long struggle with his brother Matthias weakened him such that he was unwillingly forced to grant Bohemian Protestants the 1609 Letter of Majesty.

60. The accommodation, also referred to elsewhere as the union, was an agreement made between the Protestant and Catholic estates over certain points of contention not covered by the Letter of Majesty.

61. Those who received communion in one kind (*sub una specie*) were non-Hussite Catholics. For ease of reading, however, every future use of the term "Catholic" in this document should be understood to represent the phrase *sub una specie* unless otherwise noted.

62. A general diet was a meeting of the full Bohemian parliament. In addition to serving as the principal political and legislative body, the Bohemian diet also claimed the right to elect the king.

63. Matthias, who was both Holy Roman Emperor and king of Bohemia.

also admirably and powerfully approved and confirmed this—not only generally, but also specifically.

Yet nevertheless, the above-mentioned enemies of the king, land, and general peace spared no effort to find a way to negate the concord (which had been both desired and confirmed) and to carry out their evil, extremely dangerous, and pernicious intentions toward this kingdom and our successors. Thus even at the time when the above-mentioned peace and accommodation were being made and ratified, they advanced other persons who were, like them, Catholics; and they refused to subscribe to the Letter of Majesty and the erected accommodation, or to the amnesty (by force of which we, with the help of Emperor Rudolph of blessed memory, were completely reconciled, and all desire for vengeance among us and our followers was abolished).[64] Instead they strove to abolish completely all of this, truly proving their malicious disposition and intentions toward quite a few members of the estates. . . .

[The authors accuse these men, whom they call traitors, of attempting to block the proper line of royal succession in order to undermine Bohemian Protestantism.]

Then, using the Jesuits and other tools of theirs, [these enemies] once again began to issue a variety of abuse, slander, and denunciations against Protestants, giving people to understand, both in public writings and by word of mouth, that we were heretics, with whom (according to their teaching) one was not bound to keep any faith, either promised or proscribed, no matter its importance. They also dishonored us with all kinds of ignominious names and demonstrated great contempt for our teachings and the Protestant religion, and in their libelous publications also proclaimed that Protestants and all of those who were not Roman Catholic had rejected a life of honor: thereby animating the secular authorities to use fire and sword to eradicate Protestantism.[65] And so that they could all the more easily deceive the people and provoke and bring about mistrust among the Protestant members of the estates, the enemies of this territory and of the common peace also tried to sow division among the Defenders[66] (who, with the gracious approval and

64. The amnesty was proclaimed by Rudolph II in order to protect both Catholics and non-Catholics from punishment for their actions prior to the issuance of the Letter of Majesty.

65. Protestants accused the Jesuits and their supporters of publishing numerous violent and defamatory tracts against Protestants and Protestant ministers—stating, for example, that the ministers' wives were whores, their children bastards.

66. The Defenders were a group of twenty-four men appointed by the estates, whose

ratification of His Majesty, had for very good reasons been decreed by us to be protectors of our religion—something that the oft-mentioned Letter of Majesty had granted and approved), and thereby to abolish completely the Protestant consistory,[67] . . .

[The authors then list further attempts to create disunity among the Protestants.]

Sometimes with great promises, sometimes with threats of incurring His Imperial Majesty's extreme disfavor, [the Catholic zealots] endeavored to convince the Defenders to walk away from their duties. They thus provoked some Defenders who were weak of faith to falter, and brought others to their side with promises and commitments of gaining lofty offices, encouraging them to believe that people would otherwise have little respect for them and that they would lose all worldly advantage and preference. Hence [the Defenders] chose worldly things over their consciences, forgetting the truth that they had once recognized and professed, and falling away from the faith.

Thereafter [the Catholic zealots] proceeded even further, and, after attaining higher offices,[68] they—not only by virtue of their royal and territorial commissions, but also on the authority of His Imperial Majesty— ignominiously discarded valuable old civil servants and put in their place other magistrates (along with their assistants) who, like them, were Catholics. Thereby they evilly plagued the subjects in diverse ways on account of religion, had them banished under the pretense of secular malfeasances, and wherever, in accordance with the Letter of Majesty and the union, there were priests who received communion in both kinds[69] and [Protestant] ministers, they disposed of them and put in their place others who were Catholic. In the towns surrounding Prague, furthermore, they issued a decree that Catholics be given the most distinguished positions and offices. These officials then used such diverse tricks and oaths, and so perpetrated their malice on the Protestant councilors, that the latter were forced against their will to do almost everything that was desired and commanded of them. . . .

---

job it was to protect the religious liberties and rights of non-Catholics in the kingdom. Their role was confirmed by the 1609 Letter of Majesty.

67. The consistory was the instrument of church government. The Letter of Majesty placed the Bohemian consistory under the joint control of all non-Catholic denominations in the kingdom, thereby creating an administrative union of Utraquists, Brethren, and Protestants in Bohemia.

68. In particular, as regents appointed by Matthias to oversee Bohemia in his absence.

69. Utraquist priests.

*[The authors complain that this process of stacking public offices with
Catholics, plus the emperor's appointment of new Catholic magistrates to
oversee Protestant churches, meant that for a long time they neither knew,
nor received, their full rights, including their right to convoke a general
assembly to discuss religious grievances and their right to manage all church
affairs and income without royal interference.]*

For these and other considerable reasons, we, on behalf of the above-
mentioned higher estates[70] and of our townships (which have never retreated
nor been diverted from the defense ordained for our religion), are now assembled at Prague Castle to offer our fitting apology in this matter by means
of a letter to His Imperial Majesty. And we have prevailed in this to such an
extent that all present have agreed to adopt and accept this letter. We, for
our part, have also promised to do our utmost, faithfully and sincerely, now
and in the future, with the consent of His Imperial Majesty, to preserve and
comply with the oft-mentioned Letter of Majesty and that which appertains
to it, inasmuch as everything is joined together so that the one cannot exist
without the other.

But so that we, the aforementioned Evangelical[71] estates, may oppose the
enemies of the kingdom, the territory, and the general peace, we shall now
describe what further actions they have undertaken: namely, that without
gaining the proper legal authority from the diet, which is required in such
matters, they made themselves into independent judges of the Letter of
Majesty, the union, and the resolution of the [1609] diet. In particular, as
they saw that His Roman Imperial Majesty, our most gracious king and
lord,[72] was in many ways troubled by other extremely important affairs concerning all of Christendom, and thus found it impossible to keep in mind
the entire range of territorial liberties, privileges, treaties, and accords, they
(so that they could set His Imperial Majesty at odds with the Protestant estates and move him to dispatch to them such powers as were explicitly forbidden in the Letter of Majesty) issued a written report stating that nowhere
in the Letter of Majesty and the union is it stated that those subjects belonging to cloisters[73] have any right to build churches. But such a thing is
not a matter for their personal consideration and report. Rather, as previously mentioned, the diet placed into the hands of both parties a measured

---

70. The nobles and knights.

71. The term "Evangelical" is used in this period both generally, to mean "Protestant,"
and specifically, to mean "Lutheran." Here the more general "Protestant" is meant.

72. Emperor Matthias.

73. Those who lived on land owned by the Catholic Church.

procedure for such cases, so that should some conflict arise between them, an equal number of persons appointed by both religions would establish a fair legislation. Bypassing this procedure, however, [the enemies] used the powers that their report had won for them from His Imperial Majesty and commanded the residents of the city of Braunau[74] to cease construction of the churches that they had started. The residents of Braunau complained of this to the ordained Defenders, sought recourse with them, and begged most fervently to be protected by the Letter of Majesty and the union (which they had joined at the diet).

After some deliberation, however, the Defenders decided not to resolve this affair on their own. Instead, in accordance with the substance of the diet's resolution and the instructions given to them, they called to Prague the highest territorial officers, legal assessors, members of His Imperial Majesty's two councils who knew the pertinent laws,[75] and six people from every region. After mature deliberation, they found (not only by virtue of those articles that appear and are published here in this, our *Apology*, but also on account of other reasons which we will omit here for brevity's sake) that the residents of Braunau, as well as all other subjects in this kingdom of Bohemia who belonged to the clergy,[76] were all recipients and participants of the grace and beneficence granted by His Imperial Majesty to the Protestant estates.[77] The oft-mentioned Letter of Majesty also clearly states, among other things: "That no powers or anything else contrary to Letter of Majesty and our confirmation, nor anything that might frustrate or alter it in the least," shall issue from or be adopted by His Imperial Majesty, his heirs, future kings of Bohemia, nor anyone else. And should such powers nevertheless be issued or adopted by anyone, they would be of no force, nor should there then be any further discussion or investigation of their legality or illegality.

For this reason, the estates and Defenders present made their determination and report and gave the residents of Braunau, of the little hill towns, and of Klostergrab[78] (which belongs to the archbishop of Prague) the

---

74. Brumov (known as Braunau in German) is a town approximately 140 miles northeast of Prague, on the banks of the river Steine.

75. In other words, jurists who served as councilors to the king.

76. Those who lived on land owned by the Catholic Church.

77. The Letter of Majesty and union allowed members of the three estates (but not peasants) to build churches and schools on crown land. The Protestants who attended the meeting determined that, according to Bohemian law, all land—even that owned by the Catholic Church—was technically crown land and so included in the agreement. This interpretation was not shared by the king, nor by his Catholic advisors.

78. Hrob (known as Klostergrab in German) is located in the far northwest of the modern Czech Republic, on the border with Germany.

answer that they should complete the building of their churches and use them for their church services—yet only with the express condition "That they should otherwise, and in all matters, behave peaceably, respectfully, and properly, and not give any reason for Catholics to feel antipathy and distaste. Much less should they move their superiors, the lord abbot or lord archbishop, toward agitation or rage against them, either through derogatory words or in any other way (for they well know that such would be strongly forbidden and frowned upon). Instead, they should offer all proper obedience to [their superiors] and their officials in all secular and political affairs, as is required of all loyal subjects." And we, all three Protestant estates, then approved and affirmed this answer (which had been reached with the advice of those then present) by means of a document issued by the Defenders and a full general diet held in the year 1615 at Prague Castle.

At the diet we also made known to His Imperial Majesty, as our king and lord, these and other diverse hardships and torments that had been perpetrated in the said places, to the prejudice of His Imperial Majesty's rule over the people and contrary to the express text of the Letter of Majesty and union. And we maintained the certain hope of reaching an understanding and a redress of these matters before the diet concluded.

Yet the enemies of the king, the land, and the common peace turned back to their accustomed tricks, and because they were sure they could use His Imperial Majesty's authority to do whatever they liked, they did all sorts of things to hinder us estates from getting an answer before the close of the diet. Quite a few of them presumed and dared (by peculiar means and by virtue of their legal status and official commissions) to use all their force at the general diet, until finally they achieved and arranged that we estates, loyal subjects of His Imperial Majesty despite all of the great burdens placed on us and our own poor subjects in the past, agreed to five years of tremendous and almost impossible taxes and contributions levied on us and our poor subjects for the payment of His Imperial Majesty's debts.[79] And we did this only out of the hope that this would eventually bring us some remedy for our hardships.

At the conclusion of the diet, however (and through the impetus of the oft-mentioned enemies of the land), we had still gained no answer from His Imperial Majesty, much less any remedy. Instead, these hardships piled up more and more over time, until finally, as His Imperial Majesty was staying at the castle of Brandeis after having left this kingdom,[80] he summoned (at

---

79. Note that here and elsewhere the estates carefully avoided accusing the king, but rather put the blame solely on his councilors and regents.

80. At the end of 1617, Emperor Matthias and his court moved from Prague to Vienna, stopping briefly at the Czech town of Brandeis (Brandýs nad Labem) on the way and leaving the kingdom under the control of the regents.

these people's instigation, without doubt) one of the Defenders—namely Lord Heinrich Matthias, count von Thurn, at that time Burgrave of Karl-stein, etc.,[81]—and, in the presence of two other people,[82] announced that he did not recognize as legitimate the complaint and plea of the Protestant estates, and that he had also handed all of his authority over their affairs to the archbishop of Prague and did not want to be bothered with it any further. . . .

[Thurn begs the emperor to reconsider, but to no avail.]

Instead, the lord archbishop had the newly built church at Klostergrab (which had cost a great sum of money, and toward which many electors and princes of the Holy Roman Empire and other lofty persons had contributed) pulled down, razed to the ground, and leveled, to the disgrace of our Evangelical religion. Similarly, the residents of Braunau received a command that they cede their church to the abbot, let it stand idle, and leave the keys to it in the Bohemian chancellery. As they refused to do such a thing and instead asked to be allowed to keep their churches, several of their leaders were sent to the castle of Prague and imprisoned, and they remained there despite the great lamentations of their wives, children, and friends.

This act, among many other tribulations that occurred more and more often in various places, was referred to the Defenders, who were universally blamed in the local districts for intentionally disregarding their duties. Given such significant cause, however, and following the instructions of the oft-mentioned diet, the Defenders then once again called to Prague the highest territorial officers, legal assessors, and members of His Imperial Majesty's councils, as well as six Protestants from every region.[83] At this meeting, they and we took up these matters, and because we wished to proceed with all possible mildness and modesty, we neither addressed nor took up any other concerns. Instead, we merely delivered a humble supplication to the lord regents[84] and another to His Imperial Majesty in Vienna, begging with even more lowly humility that His Imperial Majesty would give the order to stop such tribulations and would graciously allow the residents of Braunau to be freed from their imprisonment. And for this reason we also wrote to the

81. Count von Thurn had long been a leader of the Bohemian estates and played a major role both in forcing Emperor Rudolph II to sign the Letter of Majesty in 1609 and in the 1618 Defenestration of Prague.

82. A representative of the knights, Ulrich von Gersdorf, and of the burghers, Simon Kohout of Lichtenfels.

83. This meeting occurred on March 5, 1618.

84. The council of ten regents that ruled Bohemia in the emperor's absence.

estates of the margravate of Moravia, as well as the princes and estates of Upper and Lower Silesia and the lords and estates of Upper and Lower Lusatia (which are all lands incorporated into this kingdom), in order to seek their appropriate intercession with His Imperial Majesty.[85] To this end, we then conferred with the Defenders about a second meeting to be held in the college of Emperor Charles IV on the Monday after Rogation Sunday,[86] so in case some answer to our supplication came in the meantime from His Imperial Majesty, we could hear and take it into consideration. But when we appeared on the established day, we discovered that in this entire time no answer had arrived from His Imperial Majesty, nor had our hardships been redressed. To the contrary, through the provocation and instigation of our oft-mentioned enemies, His Majesty had sent a very sharp letter to the regents that placed not only the Defenders, but also us, in most extreme danger. He had also ordered that it be presented to the Defenders. Its contents are as follows:

First, His Imperial Majesty deemed that these, our meetings, had been called and employed against his own royal person.

Second, concerning the [destruction of the] church at Klostergrab and the punishment of the disloyal residents of the city of Braunau who were subjects of the cloister, both had been done by His Majesty's lawful order.

Third, we had tried to do more than was allowed by the Letter of Majesty and the accommodation between the Catholic and Protestant estates.

And fourth, we had iniquitously employed foreigners against His Majesty, defended their public disobedience and rebellion against His Imperial Majesty, and sought to fortify them in this [rebellion]: behavior that His Imperial Majesty had in no way expected from some of the people who were the authors of these acts.

He added further, that because we had abused His Majesty's good nature and also tried to do more than was our due, His Majesty would not fail to inquire further into this, and to proceed appropriately against those responsible, each according to his due. In the meantime, he also forbade the Defenders from calling any further meetings until his return to this kingdom or until he issued further orders to that effect. He instructed the lord regents, furthermore, to admonish other inhabitants that they should neither appear at nor respond to such a call. All of this was amply expressed in the letter. . . .

---

85. Moravia, Silesia, and Lusatia were part of a federal union under the Bohemian crown. The Protestant estates hoped to involve these other lands in the struggle and thus increase their leverage over Emperor Matthias.

86. The Sunday before Ascension Thursday, which is the day in the Christian calendar commemorating the bodily ascension of Jesus Christ into heaven. The day of the meeting would thus have been May 21, 1618.

[The authors state that they were horrified at the letter and argue that the blame for it falls on their enemies, who had purposely misled the emperor about them.]

Furthermore, it is more than sufficiently known and evident that, desiring to place honorable people under suspicion and cause them trouble, they brought everything to bear against them—even if it ran contrary to all right, equitableness, and every good order—and used both unusual and usual means to take numerous people's belongings and subject them to great hardships. Especially when it came to Evangelicals, they withheld, at the very least, their rights and justice, and tried to make black seem white, white black, loyal and obedient subjects of His Imperial Majesty disloyal, and, on the contrary, the disloyal loyal. Meanwhile they honored and elevated frivolous and evil people while helping to belittle and bring into contempt those who were well behaved. At the same time, they badly plagued, on account of religion, not only their own subjects but also those of the entire land, including without distinction both those under His Imperial Majesty's control and those who belonged to the ecclesiastical properties; and they used unheard-of atrocities to force people to convert to the Catholic religion against their will and against the clear language of the Letter of Majesty. Indeed, the royal judges' threats against the royal free cities brought several of these cities to the point at which they were forced to agree no longer to stand with the estates [of Bohemia], nor to be counted among their number. [The enemies] planned to do even more evil things, and when we asked them if their advice [to the emperor] had not caused the above-mentioned letter and our denunciation, they neither could, nor did, deny it.

For these above-enumerated reasons, we proceeded against two of their members—namely, Wilhelm Slawata von Chlum und Kosumberg and Jaroslav Borsita von Martinitz, otherwise known as Smeczensky—as destroyers of the law and the common peace, and also because they did not keep in mind the offices and positions in which they found themselves, but instead evilly misused them toward the belittlement of the authority of His Imperial Majesty, our king and lord, as well as toward the abolishment of the common peace in this kingdom of Bohemia. And after determining from their past publications that they were indeed such as they appeared to be, in accordance with the old custom we threw both of them, along with a secretary (their sycophant who had, among other things, caused great disruptions in the towns of Prague), out the window.[87] And we shall proceed further against

---

87. This act, the Defenestration of Prague, occurred on May 23, 1618. See Document 1.

them (for they are still living) and their goods, as well as against all those whom they represent and defend, those who wish to persecute us or anyone else by whatever ways or means, and equally all who are destroyers of the Letter of Majesty and union, or who would perpetrate similar crimes. . . .

To which end, we, at this, our assembly at the castle of Prague, have established a kingdomwide system of defense for the good of His Imperial Majesty and this kingdom (our dear fatherland), and for the protection of our wives and children from all kinds of danger. And through this action we do not intend to do anything against His Imperial Majesty, our most gracious king and lord, nor desire to cause any inopportuneness for peaceable people or our dear Catholic friends (as long as they themselves desire to live in peace). For it is commonly recognized and known that by this action no further layperson or clergyman shall be harmed, nor any tumult result, but rather good peace shall be maintained everywhere—both in the cities of Prague and in the entire kingdom—except only for the above-listed unavoidable reasons, and then only when we neither should nor can do otherwise or any less.

For this reason, we dare to hope that His Imperial Majesty, our gracious king and lord, will not otherwise interpret our actions, nor give credence to other contrary reports about us. We also do not fear that our dear Catholic friends shall either publicly or secretly show themselves to be our enemies on account of the just punishments we made in the name of our Letter of Majesty, union, and freedoms. Instead, we maintain the unquestioning hope that—either in consideration of the reasons explained above and the sufficiently described crimes of the aforementioned people, or due to the fact that we have not in the least intended to act against the Imperial Majesty (our most gracious emperor, king, and lord), against those of the Roman religion, or against the union made with them—everyone not only excuses us, but also helps us against all opponents and acts with us in doing whatever is necessary to maintain general freedoms, territorial privileges, and that which serves mutual love and unity.

Therefore we beseech His Imperial Majesty, our most gracious king and lord, that, if necessary, he will dispatch another, more detailed apology to excuse us to the entire world.

Given at the castle of Prague in our general assembly, the Friday after the feast of the ascension of Jesus Christ, that is the 25th of May new style,[88] in the year 1618.

---

88. "New style" means according to the new Gregorian calendar, which corrected the older Julian calendar by adding ten days. Since not all states had adopted this new calendar by the seventeenth century, people were often forced to specify which calendar their dating followed. They did this by adding the phrase *stylo novo* (new style) for the Gregorian calendar and *stylo vetero* (old style) for the Julian calendar.

3. Declaration of Elector Frederick V of the Palatinate (November 7, 1619)[89]

[Frederick V (1596–1632),[90] the Calvinist elector of the Palatinate, was crowned king of Bohemia on October 25, 1619 in the city of Prague. In the following declaration, which he had published across Europe, he explained both his understanding of the problems in Bohemia and his reasons for accepting the Bohemian crown. Frederick invoked his responsibilities as a good Christian, an elector, and a friend of Bohemia, but passed over in silence an issue that was perhaps of the greatest interest to the rest of the empire. For accepting the kingship had much larger constitutional implications: were Frederick to become both king of Bohemia and elector Palatine, he would then hold two votes in the electoral college. These two votes, added to the votes of the Calvinist elector of Brandenburg and the Lutheran elector of Saxony, would give Protestants a majority. At the very least, this would ensure that future emperors would likewise be Protestant; but it would also signify a radical realignment of the religious and political balance of the empire.]

Frederick, by the grace of God king in Bohemia, count Palatine of the Rhine and elector, etc.; our candid announcement of why we took up the crown of Bohemia and the rule of its incorporated territories

We, Frederick, by the grace of God king in Bohemia, count Palatine of the Rhine and elector, duke in Bavaria, margrave in Moravia, duke in Silesia and Lutzenburg, and margrave in Lusatia, etc., offer each and every Christian potentate, elector, and state our zealous service, friendship, and gracious intentions, and therefore declare:

The problem was also sometimes solved by giving the date according to both calendars: i.e., May 15/25, 1618.

89. Ludwig Camerarius, ed., *Unser Friederichs von Gottes Gnaden Königs in Böheimb, Pfaltzgraffen bey Rhein, und Churfürsten, etc. Offen Außschreiben, Warumb Wir die Kron Böheimb, und der incorporirten Länder Regierung auff Uns genommen* (Prague: Bohutsky von Hranitz, 1619). A copy can be found at the Universitätsbibliothek Augsburg, Sign. 02/IV.13.4.148angeb.02, and a slightly abbreviated version is published in Johann Philipp Abelinus and Matthaeus Merian, *Theatrum Europaeum*, Bd. 1 (Frankfurt am Main: Daniel Fievet, 1662), 248–52.

90. Frederick V, elector of the Palatinate (1596–1632), controlled the territories of the Upper Palatinate and the Palatinate of the Rhine (also known as the Rhenish Palatinate or the Lower Palatinate), an imperial state in southwestern Germany with its capital at Heidelberg. As an elector, he was also one of the seven great imperial princes who chose or elected the Holy Roman Emperor.

That we have no doubt that everyone, both within and without the empire, knows quite well the wretched and dangerous state into which the ancient and worthy kingdom of Bohemia (a most distinguished member of the Holy Roman Empire) has fallen, along with its incorporated territories and other neighboring states; and what tribulations, hardships, and hostile acts have been practiced in the past, including unceasing robbery, murder, the burning of farms and the countryside, the destruction of the territory, the spilling of much innocent Christian blood, the violation of honorable wives and maidens, the dismembering of small and nursing children, and other inhuman, barbarous excesses, maliciousness, and atrocities. Furthermore, experience and the many comprehensive reports that have emerged make the principal cause and wellspring of all such evil, misery, and distress (and of what then resulted or may yet arise) so blindingly clear that even those who supported it, by both their words and deeds (thus willfully misleading the higher sorts and bringing them into the present danger and loss), must themselves now be convinced of it in their own hearts and consciences.

For even in these recent times, when various opinions have arisen on the subject of faith and religion, one can clearly discern that according to the contents of the Holy Scripture and the foundation laid long ago by the doctors of the Church, the consciences of men may not be ordered, constrained, or overpowered; but whenever such compulsion has been either secretly or publicly attempted, it has only resulted in an evil outcome and caused marked changes in distinguished kingdoms and provinces.

Nonetheless, and especially after numerous foreign people[91] crept into the Empire of the German Nation and the kingdom and lands that belong to and border it, there emerged a new and dangerous teaching and opinion that is extremely and fundamentally dangerous to all potentates and rulers. Clothing themselves in the appearance of holiness, these people[92] insinuated themselves not only with great lords and houses, but also with their councilors and officers, and in general with the richest and most distinguished people in all places, and thereby created a noticeable growth in the false zeal to pressure, persecute, and—wherever they refused to yield—extirpate completely all those who had cut themselves off from the Roman Church.[93]

---

91. He means the Jesuits. Since many Jesuit priests in Bohemia came from outside the empire, they were branded as foreign interlopers who represented a foreign power, the papacy.

92. The Jesuits.

93. The Jesuits made it a policy to further Catholicism by becoming the confessors or teachers of kings and other important people, then using their positions to convince these rulers to clamp down vigorously on Protestantism.

From this it followed that although previous worthy regents had done their utmost to preserve the common peace (despite the above-mentioned religious disunity in the Roman Empire, and especially in the kingdom of Bohemia) and had tried to maintain a fair equilibrium between the adherents of both religions by issuing special concessions, appropriate religious settlements, and other decisions, nevertheless their successors (doubtless following others' urgings rather than their own natures and inclinations) gave such free rein to the above-mentioned ill-intentioned people and their followers that they were able to carry out one innovation after the other. Furthermore, they not only used public writings to drag into dangerous debate all past religious concessions, pacts, and related obligations and oaths, but also actively tried to weaken, annul, and abolish them entirely.

Now, we do not at this time or in this place wish to discuss everything that has been done, attempted, or practiced in this regard in past years throughout the entire Roman Empire, nor in what difficult circumstances the empire even now finds itself (for such a discussion will find its further sufficient exposition later, when and where appropriate).

But concerning, in particular, the worthy crown of Bohemia and its incorporated territories, it is quite undeniable and recognized that here the Roman religion[94] greatly waned over time while the light of the Holy Gospel[95] dawned, and that great difficulties frequently arose from this, such that in the end the only remaining solution was to make a great effort to maintain the peace through the issuance of certain compacts, concessions, and exemptions, so that peaceful coexistence and human society might not be completely dissolved and severed on account of different opinions on religion.

So long as things persisted on such terms, people on all sides were content. But the above-mentioned hot-headed people[96] were unable to abide such peaceful prosperity. Instead, as indicated above, they preferred to push things to extremes rather than set aside or abandon their deeply rooted intention of bringing everything back under the spiritual domination of the pope and the secular domination of a foreign power.[97] From this it then came to pass that throughout these territories religious grievances increased daily (especially concerning the Letter of Majesty),[98] as [these people] constantly perpetrated or practiced one act of violence after another, knocking

94. Catholicism.

95. Protestantism.

96. The Jesuits.

97. In other words, to limit both the religious freedom and the secular power of the local Calvinist Bohemian nobles.

98. The Letter of Majesty was issued by Emperor Rudolph II in 1609 and acknowledged by his successors. See note 58 for more information.

down and closing newly built Evangelical[99] churches, instigating threats against the estates, withdrawing from them their justly entitled defenses,[100] persecuting the poor subjects in an unchristian and most heinous manner, and threatening people of both high and low estate with great hardships, dishonor, danger to life and limb, and the loss of every worldly possession. Then, when the people naturally sought to use whatever means were available to resist such measures (all of which one can read about in many writings published by the estates in question), they were met with the edge of a sword and open hostility, so that henceforth the oft-mentioned crown of Bohemia, as well as its incorporated territories and provinces and other admirable neighboring lands, were most painfully and in large part ravaged, devastated, ruined by fire and sword, and, so to speak, put to ashes.

And although these territories have long (but especially in the last years) done their utmost to protect the crown of Hungary and particularly the border fortifications against the Turks (a powerful enemy), even sacrificing their own goods and blood, yet things have now come to such extremes that the fortifications have been completely denuded of troops, artillery, and munitions, and whatever was destined to oppose the Turks has instead been used against the Bohemian nation. Moreover, at the same time, and supposedly to maintain the protection of the border fortifications, not only have the old unpaid Turk taxes[101] been collected throughout the empire, but other taxes and new contributions have also been sought, and partially received, in numerous circles[102] of the empire; and in the same way, these have not been employed for the end given, but instead only for the ruin of the members of the empire and their dependencies. Hence, not only has the bulwark of Christendom, so to speak, been breached and condemned to fall, but at the same time the Hungarian nation has also been given cause and occasion to look to itself to secure its own welfare and conservation.

Now, we fully expect that it is no less well known across the empire how, in these awkward circumstances, we and numerous other kindhearted electors and princes, and even other foreign potentates, did not fail to issue faithful and sincere warnings and intercessions (both from the very beginning and as the fire grew ever hotter), hoping to avoid further disaster through more moderate means and ways. . . .

99. Protestant.

100. The Defenders.

101. Taxes levied on the people of the empire to pay for the defense of the borders against the Ottoman Turks.

102. The empire was divided into ten administrative regions, or circles, by Emperor Maximilian I in 1512.

[He states that he would have far preferred that things be settled peacefully and quickly by the parties involved. He then discusses the pernicious curtailing of Bohemia's religious and political freedoms after the death of Emperor Matthias.]

In the end, the [Bohemian] territories were suffering so greatly and had been driven to such extremes that they seized the means by which they might deliver themselves from such overwhelming hardships and more firmly establish and extend the defenses given to them by God and nature alike. To such an end, they erected a confederation with each other (for which they had also previously obtained royal assurances) and hereby moved even closer toward a complete change of their government and a new election.[103] . . .

[He argues that he had tried to be a calm mediator, acting for the good of the empire and not out of hope of personal gain.]

As, however, the election to the crown of Bohemia and its incorporated territories has fallen to us by the unanimous vote of the collected estates at a general assembly, we testify before God and with good conscience that we have always been perfectly satisfied with the electoral dignity and our inherited principality and territories, which were granted to us by God the Unwavering. Therefore we have not sought a greater elevation, nor have we tried to gain the above-mentioned crown of Bohemia by force or through any other actions, a fact to which the estates that elected us have publicly given witness (and can continue to do so). Furthermore, given the deplorable situation, we also had no reason to do so, but would instead have much preferred to have seen the return of peace, which would also have allowed the empire to maintain greater tranquillity and security for a while longer. For, not to mention many other considerations, we can quite easily estimate the burden, worry, effort, work, and danger that the present persistent warfare and ruined territories will surely bring us. We also have no doubt that sensible people will agree that to accept and take up the offer of a kingdom in such a condition requires a much firmer resolve than to refuse a peaceable kingdom, and is thus an act for which some men have been so highly praised in the history books. Moreover, we once again testify, and with a pure

103. Bohemia was joined in its rebellion by the neighboring states of Lusatia, Moravia, and Silesia, all of which signed an Act of Confederation in July 1619 to better defend themselves against the Habsburg emperor and his allies. The estates of Upper Austria later also allied with the rebels. Having "a new election" meant choosing a new king, since the Bohemian kingship was an elective one.

conscience, that had we seen some means or certainty that our repudiation of the crown would have allowed this unholy war to be contained and the noble peace truly to be obtained, or that thereby the entire Roman Empire could have been sufficiently secured, then all the honor and goods in the world would not have swayed us, but we would instead not only have completely repudiated the offered crown of Bohemia, but also gladly employed our greatest efforts toward achieving such a peace.

And we have not rushed into this great work, but first faithfully appealed to God the Almighty (who takes and gives kingdoms to whomever He will) to put the proper inclination into our heart. We also discussed the matter in confidence with our noblemen and friends, and finally we deemed that in consideration of all the circumstances, we were forced to sense the miraculous presence and firm hand of God in the entire affair. Therefore we neither could nor should have opposed His holy will and calling, all the less as we were completely convinced that the oft-mentioned estates of the crown of Bohemia and its incorporated territories had many important, established, legitimate, and sufficient reasons to make the intended change in their government, and so more firmly secure their liberty and renowned ancient right of free election (which some wanted to take away from them and enfeeble by extraordinary means). Thus the affair is in itself legal, Christian, and worthy, which is also easily proven by various ecclesiastical and secular historical examples. At the same time, however, we do not seek unjustly to dispossess or deprive any other person of that which belongs to him, but rather to legitimize those who desire their liberty, privileges, the Letter of Majesty, the free exercise of the Evangelical religion, and other just practices; to shield and preserve them against unjust violence; and also, as far as we are able and as far as God grants us His power and blessings, to rescue and emancipate this magnificent land and its many thousands of honest people from further suffering and eventual ruin.

Therefore, because we gain no temporal joy, delight, or advantage from this, but rather have before our eyes solely the honor of God, the common welfare, its subsequent consolation, protection, and conservation, and the pleas and sighs of so many pious hearts (which moved us greatly), we very much hope that God the Unwavering will not abandon us in this task, but will grant us, from on high, the means to oppose the thoughts of all men, so that through His assistance we can accomplish and implement that which (according to His inconceivable wisdom) has long since been decided through His divine Providence and omnipotence. And should we fail to perform this task, we would not only have our conscience greatly burdened, but also have to expect God's wrath and punishment.

At the same time, we have further considered that had we brushed aside this divine vocation, then presumably we would have been blamed—especially by the adherents of the Evangelical religion—for all the subsequent spilling of blood and territorial destruction. And should the adversaries have succeeded in their goal, which included an intended and obviously pending oppression of the Bohemian nation and its confederates, then we would also have provided these adversaries an opportunity to turn the weapons they had in hand against us and other Evangelical states of the empire (so they could try to effect the same thing). For the above-mentioned restless people[104] have constantly admonished and encouraged the Bohemian regents to act thusly (even using published writings), and have also stated that the regents should not even spare the little innocents—no, not even their own children, noble families, or land and people. These and various other constant threats have been heard far and wide.

Furthermore, we have had to weigh and consider that were the worthy kingdom of Bohemia—which is, after all, both a distinguished member of the empire and a bulwark against foreign nations—not immediately assisted in some way, it might well have fallen (along with its incorporated lands) into other, foreign hands, and so found itself in such a state that it would have been completely detached from the Holy Empire of the German Nation, or at least have been the cause of various difficulties, especially for neighboring Evangelical electors and princes. On account of our electoral house and principality of the Upper Palatinate, therefore, we neither could nor should have allowed such a thing—not only because of the obligation and loyalty that we possess and owe to the empire, our beloved fatherland, but also because of the ancient hereditary alliances made between our electoral house of the Palatinate and the crown of Bohemia. Due to these said reasons, therefore, we had to be all the more diligent about the conservation of this kingdom, confident that no one who sufficiently and dispassionately considered everything that had actually occurred could hold it against us.

Thus, in the name of God, for the advancement of His holy honor, for the comfort and protection of those who are so greatly distressed, for the maintenance of the common liberty and welfare, for other even more urgent motives and reasons, and in response to the diverse deferential and humble written appeals sent to us by the estates of Bohemia and all of their incorporated lands, their handsome legations, and especially their ardent desire and push for our intervention, we finally endorsed the unanimous election they offered us, and so accepted and took up the crown and government of the worthy kingdom of Bohemia and its oft-mentioned incorporated lands. Then, with God's assistance, we and our dearly beloved wife (the princess of Great Britain)[105] also moved here, in person, to Prague. A few days later, with the unanimous consent and agreement of the estates and the great

104. The Jesuits.

105. Elizabeth Stuart (1596–1662), daughter of James I Stuart (1566–1625), who was king of both Scotland and England. James had proclaimed himself "king of Great Britain," though the two crowns were not officially united until 1707. Frederick

applause of all the people, we (along with Her Highness) were crowned with the usual solemnity and were thus set upon the royal throne. May the Almighty, by His mighty arm, graciously confirm us in this, and generously grant His Holy Spirit and blessing that we direct our entire reign so that the Lord of all Lords, our savior Jesus Christ, may rule over us and our subjects, and long maintain us in both true peace and territorial prosperity.

Aside from this, we attest before God and the entire world that in this, our reign, we are firmly resolved that no one be molested or oppressed on account of religion, nor hindered in his traditional religious practice—not even those who still confess to the Roman Church (when they merely prove to be peaceful and blameless toward the basic laws of the kingdom and the territory, and especially those Letters of Majesty that concern religion). And because of this, even the above-mentioned Roman Catholics in the kingdom of Bohemia and its territories have, in great numbers and through a solemn oath and the pledging of their hands, declared their support for the commonly established defensive confederation, assented to our recent election and subsequent crowning, and pledged themselves to be obedient to us.

We are also fully determined to endeavor therein with the highest seriousness and enthusiasm, and to strive to the utmost so that, by God's grace, not only is the noble peace restored and all difficulties of war set aside in our kingdom of Bohemia and its incorporated lands, but also greater trust is sown in the empire itself, and all further danger is turned aside and averted— if only others will also similarly and commonly be disposed not to hinder us in this, nor give cause for further disorder.

We also propose, as much as possible, to cultivate and maintain the goodwill, friendship, correspondence, and trust of all Christian potentates, electors, and estates, and particularly of our neighbors. We anticipate and hereby request the equivalent from them, with friendliness, graciousness, and good intentions: that they would spring to our aid with both word and deed against all those who, with vile intentions, would set upon us or our kingdom and lands with hostile force.

We offer our services in turn to every one of them for whatever may happen that is in our power, and have judged it to be both advisable and necessary (given the state of affairs in these difficult times), to make all of this fully known through this, our public proclamation.

> Given in our Royal Castle at Prague on October 28/November 7, 1619.[106]

---

greatly hoped (in vain, it turned out) that his father-in-law would come to his aid with military and financial assistance.

106. In other words, October 28 according to the old Julian calendar, which most

4. Edict of Ferdinand II Annulling the Bohemian Election (January 29, 1620)[107]

[The Bohemian rebels and Frederick of the Palatinate had already attempted to shape public opinion by publishing their explanations of events, and Emperor Ferdinand II followed suit. The following document, which presents Ferdinand's side in this struggle, is also particularly interesting as an attempt to convince the Protestant princes of the empire that Frederick's actions set a dangerous precedent, and that they should not consider this a matter of religion, but of private property rights, law, and just punishment. If we allow local estates the right to depose and elect their own leaders whenever they wish, the emperor's argument suggested, which prince of the empire is then safe in his possessions?]

In the Year of Our Lord 1620

Ferdinand II, by the grace of God elected Roman emperor, always august, king of Germany, Hungary, Bohemia, Dalmatia, Croatia, and Slavonia, etc. . . .

Although we do not doubt that by now those both within and without the Holy Roman Empire know sufficiently well the grievous circumstances into which our kingdom of Bohemia—which is an electoral state and a principal member of the Holy Roman Empire—has fallen, along with its incorporated lands and other adjacent areas that are also part of our hereditary lands, and also what tribulations, burdens, and enmities our poor, innocent subjects have been subjected to through this newly raised and trying war, along with the general ruin of the land; yet, so that all stubbornly contrary and hostile imaginings are stripped away, we shall explain the actual nature and foundation of this war, so that all men might reach a truthful and unvarnished understanding.

---

of the Protestant states followed; or November 7, according to the recently reformed Gregorian calendar, which most of the Catholic states followed.

107. Ferdinand II von Habsburg, *Der Roem. Kay. Maj. Ferdinandi II. Edictal Cassation und Annulation, mit angeheffter Protestation, wider die angemaste Newe nichtige Wahl und Croenung in Boehaim etc.* (Vienna, 1620). A copy can be found at the Universitätsbibliothek Augsburg, Sign. 02/IV.13.4.155angeb.03. Another German version is published in Johann Philipp Abelinus and Matthaeus Merian, *Theatrum Europaeum*, Bd. 1 (Frankfurt am Main: Daniel Fievet, 1662), 300–304. A copy of an English version titled "The Manifest, or Declaration of His Sacred Imperiall Majesty. Translated Out of Latin" (1620) is available at the Bodleian Library.

The principal wellspring of this disaster and wretched distress occurred during the lifetime and rule of our dearly departed lord uncle and father, Emperor Matthias of blessed memory, who was also at that time the reigning king of Bohemia, when some members of the Bohemian estates, under the stated pretext of some hardships inflicted by some of His Majesty's regents and territorial officers against their religious privileges and the Letter of Majesty, acted on their own authority and, with an excessiveness previously almost unheard of, threw headlong out of the window several of these regents and territorial officers (who were loyal and aristocratic persons), along with other servants. They then seized and took up arms, and without the least respect for their absent but duly reigning king and lord, deposed the above-mentioned regents and officers from their offices. They then took possession of the regalia[108] of the kingdom and established a completely new form of government, in which the presumed and self-proclaimed Directors administered the government, which was employed to their own ends. They thereby far exceeded both the goal and means of the defense of religion, something they had been allowed by the terms of the Letter of Majesty (though they had never proven that this was, or could be considered, a matter of religion, nor could or might it ever be shown to be so in the future), such that all those who can and might judge this impartially and passionlessly, shall see that the above-mentioned arbitrary acts of these subjects against their duly determined authority, can be considered nothing less than a public and hostile defiance and rebellion. . . .

We hope, however, that every peace-loving German who completely favors right and justice shall, given the progress of affairs until now and the information printed about this, accept and recognize that in order to redress the hardships placed upon them (leaving aside the matter of whatever these might be) and in accordance with both Holy Writ and general justice, [these subjects] might well have found another method than, for the sake of their cause, plunging the entire fatherland into such extreme danger and ruin, with the spilling of so much innocent blood. They have even, so to speak, forced the duly established and natural authority to wield authorized counterviolence to defend what belongs to it. . . .

After the supposed Directors had rejected all such alternatives, however, they defiantly formed a bloody alliance and frightened loyal members of the estates through the defenestration of the royal regents and other such presumptuous deeds, intending thereby to be able to pursue their evil intentions with fewer hindrances. They also sought to obligate more deeply those whom they had brought over to their side, by getting them to participate in

---

108. "Regalia" is a term meaning both the symbols or paraphernalia of sovereign rulers and, more generally, the rights and prerogatives those rulers enjoy.

their schemes. They put all their efforts into arms and naked force, not only to ensure that they avoided any punishment for the above-mentioned activities, but also to repress both Protestant and Catholic[109] members of the estates who remained loyal. Then, in the name of all members of the estates, they could implement the plans they had conceived long ago.

Finally, when His Majesty, who was most highly renowned and beloved, could find no indication at all that [the Directors] would heed his completely sincere, fatherly admonition for moderation and understanding; and when he was instead forced to accept that day by day they endeavored to spread the existing fire into the lands incorporated into Bohemia and also into his other hereditary lands; he saw that, given the extreme danger of the situation, it would not be advisable to remain without military countermeasures. Yet, demonstrating his ample fatherly affection, wishing to spare poor innocent people and subjects, and desiring to return things to a state of peace and quiet, he asked the empire's completely impartial electors and princes to take the matter up as mediators. He wanted nothing more than to see that this, along with a ceasefire, could be achieved without delay (though all kinds of incidents arose that hindered this). The articles and information printed by the subjects of Bohemia, however, have already sufficiently demonstrated how little they were interested in such a mediation, and upon what kinds of conditions they insisted.

In the meantime, the most highly regarded emperor and Royal Majesty [Matthias] died, and thus, by the power of our royal coronation and the oaths of allegiance and fealty given by the estates of this same kingdom and of the lands incorporated into it, the kingdom of Bohemia and all of its possessions fell entirely to us. We then did all we could to avoid all further disaster and make without delay all arrangements that were necessitated by these changes. Principally, however, we undertook to issue a royal declaration that would put our confirmation of all territorial privileges into the hands of the supreme burgrave[110] within four weeks, and we also tried to ensure that the kingdom of Bohemia and all of its inhabitants would regain a good state of peace, and that law and justice would be promoted and granted to every man. . . .

[He argues that his efforts were rebuffed.]

109. The actual phrase is: "both those who receive communion in both kinds and those who receive communion in one kind." This includes Protestants and Bohemian Brethren on one side, and Catholics on the other.

110. The supreme burgrave of the castle of Prague, as representative of the king in his absence, was the highest member of the Bohemian government.

We then came to understand that [the Directors] were acting contrarily, so not only did they not accept our royal confirmation [of their privileges], they also rejected the ceasefire that we had earlier urged upon our army. And they did not respond to our mild, fatherly letters, in which we asked them to delegate several persons to come to us, under our royal safeguard, in order to discuss how the dreadful state of affairs that had arisen might best and most quickly be resolved. Instead, they raised a call to arms within the entire kingdom; mustered more troops daily; induced the estates of Moravia[111] also to join their secession; brought to their side the cavalry and infantry recruited by our margraviate [of Moravia] for defense; unexpectedly attacked the city of Brünn[112] and, after badly mishandling them, arrested its governor and other officers; arbitrarily and violently seized the capitol city of Olmütz;[113] deposed the city council; altered the exercise of religion in the main churches; expelled the clergy; confiscated ecclesiastical goods; incited nuns and monks to break their vows; and declared and proscribed as traitors those high-ranking people who heeded their duty and fealty and disassociated themselves from such invidious acts.

Once Moravia had been fully engulfed in flames, [the Bohemians] also set Austria alight. They besieged the city of Laa[114] on the border; shortly thereafter, they presumptuously advanced on the capital city of Vienna, came right up to us, and fired upon our imperial and archducal castle—without any hope of advantage, but only out of malice. The intention of their undertaking and pursuing such an act we leave up to others' imagination and consideration.

But they did not stop there, and at the imperial electoral diet at Frankfurt (which we were duly qualified to attend on account of our kingdom and by the power of the Golden Bull),[115] the representatives of these Bohemians made every effort to hinder our right as an elector to have a seat, a voice, and a vote: without our consent and agreement, they brought our hereditary subjects into their confederation; without any legal cause, with a willful disregard for their sworn fealty, and contrary to the privileges of our kingdom and the laws of the Holy Roman Empire, they moved to invalidate our elec-

---

111. The margraviate of Moravia was a hereditary holding of the Habsburgs. It was incorporated under the Bohemian crown but still possessed its own diet and estates.

112. The German name for Brno, a major Moravian city.

113. The German name for Olomouc, the capital city and chief religious center of Moravia at that time.

114. Laa an der Thaya, on the border between Austria and Bohemia.

115. The king of Bohemia was, by the 1356 imperial law known as the Golden Bull, one of the seven electoral princes of the empire. This meant he was one of those legally authorized to elect the new Holy Roman Emperor.

tion [as king of Bohemia], even as we were being chosen by the electors to take up the imperial dignity of the Roman Empire.

We shall not mention what actions they took in portions of Hungary after our election and coronation as emperor, also leading these subjects away from their obedience to us; they advised and abetted Prince Bethlen Gábor of Transylvania,[116] who was under the protection of our archenemy [the Turks], in his seizure of the fortress of Kaschau[117] and all of Upper Hungary; joining with his army, they again crossed the Danube and advanced on our capital city of Vienna, once again coming face to face with us. Without doubt they had every intention of completing what they had earlier begun, since they would not have been as hindered by military countermeasures. But as this was unsuccessful, they once again hostilely attacked our hereditary lands, robbing and burning them, thereby placing into extreme danger this bulwark of the Holy Roman Empire, the protection of which had cost the blood of so many German Christians and the sweat of so many poor subjects.[118] In sum, they showed themselves so opposed to us, their accepted and lawful ruling authority, by whom they had never in the least been offended, that they could not have demonstrated any greater enmity. . . . They finally went to such an extreme that they upset all at once the fundamental statutes of the kingdom, their fatherland . . . and the traditional observances of eight hundred years . . . and instead established an entirely new constitution for the kingdom. . . .

We could not in the least have anticipated that this invidious rebellious act might find approval by any law-abiding person, especially by a prince of the empire who had been granted his own subjects to rule by God the Almighty and by the Holy Empire, and who would not, without doubt, anticipate such treatment from them. Much less, however, did we expect that anyone would allow himself to become involved with affairs about which he knew nothing, or with our own or our house's rights and prerogatives within this, our kingdom, nor that he would instead take part in an entirely invalid election. But, contrary to the hopes of all men and rejecting the sincere warnings of numerous loyal, kindhearted, peace-loving electors and princes, here too our defiant subjects did not go wanting: such that one

116. Gabriel Bethlen (1580–1629), usually known in English as Bethlen Gábor, was prince of Transylvania. He used the opportunity provided by the Bohemian revolt to expand into Habsburg-controlled Hungary.

117. Košice, a city in modern Slovakia. Bethlen Gábor captured it from the Habsburgs in September 1619.

118. The combined armies of the Bohemians, Moravians, and Bethlen Gábor besieged Vienna from November to December 1619. The siege was lifted when Gábor retreated to meet the threat of an invasion of Transylvania by Cossacks.

might well suppose . . . that the leaders of this conspiracy had in mind such an innovation and development in our kingdom from the beginning. But they have not shown any evidence of their supposed right to do this, nor have they been freed or absolved of the oaths and homage the estates offered to us (and that affect all of our rebellious subjects). For another to assume our hereditary kingdom, to take our subjects up into a new oath of fealty, to violate all laws and regulations of the empire, and especially to go against the greatly affirmed public peace, creates a completely invidious and highly prejudicial example for all potentates and regents, as well as for the Turks and Tatars. And this cannot be sanctioned by God, the supreme judge of all kings and potentates and of both this world and the next. Nor, in particular, can it be sanctioned by the Holy Roman Empire, from which this office of elector and arch-cupbearer[119] proceeds as a fief, and whose electors, princes, and estates—among them also the elector Palatine himself—proclaimed and upheld us as the legitimate, accepted, and crowned king of Bohemia, and, in recognition of this royal dignity, admitted us to the election of the Roman king.[120] . . .

We hereby object to all that has indeed been done against us and our house, and what is to this day still being done, but especially the invalid election and coronation undertaken to our detriment, and, by virtue of this, the possession and occupation of our kingdom and its incorporated lands. And not only do we hereby object to this, in complete conformation with our rights, but we also hereby, by our imperial and royal authority, abrogate and annul it, proclaiming that all of this is, in itself, illegal, null, and void.

In response to such crimes, therefore, we and our praiseworthy house reserve all legally allowable means, including the completely authorized use of arms and all possible penalties and punishments that are expressly provided for by general, feudal, and imperial law, and by the constitution of the kingdom of Bohemia. And we testify before God and the entire world that we had heretofore wished nothing more than to bring forth peace and quiet in our kingdoms and lands, and to rescue our poor subjects from complete destruction and ruin. But in order to recover what has been taken from us by revolt and rebellion, and to maintain our imperial and royal authority over this place, there is no other option open to us. On the contrary, it causes us extreme pain to consider what has so far been precipitated by a few vile persons who clothed their odious rebellion under the mantle of religion, in-

119. The elector of Bohemia held the ancient ceremonial office of imperial arch-cupbearer, which came with the responsibility of presenting a new emperor with a cup filled with watered wine during imperial coronations. Each of the empire's other electors also held other high ceremonial offices.

120. Holy Roman Emperor.

flicting harm on the lives and goods of our poor subjects through the armies of one and the other side. We hereby testify as well, that we are innocent of all the spilling of innocent blood, the destitution, and the destruction that this wretched war has caused and will cause in the future—though no one suffers more than we do over it, since our assistance to our land and people called it forth—because we render before God, and with the complete satisfaction of our Christian conscience, that we gave no cause for all of this misery; rather, we rendered with complete sufficiency everything that we were bound to do by our royal declaration. And were we hereby to find something lacking, still we would have intended to comply with it, faithfully and honestly—not to encumber, nor allow to be encumbered by others, the privileges of any estate in either religious or secular matters, nor the Letter of Majesty.

We hereby also testify, that should our army, contrary to the laws of war, regulations, and military patents, proceed with robbery, arson, strangulation of innocent persons, women, or children, raping of honorable women or girls, or other forms of excess, we would feel all of this deeply, and it would go against our intentions and sentiments—indeed, against our orders. . . .

In sum, we shall maintain and uphold the rights, liberties, and prerogatives of the Holy Roman Empire, and of ourselves and our house, to the very last drop of our blood. Thereby, in such a righteous matter, we, with God's help and gracious assistance, are completely confident of the full endorsement, aid, and support of all potentates, princes, and authorities, inasmuch as all of them are also endangered by such an invidious example, since the same treason by subjects could occur against them as well. But we especially appeal, with friendship and graciousness, to the electors, princes, and estates of the Holy Roman Empire, for whom this invalid election is a matter of some concern. In return, we offer each and every one of them full imperial protection and, in particular, the protection of the highly affirmed Religious and Profane Peace [of Augsburg],[121] thereby following the laudable example of our ancestor whose name we carry,[122] and who, in similarly ruinous times, averted the danger that threatened the Holy Roman Empire, thereby ushering in the security that everyone had so desired. For with the imperial office that we bear, we shall principally endeavor that all mistrust can be set aside and instead lasting peace and unity might once again return and be maintained in all places, such that the Holy Roman Empire might be raised above all other nations in power and magnificence. . . .

121. The 1555 Religious Peace of Augsburg ended the civil conflict that had wracked the empire for years.

122. Ferdinand I Habsburg, who oversaw the completion and implementation of the Peace of Augsburg.

Given in our city of Vienna on the twenty-ninth day of January, 1620: the first year of our reign as Roman Emperor, the second year of our reign in Hungary, and the third year of our reign in Bohemia.

5. The Treaty of Ulm (July 3, 1620)[123]

[On July 3, 1620, the members of the Protestant Union, represented by Joachim Ernst of Brandenburg-Ansbach,[124] reached an agreement with the Catholic League, represented by Maximilian I of Bavaria.[125] The Union princes hoped that by abandoning Frederick of the Palatinate to his fate, they would protect the empire (and themselves) from any sparks caused by the conflict in Bohemia and other Habsburg hereditary lands.]

Accord between His Serene Princely Highness of Bavaria, for himself and on behalf of the united electors, princes, and estates, on one hand; and His Serene Highness Margrave Joachim Ernst of Brandenburg, for himself and in the name of those electors, princes, and estates, on the other hand. Made the 23rd of June of this year, 1620,[126] in the imperial city of Ulm, and published so that all might know.

Matthew 5:9
Blessed are the peacemakers

By the grace of God, we, Maximilian, count Palatine of the Rhine,[127] duke of Upper and Lower Bavaria, etc., and by the same grace, we, Joachim Ernst, margrave of Brandenburg, duke of Prussia, etc., hereby let it be known to all men:

123. *Accord Zwischen der Fr: Drl: in Bayern für sich vnd dero vereinigten Chur-Fürsten vnnd Ständ Eins: So dann Jhrer Fr: Gn: Marggraff Joachim Ernsts zu Brandenburg für sich vnnd im Namen dero mit unirten Chur-Fürsten vnd Ständ Andern Theils, den 23. Junij diß lauffenden 1620. Jahrs in deß heyligen Reichs Statt Vlm getroffen, vnd zu männiglichs wissenschafft in Truck gegeben* (Ulm, 1620). A copy can be found at the Universitätsbibliothek Augsburg, Sign. 02/IV.13.4.152angeb.13.

124. Joachim Ernst of Brandenburg-Ansbach (1583–1625).

125. Duke Maximilian I of Bavaria (1573–1651).

126. June 23, 1620, by the older Julian calendar used in Ulm, which was July 3 by the newer Gregorian calendar.

127. The dukes of Bavaria had once held the Rhenish Palatinate and still called themselves "counts Palatine of the Rhine."

That inasmuch as now and for a fairly long time, both in the Holy Roman Empire of the German Nation and in various neighboring kingdoms and lands, there has been a dangerous and hazardous situation and military rebellion; and thus the electors, princes, and estates of both the Catholic and Protestant unions have been prompted to make preparations and ready themselves for war; and, because of this, misunderstandings have arisen and the preparations made by both unions have been deemed as offenses, violations, and grievances by the adherents of one or the other union; and thereby a commotion has been aroused in the Holy Empire; therefore, and so that such misunderstandings might be abolished, and better trust might be established between both unions and within the Holy Empire, we have, through the mediation of the right honorable envoy of the Royal Majesty of France,[128] who was present here in the imperial city of Ulm, agreed to a certain binding promise, commitment, and assurance.

And first, we, Duke Maximilian of Bavaria, as general of the Catholic League, by virtue of the power we possess, and we, Joachim Ernst, margrave of Brandenburg, etc., as lieutenant general of the Protestant Union, and also by virtue of the power we possess, and in the presence of, and with the approval and agreement of other united Protestant princes and estates, and of the councilors, envoys, and ambassadors empowered by those absent, promise, commit, and assure on our behalf and on behalf of the electors, princes, and estates of both unions, by our true word, belief, and trust, and in the very strongest and most solid form it shall, can, or might take by law, that no elector, prince, or estate belonging to either one or the other union, shall in any way or manner, or under whatever appearance it might be or might be conceived of, either by us or by others, by means of one or the other union's relevant military preparations, offend, insult, complain about the [1555] Religious and Secular Peace, assail, molest, attack, disturb, or carry out an assault against one or the other. Instead, both the Catholics with the Protestants, and the Protestants with the Catholics, shall persist in righteous and unstained peace, quiet, and unity, and shall and will leave each to his own in untroubled security.

So that, however, this promise and good assurance made between neighboring princes and estates (according to the constitutions of the empire, insofar as they are pertinent) shall persist and continue for all time, the armies that both sides now have in neighboring areas shall be withdrawn as soon as possible from the places where they now are, without injury to one or the other, and no others shall be lodged in their place.

128. The French mediator for the agreement was Charles de Valois, duke d'Angoulême (1573–1650).

Second, it is also qualified and agreed upon that if an elector, prince, or estate that is an adherent of one or the other union, or if one or the other union altogether, shall, due to some claimed necessity and according to the laws of the empire, seek passage for its and its people's defense and safeguard, and shall advance a sufficient guarantee, one or the other estate shall not refuse such a thing as long as this request occurs in a timely manner and not suddenly or with only a brief warning, nor when one is already on the border with an army or actually already within another's land (whereby the subjects are burdened).

And then third, we, Duke Maximilian of Bavaria, etc., and other united Catholic electors, princes, and estates, exclude from this present negotiation the kingdom of Bohemia, its incorporated lands, and other hereditary lands belonging to the House of Austria, and include in this treaty only those electoral estates, principalities, and lands that belong to the electors, princes, and estates united to both sides; among these, we also include those hereditary lands of the elector Palatine that lie within the empire[129] (for at this time we have not experienced the above-mentioned misunderstandings with these lands, but instead hope we are on good terms with them), and it shall not be further extended. So this is the declaration of the Catholic electors, princes, and estates as concerns the kingdom of Bohemia, its incorporated lands, and other hereditary lands belonging to the House of Austria. We, Joachim Ernst, margrave of Brandenburg, etc., for our part and on behalf of the electors, princes, and estates united with us, likewise leave it at that. And we also, for our part, wish not to include here the kingdom of Bohemia, its incorporated lands, and the hereditary lands belonging to the House of Austria, but instead leave such affairs to go as they will; we equally intend that this declaration apply only to those electoral states, principalities, and lands that lie within the empire.

Fourth, since during the ongoing negotiations there were many suggestions to take up the unresolved complaints in the empire—yet because of the shortness of time and because such matters not only touch those who are members of both unions, but rather all Catholic and Protestant estates of the empire, by whom we were not at this time empowered—this has been postponed until another, more convenient time.

As for the damages done to both unions that they claim was done by their armies, but especially what occurred at Sontheim and in its neighborhood,[130] the restitution for this shall be negotiated in the future in a just manner.

---

129. By specifically including in the treaty Frederick's lands within the empire, the Protestant princes are attempting to protect them from attack by the Catholic League.

130. The armies of the Union and the League briefly skirmished at Sontheim an der Brenz, a town near Ulm, earlier in 1620.

All of this we, Duke Maximilian of Bavaria, etc., and we, Margrave Joachim Ernst of Brandenburg, etc., unswervingly, firmly, and steadfastly uphold both for ourselves as for the above-mentioned electors, princes, and estates who are fellow confederates.

And in full assurance of this, we have hereby signed by our own hands, and have had our private princely agreement put into print. Given the 23rd of June, old calendar, and the 3rd of July, new calendar, 1620.

Maximilian, etc., Joachim Ernst, etc.

6. The Battle of White Mountain (November 8, 1620)[131]

[In 1620 the army of Maximilian of Bavaria's Catholic League, under Tilly,[132] combined with the imperial army, under Bucquoy,[133] and headed for Frederick's Bohemian capital of Prague. The army of the Bohemians and their confederates, led by Christian von Anhalt,[134] followed the combined Imperial-League army and managed to cut them off shortly before they reached Prague. There, on November 8, the Bohemian army established itself on a hill known as White Mountain and prepared to defend the city. The following account of the battle and its aftermath was written by Johann Philipp Abelinus (died c. 1637), the author of the first two volumes of the Theatrum Europaeum, *a near-contemporary, German-language, illustrated history of the age, which covered the war from its beginnings.][135]*

131. Johann Philipp Abelinus and Matthaeus Merian, *Theatrum Europaeum, Oder, Außführliche und Warhafftige Beschreibung aller und jeder denckwürdiger Geschichten, so sich hin und wieder in der Welt fürnemblich aber in Europa, und Teutschlanden, so wol im Religion- als Prophan-Wesen, vom Jahr Christi 1617. biß auff das Jahr 1629,* Bd. 1 (Frankfurt am Main: Daniel Fievet, 1662), 409–12.

132. Johann Tserclaes, count of Tilly (1559–1632), a Walloon (from Flanders) who served as lieutenant general in the Bavarian army.

133. Lieutenant General Charles Bonaventure de Longueval, count of Bucquoy (1571–1621), was a French-born military commander of the imperial armies in Bohemia.

134. Christian von Anhalt-Bernburg (1568–1630) was a Calvinist prince who had long served Frederick as an advisor and who had strongly supported Frederick's decision to take the Bohemian throne in the first place.

135. The *Theatrum Europaeum* eventually stretched to twenty-one volumes and was illustrated by the beautiful, detailed copper-plate engravings of Matthaeus Merian (1593–1650).

White Mountain does not actually reach a very great elevation, nor is it very rugged, but it is uneven, strewn with hills, dales, and hollows, and is everywhere sandy. From the front it stretches to Prague; from the back it goes to a little bridge over which two can cross at a time; yet the imperialists found a partial pass across through the moors, over which those with good horses could come. Up above, on the left-hand side of the mountain, there stands a royal summerhouse named "The Star" within an animal park. The entire mountain is about a mile long. At the peak of the mountain is a flat area, which gradually slopes down into a valley toward Prague, and it was here that the Bohemian army went and raised a camp and began to entrench themselves.

As Duke Maximilian of Bavaria took notice of this, he and Tilly urged the count of Bucquoy to hurry with his troops and join with them before the enemy entrenched himself and fortified his camp such that neither could he be lured out of it, nor could it be taken from him by force.

Hereupon [Tilly] then also arranged his troops in battle order in the following way:

He made three battle formations: the first, the middle, and the last. In the first were two units of infantry (which, were they all present, were around six thousand men strong), and attached to each of these were two wings of musketeers behind and two in front. Each was also provided with three wings of cavalry of about fifteen hundred men. The middle formation consisted of three thousand Neapolitans and two wings of cavalry. The last was almost like the first, except that the wings of cavalry were to the right and left . . . and between these two units, somewhat to the rear, the Polish cavalry were arranged.

Constantinus Peregrinus[136] reported that the imperial army was not more than twelve thousand men strong, for about six thousand infantry and two thousand cavalry were absent; some of them were taking part in the campaigns of Balthasar von Marradas[137] and Wallenstein,[138] and some were out searching here and there for provisions. In the Bohemian camp, there were also no more than twenty thousand men at the battle, not counting the Hungarians.

Here they once again deliberated how the Bohemian army might most reasonably be attacked, yet this discussion was not so much about how to

---

136. A pseudonymous writer, most likely an imperial officer, who wrote a well-known description of the battle from the perspective of the imperial army.

137. Baltazar de Marradas et Vique (1560–1638), a Spanish nobleman who commanded a cavalry regiment.

138. Albrecht Wenzel Eusebius von Waldstein or Wallenstein (1583–1634), who was at this time a commander of a cavalry regiment; later, he would become the leader of the entire imperial army.

begin the encounter as about the proper time and place to carry it out. For now the Bohemians had taken their quarters and built up entrenchments on all sides of their camp, they had taken the most reasonable and comfortable place for the battle, and they had strengthened themselves with fresh troops from the city of Prague. For this reason, it looked as if it would be much better if the count of Bucquoy's troops were used here, that is, placed on the other side, toward Prague, so that the enemy might be lured from his comfortable position. There were numerous opinions about this, and they could not rightly agree on matters, but then La Motte,[139] who had in the meantime inspected the Bohemian entrenchments, arrived. From this they learned that these entrenchments were not so solid and strong that one should, on account of them, let slip the opportunity for an encounter. Principally, this was because the Bohemian artillery could do less damage from this place than from the other side, toward Prague. Given this, it was at once unanimously decided by the imperialists and Bavarians to attack the enemy immediately.

For this reason, two infantry units were taken from each army, the imperial and the Bavarian, provided with cavalry, and ordered to make the attack. Duke Maximilian made the password "Saint Mary" because the Holy Virgin Mary was depicted on the main standards. The Bavarian army was led by Tilly; the imperial army, however, was headed by Baron von Tiefenbach.[140] The imperialists were to the right and the Bavarians to the left. Three units were ordered back so they could come to help in whatever place where they were needed.

Thus as everything was now ordered, the attack finally occurred between twelve and one o'clock, and on both sides there was great zeal and bravery, and the artillery fired against each other with a great din and thunder. The battle went on for a half hour with the outcome in doubt, and both sides fought against each other with great fury and perseverance. Yet the imperial troops then began to waver, because the oldest son of Prince Christian von Anhalt pressed them with such zeal that they could no longer resist and had to retreat. Then the next regiments, those of Breuner[141] and Tiefenbach, became afraid and began to fall into disarray, especially since Colonel Breuner was also taken prisoner.

When Tilly noticed this danger, he sent Colonel Cratz[142] with five hundred of his cavalrymen to help against Anhalt. Prince Maximilian von

139. Peter de la Motte, imperial lieutenant colonel of a cuirassier regiment.

140. Baron Rudolf von Tiefenbach (1582–1653), imperial sergeant general and commander of a German infantry regiment.

141. Hans Philipp von Breuner, commander of a German infantry regiment.

142. Commander of a Bohemian cavalry regiment loyal to the emperor.

Liechtenstein and Colonel Bauer also moved with their units against the Bohemians. Then the prince of Anhalt's cavalry, which was ten companies strong, was beaten and, finally, entirely scattered; Anhalt himself was struck from his horse, suffering many wounds, and was captured by Wilhelm Verdugo.[143] Colonel Breuner, however, was once again freed.

When the Hungarians became aware of this defeat, they were frightened by it and so fled down the mountain. Then the remaining Bohemian regiments also fell into disarray, and each man sought to save himself by fleeing. In the meantime, however, Duke Maximilian, the count of Bucquoy, and their armies pursued them with great zeal and broke into the Bohemian camp, so the entire Bohemian army was beaten and scattered. The battle had not lasted more than an hour. The Bavarians captured seven heavy artillery and the imperialists three, and they gained altogether about a hundred standards and flag bearers. Written accounts vary as to the number of those who died on the Bohemian side, but the most believable claim was about nine thousand, of which six thousand were slain during the actual encounter. As for the remaining [Bohemian soldiers], some were slain during the flight, and especially within the zoo, into which a large number had fled for their lives, and others (mostly Hungarians) drowned in the Moldau. Taken prisoner were Prince Christian von Anhalt the younger, who was mentioned above, the young Count von Thurn, Count von Styrumb, a count of the Rhine, a duke of Saxe-Weimar, and many other officers, along with about five hundred soldiers.

On the imperial and Bavarian side, more than two hundred fifty were no more; but among these were many brave colonels, such as General Quartermaster Caratti (a Neapolitan), Colonel von Meggau, Captain von Prösing, Donpre,[144] and four Walloon captains. No similar battle has ever occurred in Christendom in living memory.

Indeed, nearly all the artillery and everything that belonged to a field camp were abandoned, and although many captains and commanders urged the soldiers during their flight to reassemble at Brandeis, and many of them did indeed appear, they waited in vain for ordinance, and so finally each man left for wherever he could.

Many write that before the encounter the Bohemian army, including the country people, numbered about thirty thousand men, and the imperialists, including the Bavarians and also the Bohemian country people,[145] were more than fifty thousand strong.

143. Commander of a Walloon regiment.

144. Count Meggau was colonel and commander of a German regiment; Caratti served in his regiment; Captain von Prösing served in Breuner's regiment; Cavalry Captain Dompre was a member of Colonel Gauchier's Walloon regiment.

145. Locals fighting for the imperial side.

Especially extolled on the Bavarian side was the bravery of Tilly, who ran here and there giving help where necessary, and who—along with the above-mentioned five hundred cavalrymen whom he had assigned to Colonel Cratz in order to oppose the units that were already inclined toward flight—was not a minor cause of the imperial side's victory.

Wilhelm Staden, however, reported . . . that among all other things, the greatest praise belonged to Wilhelm Verdugo, who was the principal cause of the victory achieved, as he had the greatest force of the enemy against him; but he had, with his Walloons, opposed them with cavalry, taken the prince of Anhalt prisoner, captured a standard with his own hands, seized the first three artillery pieces of the Bohemians, and then turned to face them directly, bringing the entire Bohemian army into disarray. . . .

Verdugo also gained an exquisite courtly ribbon decorated with precious stones, which King Frederick, count Palatine, had left behind in his flight, and which was a symbol of the English knightly Order of the Garter. Verdugo later gave this to the duke of Bavaria.

As now the imperialists and Bavarians had achieved a victory against the Bohemians, His Serene Highness [the duke of Bavaria] thought it would be good to attack the city of Prague, as it was the head of the kingdom. Thus, that same evening, his infantry advanced almost to the city walls, encamped themselves, and held watch there the entire night.

Count von Hohenlohe[146] and Count von Thurn, when they noticed that their affairs would come to an unhappy outcome, went from the battle to Prague, where they asked King Frederick quickly to send an emissary to the duke of Bavaria to request a mere twenty-four hours for a retreat. His Serene Highness declared that he would allow only eight hours, as long as [Frederick] would yield and agree to renounce forever all claims to the kingdom of Bohemia and its incorporated lands. After this, no further declaration followed from the king; instead, that same evening he left the castle and went into the old city, and on the following day fled in haste with his wife and entourage from Prague to Breslau.[147] Similarly, old Count von Thurn, Count von Hohenlohe, von Ruppa, and many others also left from there.

The regiment of young Count von Thurn remained, however, spending the night in the entrenchments they had begun in front of the cloister of Strahov. And many other companies of infantry that had retreated there after the battle also remained, including two companies under Captain Sigismund Schmuckherrn and Captain Georg Christoph von Heltzing at Prague Castle. These moved on the second day from their posts there into the Old

---

146. Field Marshal Count Georg Friedrich von Hohenlohe (1569–1645).

147. A town in Silesia, now Wroclaw, in Poland.

Town Square, to where His Serene Highness of Bavaria sent his commissary in order to make an accord with them (as follows).

The little city of Prague let Duke Maximilian know that they wished to surrender to His Imperial Majesty, and they asked, for this reason, that they be spared the soldiers' malice. Whereupon His Serene Highness himself went to the city so the troops would be stopped from making any mischief and the city would not be plundered. In addition, the residents of the new and old cities sent to him requesting three days' grace in order to deliberate on their affairs, with an announcement that they would thereafter live according to his orders. But he would not grant them even three hours' grace, but instead made clear to them that they should immediately surrender. At the same time, he also ordered two regiments to the two gates in order to keep the city safe from plundering, and he forbade, on pain of death, any soldier to leave his troop. And this punishment also applied to colonels and captains who failed to maintain their troops in discipline.

In the afternoon, the duke came into the city's royal palace, dismounted from his horse by the Capuchin monastery, and attended a church service. Wilhelm Popel and another five men from the estates then came and submitted to him a document in which they requested:

1. That religion be left free.
2. That they retain their privileges.
3. That no violence be inflicted by the soldiers.
4. That a general pardon be issued.
5. That no soldiers be lodged with them, the residents of the old and new cities.

The duke agreed to these terms and, in addition, made the law so much stricter that tears streamed down their faces.

On the 31st of October old style, or the 10th of November new style, there were negotiations with the Bohemian troops who had fled from the battlefield into the city, to have them move out. Colonel Heimhausen was sent to them. Once the soldiers had assembled in the marketplace in the old city, he spoke to them thusly: His Serene Princely Highness of Bavaria had the means, according to the orders given to him, to proceed against the rebels and their supporters. And there was almost no reason why he should spare those troops who had served the rebels against the Imperial Majesty and had taken part in the battle against His Serene Princely Highness. However, for certain reasons, because they themselves desired a safe conduct in order to pull out, this mercy would be shown them: they would be allowed to move out securely, with the condition that this should happen immediately. To this the soldiers replied: they would take up the safe conduct and free withdrawal that they desired, but would do so only if they were first paid their back wages by the estates that employed them. Thus His Serene Highness should order the estates to pay them. They would not consider leaving the city on any other conditions.

As they now quite seriously discussed their demands for pay with von Heimhausen, whom they might well have killed there in the middle of the marketplace, they also swore that they would not retreat before they received their pay, and aside from this, they desired that they be allowed to receive money for those goods that they had won. Von Heimhausen, however, answered them: the estates had acted against the law, in that they had hired the soldiers [to fight] against their legitimate and crowned king, who had been recognized and approved by the electors of the empire; namely, the Imperial Majesty. So these troops, who were overcome in open battle and beaten in their flight, were to be considered as the enemy. Therefore, if they would not voluntarily pull out, then His Serene Highness would stop at nothing to use all his forces to hunt them down.

Once they had heard this and other similar statements, they finally let themselves be expelled and voluntarily pulled out.

On this day it was also demanded that the magistrates and the citizens of all three cities belonging to Prague swear loyalty in the name of His Imperial Majesty, whereby this occurred, and everyone dutifully complied. Also, aside from this, they rejected and dissolved all confederations they had entered into against His Majesty, and they swore that they would offer proper obedience to their true lord and king, like loyal subjects. And this oath would be drawn up in writing, confirmed with the seals of all three cities, and presented to His Serene Highness without any announcements or conditions as to the manner of the privileges the citizens held. At the same time, however, the estates demanded that their privileges, freedoms, and customs be announced anew, and they requested that everything that had happened should be forgotten and set aside. Yet His Serene Highness answered them that now one no longer dealt with privileges, and (since they had rejected all the grace and forgiveness that had been theirs from the beginning and had proceeded so far that force and arms had to be used) His Imperial Majesty had given him no commission to consider privileges and freedoms at all. The estates should thus subordinate themselves to His Imperial Majesty now, without any conditions and stipulations, and deal with privileges, pardons, and similar matters later with His Majesty, their king.

7. Terrifying and Piteous News from Bohemia (1621)[148]

[Popular broadsheets flourished during the Thirty Years War, especially during 1620 and 1621. Many of these, often splendidly illustrated, related the great battles and events of the war or offered satirical assessments of the skills and characters of leading generals. Others scorned the influence of foreign, especially French, fashions in the empire or lashed out against the Jews or against Protestants or Catholics. Another important set of these documents, however, tried to illustrate the great horrors of the war as it was experienced by the common people. The following is a good example of this variety. It is a single sheet decorated with an image of a burning city, warring soldiers, and suffering townspeople. It appeared in 1621, in response to the indiscriminate devastation of western Bohemia by the imperialists, under Maximilian of Bavaria, as they attempted to drive out the Protestant Bohemian army of Count Ernst von Mansfeld. Entire towns were destroyed, and thousands of Czech Protestants fled. Large bands of peasants began to unite for mutual defense and, in their anger, also attacked and robbed the property of the local nobility. Like many contemporary broadsheets, this one was written in rhyming verse; it was also accompanied by a "pretty religious song" that the author helpfully instructed the reader to sing to the tune of a popular song (titled "When We Are in the Greatest Need") and that warned readers that the Last Days and the Final Judgment were imminent. For ease of reading, the translation is presented here in regular prose style.]

Terrifying and piteous news from Bohemia, how evilly the enemy has wreaked havoc there, with robbery, murder, and arson, especially in the cities of Pilsen, Saaz, Komotau, Brüx,[149] and others, as you will hear in this song.

You, dear Christians, listen to what I will sing and report to you of what has recently occurred throughout all of Bohemia. Oh, may God stand by me. I will begin shortly; now take notice, all you men and women, of how the foreign troops[150] stole, scorched, and burned, showing no compassion. Now listen further.

---

148. *Erschreckliche und erbärmliche Zeitung aus Böhmen* (Annaberg: Christian Mayer, 1621). A copy can be found at the University of Wroclaw, Poland: 357637; published in John Roger Paas, *The German Political Broadsheet 1600–1700*, vol. 3: 1620 and 1621 (Wiesbaden: Harrassowitz, 1991), #P-791, 343.

149. The modern Czech cities of Plzeň, Žatec, Chomutov, and Most.

150. The Catholic League army of Maximilian of Bavaria, under the command of Johann Tserclaes, count of Tilly.

The people ask to surrender, as they should, but it comes to nothing. The troops burn up cities and villages, and rob and kill horribly. At Pilsen, the enemy came in and did not even spare the little children or the pregnant women. He took the possessions of whomever he encountered on the lanes and streets. Twenty-seven powerful fires were seen around Pilsen in one night. There was great misery. The prophecy[151] was truly fulfilled in all the lands of Bohemia.

Now it came much closer to us, and we heard that they were at Saaz, which they began to burn. This lay five miles from Marienberg.[152] Many people began to weep and confess, for, in the villages in the night, they burned up everything with great force, and likewise the people who ran from their beds were thrown into the fire and burned.

O Christian man, behold the distress! The people have to abandon their own goods along with many supplies. Some simply run away, forced to abandon wife and child. The troops seize children from the breast, murdering them unjustly, and their parents likewise. They murder them terrifyingly, causing great misery and lamentations. Some hope to hide themselves under the hay or straw, in sheds and in barns, and they stay lying there and starving and finally even being burned.

O weep and pray alike, you people, at how they carry on with the female sex, especially with the maidens whom they rape and abuse such that one is horrified by it. Some beautiful women are forced to swear to serve the soldiers and to turn money over to them. Their husbands are forced to lose their lives, even right before the eyes of their wives. Also sold among the soldiers, and very cheaply, are wives and maids in equal numbers. They are greatly and needlessly prostituted, while their little children are forced to wait upon them.

Some people sent supplies away into Germany, to Marienberg, but the soldiers had already blocked the pass.[153] Now they are in greater need, also in danger of losing their lives.

Now hear, also, what the peasants did. Many conspired together, for they wished very much to surrender. Things would happen to them as God willed, even if it cost life and limb. They sought out their rulers and attempted to strike them dead, even should it cost them life and limb, for they had been forced to give out so much money, and yet such evil was returned to them. But in the entire land, no nobleman could be found anywhere

151. The destruction and violence done to the true Church and the faithful before the Last Days.

152. A fortress in Saxony, just across the border from Bohemia.

153. The Preßnitzer Pass was a popular route across the mountains of the Erzgebirge, which separated Saxony from Bohemia.

anymore. All of them slipped away. What the noblemen had dreaded at this time[154] could soon have succeeded.

On another night at Saaz, there were as many as sixteen fires of great strength that took many people. One and a half hundred, great and small, died at this time in the fires.

Therefore you dear Christians abandon sins—for it is high time—and come together in repentance so that we might be preserved by the Lord our God. Amen.

8. Kipper and Wipper Time (1621)[155]

[The war caused not merely direct misery from the depredations and extractions by troops, the destruction of property, or the mistreatment and murder of the people. There were also serious indirect miseries. One of the worst was the chaos caused by the reckless economic policies of the empire's various states and cities, particularly during the years 1619 to 1625. To pay for massive increases in military expenditures, governments collected existing coins with high silver content, melted them down, mixed them with cheap copper, and then reissued them at their old face value, pocketing the difference. The result was hyperinflation, beginning in Bohemia but soon spreading across much of the empire. These years became known as the Kipper and Wipper Period, named for the scales or balances (wippen) used by traveling money changers to weigh (kippen) the amount of silver in coins. The terms "kipper" and "wipper" were also expanded to mean coin counterfeiters or cheats in general, and the increasingly debased and worthless coinage came to be known as "kipper money." Some clever people did profit greatly from this economic chaos, but ordinary people were badly affected, for the money economy completely broke down in some areas, and in others prices for food and services reached impossible levels, forcing mass dislocation and despair. The sheer enormity of the problem also helped convince many, such as the author of the following 1621 broadsheet, that this was yet another sign of the imminent End of Days, and that it indicated both the moral degeneracy of the times and the active power of the Devil in the world.]

154. A successful peasant rebellion.

155. *Müntzbeschickung der Kipper und Wipper* (1621). A copy can be found at the Library of Congress, Washington D.C., Rare Book Room, Broadsheet Collection, portfolio 259–45; published in John Roger Paas, *The German Political Broadsheet 1600–1700*, vol. 3: 1620 and 1621 (Wiesbaden: Harrassowitz, 1991), #P-896, 447. See also Paas' introduction to the hyperinflation, pp. 36–9.

Alloy of Coins in the Kipper and Wipper

The Last Days of which Christ prophesied have arrived. There shall be great tribulation, with agony and misery on this earth, and great fear and concern for those things that have not come to pass since the beginning of the world. People will say about this that it indeed cannot be otherwise, for there is little fidelity and faith, compassion is not practiced, and God and the next world are not admired. All virtues are dispelled; justice has fled to heaven. Therefore it is now a time of trial, for all revenue has been debased, and every man merely robs and steals in whatever way he possibly can, and it is now as clear as day how openly this occurs.

For this reason, I will now tell you a history of what came to pass in recent days on public streets. A wagon was pulled by four strong steeds along the streets. It was almost completely loaded, so that the steeds had to pull such a heavy load that they were bent over. It is verily true and not a lie. A horseman beheld the wagon and said [to the driver]: My honest fellow, what kind of burden are you pulling there? Tell me, what do you have loaded? He replied: My dear, pious lord, it is merely old copper from kettles, pots, and pans, copper gutters, and bathtubs, all thrown together in a heap, which I haul in my wagon. The horseman said: Where are you going with it then, and tell me what will be made from it? [He answered:] Only money will be made from it. The horseman began to laugh: If that is truly going to become money, the world will be cheated. From where will the look of silver come with which the copper is to be mixed, so that one can make good money from it according to the imperial constitution? [He answered:] Don't even worry about it. Keep watch for the messengers who shall straight away follow my wagon. They can carry as much silver as one needs for mixing with this copper; it is indeed enough.

Everything must come to an end. It cannot last forever. For now we have the fruit of the Devil, from which comes a noble breed called Kipper and Wipper. Those with great understanding can consider if it is truly the Devil's wicked deed. Yes, consider it a masterpiece that allows people to defraud the poor of their belongings under the semblance of justice. To this end, the godless rush night and day to ruin the poor and do not spare anything of which they catch sight. They do not ask about any ancient punishments, but allow the Devil to prevail. They say: We do as we will, only as we can and should. Everyone must now take his due, and whoever does not is much too weak and good for nothing in this world, lacking both in possessions and money.

Such fiends are, without doubt, bound to their father, the wretched Devil, for he keeps all of them together captive within his kingdom. As they are his bondsmen, performing what he suggests to them, he will also powerfully strengthen them, so that, with words and deeds, they are tied so deeply to these sins that he leaves none of these godless people behind. In these difficult times, they are the reason that such debased money is introduced throughout the world. For the more the *reichsthaler* is worth, the more people fraudulently obtain coins, making debased *groschen, schreckenberger,* and eight-*groschen* pieces,[156] and causing a great deal of trouble. It harms only the poor; may God notice this and take pity on them. For nowadays not only the shopkeepers and merchants wish to debase coins,[157] but it has also come into practice among the educated. For many a genteel, respectable man who has studied for a long time, has few skills, and carries a lofty title, earns a living from debasing that he would not otherwise have. If he had studied so much, he could have earned a living from that, and he could have avoided debasing coins. But the avarice and splendor of the Devil have filled the world with counterfeiters.[158] Although no one here calls them by that name, yet one meets them soon enough when these men need to accumulate lots of money to buy beautiful houses and gardens, estates, pastures, and also fields with such debased kipper money. Thus they can quickly be rid of it, so that when it one day receives a blow and they can no longer do business, they will still have their property.[159]

How does the craftsman manage when he has to be paid for his difficult work and toil with such money? The merchant, on the other hand, sells all of his wares more expensively so that he has enough in his coffer. He has to do it, he would say, because the *reichsthaler* has shot up in value. So may God give to him who made the *reichsthaler* so expensive a life only so long, and not one more hour alive, and then after this life, the fires of hell.

9. Letter of Archbishop Ferdinand of Cologne (July 6, 1622)[160]

[By the winter of 1621 to 1622, the war had spread far from Bohemia and the surrounding Habsburg hereditary territories. One of Frederick's generals,

156. Various small coins. The *groschen* was set at 1/24 of a *thaler,* and the *schreckenberger* was an old coin that was recreated in the Kipper and Wipper period as a debased coin fixed at 1/21 of a *thaler.*

157. *Kippen.*

158. *Kipper,* or counterfeiter.

159. Indeed, this was the case. Albrecht von Wallenstein, for example, used debased coinage to obtain vast estates in Bohemia, which he later used as a means to finance his rise to power as head of the imperial armies.

160. Ferdinand, Archbishop of Cologne, to Count Franz Christoph Khevenhüller, Bonn, July 6, 1622, Státní archiv Praha (Mnichovo Hradiště), Rodinný archiv Vald-

Christian of Brunswick,[161] who was sometimes called "the mad Halber-stadter" because of his reputed cruelty and lack of restraint, moved his troops into northwest Germany in the area of Westphalia, where he lodged them with the locals and let the soldiers loot and pillage at will. The ruler of these lands, Archbishop Ferdinand of Cologne,[162] who was the brother of Duke Maximilian of Bavaria, found himself powerless to stop the mistreatment. In July 1622, therefore, he wrote the following letter to the imperial ambassador to Spain, Franz Christoph Khevenhüller,[163] in which he described the results of Christian's military occupation in Westphalia and asked for assistance from the Spanish, whose armies controlled the nearby Lower Palatinate and Spanish Netherlands.]

Bonn, July 6, 1622

Our dear friend and lord brother Duke Maximilian of Bavaria has written us recently with praise for the zealous and good services you have employed in order to aid our highly valued Westphalian lands, and how graciously willing you have been to offer to oblige us further. . . . Thus we graciously thank you for this, and are prepared to take every possible opportunity, in turn, to promote you with His Highness. . . .

You without doubt already know how Duke Christian of Brunswick, administrator of the diocese of Halberstadt, set himself up against the beneficial imperial constitution and against all equitableness in order to help the proscribed count Palatine with a unit of arrogant, malicious riffraff serving as his infantry and cavalry. And as we, following our duty, obediently sided with our leader, he, completely unexpectedly and without any provocation, invaded our dioceses of Münster and Paderborn and the principality of Westphalia with the naked power of an army. He took the subjects prisoner, bound them, beat them, martyred some of them to death, similarly maltreated others, and ruined and emaciated people such that they—out of pure terror, misery, and distress—ran to and fro into the woods and valleys,

---

štejnové, AII-34, in Miloš Kouřil et al., eds., *Documenta Bohemica Bellum Tricennale Illustrantia, T. III, Der Kampf des Hauses Habsburg gegen die Niederlande und ihre Verbündeten. Quellen zur Geschichte des Pfälzisch-Niederländisch-Ungarischen Krieges, 1621–1625* (Prague: Academia, 1976), 128–30.

161. Duke Christian of Brunswick-Lüneburg (1599–1626) was also secular administrator of the bishopric of Halberstadt.

162. Ferdinand of Bavaria, archbishop and elector of Cologne (1577–1650), was also bishop of Münster, Liège, Hildesheim, and Paderborn. He was a strong supporter of the Catholic Counter-Reformation.

163. Franz Christoph Khevenhüller (1588–1650).

scattering along with their wives and innocent children, who, because of the extremely cold winter and the raw weather, must surely wither and die from hunger and pain. In the meantime, he seized for himself or spoiled all of their supplies, livestock, grain, and more, and finally burned their houses to ashes; he took possession of entire villages, market towns, princely and noble houses, and cities, and along with the cathedral college and the parish church, he plundered, ruined, and burned them down, one after the other; he assumed the government, commanded and forbid the calling up of the militia, and disarmed the residents; he took our cannons, munitions, and the silver plate left behind in the dioceses; he went after our advisors, servants, and officials, and also our very person, such that he took prisoner our privy council and our old meritorious servant, Arnold von Buchholtz, the cathedral provost of Hildesheim and Liège, among others; and he dragged them here and there until he was paid ten thousand ducats. But he did not stop there. Instead, as he had first done with Brunswick, he imposed a large general tax on all archdioceses and dioceses, which came to many hundreds of thousands of *reichsthalers;* he promised to spare our lands from actual subjugation through the delivery of a written declaration and assurance, confirmed by a signature and seal, yet nevertheless he put the lesser nobles and nonnoble residents under contribution[164] and, to this end, sent out urgent notices, burned on all four corners, and said that otherwise he would impose his wicked intention with a fiery hand; and in sum, in this way he drove the poor, innocent people to the most extreme degree and ruined their lives, possessions, and goods, so that those who still managed to eke out an existence found it impossible to recover once again. This is not to mention the kinds of bad words, unbecoming of a prince, he and his supporters used, and the deeds, disgraces, sacrileges, and blasphemies they perpetrated. And were we to mention even more particulars in this case, you would certainly see and sense that he is a blatant and declared enemy, as he has publicly displayed and professed himself in opposition to us. Yes, Turks and Tatars think and act no worse and no less Christian. Since then we have been unavoidably and urgently required to seek the preservation of our remaining areas and to try to regain from our declared enemy (and blatant spoiler of land) those lands in question that were taken from us by force. And we shall do so by means of very strong support and by providing sizeable countermeasures, in addition to seeking help elsewhere.

164. Contributions were the forced payments, either money or supplies, demanded by occupying armies during the war. This system allowed an army to live off the land and so freed military commanders from having to find pay and support for their troops elsewhere.

So you can easily imagine what a heavy burden and what marked costs all of the above has imposed upon us and upon our lands, which have thereby been ruined and wrecked, and what kind of great and inevitable difficulties, losses, and devastation our territory and the boundary defenses have had to bear during this war. Yet we do not know how to gain our soldiers' necessary subsistence from the mostly poor and ruined subjects, as even our own electoral and princely subsistence suffers from dearth. This is not to mention that the States of the United Netherlands[165] very strongly resent and punish us because we openly show our devotion and friendly affection toward the Imperial Majesty and his commendable House of Austria.[166] Therefore, not only did they use their army to inflict great and ruinous losses on our dependents, they also wrote with severe threats to our estates in every location, telling them not to give us either contributions or help.

If we now, through our obedient faithfulness and constant devotion to the maintenance of the Imperial Highness and the commendable House of Austria, are to be plunged into such suffering and ruin, we persevere in the consoling confidence that His Royal Majesty of Spain shall not patiently allow us—as his friends who, up to now, have missed no opportunity to be of service to the crown—to be abandoned to such vile robbery; but rather that he shall, by his mighty hand, help to protect and shield us against such unjust violence.

We humbly beseech that you promote this, faithfully concern yourself with it, and assure His Royal Majesty that we shall not allow ourselves, on account of the aforementioned tribulations and burdens, to stray from our devotion; rather, we shall persist in it to the death.

10. Letter of Elector John George of Saxony (February 23, 1623)[167]

[John George, the Lutheran elector of Saxony and an ally of the emperor, was unable to attend the 1623 meeting at Regensburg at which the emperor transferred Frederick's electoral title and lands to Duke Maximilian of Bavaria, but he made known his opposition through his deputies. He also expressed his deep concern in the following letter to his fellow prince, the elector of Mainz,

165. Also known as the United Provinces or the Dutch Republic.

166. The Austrian Habsburgs. The Dutch were then at war with the Austrian Habsburgs' cousins and allies, the Spanish Habsburgs.

167. Johann Philipp Abelinus and Matthaeus Merian, *Theatrum Europaeum*, Bd. 1 (Frankfurt am Main: Daniel Fievet, 1662), 725–6.

complaining that the emperor's act directly challenged the princes' rights and constitutional privileges, often termed the German Liberties. He was particularly concerned, however, about the dignity and power of one small elite group of imperial princes: the electors.]

First of all, we were very happy to learn that you abundantly sensed the care that we have for the well-being of the Holy Roman Empire, the maintenance of its erected fundamental laws, the imperial constitution, and the dignity and preeminence of electors; but especially the inclination we have for a worthy peace, which is desperately needed; and we were also happy that at this convention you were able to bear witness to this on our behalf. We shall also testify before God, that although due to urgent reasons (of which you are aware) we were not able to attend in person, we desired no other result for this meeting than to reach the goal of peace; to revive the mortally wounded Roman Empire, which has already been in large part destroyed, burdened with all kinds of vileness, filled with dissensions and disagreements, and so on; to keep what remains from total ruin and devastation; to establish friendly relations among all of the estates; and, one hopes, to serve the public by achieving peace and its fruits, which are of great price and value. We also would have hoped that one would have heeded the good advice and warnings that were based not on mere popular delusion, but on fundamental, imperial legal precedents and other statutes, and not instead seized upon a means that will create further division, embitterment, turbulence, and unpleasantness. We, for our part, could so much more willingly bear such things if our innocence and the fact that we were unable to anticipate what would happen (due to the above-mentioned extremely important reasons and causes) were known to you and to every man, and also perhaps if our protestations were also better known.

Yet we are thus not a little aggrieved that this would happen in our time and that matters would come to such a point, and we estimate that there is little hope for a remedy. . . . We thereby entreat the Divine Omnipotence to mercifully divert all misfortune from the Holy Empire and from its members. For that which can no longer be remedied, however, we ask that He, like a father, grant that faithful, well-meaning advice kept in mind.

As an old, extremely experienced elector who is knowledgeable about the empire, you require no explanation of the function of electors within the Roman Empire, nor of what this office and its preeminence and dignity consist, nor upon what they are based. The Golden Bull,[168] the union confirmed

---

168. The Golden Bull of 1356 was an imperial decree that established the seven electors who were henceforth responsible for choosing the emperor.

and sworn to by the electors, and the observances of many years show this superbly and handsomely. The electors have also maintained these [privileges] until today. Now, however, we think they are afflicted by a not inconsiderable assault.

For, not to mention the condemnation of the electors and princes who attended this convention, which proceeded contrary to our advice, this same example [of maintaining the electoral privileges] was not on display when the electoral college, which was incomplete at this convention, was dissolved despite the protestation that had already been made and taken into the protocols, such that it was, in fact, deemed legally registered. But the electors should be the closest and most secret councilors of the Roman Imperial Majesty, and they should be consulted in all extremely important matters, and especially in those concerning the Roman Empire; and these matters should be handled with their foreknowledge. Yet you know, and it has been sufficiently indicated at this convention, how things proceeded with the outlawing of the count Palatine (the fact and acts of which we have still not yet assayed) and the transference of the electoral title. Since the electors were not consulted when an elector was declared an outlaw and ejected from the electoral college, and another man was placed therein, we do not know in what the electoral dignity consists. And what kind of difference might there be between this and the other estates, except for the names? And how might the electors be safeguarded against the empire because of the danger that might quite easily arise from such lofty matters? Also, this matter cannot be justified by the excuses that it was necessary or that it does no prejudice to the electoral college. For the strict legal interpretation of the capitulations[169] does not allow for any exceptions. . . . For many reasons, we consider the transference of the electoral title, and what followed from this act, not as a means for peace, but rather as one for perpetual war, and thus we cannot justify it—especially as there exists no single example of something similar ever occurring since the establishment of the Golden Bull . . . and we do not know if the clause concerning the children and heirs [of Frederick],which appears in the resolution given to the electors and princes by the Roman Imperial Majesty, will wreak more division and embitterment than it will bring peace. . . .

We are proud to declare that we have rendered service and assistance to the Roman Imperial Majesty, our gracious lord, in his time of need and, when one considers this in particular, have done so both willingly and gladly, beyond what any other estate of the empire has done, ready to sacrifice our own life and limbs, land and people, and all of our property. But at the same

---

169. The imperial capitulations were those legally binding recognitions of princely power to which each emperor was required to swear upon his election.

time, despite our various letters, petitions, and requests, we have to this point still been unable to obtain a lasting resolution concerning the [Catholic] Reformation that has occurred. Instead, we learn even more that it continues, increases, and is extended onto the innocent and, yes, even onto widows and orphans, who flee in droves into our lands and, weeping and crying, beg us for help, such that it would move a stone to pity. We have so far suffered and borne this with patience, but we now urge you to act instead, so that one day a lasting resolution might occur, mercy and leniency might be granted, closed German churches might be opened, the free exercise of the true Augsburg Confession[170] might be allowed, and our loyal, upright, and useful service might one day be respected and considered.

170. Lutheranism.

II

THE INTERVENTION OF DENMARK
AND SWEDEN (1623–1635)

By late 1623 Emperor Ferdinand II's bold strategy had overwhelmed all op-position within the empire, and Tilly's army was encamped near the Lower Saxon Circle, ready to oppose any new outbreak. All resistance in Bohemia and its surrounding territories had been suppressed, the duke of Bavaria and elector of Saxony had been rewarded for their assistance with lands and hon-ors, and the Spanish Habsburgs were comfortably ensconced in Frederick's territories along the Rhine, allowing their troops easy access to the renewed war in the Netherlands. These very successes, however, now began to raise alarm among a number of European powers. Many had long feared that the Habsburgs secretly desired universal dominion, and worried that such easy victories in the empire might encourage them to turn their attentions to the rest of Europe. The Dutch, of course, were already feeling the ill effects of this Habsburg revival, and they now joined the English and the French in a defensive alliance to try to protect themselves from further aggression. After some initial failures, the allies sought additional help from both the king of Sweden, Gustavus Adolphus, and the king of Denmark-Norway, Christian IV, but the long rivalry of these two Scandinavian powers blocked their joint cooperation. In the end, the allies chose the enormously wealthy Christian IV as their sole champion and offered him further financial support if he would invade the empire and retake the Palatinate and Bohemia for Fred-erick V.

Christian IV was a Lutheran who supported the rights of his fellow reli-gionists, but he also had numerous practical interests in the affairs of the em-pire. As duke of Holstein, he was himself a prince of the empire and a member of the Lower Saxon Circle. Furthermore, Christian's son had been elected ad-ministrator of the secularized bishoprics of Halberstadt, Bremen, and Ver-den, and Christian's ambition was to bring these territories under the permanent hereditary control of his family. He also hoped to expand his con-trol over Baltic shipping and increase the already sizeable numbers of customs duties and tolls that he collected from passing ships. Thus, with his religious, political, and economic interests coinciding, Christian accepted the allies' proposal. In May 1625 he used his influence to have himself named director of the Lower Saxon Circle and began to raise an army.

While Christian IV had been negotiating with his potential supporters, the emperor had been maneuvering to meet this new challenge. In April

1625 he decided to raise his own army and turned to Albrecht von Wallenstein for help. Wallenstein had served the emperor in the pacification of Bohemia, and after White Mountain had used his position as military commander of Prague to increase his already extensive land holdings. Wallenstein now offered to raise, at his own expense, a brand-new imperial army of as many as fifty thousand men. He would support these troops off the lands that he conquered, requiring from the emperor only the soldiers' pay. The emperor agreed, and within months, Wallenstein had managed to raise twenty thousand to thirty thousand troops, with which he occupied the bishoprics of Magdeburg and Halberstadt. Meanwhile, the Bavarian army under Tilly also advanced into the Lower Saxon Circle, and both armies settled into occupied territories for the winter. These lands were not treated well by the occupying armies, but Wallenstein in particular began to regularize the extractions of his troops by requiring the local governments to pay large "contributions" toward the support of his army.[1]

By the winter of 1625, with the armies of Tilly, Wallenstein, and Christian IV all hovering in and around the Lower Saxon Circle, the stage was now set for a major campaign in the spring (see Document 11). But although he was aided by the reconstituted armies of Ernst von Mansfeld and Christian of Brunswick, as well as by a diversionary attack launched by Bethlen Gábor into Silesia and Moravia, Christian IV did not fare well in 1626. Unable to work successfully with Mansfeld and Christian of Brunswick, whose armies were defeated almost as soon as they took to the field, Christian IV was then utterly crushed by Tilly in August 1626 at the battle of Lutter-am-Barenberg. Mansfeld, meanwhile, had managed to regroup and march on Silesia to try to unite with Bethlen Gábor; but by the end of the year, both Mansfeld and Christian of Brunswick were dead, and Bethlen Gábor had sued for peace. The new Protestant party was suddenly in tatters.

Things were just as grim for Protestants within the Habsburg hereditary territories and the conquered lands of Frederick in the Palatinate. Their situation had, if anything, deteriorated since the bloody conclusion to the Bohemian uprising, for in addition to suffering the effects of the long "Kipper and Wipper" years of economic disruption and inflation, the people of these areas were also living with forced re-Catholicization and extraordinarily high taxes. In 1626 the peasants of Upper Austria, pushed to the breaking point, rose up in open revolt. "The salvation of the righteous is of the Lord," the peasants proclaimed. "He is their strength in the time of trouble"(Document 12). Yet the duke of Bavaria, who had been holding Upper Austria until the emperor repaid his war expenses, brought in his general von Pappenheim, who scattered the rebels and brutally ended their uprising.

1. For more on contributions, see the General Introduction.

Christian IV fought on in 1627, but his armies were under constant pressure from both Tilly and Wallenstein. By the end of the year he had been pushed back into Denmark. King Sigismund III of Poland sent Wallenstein his hearty congratulations on this success, urging him to continue the fight, "which is so useful for our Catholic religion" (Document 13). The expulsion of the Danes from the empire[2] was indeed an enormous victory for the emperor, who took for his own son the bishoprics of Magdeburg and Halberstadt, and who began to think of pushing his influence into the Baltic by creating a new imperial navy. This was also of considerable interest to the Spanish, who were eager to block Dutch access to the Baltic trade, and to Wallenstein, who gained from it the grand title "Admiral of the Baltic."

Wallenstein's reputation as a military genius had been cemented by his victory over the Danes, and his method of supporting armies from occupied lands (and the freedom given him by the emperor to recruit as many men as he liked) had by now allowed him to establish an army of over one hundred thousand men, bigger than any other at the time. As an added bonus he had acquired from the emperor the territory of Mecklenburg, which had been confiscated from its dukes for their support of Christian IV. Wallenstein was not invincible, however. In 1628, for example, the residents of the city of Stralsund, whose duke had agreed to lodge some of Wallenstein's troops there, rejected the presence of the garrison. Wallenstein attempted a siege, but the city was resupplied and garrisoned by the Danes and Swedes. Other Baltic cities also rejected Wallenstein's garrisons, joining together in a defensive league, and his indiscriminate quartering of troops led to increasing complaints by many other imperial princes, both Protestant and Catholic.

These were but minor problems, and by 1629 Emperor Ferdinand's armies controlled almost all of the empire. As a sign of his self-confidence, he determined that this was the moment to roll back seventy-five years of Protestant advances with one imperial edict (see Document 14). This proclamation, known as the Edict of Restitution, was an attempt to enforce the 1555 Peace of Augsburg, which had allowed Protestant princes to keep all ecclesiastical properties they had seized before 1552, but had stipulated that no further ecclesiastical properties could be reformed and secularized. Over time, many princes had failed to abide by this stipulation, and numerous additional bishoprics and archbishoprics, along with lesser church lands and goods, had fallen into the hands of Protestants. The Edict of Restitution, therefore, was a revolutionary document. Its implementation would dispossess hundreds

---

2. Christian did try one more invasion of the empire in 1628, but he was driven back again. He finally signed a peace with Wallenstein on May 22, 1629 at the city of Lübeck.

of princes and tens of thousands of ordinary people of their properties. For Calvinists the edict was even more frightening, for it expressly stated that only those belonging to the unaltered and original Augsburg Confession (namely the Lutherans) enjoyed legal recognition. Thus the edict both made Calvinism illegal and deprived Calvinist princes of the right to even those Church lands seized before 1552.

Opposition to the edict was fierce and immediate, and Protestants who had previously supported the emperor were now outraged and frightened. Hans Heberle, a resident of the Protestant territory of Ulm, described the edict in exaggerated terms, writing that "Lutheranism was now abolished everywhere by the emperor, and [formerly] Catholic property or ecclesiastical property was supposed to be given back to the Catholics. This frightened the Protestant estates while greatly pleasing the Catholics. Then there was a great outcry and lack of trust, and everyone was afraid that his property would be extracted and taken away."[3] Even some Catholic princes were becoming uneasy about the rapid extension of imperial power, for the emperor had shown himself disturbingly willing to rule by fiat instead of following tradition and bringing matters before an imperial diet. This disquiet worsened when Wallenstein was given the job of providing military support to the imperial commissioners tasked with implementing the edict, for this only reinforced the impression that the imperial army gave the emperor unprecedented power to impose his will on the empire.

It was at this very moment that Gustavus Adolphus, the Lutheran king of Sweden, finally decided to enter the war. Gustavus Adolphus was a brilliant and charismatic general, battle-tested in the recent wars between Sweden and Poland. After the defeat of Christian IV of Denmark, the French prime minister, Cardinal Richelieu, had offered the Swedish king subsidies in return for his intervention in the empire. Now he finally agreed. Like Christian IV's, his motives were varied. He saw the danger an overly strong emperor posed to Sweden, he wished to aid his fellow religionists, and he did not care to allow Wallenstein and the Habsburgs to control the Baltic and its trade. On June 26, 1630, therefore, he landed his fleet with around fourteen thousand men on the island of Usedom in Pomerania (see Document 15). The seemingly miraculous appearance of the "Lion of the North" aroused great hope among the Protestant powers of Europe, but only a few imperial princes leaped at the new opportunity. The landgrave of Hesse-Cassel, who was a Calvinist and whose lands had largely been stripped away by the emperor, rushed to join the Swedish king in an alliance; so did the elector Palatine. But these were isolated cases.

3. Document 38.

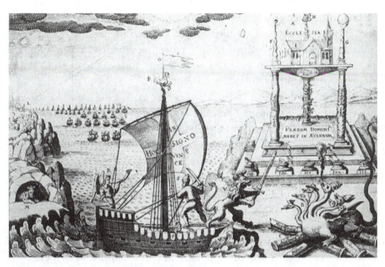

"The Swedes Save the Christian Church," 1631 (Nürnberg, Germanisches National-
museum, Graphische Sammlung, HB 477)

The Swedish king was aided, however, by the general dissatisfaction of the
princes of the empire, who used the Regensburg electoral diet of July 1630
to express loudly their anger over the recent course of events. The princes'
hatred for and fear of Wallenstein—together with their great resentment of
the emperor's repeated insults to their liberties—boiled over at this meeting,
and they managed to prevail upon the emperor to dismiss Wallenstein and
reduce the size of the imperial army. Tilly, still in charge of the Catholic
League army, was also given command of the remaining imperial troops.
This reshuffling and reduction of imperial forces could not have been better for the Swedish king, who focused his attacks on the Oder River and tried
to determine a strategy that would ensure a quick and satisfying victory. Indeed, his armies met little opposition, in part because Tilly's army was far to
the west, and in part due to still-simmering local resentment of Wallenstein's
heavy-handedness along the Baltic coast. Gradually Gustavus Adolphus conquered almost all of Pomerania and Mecklenburg, aided by a treaty with
France that now guaranteed him the promised financial support.[4]

Meeting at the city of Leipzig in February 1631, the Protestant princes of
the empire, led by the Calvinist elector of Brandenburg but also including delegates from leading Lutheran princes, such as the elector of Saxony,

4. The Treaty of Barwälde, January 13, 1631.

responded to the twin dangers of an overly strong emperor and an invading foreign army by suppressing their mutual distaste and attempting to create a third, neutral party. In April 1631 the meeting produced a manifesto that proclaimed their formation of a strong defensive alliance and demanded that the emperor withdraw the Edict of Restitution.

Gustavus Adolphus, of course, did his best to gain the trust of these and other princes and estates by proclaiming himself the defender of the German Liberties. He was not seeking personal gain, he argued, but attempting to restore the imperial constitution and to end the illegal suppression and persecution of Protestants. This strategy worked, and among the new allies who slowly began to flock to his side was the great free imperial city of Magdeburg, part of a Lutheran bishopric endangered by the Edict of Restitution. The city's rebellion was somewhat premature, however, for its own small army was almost immediately forced to retreat behind the city walls, which Tilly then settled in to besiege. Yet despite his promises, Gustavus Adolphus failed to come to the rescue, and after months of desperate expectation, on the morning of May 20, 1631, the city council finally decided to come to terms. But it was too late. At that very moment, Tilly's forces breached the walls and his troops poured into the city. Frustrated and hungry, the troops had no mercy on the citizens. "Through such enduring fury," Magdeburg resident Otto von Guericke reported,

> which laid this great, magnificent city, which had been like a princess in the entire land, into complete burning embers and put it into such enormous misery and unspeakable need and heartache—many thousands of innocent men, women, and children were, with horrid, fearful screams of pain and alarm, miserably murdered and wretchedly executed in manifold ways, so that no words can sufficiently describe it, nor tears bemoan it.[5]

The city was engulfed in flames, and as many as twenty thousand people were killed, their bodies burned or left floating in the river.

Magdeburg had been a jewel of the empire. Now it was a burned husk, and its utter destruction shocked the princes of the empire into action. Over the course of the summer and fall, the Leipzig colloquy princes raised an army, the elector of Brandenburg allied with Sweden, and then John George of Saxony finally joined as well, bringing his considerable military forces into conjunction with the Swedish king. The allied army of Saxony and Sweden then formed a powerful force, which chased Tilly's outnumbered troops into

5. Document 16; for additional descriptions of the sack of Magdeburg, see Johann Philipp Abilenus and Matthaeus Merian, *Theatrum Europaeum,* Bd. 2 (Frankfurt am Main: 1646), 368–70.

southern Saxony. There, near Leipzig at the town of Breitenfeld, the two armies met on September 17, 1631 (Document 17). The battle was a rout. Tilly's army was completely defeated, his troops killed and scattered, and he was forced to retreat into the Upper Palatinate with only a small remnant of his troops.

The victorious Protestants then split up, with the elector of Saxony invading Bohemia and Moravia, while Gustavus Adolphus marched his armies west toward the Rhineland. By the end of the year, Saxon armies had occupied Prague and Gustavus Adolphus had conquered huge areas of north and western Germany, including the archbishopric of Mainz, the bishopric of Würzburg, the Lower Palatinate, and the destroyed bishopric of Magdeburg. In the spring of 1632 the Swedish king advanced into Bavaria; there, after defeating and mortally wounding Tilly, he took the capital city of Munich. As he advanced through these firmly Catholic areas, Gustavus Adolphus mostly (though not always) kept his promise to the French that he would not intentionally persecute Catholics in conquered territories. On the other hand, he used these lands much as Wallenstein had used the lands he had once controlled: extracting forced contributions, tolerating controlled looting, and demanding that locals pay for the maintenance of the troops (see Document 19). Tens of thousands of Catholic civilians were displaced, fleeing before the victorious Protestant troops and protecting whatever belongings they could manage.

Local Protestant minorities also took advantage of the new shape of affairs to indulge in a bit of bloody payback. In Prague, for example, the *Theatrum Europaeum* reported that after "fifteen cornets of cavalry and thirteen companies of infantry were brought into Prague and quartered,"

> thereafter the Lutherans, who up to now had been dispossessed and forced to go around in misery, returned to the cities and the countryside and their houses and possessions, which had been taken from them by the Catholics. The peasants also began to join the Saxons, plundering their overlords and ecclesiastical possessions, and whenever they met their lords, they beat them almost to death. They did the same to the imperial soldiers whenever any fell into their hands.[6]

The Swedes' grand success overjoyed grateful Protestants across the empire. In the Protestant city of Ulm, for example, the city council had been forced to form the local peasants and burghers into a militia in order to try to defend itself from depredations by imperial troops. But in February 1632, the city formed an alliance with the Swedes and agreed to support a garrison of real troops under the command of Colonel Patrick Ruthwen, one of the

6. Abelinus and Merian, Bd. 2, 485–6.

CRUCENACVM A SVECIS OCCVLATVR

Gustavus Adolphus takes Kreutzenach in the Lower Palatinate, 1631 (*Theatrum Europaeum*, II, p.602+, Universitätsbibliothek Augsburg Sign. 02/IV.13.2.26-2)

many Scottish officers serving the Swedish king. As Ulm resident Hans Heberle described it, "The twenty-eighth day of February, the government asked the burghers whether they would want to be Swedish, and this was accepted from the heart with joy. The fourteenth day of March the young fellows in the land of Ulm were put under the Swedish troops so that resistance could be offered to the enemy."[7] Protestant princes were similarly pleased at the glorious victories of the Swedish king and his allies, and they began to dream of their ultimate takeover of the empire (see Document 18).

The spring of 1632 was a high point for Protestant forces. By May, however, the tables began to turn once again. In his panic over the Swedish advance, Ferdinand had recalled Wallenstein and given him vast new powers over the imperial forces. Wallenstein quickly retook Bohemia and, in the fall, advanced into Saxony. Gustavus Adolphus moved to intercept him, and on November 16 the two armies met at Lützen, once again right outside the city of Leipzig. The battle of Lützen was another victory for the Protestants, for Wallenstein was forced to fall back into Bohemia. But in one way the imperialists were also successful: Gustavus Adolphus was killed in combat.

The death of the Swedish king left his government in the hands of a regency council led by his chancellor, Axel Oxenstierna.[8] Oxenstierna was determined that Sweden would not withdraw from the war without some gains to show for it, and he convinced the council to concentrate the army on maintaining Gustavus Adolphus' territorial conquests in Pomerania and along the Baltic. Oxenstierna also pushed forward with the king's earlier efforts to create a more permanent defensive alliance with his imperial allies. This new Heilbronn League, signed into existence on April 23, 1633, brought together princes from the imperial circles of Swabia, Franconia, and the Lower Rhine. They agreed to pay for a new, united league army and to keep fighting until the empire's constitutional and religious problems were resolved—and until Sweden was guaranteed compensation, or "satisfaction," for its troubles. The league was further supported by subsidies from the French and contributions extracted from both occupied and allied territories. The two Protestant electors of Saxony and Brandenburg refused to join the Heilbronn League as signing members, but agreed to keep fighting as allies of Sweden. Yet both were strongly inclined toward peace and, throughout 1633, entertained numerous separate negotiations with Wallenstein (see Document 20).

Wallenstein had by now become the most powerful man in the empire and was acting with increasing arrogance and impulsiveness, demanding

---

7. Document 38.

8. Axel Gustafsson Oxenstierna, count of Södermöre (1583–1654), Swedish chancellor and Gustavus Adolphus' closest advisor.

even that the Spanish army in the empire be placed under his command. His enemies had only grown in number since his earlier dismissal, and in early 1634 the emperor began to plot his removal again. This would quiet Wallenstein's critics, appease the Spanish, and allow the emperor's own son, King Ferdinand of Hungary,[9] to take Wallenstein's place as head of the imperial army. The plot was carefully executed, and on February 25, 1634, some of Wallenstein's own officers led his assassination. According to a contemporary English account, at the final moment, Wallenstein's assailant called out his triumph, stating "Thus shall dye all that doe rebell against the Emperour" (Document 21).

Despite the death of Wallenstein, the Protestant parties could not agree among themselves, nor unify their military operations. The Swedish–Heilbronn League army, under the uncertain command of both Bernard of Saxe-Weimar and Gustav Horn,[10] advanced into Bavaria, while the Saxon army, under the command of Field Marshal Arnim,[11] pushed into the Habsburg hereditary territories of Silesia and Bohemia. The emperor's forces, now under Ferdinand of Hungary's command, fought back, retaking Regensburg and Donauwörth from the Protestants and besieging Nördlingen. There, on September 6, 1634, Ferdinand of Hungary, aided by the army of his cousin, the Spanish cardinal-infante Ferdinand,[12] met the Swedish forces and utterly destroyed them. After the battle, at which Horn himself was captured, the Swedish troops and Bernard of Saxe-Weimar fled west toward the Rhine, chased closely by the imperialists. The countryside was subjected to two separate armies, neither of which took any heed of the loyalties of the people they brutalized and looted. The pastor Johann Daniel Minck described the total devastation of the entire area, explaining that because of the soldiers,

> no man could dare to be spotted in the countryside, lest he be hunted down like game; were he captured, he would be mercilessly battered and bound—worse than the methods used by the Turks—until he disclosed money or cattle or a horse; he would be tied up naked in a hot oven, suspended, and steamed with smoke; he would be saturated with water and dirty water by the people who poured it down his throat using a tube and then jumped on his engorged stomach with their feet.[13]

9. King Ferdinand of Hungary (1608–1657), later Holy Roman Emperor Ferdinand III.

10. Duke Bernard of Saxe-Weimar (1604–1639), an ally of Gustavus Adolphus since his landing in 1630; and Count Gustav Horn (1592–1657), Swedish field marshal.

11. Hans Georg von Arnim-Boitzenburg (1583–1641), the elector of Saxony's field marshal.

12. Cardinal-Infante Ferdinand (1610–1641), the son of King Philip III of Spain.

13. Document 22.

After Nördlingen, the imperial and Spanish armies advanced easily through Franconia, Swabia, and Württemberg. Entire towns were emptied as the people fled, and Protestants everywhere agreed with Minck that this was "a grievous and very injurious year for all Evangelicals" (Document 22). Despite the renewed aid promised by the almost panicked French court, the victory of the emperor and his allies now seemed almost assured (see Document 23). Sensing the moment, in the Saxon city of Pirna on November 24, 1634, the elector of Saxony reached a preliminary peace agreement with the emperor.

11. Letter of King Christian IV of Denmark (February 21, 1626)[14]

[In 1625 the Danish king Christian IV decided to intervene in the war. As a Lutheran prince of the empire and member of the Lower Saxon Circle (as duke of Holstein), he strongly opposed the emperor's recent constitutional and religious changes. As king of Denmark, he hated to see an overly powerful emperor as his neighbor to the south. Christian also had strong economic reasons for wanting to become involved. With the support of the French, Dutch, and English, therefore, who were eager to find someone willing to counter the power of the Austrian Habsburgs, Christian pressured the estates of the Lower Saxon Circle to elect him as their director and allow him to recruit an army. Meanwhile, however, the Bavarian army under Tilly and the new imperial army under Wallenstein[15] were moving to meet this new threat, and by the winter of 1625 to 1626, they had entered the Lower Saxon Circle and settled in for the winter. The very existence of Wallenstein's army had come as a nasty shock to Christian, and the campaign season of 1626 now promised to be much tougher than he had expected. The following document, which was written by Christian to the leading Catholic princes of the empire, shows his attempt to limit the forces allied against him and so improve his chances of success in the coming campaign. It is also interesting to see how firmly he justified his intervention in the empire in terms of the German Liberties,[16] a

14. "Copia Königl May zu Dennemarcken, . . . an die zu Meintz, Trier und Cöln Ertzbischoffe vund Churfürsten, wie dann auch Maximilian vnd Wolffgang Wilhelm, Pfallzgraffn bey Rein vnd Hertzoge zu Beyern xc abgangnen Schreibens, sub Dato Rotenburg den 21 Januarij [*sic*] Anno 1525 [*sic*]," February 21, 1626, Det Konigelige Bibliotek, København, E 4261 4°.

15. In April 1625 the emperor had asked Wallenstein to raise a brand-new army of about twenty-five thousand men to serve the emperor directly.

16. The constitutional rights and privileges of the individual imperial princes and estates who were in opposition to the centralized power of the emperor.

call designed to appeal to the concerns of all imperial princes, not just Protestant ones.]

His Royal Majesty of Denmark, Norway, etc.; letter sent to the archbishops and electors of Mainz, Trier, and Cologne, and also to Maximilian and Wolfgang Wilhelm, counts Palatine of the Rhine and dukes of Bavaria, etc.; Rotenburg,[17] the 21st of February 1626

We do not doubt that you are sufficiently aware how His Roman Imperial Majesty is now trying to cast doubt on our and the praiseworthy Lower Saxon Circle's defensive organization, as if it were intended for something other than the alleged defense. He has also used this as a pretense and pretext in order to overrun this circle with two hostile armies, and to allow them free rein to ravage utterly and devastate as much as they wish, which they are still doing. Similarly, we are told that ill-intentioned people are being found who pretend that our confederation, which was established for the maintenance of the German Liberties (with several neighboring potentates and sovereigns who are extremely interested in the conservation of the traditional constitution of the Roman Empire), was instead supposed to oppress those princes and estates of the Roman Empire who belong to the Roman Catholic religion.

Since so much that was hostile on one or another point was directed toward us and the princes and estates of the circle, we decided that it was very important to explain to you in somewhat greater detail both the reasons that compelled us to form the defensive organization and confederation, and the purpose for which these were actually intended. . . . We fully hope that this, our plea and intercession—which flows forth from our well-intentioned heart and soul—shall not fail to bear fruit. This is particularly because of the various letters (especially those of July 20 and December 3, 1620, and then of April 14 of the following year) that His Imperial Majesty had sent out to us. These quite firmly pledged that he had resolved to use his Lower Burgundian and other armies neither to demolish the statutes of the empire and the Religious and Secular Peace [of 1555], nor to aggrieve or assault any obedient electors, princes, and estates of the empire. Instead, his actions were solely intended to preserve all of these and regain that which he had been deprived of in the kingdom of Bohemia and its incorporated principalities and lands. Thus the other princes could remain securely peaceful and so set aside any unnecessary military preparations and costs.

Yet we found that, in fact, our hopes had been in vain. For although His Imperial Majesty regained and took back into his possession all of the above-

---

17. Christian's headquarters were in the Lower Saxon town of Rotenburg near the Wümme River.

mentioned lands, we came to see (and the electoral prince Palatine also made multiple efforts to show us) that only if [Frederick of the Palatinate] agreed to renounce completely all claims that he might have to these lands—and would also submit to and humble himself before His Imperial Majesty— would he then be allowed to keep his own hereditary lands and dignities. . . . Instead of this, armies were raised by one means or another, and other princes and estates of the empire who had had nothing whatsoever to do with the Bohemian matter were completely ruined and spoiled through the quartering of troops and other afflictions of war. Among these was the Lower Saxon Circle, which His Imperial Majesty himself had much praised on account of the staunch obedience that it had consistently demonstrated, and which no other person had ever denounced. But it was nevertheless not spared in the slightest, and rather was made desolate in many places through the quartering and passage of troops. Our cousin and brother-in-law the duke of Lüneburg[18] alone estimates the damages done to his lands at several tons of gold, such that it would be much more bearable for him to keep several thousand men in the field instead. Thus the princes and estates of this circle sought some help and rescue through serious letters and numerous discussions. . . . Subsequently, some of these princes and estates of the circle were induced to come together, where they thought to form an organization to ward off such territorial damages.[19] This was all the more urgent as, in the meantime, the armies of other potentates were being established in the Roman Empire, led by Duke Christian of Brunswick and the count of Mansfeld.[20] Thus General Tilly himself urgently warned the circle to see to its own protection and to ready itself for its own defense, and this was agreed to by majority vote in the general diet[21] of the circle, although some few estates were not in agreement. We were then assigned to lead this defense because shortly before, with the urgent prompting of the estates, we had been charged with the office of director of the circle, which had become vacant on the resignation of the aforementioned Duke Christian of Lüneburg.[22] We then specifically notified His Roman Imperial Majesty and the entire

18. Duke Christian the elder of Brunswick-Lüneburg (1566–1633), bishop of Minden.

19. This meeting was held in April 1625 at Lauenberg and was attended mostly by supporters of Christian IV.

20. Duke Christian of Brunswick (the "mad Halberstadter") and Count Ernst von Mansfeld.

21. A meeting of the estates.

22. Christian of Brunswick-Lüneburg resigned in early 1625, and the diet, which met at Lüneburg, then elected King Christian IV director of the circle, or *Kreisoberst*, in May 1625.

circle about this organization and the goal for which it was intended: that is, solely toward the defense of the circle, not to offend any person. And neither we nor the circle could have believed that it would be interpreted in this way, as did indeed happen subsequently, given that the imperial constitution allows such a thing to the circles and that Tilly himself had desired it. . . .

In addition to the previous explanation that we made to His Imperial Majesty and also to the general [Tilly] (although we are in no way responsible to give him an account of our actions), nevertheless, for even more evidence of our peaceful disposition, we avow that this was only to be a defensive project, and this is also sufficiently proven in fact, in that we offended no man with our army, but instead remained at the river[23] on the border of the circle in order to secure it. But despite all of this, General Tilly hostilely led his army into the circle in the month of July [1625], and did so with such rampant robbery, murder, and arson that the Turks and Tatars would not have behaved worse. . . . In a letter dated Neustadt on the 3rd of August 1625, which was delivered to us on the 22nd of that month, [His Imperial Majesty] advised us that he had empowered the duke of Bavaria to grant an ordinance to his lieutenant general, Count Tilly, that he should move into this circle (or to wherever our or the circle's suspicious armaments were to be found); and he had also ordered his own general, the duke of Friedland,[24] to do the same thing and not to leave the circle until his army was given leave to do so.

As for why our armaments were suspicious, no other reason was given than that they were unnecessary and much too strong. Yet it should have been evident that as for the resolution that His Majesty had given, one would have to tread outside the reins of the imperial constitution before one could justifiably condemn the organization and hostilely invade the circle. But without considering this, both armies authorized by His Imperial Majesty proceeded with their perpetration of this hostile act, ignoring the requests for peace and amicable negotiations by both us and the estates of the circle. They even went so far that in his reply (dated Holßmünden the 5th of August) to our vice regent and commissioner—who had similarly proposed amicable negotiations and, in order to promote this, had offered to pull back our army—General Tilly had quite arrogantly declared that he would not be satisfied by the proposed negotiations and pullback of the troops. Instead, he said the army of the kingdom of Denmark and the circle must be disbanded, broken up, and eliminated, and should it remain any longer, one could not blame him were he personally to see to such a breaking up and elimination.

23. The Elbe.

24. General Wallenstein (he had been rewarded by the emperor with the title of duke of Friedland after his earlier victories over Frederick and his allies).

From such threats, but also from the actions themselves, we sense that the final goal here is to beat our army, occupy the circle, and stain the laudable royal reputation that we have held until now. Thus we had to grab hold of our defenses and take up all appropriate means in order to save ourselves and the circle. Yet before we acted to involve other potentates in this matter, we once again decreed and attested to the resolution of August 24 of the past year [1624], which we had given to His Imperial Majesty and also to the king of Spain (who at that time had an envoy with us), stating that we were inclined toward peace, would gladly be freed from the defense we had been compelled to undertake, and wished to be excused before God and the world for all of the judgments and bloodletting that would ensue. Because, however, there was still no answer forthcoming, and we and the circle were instead, day by day, increasingly pressed to the limit by hostile forces, we finally stopped resisting the assistance that had long been offered to us by our relatives and neighboring potentates and sovereigns.[25] In order to save this circle, which, though completely innocent, had been attacked contrary to the imperial constitution and the sworn capitulations,[26] and to save German liberty, which is everywhere suffering, we joined with them in a confederation so that thereby, with the grace of God the Almighty, liberty and the Religious and Secular Peace [of 1555] might not be lost, but conserved through those means allowed by God and nature, and transferred to our dear posterity. . . .

And we hereby not only publicly deny that this conjunction is only designed to oppress you or the adherents of your religion . . . but also firmly and most persistently stipulate and attest that it was never, even in the least, our intention, nor is it now. Instead, we profess only friendly feelings toward you and the adherents of your religion, and, for our part, we will not rest until it comes to pass that the princes and estates of the Roman Empire—of both one and the other religion—shall all live together in abiding peace, quiet, and unity as Christians and patriots, and that the liberty in religious and secular affairs that was inherited from our ancestors might also be transferred to posterity as a hereditary law. This [we attest] with a very Christian and serious consideration of the extent to which it concerns all of Christendom that the standing of the Holy Roman Empire (in which neighboring potentates and states are so noticeably interested) be restored to its former state.

25. The Hague Alliance, signed in November 1625 by the Danes, English, and Dutch, had as its ultimate goal that Christian work to restore Frederick of the Palatinate.

26. The capitulations are the sworn statements made by incoming emperors to preserve the rights and privileges of the estates of the empire—that is, the German Liberties.

Also, you should not think badly of Count von Mansfeld, for he did not come here on his own behalf, but was sent here by the kings of France and Great Britain in order to further the oft-mentioned goal [of self-defense]; and he is, moreover, not to treat anyone with hostility.

Should, however, things proceed contrary to our hopes, such that disorder is fomented and the armies that rampaged into this circle advance, we would be forced to take action, though this would be contrary to our intentions. We console ourselves fully, however, with the thought that you, as leading electors of the Roman Empire, shall moderate matters among your co-electors and other Catholic princes and estates of the Roman Empire, so that we shall be given no reason to act. . . .

12. The Austrian Peasants' Rebellion (1626)

[In 1619 the people of Upper Austria,[27] also known as Austria above the Enns River,[28] joined the Bohemian estates in their rebellion against their Habsburg overlords. Their rebellion was brutally crushed in 1620 by the army of Duke Maximilian of Bavaria, who was then given temporary control of the area by Emperor Ferdinand II as partial payment for his efforts on the emperor's behalf. Upper Austria had been almost fully Lutheran since the middle of the sixteenth century, but Maximilian brought in the Jesuits, who led the re-Catholicization of the area. The duke banned Lutheran practice and teaching for all—even the nobility—ordered all Lutheran ministers ejected, and seized all land and property that had formerly belonged to the Church. These restrictions greatly intensified popular frustration with the Bavarian army's occupation, and in 1625 the peasantry of Upper Austria broke into open revolt. Maximilian's governor, Count Adam von Herberstorff, mindful of historical similarities with the great Peasants' War of 1525, brutally crushed these uprisings, killing half the ringleaders after forcing them to roll dice for their lives. Rather than resolve the problem, this only further enraged the peasantry and gained them the support of craftsmen, small businessmen, and lesser nobility. Then, in May 1626, thousands or perhaps even tens of thousands of peasants, under the leadership of the farmer Stefan Fadinger, staged another carefully planned uprising. Unlike the rebellion of 1525, the peasants' demands of 1626 did not include social revolution, but focused instead on the twin goals of evicting the Bavarians and restoring Lutheran worship. The well-armed and organ-

---

27. Upper Austria includes the modern Austrian state of the same name, located in northwestern Austria.

28. A tributary of the Danube River.

ized peasant army occupied a number of major towns and regions of Upper Austria and then marched on the capital city of Linz, which they besieged. Fadinger was killed in the attack, but after his death the peasants regrouped under his brother-in-law, the innkeeper Christoph Zeller. When he too was killed, command finally fell to Achaz Wiellinger, a minor nobleman. In all, Linz lay besieged for two months before the combined forces of the Linz regiment and fresh imperial reinforcements broke the siege on August 29, 1626. The Bavarian General von Pappenheim and the imperial regiments quickly reconquered Upper Austria and crushed all remaining resistance. As many as twelve thousand peasants may have died in the rebellion. Both of the following documents appeared as printed broadsheets in 1626. The first (I)[29] gives the peasants' demands and was accompanied by an image of peasants carrying banners, one bearing a poem against the duke of Bavaria and one bearing the date and slogan "It must be," which signified their readiness for death. These may match the banners the peasants actually carried into battle. The second broadsheet (II)[30] relates the peasants' siege of Linz and its immediate aftermath, and it is accompanied by an image of the besieged city at the moment when the peasants were beginning to flee.]

Broadsheet I: Remembrance of the Peasant War in the Year 1626

> Psalm 37: But the salvation of the righteous is of the Lord. He is their strength in the time of trouble.[31]
> Psalm 20: In the name of our God we will set up our banners.[32]

This story, recounted on little banners, is not told out of malice, but concerns only the honor of God and His word, according to Doctor Luther's[33] teaching.

---

29. *Gedechtnis des Bauren Kriegs im Jahr 1626* (1626). A copy can be found at the Oberösterreichischen Landesarchivs; published in John Roger Paas, *The German Political Broadsheet 1600–1700*, vol. 4: 1622–1629 (Wiesbaden: Harrassowitz, 1994), #P-1099, 232.

30. *Wahre unnd eigendtliche Contrafectur der Statt Lintz* (Augsburg: Johann Georg Mannasser, copperplate engraver, 1626). A copy can be found at the Linz Stadtmuseum, Inv. Nr. 2057; also published in John Roger Paas, *The German Political Broadsheet 1600–1700*, vol. 4, #P-1103, 236.

31. Ps. 37:39. These are from Martin Luther's translation of the Bible. Here I have given English translations from the King James Version.

32. Ps. 20:6.

33. The Protestant reformer Martin Luther.

[**Left banner:**]   O dear Lord God, free us from Bavarian yoke and tyranny and from his great oppression. For it concerns both soul and property, as it also concerns our lives and blood. God give us bravery.

[**Right banner:**]   It must be.

Anno 1626

The demands of the collected peasantry of Austria above the Enns to His Imperial Majesty consist of the following twelve articles.

1. The word of God.
2. The emperor as ruler, and not the prince of Bavaria.
3. To remove the governor of Linz.[34]
4. A provincial governor who resides in the province.
5. To place Lutheran judges and mayors in the cities; the Catholics are not to be trusted.
6. To remove prelates from the council[35] and to put in peasants, as is the custom in Tyrol.[36]
7. That the soldiers be expelled legally from the province, for we peasants wish to protect the province.
8. To remove the garrisons from the cities; some money shall be given annually for this.
9. To clear from the province the rabble of Jesuit clergy, in addition to the prelates.
10. A general pardon of all poor and rich, of high and low estate.
11. By dint of the capitulation that Emperor Matthias promised,[37] every provincial lord to be able to keep a preacher on his property.
12. All exiles to be entirely restored to their property and be placed once again in peaceful possession of it.

Given in the small land above the Enns.

---

34. Adam, count von Heberstorff (1585–1629), Bavarian governor, was despised by the people of Upper Austria for enforcing the re-Catholicization of the region.

35. The estates of Upper Austria.

36. Another Habsburg hereditary territory consisting of the northern portion of modern Italy and much of the western portion of modern Austria.

37. In 1609 Emperor Matthias had granted religious toleration to Protestants in his territories.

Broadsheet II: True and actual depiction of the city of Linz: how the same was besieged by the peasants of Enns in 1626, and stormed on the 19th of July.[38] But in the end they were finally forced to withdraw once again with great losses.

In 1620, as one counts the years, Elector Maximilian of Bavaria, after the territorial diet held at Ulm, traveled with his army over the Danube River into Austria, punished the rebels and all of those who belonged to the confederation against His Imperial Majesty, occupied the entire area above the Enns, and brought it into obedience to him. But the peasantry, which constantly thought of mutiny, never let it drop, instead daring to rebel often and seriously against its own ruling authority, as we have sufficiently seen in this year, 1626. For not only have the peasants revolted in their hamlets and villages, but they have also put in an appearance in the open, with flags flying, almost according to the custom of war. And because their power quickly increased and to such an extent, they were even more firmly reinforced in their intentions, such that they incinerated with fire several hamlets, stormed cloisters, occupied small towns, and so proceeded and continued with equal speed until they even intended to overwhelm the city of Linz; but their attack on it failed by far. For on the 15th of July, as, up to seventy thousand strong,[39] they attacked the city hard and by storm over both water and land, they met fierce resistance from the soldiers and garrison of the place, such that this assault lasted almost thirty days. The peasants were thwarted again and again, with great losses to themselves; yet, with the greatest fervor, they fired upon the city with great *kartaune*[40] until they finally knocked down a large portion of the wall between the Wels Gate and the little Student Gate, at which they were almost jubilant and were convinced that they had won the day, and so rushed in force to the broken-open hole. Then as more than six hundred of them were allowed in, by order of the lord governor himself, the area was bombarded with great cannons from the castle, and all but forty of those who had climbed in were chopped down quite wretchedly by the concealed Croats.[41] The lord governor had those forty swear never again to revolt against their ruling authority, to make their way back home, and also

---

38. The author is inconsistent about the day the city was stormed (here the 19th, later the 15th). Other sources suggest it may have occurred on the 21st of July instead.

39. This number is probably exaggerated. Scholars estimate the peasant army at its height to number about forty thousand.

40. *Kartaune* were large siege cannons.

41. Croatia was a Habsburg territory, and Croatian troops served the imperial side in the Thirty Years War. They were infamous for their viciousness.

to advise their fellows, who had already fled, to abandon their intentions. In addition, Lord Löbel,[42] a colonel of His Imperial Majesty, did not hesitate. For as soon as he heard of the matter, he quickly had the dismantled scaffolding once again raised on the Enns bridge, and then, on the 24th of this month, near Enns,[43] he attacked the peasants to such an extent that he put more than twelve thousand of them to flight, killed fully nine hundred, and seized a lot of livestock along with ten cannons. This then moved the peasants to such fear that they soon refused to continue to obey their leader, Achaz Wiellinger, a shoemaker by trade.[44] Instead, they gradually—one here, another there—made their way back home.[45] And so one can see that the outcome of this war can be compared to the Peasant War of a hundred and some years ago.[46] May God direct everything for the best.

13. General Wallenstein on Two Fronts (August–November 1627)

[The 1627 campaign season was an excellent one for the emperor and General Wallenstein. After the August 1626 defeat of King Christian IV of Denmark at the battle of Lutter-am-Barenberg, Wallenstein had been able to push the Danish army back almost to the Baltic. Yet at the same time that Wallenstein was driving the Danes to the north, he also had to be prepared for the contingency that his long-time enemy, the prince of Transylvania Bethlen Gábor,[47] would take this opportunity to attack again from the east. The following documents illustrate a number of interesting points concerning this campaign. The first letter, sent by the emperor to the governor of Moravia, Cardinal von Diet-

42. Hans Christian Löbel, or Löbl, was one of a number of commanders who led the imperial reinforcements sent to aid the Bavarians against the peasant armies.

43. The city of Enns.

44. Other records suggest he was a member of the lesser nobility and owned a farmstead.

45. Colonel Löbel's regiment of imperial troops defeated the remaining peasant army at the town of Neuhofen on August 17, killing many and wounding Wiellinger himself. By the end of September, imperial commanders had ended most peasant resistance, but the last battle of the rebellion took place toward the end of November.

46. 1525.

47. Bethlen Gábor (1580–1629), prince of Transylvania. He had been at peace with the emperor since the 1626 Peace of Pressburg, which had affirmed an earlier peace and by which Bethlen Gábor had agreed not to ally with the Ottoman Turks against the emperor. In return, he gained portions of Habsburg Hungary and confirmation of religious freedom for Transylvanian Protestants.

*richstein,[48] suggests how burdensome the princes of the empire found Wallen-
stein's practice of foisting the support of his armies onto local populations. This
was to be a constant complaint throughout the war, but this method of maintaining troops by extracting forced, regular contributions of money and supplies
was one of the principal reasons the war could drag on for so many years. The
second letter, from King Sigismund III of Poland to Wallenstein, gives another
clue as to why the war stretched on so long. Every time one or another power
enjoyed a great success, he and his supporters glimpsed the possibility of absolute victory. Just one more push, and religious unity could be possible. Just
one more push, and all political goals might be met.]*

Letter of Emperor Ferdinand II to Cardinal Franz von Dietrichstein[49]

August 7, 1627

We saw from the contents of your letter, dated the 4th of this month, how you
humbly and with several meek warnings referred our attention to the matter
of the regiments of cavalry and infantry that are to be brought into our hereditary margraviate of Moravia, by force of orders given recently by our military
advisor, councilor, and generalissimo, the duke of Friedland.[50]

We ourselves still look forward to learning from our Aulic councilor,[51]
Baron von Questenberg,[52] about the further particulars of both the orders issued by our generalissimo, and about what you discussed with von Questenberg in this regard.

Meanwhile, however, we, with our gracious good intention that you have
full knowledge of events, do not wish to conceal from you that we heard
from the commissioners whom we had sent to the peace negotiations with
the Turks,[53] that the Turks had proposed, obstinately sought, and asked such

48. Cardinal Franz von Dietrichstein (1570–1636).

49. Emperor Ferdinand II (letter sent) to Cardinal Franz v. Dietrichstein, August 7,
1627, Vienna, Státní archiv Brno, Rodinný archiv Ditrichštejnové, Sign. 223, in
Josef Kollmann, ed., *Documenta Bohemica Bellum Tricennale Illustrantia, T. IV, Der
Dänisch-Niederdeutsche Krieg und der Aufstieg Wallensteins. Quellen zur Geschichte der
Kriegsereignisse der Jahre 1625–1630* (Prague: Academia, 1974), 207–9.

50. Wallenstein was given the duchy of Friedland by the emperor and also held the
title of *Generalobristfeldhauptmann,* or generalissimo, which meant he was the head
of the entire imperial army.

51. A member of the Imperial Aulic Council (*Reichshofrat*).

52. Gerhard von Questenberg-Jarmeritz (c. 1586–1646) was an imperial councilor
and a personal friend and advisor to Wallenstein.

53. The Ottoman Turks, whose large empire lay to the east of the Holy Roman
Empire.

unexpectedly unjust conditions that we neither could in any way, nor shall in the least, agree to them without a belittlement of our dignity and a marked disadvantage to beloved Christendom. Furthermore, according to the news that has been arriving, both the Turks and Bethlen Gábor are daily making such extremely suspicious military preparations and provisions that we can count on another incomprehensible break in the peace, a territorially damaging invasion and attack into those lands that neighbor them. They will, especially, not simply depart after receiving our persistently negative reply to their unjust conditions. Instead, we can and must assume the exact opposite, so that we consider it to be an absolute emergency and have, for that reason, consulted with our above-mentioned generalissimo to arrange for a considerable number of cavalry and infantry troops to be set on the border between Moravia and Hungary as soon as possible. Thus, with a single blow, one would not only be able to reverse, immediately and without losing any time, the territorially ruinous violence and crimes committed by the rebellious Wallachs[54] against this same land of Moravia (the remediation of which was the topic of your written petition of the 1st of this month), but one would also be able to respond to the emergency by protecting and securing this land (and other surrounding and neighboring lands that have remained loyal to us) from the above-mentioned repeated violence and incomprehensible attack by the Turks and Bethlen Gábor.

You, and the entire territory that is loyal, may and should take an abiding consolation in the knowledge that since we have a constant, gracious, and fatherly remembrance and regard for the current condition of this land and the misery it has suffered, we would have graciously preferred to have spared you everything, including the quartering of troops that will occur for a short time, if we had not determined and considered it more advisable and completely necessary to prefer such a minor inconvenience over the danger that a much greater disaster, and even complete ruin, might occur.

We have thereby neither thought nor intended that this army, as we mentioned, would remain for long. Instead, as soon as we have gained greater and more certain news of the intentions and final movements of the Turks and Bethlen Gábor, we shall either respond to a manifest emergency by immediately sending the army out against them in order temporarily to cut off their advance and keep our eyes on them (because this advance might most reasonably and advantageously be made from this same Moravian border

---

54. The Wallachs, or Vlachs, were the peoples living in the border regions of Moravia. They had adopted Protestantism and were violently opposed to the re-Catholicization and tightened political control Emperor Ferdinand demanded. Even after the Bohemian and Moravian rebellions had collapsed, the Wallachs continued to harry Habsburg forces with raids and revolts. Only in 1644 would the Wallachs finally be defeated and brutally punished by the emperor's forces.

against all those places that are dependent on us), and would then lodge the army farther out in Hungary; or instead, should the nature of things improve, we shall graciously order the army once again to move out entirely and proceed back into the empire.

Meanwhile, in such circumstances it is very important that this unavoidable quartering of troops be done with the best order and greatest sparing of the land possible. Thus you should settle and regulate this with our appointed colonel, Lorenzo del Maestro, who shall presently be leading this particular army, so that this army can live on the border with Hungary either in the open woods—which as far as we know would be most reasonable in this good summertime—or placed and dispersed into comfortable quarters in such a way that one could, at any time, in response to any emergency that might occur, quickly move them against an expected advancing enemy, and so might rescue the fatherland from ruinous disaster.

As for the matter of provisioning, because this and other regiments have fully enjoyed the previous winter and summer with the good advantages and conveniences offered by their present quarters, we have issued an order (which is attached here) to our appointed colonel, Lorenzo del Maestro, instructing him to act with the utmost zeal so that they remain satisfied with greatly reduced provisioning, which will be much more bearable for the land. Furthermore, it is also our final gracious desire for it to be ordered and decreed that both for the high and lesser officers as well as for the common soldiers, such provisioning shall include nothing more than that which the common people of the land themselves enjoy.

So that, however, these border places in which the soldiers will be quartered might be able to bear the burden somewhat easier, and the burden might be borne with greater equity, you shall provide for a distribution and regulation such that those areas that are farther away provide a correspondingly greater contribution, so that those who have been spared the quartering compensate for this and help carry the unpleasant burden.

We trust that in other matters you will do the right thing and report to us on further successes as they occur.

Letter of King Sigismund III of Poland to Wallenstein[55]

November 10, 1627, Warsaw

We have come to know with certainty that you, by means of divine grace and assistance, have won a considerable victory in the principality of

55. King Sigismund III of Poland (letter sent) to Wallenstein, November 10, 1627, Warsaw, Státní ústřední archiv Praha, VL F 67/52, in Kollmann, ed., *Documenta Bohemica Bellum*, T. IV, 226–7.

Holstein[56] against the king of Denmark, the enemy of His Majesty the emperor, and have now brought this land into devotion to His Majesty, which not only fills us with exceptional affection and pleasure, but also with great joy. Thus we did not want to fail to congratulate you for such a happy success, and also to offer up our thanks to the Almighty for it, and to ask that He graciously favor you even further in the work you have begun—which is so useful for our Catholic religion—and in the due extirpation of all such extremely destructive conflicts. In addition, we do not want to fail cordially to advise you that a particular report reached us that Denmark is now supposedly asking, and eagerly wishes, to hold peace negotiations with His Majesty the emperor. But we are certainly not pleased to hear of this, for such peace negotiations would be more damaging than beneficial for Their Majesties, the emperor and the king of Spain,[57] as well as for ourselves. Since, praise be to God, triumph and victory are within His Majesty's grasp, were one to continue further such military activities as have already been started, one might easily be able to use such a sizeable armada to seize the Sound[58] and other places (because of the great fear caused by the troops) and, from there, the entire kingdom of Denmark. The king of Spain would also thereby be empowered against his enemy, and we too would then be able to regain our kingdom of Sweden much sooner and easier through the aid and assistance of the king of Spain—something of which he has already assured us.[59]

Since affairs are happening in the above-mentioned ways—which you yourself, with your powers of discernment, realize—and because of the affection that we bear for you, we did not want to fail cordially to request your good opinion on whether also to seek assistance against Sweden from His Majesty the emperor in the same way that we were promised assistance by the king of Spain, and if this might be something that we could obtain; for were we to gain this support, Sweden might then be attacked from both one side and the other.

56. Holstein was a territory to the far north of the Holy Roman Empire near Denmark.

57. Philip IV Habsburg, the cousin and ally of Holy Roman Emperor Ferdinand II.

58. The Sound, or Øresund, is the narrow strait between Sweden and Denmark. Danish control of this important waterway provided the crown with enormous sums in shipping tolls. This had allowed the Danish king Christian the freedom to undertake his costly military adventure in the empire.

59. Sigismund III had inherited the kingdom of Sweden in 1592 and had ruled until 1599, when he was deposed by his uncle, Charles IX. Charles had the full support of the Lutheran clergy, who feared that the Catholic Sigismund would try to impose Catholicism on the now almost fully Lutheran country. Despite being long since deposed, Sigismund had not given up his claims to the kingdom.

14. The Edict of Restitution (March 6, 1629)[60]

[By the beginning of 1629 the imperialists had pushed back their enemies and dominated the empire. With his armies triumphant, the emperor now decided to advance one of his original war aims: weakening the influence of Protestantism in the empire. To do this he seized on the legal precedent of the 1555 Peace of Augsburg and its preliminary, the 1552 Peace of Passau. The Peace of Augsburg had recognized and legalized the practice of the Augsburg Confession (Lutheranism), accepted the loss of all Church property confiscated by Lutherans before 1552, and granted each prince the right to establish the religion of his territories. Individual subjects did not have freedom of religion, but were granted the right to emigrate—at least those who could afford to pay an exit or escape tax. An important exception to the terms of the peace, added despite the opposition of the Lutherans, was a paragraph known as the Ecclesiastical Reservation. This stipulated that ecclesiastical rulers (such as prince-bishops) must give up their offices and rights should they change religions. In the decades following the peace, however, Protestants had ignored this exception and had also continued to seize Church lands in their own territories. By 1629, therefore, large swaths of the empire—especially in the regions of Lower Saxony, Swabia, Alsace, and Franconia, and including such major archbishoprics and bishoprics as Bremen, Magdeburg, Halberstadt, Verden, Minden, Merseburg, and Brandenburg—had been secularized. By issuing the following imperial edict, Ferdinand expressed his determination to reverse these Protestant gains. He also took this opportunity to oppose what both Catholics and Lutherans agreed was an alarming trend: the rapid growth of Calvinism since 1555. Though Calvinists claimed that they followed a variant of the Augsburg Confession and were thus included within the Peace of Augsburg, in this edict Ferdinand made clear his opinion that Calvinists (and other Protestants) had been expressly excluded—and thus shared none of the legal, territorial, and religious rights possessed by Lutherans.]

We, Ferdinand II, by the grace of God elected Roman Emperor, always august, king of Germany, Hungary, Bohemia, Dalmatia, Croatia, and

---

60. Ferdinand II von Habsburg, *Der Roem. Kays. auch zu Hungarn und Boeheimb Koen. May etc. Ferdinandi II. Außspruch Decision, und Kayserlich Edict, Uber Etliche Puncten den Religion-Frieden sonderlich die restitution der Geistlichen Gueter betreffendt Franckfurt am Mayn bey Johann Schmidlin zu finden, Anno M.DC.XXIX* (Frankfurt am Main: Johann Schmidlin, 1629). A copy can be found at the Universitätsbibliothek Augsburg, Sign. 02/IV.13.4.177angeb.02; published in Johann Philipp Abelinus and Matthaeus Merian, *Theatrum Europaeum*, Bd. 2 (Frankfurt am Main, 1646).

Slavonia . . . etc., offer our friendship, grace, and goodwill to each and every ecclesiastic and secular elector, prince, prelate, count, baron, knight . . . and also to all other subjects and loyalists of ours and of the empire, of whatever dignity, estate, or nature they may be.

It is beyond doubt that you and yours, and also every man, understand and know far too well the state of injurious disagreement and disruption in which our beloved fatherland, the German nation, has now hovered for so long, and how the mistrust and extremely dangerous division owe their original beginning and wellspring, and their current state, to the tiresome schism of religion. Next to this, however, is the fact that, contrary to the Religious and Public Peace[61]—which was principally established so that the estates of both religions would, in accordance with this peace, behave peacefully toward each other, and no party would invade, damage, or disadvantage any other in his rights, property, lands, and people—not only were various forms of robbery and other extremely harmful attacks performed, but also, extremely harmful arguments were proffered, under all kinds of pretenses, against the Religious Peace itself and against those who would have justified and defended the contents of the Peace against its enemies.

From this then followed, that after these troublemakers had lost several legal verdicts, and, due to their illegal encroachments, had to expect even further losses, they then finally refused to tolerate another magistrate, but instead (contrary to the clear contents of the Religious Peace itself as also other imperial laws) tried to force everyone else to make a new accord so that they might gain all of their demands and claims in full under the pretext of an agreement. To obtain such an illegal intent, they initially pursued all kinds of clandestine schemes, secret coalitions, various correspondences, and finally an open union. Then, when the Bohemian rebellion occurred and they thought they had gained the advantage they had desired, they made even further confederations and alliances with domestic and foreign sovereigns and municipalities in order to bring about their plans, and even brought in the hereditary enemy of all Christians, [the Turks] themselves, until finally, through such machinations, the entire fatherland was set afire and placed into the situation in which it still finds itself: filled with the most extreme sighs and lamentations of the poor, destitute subjects. . . .

Given our imperial office, we then gauged not only how we might face the difficulties of the Holy Roman Empire and place it at peace once again, but also, at the same time, how we might arrange assiduously so that the estates of the empire would not incur further discord and disagreement among themselves because of disparate interpretations and readings of the Religious Peace. For these reasons we were also asked by the electoral congress at

---

61. The 1555 Religious Peace of Augsburg.

Mühlhausen (out of their most humble and loyal concern for the well-being of the Holy Empire) to make the most gracious provision so that, in order to bring about good and reasonable confidence, the complaints brought and filed so often by the estates would be submitted and debated to an extent and amount allowed by the contents of the Imperial constitution and of the Religious and Secular Peace, and that no estate would continue to be offended and aggrieved contrary to these.

Thus we neither ought to nor wished to delay the declaration and resolution that were bound to our imperial office in the matter of the Religious and Secular Peace (and according to the contents of the imperial recesses, principally that of 1566), especially . . . as even long ago, in the 1576 supplication presented by the Protestant estates to our ancestor Emperor Maximilian, which asked for settlement of their complaints, they themselves clearly stated with good reason that it was unnecessary to look to or await the approval of one or another party; but instead the Imperial Majesty, as the leader and dispenser of all statutes and laws and the protector and guardian of the oppressed, is rightfully entitled to use every absolute power and authority, to interpose his imperial office, and to command whatever might be beneficial for the propagation of the common welfare and the abolition of every injurious misunderstanding and disaster in the Roman Empire, in accordance with previous imperial statutes. . . .

To come now to the matter itself, we first find that, contrary to the Religious Peace (and to the previous imperial statutes that were not completely abrogated on account of it), a completely unnecessary dispute has arisen, which has in large part caused the current ills in the Holy Roman Empire. This concerns whether those foundations, cloisters, and prelatures that are under the command and rule of the princes and estates are included within the Religious Peace, and if those under princely or other territorial authority and over which one had or still has power can be confiscated, reformed, or granted in another way, or can otherwise be used as one desires.

This shall not be, for the Religious Peace clearly and expressly states that such interference in ecclesiastical property, whether or not it is immediately subject to the Holy Roman Empire, is not allowed to ruling authorities. . . .

Then, second, there is more to be found in the paragraph beginning "Because, however," etc. For here it provides that those dioceses and cloisters that do not belong to imperial estates and that were not in the possession of ecclesiastics at the time of, or subsequent to, the Treaty of Passau,[62] but instead were confiscated by estates belonging to the Augsburg Confession

---

62. The 1552 Treaty of Passau served as a preliminary to the Peace of Augsburg, and its date was the one used in the Peace of Augsburg to determine ownership of most ecclesiastical territories.

before the Treaty of Passau, shall remain with the adherents of the Augsburg Confession, and this shall no longer be contested any further. . . . But this indisputably excludes those mediate[63] dioceses and cloisters that were not confiscated before the Treaty of Passau, but only afterward, and since the Religious Peace. And the adherents of the Augsburg Confession are conceded no right at all to reform or confiscate these same lands. Instead, such a thing is not permitted, and should it still have occurred, the offended parties are to be provided their rights and prerogatives undiminished.

Third, it thereby also appears that it is nowhere to be found in the Religious Peace that adherents of the Augsburg Confession might thereafter confiscate further dioceses and cloisters. Instead, the intent was much more the contrary. For indeed, while such a thing was not therein explicitly forbidden, because it was also not expressly allowed it would then be judged by the disposition of general ecclesiastical and secular laws, and by the common public peace. And by dint of these no one ought to divest another of his possessions, no less should he alter another's ecclesiastical institutions and property—especially as these, by their very foundations, are ruled by divine law and belong solely to God and the Church. . . .

And it is indeed true that the Religious Peace states, in the paragraph beginning "And so that," etc., that the estates belonging to the Augsburg Confession should be and remain unhindered in the faith, ceremonies, and Church statutes that they erected or shall erect in their principalities, lands, and dominions. From this some have thought to conclude that they also have the power to reform those cloisters that lie within their lands. Yet although these same cloisters respect the obligations they admittedly owe to the secular powers, in their foundations and in ecclesiastical matters they have nothing to do with the lands and dominions. Instead, as mentioned previously, they belong to God and the Church; thus they are then, in this case, exempt and free from the secular domain and rule. . . .

In addition, it is now well known in the empire that several Protestant estates presume to act contrary to the express wording of the Religious Peace (in the paragraph beginning "And after," etc.), which provides in clear words that where an archbishop, bishop, prelate, or any other cleric of our old religion shall abandon it, he shall quit his archbishopric, prelature, or benefice, along with all profit and income that he had from it, at once and without any reluctance and delay, yet without any prejudice to his honor. Also the chapter and those to whom it belongs by common law or by the traditions of the churches and foundations, shall be permitted to choose and ordain a

63. Mediate territories were those that were subject to at least one legal overlord below the emperor. Territories or states directly below the emperor were known as immediate territories.

person who adheres to the old religion, who, along with the ecclesiastical chapters and other churches, shall also be left unhindered and in peace, etc., with the endowments, elections, presentations, confirmations, old conventions, prerogatives, and property. Yet despite this, after they had abandoned the Catholic religion, not only did they dare to keep their bishoprics, prelatures, and prebendships,[64] but those who were not provided with such bishoprics and prelatures endeavored to gain them. This they did under the affected pretext and pretense as if this paragraph, which seems all too clear to their eyes, were not a part of the Religious Peace and was something to which they never agreed, but instead had protested.

Therefore, we then diligently informed ourselves from imperial records about the actual nature of such a paragraph, which people in general usually call the Ecclesiastical Reservation, and about how it came to be in the Religious Peace (although to us, the very wording of the Religious Peace should have been sufficient). From this we then determined that, notwithstanding the contradiction and lack of consent by the Protestants, on the contrary, the oft-mentioned Religious Peace did indeed include this point within its contents; that it was made, concluded, and so executed with the advice and goodwill of the collected electors and estates of both religions; that it was, at the same time, confirmed and sworn to by all of the estates with a solemn oath that it would be upheld unhesitatingly, firmly, and unswervingly in each and every one of its points, clauses, and articles; and that it would not in the least be either contradicted or opposed. . . .

Then also third and finally, the matter is once again raised . . . whether the subjects of imperial estates are also able to enjoy the Religious Peace and so likewise cannot be expelled on account of religion by their authorities. . . . We then found in this regard that in the beginning a great deal of conflict occurred over this, and the adherents of the Augsburg Confession strongly urged that the subjects of other estates might be left equally free to practice the Augsburg Confession, and thus a special clause was proposed for the Religious Peace. Yet the Catholics absolutely refused to agree to this, but instead said that such a thing would give cause for raucous revolt, disobedience, and indignation between sovereigns and subjects. Thus it would be unjust for them to want to impose such a law and statute on the Catholics. They, the Catholics, meant to provide for their own souls, as well as those of others, and for this reason they could not tolerate that their subjects would be given room and air to follow a different religion than their own. . . .

As, however, the estates belonging to the Augsburg Confession no less strongly urged for freedom of conscience, the Catholics finally relented

64. A Church office in which one is entitled to an endowment or pension, often a share of church revenue.

insofar that the subjects should be free to emigrate from the land. With this the estates let the above-mentioned clause fall and the matter was agreed to with His Majesty and the Catholics as it stands today in the Religious Peace. . . .

From these above-mentioned three main articles, which we have resolved according to the contents of the Religious Peace and other recesses, negotiations, and acts of the Holy Empire, we then thereby recognize and declare: first, that the Protestant estates have no cause to complain and to take up as a grievance that the heads of religious orders, abbots, prelates, and other clerics who are not subject immediately to the empire, pursued necessary litigation with us or our imperial supreme court on account of their confiscated dioceses and property, hospitals, and other religious foundations; that the same were then granted back to them; and that these cases thereby proceeded even to judgment and execution. On the other hand, the Catholic estates are justly and legitimately aggrieved (in agreement with these mediate ecclesiastics) that the cloisters and ecclesiastical property that they held at the time of the Treaty of Passau, or subsequently, were then confiscated from them contrary to the clear contents of the Religious Peace, their rents and revenues were suspended, and they were also completely stripped of every right and claim over them, as if they were not at all included within the Religious Peace, while their property was given over to the arbitrary occupation of the authorities, contrary to the intention and sentiments of [the cloisters'] pious founders, and also against the clear wording of the Religious Peace.

As to the second article, we equally recognize that the adherents of the Augsburg Confession have no cause for any complaint that the Catholic estates do not wish to recognize their co-religionists [Lutherans] who occupy ecclesiastical dioceses, bishoprics, and imperial prelatures that are immediate to the empire (or who are endeavoring to gain the same status) as being bishops and prelates, nor allow them a seat and vote at the imperial diets, nor grant them regalia and fiefs. For, on the contrary, following the contents of the Ecclesiastical Reservation and its indisputable wording, the Catholics, for their part, have not unjustly complained of manifest grievances: that such ecclesiastical bishops and prelates who have deviated from the Catholic religion have nonetheless remained in their bishoprics and prelatures, kept all rights and privileges that they had with the Catholic religion, and expected to be regarded as estates of the empire on account of such bishoprics and prelatures. Also, that those who are not of the Catholic religion, much less otherwise qualified for the clergy, have nevertheless pushed their way into such bishoprics and prelatures, and thereby eventually intend, as far as they are able, to abolish the entire Catholic clergy along with the religion.

We then also, for the third point, find the grievances brought by several Protestant estates to be completely insignificant: including that the Catholic estates should not be allowed to press the subjects in their territories to join their religion and, if the subjects refuse to devote themselves to it, to extract whatever escape fee and supplementary tax that they feel are proper and to deport them; nor should they be allowed to forbid their subjects from traveling to a foreign place to seek other preaching and religious exercise, under the argument that they were indeed fully warranted to abolish such exercise completely. On the other hand, however, and following the observations given above, it is obvious that the Catholics justly feel aggrieved that limitations were placed on their own reformation by the other party, and that from this basis their subjects were incited and stirred toward a complete defection and secession from their authorities. And this grievance made on the Catholic side is all the stronger, because it is on account of such a reformation that the adherents of the Augsburg Confession argue as if the Catholics do not share the same rights they enjoy. Instead, they claim that while the adherents of the Augsburg Confession are indeed allowed to reform their subjects and deport the obstinate (and have indeed openly demonstrated such acts), for the Catholics, however, such a thing is not acceptable. . . .

Thus we are finally resolved, for the genuine implementation of the Religious and Secular Peace, to delegate forthwith our imperial commissioners to go into the empire; to reclaim from their illegal holders those archbishoprics and bishoprics, prelatures, cloisters, and other ecclesiastical property, hospitals, and foundations that the Catholics possessed at the time of the Treaty of Passau, or subsequently, but that they were illegally deprived of (whether these drifted away or were confiscated by force or otherwise); and to have them suitably staffed with duly appointed and qualified persons, according to their foundations and endowments, and thus to restore to each person his due and what, according to the stipulations of the oft-mentioned Religious Peace, is legitimately his, without the requisite digression and delay.

We also hereby . . . declare and recognize that the Religious Peace concerns and includes only those of the ancient Catholic religion and the adherents of the unaltered Augsburg Confession, as it was presented to our beloved ancestor Emperor Charles V in the year 1530 on the 25th of June. All other contrary doctrines and sects, of whatever name and whether they have already arisen or are still to arise, shall be impermissible, excluded from the peace, forbidden, and neither tolerated nor suffered.

We thus command your graces and each and every one of you, under penalty of the Religious and Public Peace, not to defy this, our final decree, but instead to promote it in your lands and territories, to help it succeed, and also to offer a helping hand to our commissioners when they call upon you. As for those, however, who possess these archbishoprics and bishoprics, prelatures, cloisters, hospitals, prebendships, and other ecclesiastical property and foundations: they are to be prepared to relinquish and restore these bishoprics, prelatures, and other ecclesiastical property immediately after the issuance of this, our imperial edict, and to grant and restore them, along with all of their trappings and appurtenances, to our imperial commissioners on demand. Should they not comply with this order, or prove to be slow in doing so, not only will they, on account of their notorious defiance, be subject to the penalty of the Public and Religious Peace—namely the ban of empire and final proscription, as well as the loss of all of their privileges, rights, and prerogatives ipso facto and without any further sentence and judgment— but immediately afterward, we will also inevitably have the actual execution carried out and enforced.

We also command, order, and desire that this, our imperial edict, resolution, and declaration, be openly published by each and every circle executive prince,[65] and that it be made known to everyone, such that everyone gives the same absolute credence to the copies sent here and there by the circle executive princes as they do to the original itself. We mean this seriously.

Given in our city of Vienna, the 6th of March 1629: the tenth year of our Roman, the eleventh of our Hungarian, and the twelfth of our Bohemian reign.

15. Gustavus Adolphus' Invasion of the Empire (July and October 1630)

[Gustavus Adolphus' landing on the island of Usedom on June 26, 1630 marked the beginning of his involvement in the military affairs of the empire. It also marked the beginning of a veritable flood of broadsheets and pamphlets about the Swedish king that appeared in the empire from 1630 to 1632. One of the principal goals of these broadsheets was to explain and legitimize Swedish intervention in the war, and here the most popular and enduring interpretation was that Gustavus Adolphus came as a champion of Protestantism, "the Lion of the North" or a new Joshua, selflessly endangering himself in order to save his fellow religionists and preserve the true religion. This was a theme encouraged by Gustavus Adolphus himself, who timed his entry into the empire to coincide with the hundred-year anniversary of the Augsburg Confession. Another important theme sounded by Gustavus Adolphus and his

---

65. The circle executive princes (*Kreisausschreibenden Fürsten*) were usually the one or two highest-ranking princes from each of the ten imperial circles (or regions). The executive princes maintained correspondence with other circles and publicized imperial edicts and laws within their own circles. This position differed from that of circle director, or *Kreisoberst,* who had command of a circle's army.

*supporters was a constitutional one. In this interpretation, which had also
been used by King Christian of Denmark, the Swedish king was a true champion of the German Liberties and a federal empire against the unconstitu-
tional and dangerous attempt by the emperor to impose his will as an
absolute monarch. The manifesto below, however, which was an official justification for Swedish intervention (written for the king by Johan Adler
Salvius,⁶⁶ his secretary of state, and published in the city of Stralsund immediately after the king's landing), avoids the issue of the Lutheran king's religious
motivations—which might offend Catholics—and also skims over the issue of
internal imperial politics. Instead, it focuses on matters of commerce, international law, and regional political balance. The second document below is on
the same topic as this manifesto, but it was not intended for public consump-
tion. Instead, it was a letter sent from Gustavus Adolphus to his closest confidant and chancellor, Axel Oxenstierna, and so gives a fascinating inside look
at the king's private thinking. The letter describes the reasons he thought the
war was worth fighting, and one may also note the strategic importance he
placed on contributions (forced extractions from local populations, which were
used to maintain armies), as well as his hope for an Ottoman advance to dis-
tract the emperor in the east.]*

Gustavus Adolphus, Manifesto on Invading Germany (July 1630)⁶⁷

The reasons why the most serene and powerful prince and lord, Lord Gustavus Adolphus, king of the Swedes, Goths, and Wends, grand duke of Finland, duke of Estonia and Karelia, lord over Ingermanland, etc., has finally
been forced to cross over and advance into Germany with an army.

66. Johan Adler Salvius (1590–1652).

67. *Orsachen, Dahero Der Durchleuchtigste unnd Grossmächtigste Fürst vnnd Herr,
Herz* [sic] *Gustavus Adolphus der Schweden, Gothen vnnd Wenden König, Gross Fürst in
Finland, Hertzog zu Ehsten vnd Carelen, Herz* [sic] *zu Ingermanland etc. Endlich gleich-
fals gezwungen worden, mit dem Kriegsvolck in Deutschland über zusetsen vnnd zu
verzucken, Stralsund, Im Monat Julio Anno M. DC. XXX, in der Ferberischen Druck-
eren* (Stralsund: Feberishen Druckerei, 1630). A copy can be found at the Krigsarkivet
bibliotek, Stockholm, Hyllplacering Årstryck 1630 juli; published in Sigmunt Goetze,
Die Politik des schwedischen Reichskanzler Axel Oxenstierna gegenüber Kaiser und Reich
(Kiel: Kommissionsverlag Walter G. Mühlau, 1971), 349–65; also published in
Sverker Oredsson, *Geschichtsschreibung und Kult. Gustav Adolf, Schweden und der
Dreißigjährige Krieg* (Berlin: Duncker und Humblot, 1994), appendix 2, 286–93. For
an English-language version of Gustavus Adolphus' similar June *Declaration,* which
gained extremely wide European circulation, see Geoffrey Simcox, ed., *War, Diplo-
macy, and Imperialism, 1618–1763* (New York: Harper Torchbooks, 1973).

Stralsund, July 1630

It is an old adage that no one can be at peace any longer than it suits or pleases his neighbor. His Royal Majesty of Sweden has, to his great loss, experienced the truth of this adage in past years and still experiences it daily. For although there is nothing for which he has more assiduously endeavored and striven during the entire time of his royal rule, than that he might maintain a genuine friendship with all of those adjacent to him, and especially with the estates of the German Nation, in order that peace and tranquillity might flourish everywhere and commerce and other things that depend on peace might be maintained to the benefit of neighboring peoples; yet he could achieve nothing more than that greater and greater schemes were made against His Royal Majesty's security from one year to the next . . . by some who hated the common peace, after they had destroyed almost all of Germany through murder and fire.[68] Long ago, while this fire still burned in upper Germany, His Royal Majesty was indeed advised by many German estates to tread warily and opportunely, and not to think that the enemy would behave in a friendlier manner were one to allow him to approach somewhat closer; but instead, they advised His Royal Majesty immediately to take up arms, come into Germany, and, with a common force, extinguish the general fire; for they firmly advised that the affairs of His Royal Majesty were also touched when neighboring provinces were ablaze.

Nor at that time did His Royal Majesty lack either a superb opportunity— for his residents requested it and foreigners pushed him to it—or a just cause—for his friends were oppressed and his allies had most strenuously requested his aid and assistance.

Nevertheless, since His Royal Majesty still hoped that the adversary would, in the end, proceed much more moderately instead of impatiently pressing the neighboring provinces, and as he judged others to be like himself, with the same morals and naturally implanted virtue, he decided that it would be much better to see to his own security, submitting to God and maintaining an innocent conscience, rather than to act in this matter prematurely.

But then, back in the year 1626, when—by reason of His Royal Majesty's own war that had developed against the king and kingdom of Poland—he moved into the country of Prussia (which was subject to the kingdom of Poland), he began to notice much more closely what he might expect from these spoilers of Germany. Indeed, he found little that was false in the warnings of his friends and instead perceived, even more, that the closer the en-

68. Note in the margin of the original pamphlet: "The Jesuits and their accomplices."

emies thrust themselves into the Baltic provinces of Germany, the more and greater opportunities they sought, day by day, to war against His Royal Majesty. . . .

And so that they might achieve in fact what they had promised with words, and so that they could also, using all possible means that they could bring to bear, strip the kingdom of Sweden of power and strengthen the Poles, they not only forbid the transference of any troops and arms to His Royal Majesty in Sweden, while freely allowing it to the then-enemies of His Royal Majesty, the Poles; but when this accomplished little and, despite this prohibition, a large number of soldiers rushed to join the powerful king of Sweden (coming not only from other places, but also from Germany, which was even more in opposition to the enemy's will), in the following year, 1627, they also dispatched the duke of Holstein[69] with a great army against His Royal Majesty, and it marched not under the colors of this duke or of the king of Poland, but rather under those of the Roman emperor. And not being satisfied with this enmity, but instead, so that they might bar the kingdom of Sweden from all human associations, when innocent subjects of His Royal Majesty landed at German seaports on business, they relieved them forcefully of their goods, seized their ships, and robbed them unjustly. Also, they did not stop there, but rather they sent out men to Lübeck and other Wendish and Hanseatic League[70] cities under the pretense that they wished only these places to benefit from commerce, but actually intending thereby that the subjects of the kingdom of Sweden would be completely excluded; and so through this opportunity, [these enemies] could then ready ships and naval weaponry by which they could spit out into the Baltic Sea itself the poison contained within their minds. And this was then much more manifestly demonstrated by their issuance [to the imperial General Wallenstein] of the monstrous title of Generality of the Baltic Sea, and also by their taking of principal places and fortresses throughout Mecklenburg and Pomerania, along with their seaports and harbors, and also by other subsequent acts.

At this any man might perhaps judge that as long as his opponent remained on the opposite side of the border, these things should have been tolerated and borne in patience, lest it seem as if one wished to meddle in another's affairs. Yet after they chose the seaport of Stralsund as a base for their piracy and moved to extend their power over the sea itself, it was clear that this was a matter of great prejudice or loss to everyone who depended

---

69. Frederick III, duke of Holstein-Gottorp (1597–1659).

70. The Hanseatic League was founded in the thirteenth century as a defensive and economic league for urban merchants in northern German and Baltic cities. Leading Hansa cities included Lübeck, Hamburg, Danzig, Bremen, Stralsund, and many others.

on this sea, though especially to the German estates. And it was thus even less tolerable to the most serene king of Sweden, principally because the rightful protection of this sea had remained in the hands of the kings of Sweden since time immemorial.

Therefore, once the most serene king of Sweden considered that . . . the pleas of the tormented city [of Stralsund] were grounded upon divine and secular rights; and further considered that the city had always been attached to His Royal Majesty's ancestors, to the kings and empire of Sweden, by the bonds of honor, proximity, common religion, liberty, and commerce; and finally [considered] what great danger would arise, not only to himself and the kingdom of Sweden, but also to all of his neighbors, if anyone, out of private ambition, were to establish in this port a nest from which to launch piratical raids; His Royal Majesty could then not, in any fashion or by any right, wait any longer to come to the assistance of the oppressed, who had so urgently requested help, solace, and advice; nor to act for the benefit of neighbors and friends, and also for both his own and the public and common security.[71] . . .

So many and such great insults have truly been made against His Royal Majesty—letters intercepted and opened; subjects, servants, and soldiers robbed and carried off into servitude; commerce, which is naturally common, prohibited; his enemy [the Poles] so often dissuaded from peace, and powerful auxiliary troops sent out in order to ruin the kingdom of Sweden, while the king of Sweden was not even granted a peaceful passage; even worse, his friends, neighbors, and blood relatives oppressed because of their association with him, their dominions robbed and almost utterly destroyed; envoys who, unlike barbarians, were to negotiate the peace, ignominiously expelled; and, for the second time, a hostile army set out; and all of this without any cause or pretext. Are these not, either altogether or each portion by itself, and given the unanimous assent of all peoples, the counsel of reason, and almost the instigation of nature itself, of the most vital importance? And, if no just restitution is made, do they not warrant a most justified vengeance? And meanwhile so many threats, such great preparations, and so many attempts have, as of yet, to be manifested, mocking all of the Baltic ports and the sea itself. From which it appears that all plots, assaults, and arrangements by land and sea conspire toward His Majesty's ruin. Do they not then impose upon him, though unwilling, the right of self-defense, such that, according to the military custom of all peoples, he might render a measure of justifiable defense? Because, having sought so many remedies in the law, no further legal methods were allowed him. Indeed, he was offered only hostil-

---

71. Sweden agreed to a defensive alliance with Stralsund in 1628, designed to keep the emperor from dominating trade throughout the Baltic.

ity. Does not, then, the law itself finally demand that this matter be settled by force, so that force counters force?

Therefore, because there is no other way for [the king] to be safe except that he, alongside God, gain security for himself and his people through force of arms, he hereby wished to allow all of Christendom to judge his conduct and how unwillingly he had been forced to proceed to such extremities. . . .

Hence the king hereby protests that he has not taken up these arms to the detriment of the Roman Empire (for whom he bears no ill will), but looks only to the protection of himself, his people, and the general liberty, until such time as his friends and neighbors are returned to the state in which the entire neighborhood peacefully flourished before this war, and, principally, until the city of Stralsund, the Baltic Sea, and the kingdom of Sweden may assure themselves that they will have more definitive security in the future. The king therefore has no doubt that the law-abiding reader and the popular welfare itself shall see through and condemn the unjust proceedings of the opposition (a response that they have earned). And he certainly hopes that all Germans, and also the entirety of Christendom, shall support and be favorably inclined toward his innocent and just move to take up arms in order legitimately to oppose such unjust persecution.

Letter of Gustavus Adolphus to Axel Oxenstierna (October 8, 1630)[72]

Gustavus Adolphus, etc. Our particular favor, etc.

There is no need to repeat to you, lord chancellor, which highly important reasons and occasions have brought us to this war. For you have considered amply these matters with us and have concluded that for the security of the fatherland from the designs of our enemies, we could not act differently or transfer our arms over there at a more suitable time than has now transpired. It now remains for us to consider how this war can be waged so that we can reach the desired goal, the safety of the fatherland, and where we can find the means to complete our intentions so that this war, with God's most merciful assistance, can most likely be brought to a good conclusion.

---

72. Letter of Gustavus Adolphus to Axel Oxenstierna, Ribnitz, October [8], 1630, in *Rikskansleren Axel Oxenstiernas skrifter och brevvexling*, Afd. 2. Bd. 1, *K. Gustaf II Adolfs Bref och Instruktioner* (II, 1, #476), 653–7 (Stockholm: P. A. Norstedt & Söner, 1930). The enclosed proposals are to be found in *Archiv till upplysning om Sveriges Krigens och Krigsinrättningens historia*, I, sid. 230. The letter of the electors of August 4, 1630 and Gustavus Adolphus' reply are published in Olaf Rydberg and Carl Hallendorf, eds., *Sverges Traktater med främmande magter*, V (Stockholm: P. A. Norstedt & Söner, 1877), 820–6. My great thanks to Erik Thomson and Paul Sonnino for their work on this translation, though any errors are mine.

We do not doubt that you completely agree with us that the House of Austria fully intends to overthrow all of Germany and bring it to another state. And then, when the House of Austria has imposed its will, the Evangelical religion[73] will be uprooted from all of Germany and erroneous papal teachings implanted again in its place. We also know well that you have diligently considered what a danger this is for us, the fatherland, and all of our dependent neighbors, because we have so often debated this. Therefore, even though we have learned from the letters of the elector and, especially, of the emperor (which now have reached us in such a form that we have no reason to doubt them), that both the emperor and the estates of the Holy Roman Empire incline to treat with us, and would be glad to be finished with this war, yet from these same letters, we can see too well that as things stand no peace terms are proposed to us such that we could, without further consideration for our and our interested neighbors' and friends' own interest and security, return to our prior uncertainty and abandon everything that we have acquired with great trouble and expense. For these reasons we cannot reasonably maintain that we should let ourselves come to such an intolerable accord, which would leave us to waste uselessly such great expenditures; would cause us, instead of security, greater danger and a great loss of reputation; and, finally, would give our enemies the opportunity—once they have subjugated all of Germany without further opposition and according to their desire and intention—to attempt to do the same to us and to the crown of Sweden, since they are still proceeding relentlessly against the Reformed[74] in all places for good and ill, and all of their counsels are directed so that they can put into effect their above-mentioned plan.

We are for this reason of the opinion that we cannot enter into any reconciliation with our enemies unless a new religious peace can be reached and confirmed for all of Germany, and our neighbors and friends are returned to their previous state and condition, so that we, through their safety, may be secure and safe in our fatherland. To which end, we see no other way and means than that we more closely assault the emperor himself, and with him the clergy who are on his side, so that we can bring them to be tired of this war. For if it were so that we could come into the emperor's hereditary lands and deprive him of his own means, and also have the joy and opportunity to cut off from him the contributions that he now extracts from the adherents of our religion in order to maintain his armies, so that the whole burden of the war could devolve entirely upon him and the papist clergy alone, then we would certainly believe that we could sooner obtain, both for us and

73. Protestantism.
74. Calvinists.

for those of our religion, peace terms that we could trust and from which we would gain a reputation.

To put this into practice, we have considered and thought it best and most proper that we should be strong enough in the coming spring to establish five separate armies that we can use in the following ways. first, that with one army under our own direction, we maintain the lands that we have already occupied, and thus hold the Baltic coast in security. Then, that Gustav Horn and Lord Teuffel,[75] with two armies, procure for us the possession of the Oder River and also do their best to bring the Mark Brandenburg to devotion to our side; and then penetrate into Silesia and, from there, consolidate themselves in the emperor's own land. We now have an excellent opportunity to establish the fourth army at Magdeburg, because the administrator of Magdeburg has already assembled three thousand foot and several hundred horse;[76] we would hope to use that to hold the Elbe, so that with it and with our own army, with which we could always combine it, we could give the electors of both Saxony and Brandenburg some room and opportunity to cooperate with us. For the fifth army, we have reason to think that the archbishopric, bishopric, and city of Bremen, as well as the cities of Brunswick, Hildesheim, and others, incline toward us and correspond secretly with Doctor Salvius[77] to this end, and we must only see to it that we have some people with them upon whom they can depend. Therefore we intend to order to these places the Hamiltons[78] with the ten thousand English and Scottish soldiers whom they wish to recruit for us and whom we now hear the king in England will himself support and help. Then we intend that Colonel Leslie,[79] whom we will order to follow the Hamiltons, will recruit four regiments of foot and one thousand horse, which troops will bear down on the Weser River and do everything possible to attract the enemy to that side.

With these five armies, which we could always use with ease in all the best places, according to conditions and the enemies' countenance, we can confidently expect that the enemy will become exhausted, so that soon, in all of Germany, a general call and vote for peace shall be heard, along with an

---

75. Gustav Karlsson Horn, count of Pori (1592–1657), Swedish commander and son-in-law to Axel Oxenstierna; and Maximilian Teuffel, baron of Güntersdorf (d. 1631).

76. Infantry and cavalrymen.

77. Johan Adler Salvius (1590–1652), Swedish councilor and ambassador.

78. Hugo and Ludvig Hamilton were Scottish brothers in Swedish service.

79. Alexander Leslie, 1st earl of Leven (c. 1580–1661), a Scottish officer in Swedish service.

inclination to give satisfaction to us, our friends, and the adherents of our religion. For the enemy's army, even though it is much smaller in effective numbers, must be paid as if it held complete regiments and regimental staffs, which requires a remarkably great sum of money that will at length be very troublesome for them to bring together (since our success here in Mecklenburg and Pomerania has already removed from them a portion of the means to do this, and we hope to take even more from them in the abovementioned way); for after all, there has already been a noticeable unwillingness in the electoral college to grant further contributions.

On top of all this, one should also consider, although not depend upon it, that great empires that border one another rarely allow each other to remain unmolested, and thus it could easily happen that during the time that we would undertake this war, the Roman Empire could end up in a war with the Turkish Empire. For all the news sheets confirm that even though the Turk has had great happiness and success in Asia, he is, in any case, more inclined to peace on that side; and thus they believe that as soon as he were to find some peace there, he would then (for he is not in the habit of staying still for long) wage war on the Roman Empire, all of which could cause a great change for us and possibly help us to a much quicker and more beneficial settlement.

And so this was our counsel, which we expect could, with God's help, have the effect that if we could bring such armies to their feet in time, then, as much as our credit allowed, we could probably arrange for the first months and until it could be brought to pass that each and every head of an army could get some help for the soldiers' subsistence from the new harvest. On your side is it particularly vital to us that this winter you recruit the regiments that are lacking, and also that you support us in the spring with a barrel of *reichsthalers*,[80] at the very least. We hope that when we also get the above-mentioned help from Sweden, our design will happily be able to go ahead, for the gain and benefit of the fatherland.

We most graciously desire, therefore, that you consider all of this counsel and send us your thoughts about it as soon as possible. We desire particularly, in case it would be possible for you to arrange for the above-mentioned recruiting, that during the winter, you can collect enough so that you can second our efforts on the first spring day with a barrel of gold, and also be ready with the other credit that we have placed in your hands, so that it can be furnished to us at the right time. You will see from the proposal we include, upon what credit from Sweden and Livonia we will then be basing our design, which we certainly expect will prove to be accurate. Above all,

---

80. One hundred thousand *reichsthalers*.

we expect your council and thoughts as soon as possible. And we commend you to Almighty God. From Rebnitz, October [8], 1630.

Gustavus Adolphus

16. The Sack of Magdeburg (May 20, 1631)[81]

[Gustavus Adolphus' landing in Pomerania was met with some initial hesitation from those he was theoretically rescuing. But while most princes of the empire did not rush to ally with the Swedish king, some, such as the dukes of Mecklenburg and the landgrave of Hesse-Cassel, were indeed energized. Among those who eagerly welcomed the king of Sweden was the free imperial city of Magdeburg, which took this opportunity to rebel against the emperor. Too weak to withstand the imperial forces in the field, however, the city found itself besieged, able to do little but wait for promised aid from Gustavus Adolphus— which never came. Finally, unable to hold out any longer against the encamped army of General Tilly, the city council agreed to come to terms on the morning of May 20, 1631. But the council had deliberated too long, and before they could surrender, the city walls were breached. Tilly's troops—hungry, lacking pay, and angry at the long resistance of the city—looted with abandon. They carted off every valuable they could carry and destroyed everything else. Fire, which either sprang up accidentally or was purposely set by one side or the other, swept through the entire city. As many as twenty thousand people died. The following account comes from the pen of Magdeburg resident Otto von Guericke (1602–1686), later known as a skilled inventor and early expert on vacuums. Guericke's full report chronicles the events of the days leading up to and immediately after the city's destruction. Below is an excerpt from the last few pages, which describe the sack itself and its horrible aftermath.]

As for the hornwork[82] before the Kröcken Gate and the two half-moons[83] before the Ulrich and Strotdorf Gates, they were also severely assailed, but were not taken from outside nor overpowered; instead, as the imperialists took possession of the entire rampart from the Neustadt[84] and the Elbe up

---

81. Otto von Guericke, *Die Belagerung, Eroberung und Zerstörung der Stadt Magdeburg am 10/20 Mai 1631* (Leipzig: R. Voigtländers Verlag, 1912).

82. A complex type of fortification composed of two half-bastions connected by a curtain.

83. Also called demi-lunes, these were small bastions placed outside the main bastion and trench.

84. A newer part of the city.

to here, all of [the defenders'] resistance became impossible, so they could only beg for mercy and quarter. The lord administrator,[85] under continual onslaught, had to abandon completely the crownwork[86] on the marsh and the ravelin[87] before the short Elbe bridge, and so ordered that the planks and beams from one piling of this bridge be brought down. But with such a hasty retreat, most of the beams were left lying. Nevertheless, because of the citizens' watch that had been placed in the Bridge Gate and the millhouse, the imperialists were not able to cross here until the city had otherwise been completely overpowered—though many imperial cavalrymen, having watched from the other side of the Elbe and being greedy for booty, had tried to ride across the river and so drowned in the water.

Then General Pappenheim[88] brought a good number of troops onto the rampart by the Neustadt, and from there into the alleys of the city, and von Falkenberg[89] was shot and fires were set in every corner. Then the city was lost, and all resistance came too late and was useless. For although citizens and soldiers in some places tried to put up some opposition and come to arms, meanwhile the imperialists always had more and more troops to help them, as well as enough cavalry (for the trench at the top of this bastion had not yet been completed, and the new rampart was very flat, so that they could ride over it into the city), and finally they opened the Kröcken Gate and let in through it the entire army of the imperialists and Catholic League, made up of Hungarians, Croats, Poles, Heyducks,[90] Italians, Spaniards, French, Walloons, Lower and Upper Germans, etc. Thus it happened that the city, with all of its inhabitants, fell into the hands and under the power of its enemies, whose fierceness and cruelty came partly out of a common hatred of the adherents of the Augsburg Confession,[91] and partly from the fact that people had shot at them with crossbar shot[92] and other things from the ramparts, belittling them, provoking them, and leading them to become enraged. Then there was nothing but murder, burning, plundering, tor-

---

85. Christian William, the Protestant administrator of the secularized bishopric of Magdeburg.

86. Another form of fortification.

87. Similar to a half-moon.

88. Gottfried Heinrich, count zu Pappenheim (1594–1632), the imperial commander who was serving as General Tilly's lieutenant.

89. Colonel Dietrich von Falkenberg (1580–1631), a Hessian nobleman sent by Gustavus Adolphus to serve as military commander of Magdeburg.

90. A class of Hungarian mercenaries.

91. Lutherans.

92. Bullets with an iron spike in the middle of each ball.

ment, and beatings. In particular, each of the enemies sought more and greater booty. When such a party of looters entered a house and the head of the household had something he could give them, then he could use this to save and preserve himself and his family until another soldier, who also wanted something, came along. Finally, however, when everything had been given out and there was nothing left to give, then the misery really began. For then the soldiers began to beat, frighten, and threaten to shoot, skewer, hang, etc., the people, so that even if something had been buried under the earth or locked away behind a thousand locks, the citizens would still have been forced to seek it out and hand it over. Through such enduring fury—which laid this great, magnificent city, which had been like a princess in the entire land, into complete burning embers and put it into such enormous misery and unspeakable need and heartache—many thousands of innocent men, women, and children were, with horrid, fearful screams of pain and alarm, miserably murdered and wretchedly executed in manifold ways, so that no words can sufficiently describe it, nor tears bemoan it.

This dismal time in the city, however, did not actually last much more than two hours, but in this time the fire, which had originally been ordered set by Count von Pappenheim in order to perturb and frighten the citizens and inhabitants, but which had afterward been used by the common soldiery without discretion or pause, took the upper hand by means of the sudden appearance of the wind, so that by ten o'clock in the morning everything was afire; and by ten o'clock in the evening the entire city, including the beautiful courthouse and all the churches and cloisters, had been reduced to ashes and heaps of stone. Thus the imperial army, lest it incinerate itself, had to withdraw from the city and retreat to its encampment.

Thus this renowned and genteel city, the ornament of the entire land, went up in flames and smoke in a single day, and its remaining inhabitants, with their wives and children, were taken prisoner and driven out by the enemy, such that the shouting, crying, and howling could be heard from far away, and the seething embers and ash from the city were transported by the wind as far away as Wanzleben, Egeln,[93] and other places.

And as for those from Magdeburg who had escaped the fire and sword, each was forced to pay a ransom in order to obtain his and his family's life and honor and, depending on the status of the person, would have to buy them back by paying as much as a thousand or more *reichsthalers*. If he did not have this amount, he would be held and even kept in prison until he could obtain the ransom money from other outside people, whether as an active debt, a petition, or a loan, or until he could make some other sufficient

93. Wanzleben is a town ten miles southwest of Magdeburg, Egeln is seventeen miles southwest of Magdeburg.

guarantee. As to common craftspeople, day laborers, servants, and apprentices, as well as soldiers who had served on the side of the Swedes and the city and could give nothing, they had to carry the booty and bundles of the enemy for a while, to do all kinds of service for them, or even to join the enemy's service and so be supported by them. However, things went very badly for many of those women, girls, daughters, and maids who either had no men, parents, or relatives who could pay a ransom on their behalf, or could not appeal to high officers for help or advice; some were defiled and disgraced, and some were kept as concubines. However, there were also many who similarly had no friends or means, but who still, amazingly, kept their honor—partially due to honorable soldiers who, by dint of the decency of those they had taken prisoner, simply let them free or even married them. . . .

As to what concerns His Princely Highness the lord administrator, he was underway on the street, wishing to ride out to face the imperialists, when he came across them and was badly beaten by guerilla troops and musketeers, and was shot in the left thigh. Finally, a lieutenant[94] seized him and had him carried to Pappenheim's tent. In subsequent days he was taken to Wolmirstedt[95] and there placed in prison. The lord steward von Falkenberg, after he was shot and carried into the house of a citizen near St. Jakob's, was incinerated in the conflagration along with others who had been slain, and thus remained in the city.[96] Ambassador Stalmann,[97] however, had a good deal of luck, since a few days afterward, at the enemy camp at Fermersleben[98] and through the help of a Jew who was well known to him, he was able to get out of the iron bands on his hands and feet and by setting the camp on fire, or so people say, then escape and flee to the king of Sweden. Of the city council, the burgermeister Martin Brauns and the councilors Dietrich Brewitz, Kaspar Steinbeck, and Martin Bauermeister died; and the other three burgermeisters, Georg Schmidt, Georg Kühlewein, and Johann Westphal, along with the councilor Otto Guericke[99] and many other people, retreated with their families into the house of Johann Alemann, from where, after experiencing a variety of dangers to life and limb, they were finally rescued by imperial Commissary General von Walmerode[100] (who had come to save Johann Alemann's wife) and were brought out safely to Schönebeck. . . .

94. Lieutenant Fahrensbach, the adjutant-general of Field Marshal Tilly.

95. A town nine miles north of Magdeburg.

96. His ashes were later collected and placed in the cathedral.

97. Stalmann was an agent of the administrator, Christian William.

98. A small town just south of Magdeburg.

99. The author himself.

100. Reinhard von Walmerode.

Almost four thousand people were in the cathedral church, where they had retreated and holed themselves up; and although, in the beginning, some of the imperial troops had gotten in, killing several people and raping two women, soon they set up a watch at the doors and further violence was averted. . . .

As for the number of those slain and dead in the city, since many people were devoured not only by the sword, but also by the fire, one cannot really know. For not only did General Tilly, soon after this wretched incineration, have the burned corpses and other dead from the alleys, ramparts, and other places loaded onto wagons and driven to the water of the Elbe, but also for almost an entire year after this time we found many dead bodies—five, six, eight, ten, or more at a time—in ruined cellars where they had suffocated and died; and also, because those bodies that had lain in the alleys had been so badly consumed by the fire and then been smashed to pieces by the collapsing buildings, one often had to load up the pieces using a pitchfork. Thus no one can name the actual number. Altogether, however, one could say that including the two suburbs and those imperial troops who had died and were burned (for many had fallen here and there during the attack, or had been too long in searching cellars or houses or had otherwise gotten lost), it was about twenty thousand people, young and old, whose lives were ended in such cruel conditions or who otherwise had to suffer from bodily injury. The dead corpses, which had been carried out to the Elbe in front of the Water Gate, were not soon able or willing to flow away, for in that place all the water forms a ripple or eddy, such that many of them floated around for a long time, some with their heads out of the water, others reaching out their hands as if toward heaven, giving onlookers quite a horrible spectacle. Many blatherers suggested that it was just as if these dead people still prayed, sang out, and cried to God for vengeance; and then, in the same way, people spoke of many visages, wraiths, and other such things, but no one wished to affirm this in the light of day.

As soon as the heat and embers had somewhat died down, the imperial artillery general . . . had all the brew kettles, bells, and other copperware brought together into variously sized heaps and had them kept as his booty. . . . In addition, a great many magnificent and irrecoverable household effects and all kinds of stately personal effects—including old books, writings, statues, paintings, and so on, which had belonged partly to the genteel nobility of the city who had fled, partly also to the most genteel citizens, and which were now priceless—were burned with everything else or taken by the troops as their booty. One could also walk around in many cellars up to the knee in beer and wine, because the high spirits and iniquity of the common soldiers had grown so great that when one had drawn a bucket of beer or wine from a barrel, he had not bothered to replug the tap, and so had simply let the remaining beer and wine flow out. The stately clothes, covers, silks, gold and silver cords, all kinds of linen, and other household equipment were acquired for a song by the sutlers[101] and then transported and sold by the wagonful throughout the archbishopric of Magdeburg and the lands of Anhalt and Brunswick. One could also barter for and buy golden chains, rings, gems, and other gold and silver utensils from common servants for more than ten times less than their true worth.

Where the city archives, letters and seals, privileges, registers, protocols, and other documents had gotten to, no one knows, inasmuch as the leading councilors and citizens, at least those who had remained after the fire and the sword, could neither return to the city nor find any lodging there. Whether such documents, letters, and manuscripts were removed by anyone is debatable, because everything was in vaults and was badly burned; nonetheless, the city hereby suffered an irreparable injury. Whatever still existed in the cellars was used by Tilly's soldiers, who built huts on the deserted scenes of the fire.

The clergy and other members of Catholic religious orders, monks and so on, who had long awaited such an opportunity to come in and reform the cathedral (which, standing in the wide, spacious area of the new market, had remained standing and unburned along with several houses), have begun to create a new institution of both this and of other churches.

The king of Sweden, surmising that this sad circumstance, whereby the city was not relieved in time, would cause some to have unfavorable thoughts about him, had a manifesto published in which he first described the expulsion of the people of Magdeburg in its beginnings, and then laid out the reasons: that they had not wished to pay the considerable sums required for new recruitments and similar necessities of war. . . .

After this unspeakable misfortune happened to this city, which had been the residence of the first German emperor, and those Magdeburgers who were still alive had been scattered here and there, there was a great deal of inquiry by those foreigners to whom the displaced Magdeburgers had come. How had it happened that the city had gotten into such misery and need? Had the people perhaps not resisted or not given the soldiers the proper support so that they could fight? Or had the citizens given up hope and fled from the ramparts? Or had they fallen asleep on watch? Or had they become so godless that God had had to punish them in this way? Or had it happened in some other way?, etc., since one person put forward one cause, another a different one. Overall, however, because there had been two parties in the city (the one, which had advised and promoted the conjunction with the lord administrator, and the other, which had advised against this, declaring

---

101. Sutlers were civilians who sold goods and merchandise to soldiers.

even that it would lead to a disturbingly large calamity), each laid a part of the guilt on the other and were thus, both before and after the conquest, fierce opponents. Those who had prophesied the misfortune could manifestly show that it had happened as they had said; the others, however, who had initiated the work and then had, by leading the common man astray, accomplished it, renounced those who had not joined in; these had been good imperialists, they claimed, and had secretly conspired with them (the imperialists) and had, indeed, even betrayed the safety of the city to the enemy, for otherwise the situation would have gone differently, etc.

This is thus the correct, true progression of events during the conquest of this good city, Magdeburg. No one can gainsay this, for the truth shall be known.

17. The Battle of Breitenfeld (September 17, 1631)[102]

[After the horrible sack of Magdeburg, many Protestant princes of the empire decided to join the Swedish side and rise up against the emperor. Among these was John George, the elector of Saxony, whose army then combined with that of Sweden. Together, the two armies pursued the imperial army, led by General Tilly, who retreated into southern Saxony. On September 17, 1631, the two armies met near Leipzig at the town of Breitenfeld. Outnumbered and outmaneuvered, Tilly's army was completely shattered. The following account of the battle appeared in the diary of Robert Monroe, one of many Scottish soldiers who served in the army of Gustavus Adolphus. It is shown here with its original spelling and punctuation.]

As the Larke begunne to peepe, the seventh of September 1631.[103] having stood all night in battaile a mile from Tillies Armie, in the morning, the Trumpets sound to horse, the Drummes calling to March, being at our Armes, and in readinesse, having before meditated in the night, and resolved with our Consciences; we begunne the morning with offering our soules and bodies, as living Sacrifices unto God, with Confession of our sinnes, lifting

102. Robert Monro, *Monro his expedition with the worthy Scots Regiment (called Mac-Keyes Regiment) levied in August 1626. by Sr. Donald Mac-Key Lord Rhees, colonell for his Majesties service of Denmark, and reduced after the Battaile of Nerling, to one company in September 1634. at Wormes in the Paltz,* Part II (London: Printed by William Iones in Red-Crosse streete, 1637), 63–67. A copy can be found at the Henry E. Huntington Library.

103. By the old calendar. In the new Gregorian calendar, the date was September 17, 1631.

up our hearts and hands to Heaven, we begged for reconciliation in Christ, by our publique prayers, and secret sighes, and groanes; recommending our selves, the successe, and event of the day unto God, our Father in Christ; which done by us all, we marched forwards in Gods name a little, and then halted againe, till the whole Armie, both the Duke's [of Saxony], and Ours, were put in good Order: our Armie marching on the right hand, and the Dukes on the left, our commanded Musketeres marching in the Van-Guarde. . . . we marched thus, both the Armies in Battaile, Horse, foote, and Artillerie, till about nine of the Clocke in the morning, wee halted halfe a mile distant from the Emperiall Armie; that were attending us in Battaile; consisting of fortie foure thousand men, horse, and foote, our Armie, con-sisting of thirtie thousand men, whereof, to my judgement, His Majesties Armie; were eight thousand foote, and seven thousand horse; The Duke also, would be eleven thousand foote, and foure thousand horse; having refreshed ourselves with victuals, leaving our Coaches behind us. The whole Armie did get greene Branches on their heads; and the word was given, God with us: a little short speech made by His Majestie, being in order of Battaile, we marched towards the enemie, who had taken the advantage of the ground, having placed his Armie on a place called Gods Acre; where their Generall did make choice of the ground most advantagious for his foote, Artillerie, and horses; he also did beset the Dorpes,[104] that invironed the ground, which was left for us, with Dragoniers and Crabbats:[105] to incomber our wings by their evill Neighbourhood: yet, notwithstanding of all the advan-tages hee had of Ground, Wind, and Sunne; our magnanimous King and Leader; under God, inferiour to no Generall we ever reade of, for wisedome, courage, dexteritie, and good Conduct, he was not dejected; but with mag-nanimitie, and Christian resolution, having recommended himselfe, his Armie, and success to God, the Director of men and Angells; able to give victory with few against many; He ordered his Armie, and directed every supreame Officer of the Field, on their particular charge and stations com-mitted unto them, for that day: As also he acquainted them severally, of the forme he was to fight unto, and he appointed Plottons of Musketiers, by fifties, which were commanded by sufficient Officers to attend on severall Regiments of horse; and he instructed the Officers how to behave themselves in discharging their duties on service. . . .

The Felt-marshall Horne, Generall Banier, and Lieutenant Generall Bawtish were commanded to over-see the Horsemen, his Majestie, the Baron Tyvell, and Grave Neles, were to command the Battaile of foote; Sir Iames Ramsey, as eldest Colonell, had the command of the fore-Troopes, or com-

104. Villages, from the Dutch word for village (*Dorp*).
105. Croatians.

manded Musketiers; and Sir Iohn Hepburne, as eldest Colonell, commanded the three Briggads of Reserve:[106] Our Armie thus ordered, the Duke
of Saxon and his Feltmarshall Arnhem, having ordered their Armie (whereof
I was not particularly inquisitive of the manner) they were ordained to draw
up on our left hand, and being both in one front thus ordered, we marched
in Battaile a little, and then halted againe, till his Majestie had commanded
out some commanded Horsemen, on the wings of the Armie, a large distance from the body, to scoure the fields of the Crabbats; we marched againe
in order of Battaile, with Trumpets sounding, Drummes beating, and
Colours advanced and flying, till we came within reach of Cannon to our
enemies Armie, then the magnifick and magnanimous Gustavus the Invincible, leads up the Briggads of horse one after another to their ground, with
their Plottons of shot to attend them: As also he led up the Briggads of foote
one after another to their ground, during which time we were drawne up according to our former plot, the enemy was thundering amongst us, with the
noise, and roaring whisling and flying of Cannon-Bullets; where you may
imagine the hurt was great. . . .

By twelve of the Clock on wednesday the seventh of September, in de-
spight of the fury of the enemies Cannon, and of his advantages taken, they
were drawne up in even front with the enemy, and then our Cannon begun
to roare, great and small, paying the enemy with the like coyne, which thundering continued alike on both sides for two houres and an halfe, during
which time, our Battailes of horse and foote stood firme like a wall, the Cannon now and then making great breaches amongst us, which was diligently
looked unto, on all hands, by the diligence of Officers in filling up the voide
parts, and in setting aside of the wounded towards Chirurgians,[107] every Officer standing firme, over-seeing their Commands in their owne stations,
succeeding one another as occasion offered.

By halfe three, our Cannon a little ceasing, the Horsemen on both wings
charged furiously one another, our Horsemen with a resolution, abiding un-
loosing a Pistoll, till the enemy had discharged first, and then at a neere distance our Musketiers meeting them with a Salve; then our hoursemen
discharged their Pistolls, and then charged through them with swords; and at
their returne the Musketiers were ready againe to give the second Salve of Musket amongst them; the enemy thus valiantly resisted by our Horsemen, and
cruelly plagued by our Plottons of Musketiers; you may imagine, how soone
he would be discouraged after charging twice in this manner, and repulsed.

Our Horsemen of the right wing of Finnes and Haggapells, led by the val-
ourous Feltmarshall Horne, finding the enemies Horsemen out of Order,

106. Brigades of reserves.
107. Surgeons.

with resolution he charged the enemies left wing, forcing them to retire disorderly on their battailes of foote, which caused disorder among the foote, who were forced then to fall to the right hand; our Horsemen retiring, his Majestie seeing the enemy in disorder, played with Ordnance amongst them, during which time, the force of the enemies Battailes falls on the Duke of Saxon, charging with Horse first in the middest of the Battailes, and then the foote giving two Salves of Musket amongst them, they were put to the Rout, horse and foote, and the enemy following them cryed Victoria, as if the day had beene wonne, triumphing before the victory; But our Horsemen charging the remnant of their horse and foote, where their Generall stood, they were made to retire in disorder to the other hand towards Leipsigh;[108] our Armie of foote standing firme, not having loosed one Musket; the smoake being great, by the rising of the dust, for a long time we were not able to see about us; but being cleared up, we did see on the left hand of our reserve two great Battailes of foote, which we imagined to have beene Saxons, that were forced to give ground; having heard the service, though not seene it, we found they were enemies, being a great deale neerer than the Saxons were: His Majestie having sent Baron Tyvell to know the certaintie, coming before our Briggad, I certified him they were enemies, and he returning towards his Majestie, was shot dead; his Majestie coming by, gave direction to Colonell Hepburne, to cause the Briggads on his right and left wing to wheele, and then to charge the enemy, the Orders given, his Majestie retired, promising to bring succours unto us.

The enemies Battaile standing firme, looking on us at a neere distance, and seeing the other Briggads and ours wheeleing about, making front unto them, they were prepared with a firme resolution to receive us with a salve of Cannon and Muskets; but our small Ordinance being twice discharged amongst them, and before we stirred, we charged them with a salve of musket, which was repaied, and incontinent our Briggad advancing unto them with push of pike, putting one of their battailes in disorder, fell on the execution, so that they were put to the route.

I having commanded the right wing of our musketiers, being my Lord of Rhees and Lumsdells, we advanced on the other body of the enemies, which defended their Cannon, and beating them from their Cannon, we were masters of their Cannon, and consequently of the field, but the smoake being great, the dust being raised, we were as in a darke cloud, not seeing the halfe of our actions, much lesse discerning, either the way of our enemies, or yet the rest of our Briggads: whereupon, having a drummer by me, I caused him beate the Scots march, till it cleered up, which recollected our friends unto us, and dispersed our enemies being overcome; so that the Briggad coming together, such as were alive missed their dead and hurt Camerades.

108. Leipzig.

Colonell Lumsdell was hurt at the first, and Lievetenant Colonell Musten also, with divers other Ensignes were hurt and killed, and sundry Colours were missing for that night, which were found the next day; The enemy thus fled, our horsemen were pursuing hard, till it was darke, and the blew Birggad, and the commanded musketiers were sent by his Majesty to helpe us, but before their coming, the victory and the credit of the day, as being left ingaged, was ascribed to our Briggad, being the reserve, were thanked by his Majesty for their service, in publique audience, and in view of the whole Army, we were promised to be rewarded.

The Battaile thus happily wonne, his Majesty did principally under God ascribe the glory of the victory to the Sweds, and Fynnes horsemen, who were led by the valorous Felt-marshall Gustavus Horne; For though the Dutch horsemen did behave themselves valorously divers times that day; yet it was not their fortune to have done the charge, which did put the enemy to flight, and though there were brave Briggads of Sweds and Dutch in the field, yet it was the Scots Briggads fortune to have gotten the praise for the foote service. . . . The victory being ours, we incamped over night on the place of Battaile, the living merry and rejoycing, though without drinke at the night-wake of their dead Camerades and friends, lying then on the ground in the bed of honour, being glad the Lord had prolonged their dayes for to discharge the last honourable duty, in burying of their Camerades.

Our bone-fiers[109] were made of the enemies Amunition waggons, and Pikes left, for want of good fellowes to use them; and all this night our brave Camerades, the Saxons were making use of their heeles in flying, thinking all was lost, they made booty of our waggons and goods, too good a recompence for Cullions that had left their Duke, betrayed their country and the good cause, when as strangers were hazarding their lives for their freedomes.

Our losse this day with the Saxons, did not exceede three thousand men, which for the most part were killed by the enemies Cannon: of principall Officers we lost a number. . . .

To the enemy were lost on the field neere eight thousand, besides Officers of note, such as the Felt-marshall Fustenberg: the Duke of Holsten, the Count of Shomeberg; old Generall Tillie hurt and almost taken; a number of other Officers of the Field were killed, and taken prisoners. They lost also thirty two peeces of Cannon, with three score waggons of Amunition, and their Generall, and Papingham were chased towards Hall, and from thence were forced with a small convoy to take their flight for refuge to Hamell on the Waser.[110]

109. Bonfires.
110. Hameln on the Weser River.

18. Protestants Triumphant (March 5, 1632)[111]

*[The victory at the battle of Breitenfeld in September 1631 and the subse-
quent victories by the Swedish King Gustavus Adolphus and his allies, filled
the Protestants with a new hope of absolute victory against the Catholics. In
response, some princes began to increase their war aims and demands radically.
This letter of March 5, 1632, from Landgrave Wilhelm V of Hesse-Cassel to
King Gustavus Adolphus, is a good example of this new confidence and hunger
for both payback and profit. It shows a desire not only to return to the* status
quo ante bellum *by eliminating anti-Protestant legal changes that had occurred since 1618 (particularly the 1629 Edict of Restitution), but also to
remake the very institutions of empire in order to increase the power of Protestants over Catholics and of imperial princes over the emperor. Furthermore,
Wilhelm's demands show the ongoing struggle by Calvinists to gain some of the
same legal recognition and rights over their territories as Lutherans enjoyed.
This was especially important after the Edict of Restitution, which had declared Calvinism illegal and thereby threatened the control of Calvinist princes
over their lands and people.]*

At our recent visit to Mainz, Your Royal Majesty most amicably wished to
know our humble thoughts on perhaps holding and concluding the friendly
negotiations suggested by our dear cousin, brother, and relative, Landgrave
George of Hesse,[112] between Your Royal Majesty and the Catholic League,[113]
and what sort of abiding security would be required and desired for that
which might be agreed on by both sides amid reports of victory. . . .

  To come right to the point, in our opinion, that which Your Royal Majesty
has asked of us consists of three parts, and first is in what form, measure, and
way this extremely important action might be conducted. The second,
should we reach this point, is what conditions and means for making peace
would be proposed. Third, should, by means of divine grace, a hoped-for
universal peace be made in the Holy Roman Empire of the German Nation,
which remedies and means could and should be considered and found by

111. Attachment to Wilhelm V of Hesse-Cassel (minute) to Gustavus Adolphus,
Hörter, February 24/March 5, 1632, Hessische Staatsarchiv Marburg, in Georg Irmer,
*Die Verhandlungs Schwedens und seiner Verbündeten mit Wallenstein und dem Kaiser
von 1631 bis 1634,* vol. I, 1631 und 1632, nr. 47 (Leipzig: Verlag von S. Hirzel, 1888),
125–33.

112. Landgrave George of Hesse-Darmstadt (1605–1661).

113. The league of Catholic princes of the empire, led by Duke Maximilian of
Bavaria.

which the Evangelicals[114] and their most beloved posterity might thereby truly be assured. . . .

As for what concerns the second point in particular, the means for peace: although this was already, in good measure, quite prudently deliberated and pondered at the recent meeting in Leipzig, since then, however, by a divine merciful grant, affairs have taken a quite different and more delightful turn, for which we give praise and thanks to the benevolent, gracious God. And therefore, things must and can justly be expanded. . . . So for Your Royal Majesty's betterment, we think that these matters can again be divided into three distinct components: first religious, second secular, and third the private complaints and interests of those Evangelical estates with which Your Royal Highness formed a union, and to whom you have agreed to oblige yourself.

And as for the religious:

1) First, since the primary cause of the arming of the Evangelicals was freedom of conscience . . . both those called Reformed[115] as well as those called Lutherans should expressly be included in the Religious Peace[116] without any distinction, and (by virtue of ancient compacts) no Roman emperor ought to presume to make any inquiry, interpretation, or declaration concerning the understanding of the Augsburg Confession[117] and the subsequent Religious Peace, nor to make any restriction or extension of it. Instead, should some such thing occur, it is a matter for all of the imperial estates. Regardless of this, however, the current Roman Imperial Majesty was pleased to issue an edict in which he inquired about and made a decree concerning ecclesiastical property, and also who was to be understood to be within the Augsburg Confession.[118] This, being null and void and intrinsically

114. Protestants.

115. Calvinists.

116. The 1555 Peace of Augsburg, which, along with its preliminary, the 1552 Peace of Passau, gave each prince the right to reform his territories. Lutherans and Catholics claimed that only they were included, not Calvinists.

117. Calvinists claimed that their faith was merely a variation on the 1530 Confession of Augsburg, and thus they should be granted the same rights as Lutherans within the empire. The emperor and others had rejected this argument.

118. Here he is referring to the 1629 Edict of Restitution, in which the emperor demanded the return of all ecclesiastical properties that Protestants had seized since 1552. The edict also expressly excluded Calvinists from the Augsburg Confession, thereby depriving Calvinist princes of all legal protections and of the right to keep Catholic lands seized even before 1552. This was an especial threat to the Calvinist Landgrave Wilhelm of Hesse-Cassel, and one of the principal reasons he had soon thereafter come to an agreement with Gustavus Adolphus of Sweden. See Document 14.

unbinding and without power, should be soon revoked, annulled, and nulli-fied, and no Roman emperor, nor any estate of the empire (under whatever name they may be), should ever invoke or try to apply it in the future; rather it shall be considered and seen as revoked and as if it had never been conceived.

2) Second, that all dioceses, cloisters, and ecclesiastical property, without distinction of whether they are mediate or immediate to the empire,[119] that Evangelicals held and possessed before and after the Treaty of Passau shall ir-revocably and peacefully be left to them. Furthermore, that all of the dioce-ses, cloisters, property, rents, dividends, and income, as well as any rights, dues, and prerogatives that all Protestant estates might have gained during the Bohemian trouble and until the conclusion of a peace, shall remain to them irrevocably and indisputably. . . .

3) That each and every Protestant, without any distinction, shall be free and available to reform those dioceses and cloisters that lie in their territo-ries or that they have otherwise possessed and gained, whether mediate or immediate; to dispose of their revenue, proceeds, and income, and from this to maintain the churches and schools; and to enact provisions for their sec-ular rule so that one might always have well-qualified, useful, and functional persons. . . .

4) Fourth, that all high and low Catholic dioceses, cloisters, colleges, and chapters, both in general and for any specific person who is included within any of them, whether male or female, shall certainly and without hindrance be free and available to convert from the Catholic papist religion without detriment to their ecclesiastical offices, titles, and dignities, and to take up the Protestant religion. . . .

5) Fifth, that in all Catholic places and areas, the Evangelicals, once again without distinction, shall not only be tolerated unmolested, allowed to en-joy all privileges, freedoms, and prerogatives just like Catholic subjects, and, without distinction, be called to and promoted to all offices in the churches and for the general good; but also shall be allowed the free exercise of reli-gion and the right publicly to practice, to teach, and to confess it. . . .

But to focus on those points that concern secular matters, here we think it should be as follows, without any amendment:

1) Since the Catholics intended to exclude the Protestant electoral estates from the electoral college,[120] [we propose] that one now do the same thing

---

119. Mediate territories were those that were subject to at least one legal overlord below the emperor. Territories or states directly below the emperor were known as immediate territories.

120. The electoral college consisted of seven great princes of the empire, who, by

to them by an equal legal edict, and, in order to cut off in the future all similar practices and to assure the Evangelicals of a much better and more enduring peace, that one no longer draw on the ecclesiastical electors for an election of a Roman emperor, . . .

2) When an imperial fiefdom becomes open, a Roman emperor or king alone does not have the power to confer it . . . but the concession of it shall be debated at a general Reichstag, and then such a fiefdom shall be conferred to one or more estates by majority vote.

3) That all Aulic Council[121] lawsuits be discontinued in the future and at all times, and no further imperial estates be called to the Aulic Council, whatever the matter or circumstances. Instead, when one or another estate of the empire faces prosecution, then this should be left to the existing judgments of the estate; or, should such not exist, the matter should then be heard by the Imperial Chamber Court[122] and should be begun, pursued, and debated according to its form, qualities, and character, by virtue of the rules of the Chamber Court itself. . . .

As for what concerns the private interests:

1) It is especially fitting that, above all else, what Your Royal Majesty—as a divinely chosen instrument and armament and tool, risking life and limb and incurring untold costs in ecclesiastical and secular matters—has already and up to now demonstrated and contributed, is not forgotten; nor are those things that, by the grace and blessings of the Almighty, Your Majesty can and will further do. Thus we would wish that the gratitude that is, for this reason,

---

law, were empowered to elect the emperor. Before the war, these included three ecclesiastical princes—the archbishops of Mainz, Trier, and Cologne—and four secular princes—the duke of Saxony, the king of Bohemia, the margrave of Brandenburg, and the count Palatine of the Rhine. In the course of the war, however, Emperor Ferdinand transferred the electoral office of the Calvinist count Palatine to his ally, the Catholic duke of Bavaria, thereby increasing the number of Catholic electors to five and ensuring a Catholic majority in all important imperial matters—including imperial elections.

121. The Imperial Aulic Council, or *Reichshofrat,* was the first of the great courts of the empire.

122. The Imperial Chamber Court, or *Reichskammergericht,* was the second of the two great courts of the empire. It was the highest, or supreme court, and was designed to resolve conflicts between the estates of the empire. Membership in the court was controlled by the princes and estates themselves. The court, which met in the city of Speyer, had become paralyzed before the war by religious divisions within the empire, leaving the *Reichshofrat* as the only functioning court. The Hessians believed the *Reichshofrat* to be biased toward the emperor and the Catholics.

owed by the Protestant estates might then be demonstrated and recognized everywhere in the same way that we truly do: from the bottom of our hearts, without rivalry, consideration, or thought. Because, however, your royal demonstrations of friendship are so great that sufficient gratefulness could never be demonstrated . . . no one would blame Your Royal Majesty if you were to see to your own recompense, as, thanks to God, you now have the means to do so in your own hands. We are also reminded by a protocol from our former councilor, Doctor Wolff . . . of the discussions that occurred in the negotiations undertaken between himself and Your Royal Majesty's secretary Philip Sattler. These discussions concerned conquered property in payment for our efforts, risk, and expenses; and, on this account, it was proposed that you make a secret accord with us. Although, because of the enormous advances of the enemy in the past, this accord has not yet been agreed to nor implemented, yet not only are we completely prepared to act on this once again, but instead—just as our alliance specifies that no party shall enter into any peace without the other's satisfaction and consent, nor shall establish another confederation and friendship that runs contrary to this alliance with any other, whether he be either within or without the empire, or whomever he might be—we declare ourselves such that we not only confidently and eagerly await Your Royal Majesty's thoughts, but also intend to prove ourselves with a further offering of our body, property, and blood, and therefore will firmly continue with Your Royal Majesty in military preparations until this goal is reached, so that you can truly sense and see the abiding, pure, and loyal affection and devotion to serve yourself and your crown, with which, to the best of our ability, we work.

2) Concerning, however, our particular interests, when, by means of divine blessing, an acceptable general peace is obtained, Your Royal Majesty will—not only due to our close blood relationship, but also on account of the specific alliance we have made—cordially acquiesce that we, our princely children and posterity, land and people, and those of our (and Your Majesty's) councilors whom we have used in this war, and our officers, servants, and soldiers, and their property, are included and provided for in the general amnesty, and that whatever is suitable to recompense them on account of their efforts and loyal service . . . might remain to them.

3) The Catholics, without considering that they brought the war to the land and poor people of the Protestant estates, nevertheless presented a bill for their pretended war costs to the Evangelicals, and under this pretext wished to take the rest of their land and people so that the Evangelicals would even be driven from the empire and their emergency food supplies would be stolen from them. And we can declare that . . . for us and our lands and people, both conjointly and separately, we suffered such damages through these robbers . . . that, as of two years ago, we already owed twenty million

in gold; and at the same time, there was that which our lord father had to pay for defense and military preparations for us and our lands and people; and we too, insofar as they had even taken our food, had to incur many debts and take in great sums in order to sustain our life. And therefore we have a reason to claim to be restituted, made good again, and given proper satisfaction, either in money or in land and people, for what the Imperial Court and the [Catholic] League have done to us in the Marburg succession matter.[123] . . .

Finally, and in conclusion, as to what concerns the point of assurance for the hoped-for general peace and agreement . . .

1) That, as Your Royal Majesty indicated to us, the Catholics should be completely and totally disarmed.

2) . . . . That Your Royal Majesty firmly remain with us in certain military preparations as protector of Protestantism . . . and allow us to occupy all of the principal rivers and fortresses, and to be able to take from them the support needed for the soldiers. . . .

3) That on account of the damages we have sustained, and just as they intended to do with us, they, the papists, must pay Your Royal Majesty and us Evangelicals with their lands and people; and though they maintain in their hearts an evil desire to break capitulations, compacts, transactions, and oaths, one might yet, through this impoverishment and circumcision, make impotent their rage and evil intentions.

4) That wherever possible, one should not only, as stated above, take from the Catholic electors their right to vote for the emperor . . . but because the papists, where they have not directly acknowledged a desire for revenge, have, under the pretext of their administration of justice, really brought things to a bad point, one should also exclude them from the Imperial Chamber and all courts, and should abolish the Aulic Council.

5) That in order to prevent all of the divisions that have arisen among the Evangelicals . . . the Reformed religion ought to be mentioned with a few words in such a way that those who account themselves among the Reformed are understood to be within the Augsburg Confession and therefore contained within the Religious and Secular Peace. . . .

---

123. The emperor had favored his ally, George of Hesse-Darmstadt, over Wilhelm's father, Moritz of Hesse-Cassel (who opposed the emperor), in their argument over who was the rightful successor to the territory of Marburg. Such imperial partisanship most likely influenced the judgment of the Aulic Council, which awarded the territory, plus large reparation costs, to Hesse-Darmstadt in 1623. This left both Moritz and his son embittered and angry about the emperor's influence over the imperial court system.

7) That the entire meddlesome Jesuit gang and horde, with all of their followers, from whom all of this misery originated and from whom this misfortune and fire issued . . . be quickly and entirely removed from the Empire of the German Nation. . . .

8) Since the House of Spain, whose Spanish monarchs have an appetite for revenge and other dangerous practices, has thus made all kinds of codicils and has splendidly studied rhetoric, from this it is clear to see how, one way or another, its power must be placed into such an equilibrium that it and its followers are satisfied and removed. Your Royal Majesty should then endeavor to see to it that the Spanish leave imperial soil and are dismissed from all of the places that they hold or are owed, and that they once again evacuate the empire, a goal which all Evangelicals will, without doubt, loyally support. . . .

And we hereby present these humble thoughts, which we have composed in the total, certain hope of Your Royal Majesty's reasonable consideration. And at the same time, we have always faithfully, staunchly, and honestly demonstrated our loyalty, setting aside all our temporal well-being and also ancient compacts that we have had with other potentates, and thereby shall persist until we are in the grave—not only without any vacillation, but also directing our princely posterity to comport itself toward Your Royal Majesty and your royal posterity and crown in the same way, and, should you be prepared and inclined to erect the above-mentioned secret agreement, to bind themselves to you now and also hereafter. Your Royal Majesty will also always consider us with good, friendly affection, and always assist us and our whole house of the Cassel line to gain that which we are owed by God and the courts, and which is confirmed by the Christian alliance made between us. . . .

Wilhelm
To the Royal Majesty of Sweden

19. The Swedish Discipline (1632)[124]

[The Swedish ruler Gustavus Adolphus was renowned for his skill as a general. His innovations—based, to a large degree, on the earlier reforms instituted in the Dutch Republic by Maurice of Nassau—included his stress on increasing

124. William Watts, *The Swedish discipline, religious, civile, and military . . . The second part, in the excellent orders observed in the armie; whereof we here present you the articles, by which the souldiery is governed* (London: Printed by Iohn Dawson for Nath: Butter and Nich: Bourne, 1632). A copy can be found at the University of Michigan Libraries, Special Collections DL 706 .W35 1632.

his army's firepower and his use of a new tactical formation (the brigade). He also insisted that his army, filled with both Swedish recruits and, increasingly over time, German mercenaries, both serve his needs precisely and present a civilized face to the princes of Germany, whose liberties he claimed to be fighting to preserve. He thus stressed constant training and military drills for his troops, and instituted unusually strict rules concerning their religious, civil, and military discipline. His extraordinary military successes spurred many other generals to follow his model, broadly affecting the prosecution of the Thirty Years War. The document below is a portion of the Swedish rules of war. It was published in English in 1632 by an admirer of Gustavus Adolphus, the chaplain William Watts (c. 1590–1649), who also provided readers with sections containing such details as the prayers used by the Swedish army, how the king organized and quartered his regiments, and how he fortified a town. Watts' spelling and punctuation have been maintained here.]

The Second Part of the Swedish Discipline: Containing those Orders, and Articles of Warre, which have beene commanded by the King of Sweden, to be under their severall Penalties observed in his Majesties Camp, Garrisons, or elsewhere.

Gustavus Adolphus By the Grace of God King of the Swedens Gothes and Vandals, Great Prince of Finland Duke of Esthonia and Carelia, and Lord of Ingria, &c. Whereas the exactnesse of Auncient Discipline and Justice is now almost utterly forgotten: and in place thereof many strange and enormous abuses, crept in amongst our soldiers: Wee therefore taking the matter into our tender care and consideration; will by the assistance of Almighty God endevour to doe our uttermost, both for the reducing of the said forme of Discipline, and the rooting out the same abuses, using to that purpose the way of gentlenesse and admonition unto some; and resolving to take the course and strictnesse of Justice unto others, That therefore our soldiers may the better be trained up to the right use and handling of their Armes, so as may best enable them for our service and defence of our native Country: and that every man in like manner, may the better eschew what may fall out to be inconvenient: Wee have once againe overseene our former Articles of warres, calling out from thence these following Articles; which wee have thought most fit and expedient, both for our service and their ordering. Streightly willing or commanding all our soldiers, both natives of our Kingdome as well as Strangers, serving both on Horse and Foote;[125] that from the time of their comming into our service, they doe duely and obediently observe these following Articles: unto which, if any upon presumption doe the contrary, he shall be Punished as here after followeth.

125. In other words, both cavalry and infantry.

1. Seeing therefore that all our wellfare and prosperity, proceedeth from Almighty God; and that it is all mens duty to feare and serve him above all: Wee streightly hereby charge all manner of Persons whatsoever, that they by no meanes use any kind of Idolatry, Witch-craft, or Enchanting of Armes, by Devils inchantment any manner of way whatsoever. And if any herein be found faulty he shall be proceeded against according to Gods law and the Swedens: And so much as the law in that case enjoyneth, shalbe put in execution against them. And it is further provided, that such manner of Malefactors shall by no meanes be suffered to come in Company with any soldiers whatsoever.

2. If any shall blaspheme the name of God, either drunke or sober; and the thing be by 2. or 3. witnesses proved against him, he shall be put to death without all mercy.

3. If any shall presume to deride or scorne Gods word or Sacraments, and be taken in the fault; they shall forthwith be convented before the Consistory or Commission Ecclesiasticall, to be in presence of the Commissioners examined: by whom if he be found guilty and condemned; he shall lose his head without all mercy. But if the words by him so uttered, were spoken out of hast or unadvisednesse; he shall for the first offence be put in Irons for 14. dayes: And give unto the next hospitall one halfe Months pay. After which if he presume againe, he shalbe shot to death.

4. He who in his anger shall sweare by the name of God, and be taken therewith; whither it were done in hastinesse or not, or otherwise in the executing of his office: he shall forfeit halfe a Months pay unto the poore. In like manner, if any be in time of Prayers found drinking, or at any other evill exercise, the shall give one halfe months pay unto the next Hospitall, and at the next Preaching or Prayers that is, he shall be brought upon his knees in the midst of all the Congregation, there to crave pardon of Almighty God; and so continue the whole time of Divine service and Sermon. This shall the Minister see executed.

5. And to the end that Gods word be by no meanes neglected, our will is, that publick Prayers be every day said both morning and Evening throughout our whole leaguer.[126] For which purpose, shall some token or warning be given by our Generall; and in his absence by our Marshall of the Field, or other chiefe officer. Which token or warning, shall be made by sound of trumpet, playing the tune of some Psalme: unto which the other trumpettors shall likewise answer in the tune of a Psalme: and so shall the Drummers of every Regiment. Then shall every Priest or Minister in our Army say Publick Prayers in his owne Quarter.

---

126. Military camp.

6. Whatsoever Minister shall neglect his time of Prayer (except by sicknesse or other lawfull occasion he be hindred) he shall for every absence forfeit one halfe moneths pay unto the next Hospitall.

7. Whatsoever soldiour shall neglect the time of Prayers, & is therefore once, twice, or thrice admonished by his Captaine, he shall lye in prison 24. houres: except he had a lawful occasion to be absent.

8. If any Minister shalbe found drunken at such time as he should preach or reade Prayers; he shall for the second offence be gravely advised by Consistory or Commission to forsake his sinne; but if he be found drunken the third time, he shalbe put out of the Leaguer.

9. Every Holy day, or every Sunday at least, shalbe kept solemne with Preaching; to be holden in the fittest place for such a purpose. This also to be done twice every weeke if the time will permit. If there be any Holy dayes to come in the following weeke; the Minister shall after such Sermon or Prayers publickly bid them. Who so shall neglect the time appoynted, unlesse he have some lawfull let or occasion; shalbe punished as aforesaid. . . .

14. To the intent that all Church businesse, as well in the Field as otherwhere, may have an orderly proceeding; wee ordaine, that there be one Ecclesiasticall Consistory or Commission in our Leaguer. The President or chiefe person whereof shalbe our owne Minister when wee our selues, are personally present in the field. In our absence, shall the chiefe Minister to our Generall, be the man. His fellow Commissioners or ordinary Assessors, shalbe the chiefe Ministers to every Regiment of Horse and Foote: unto whom wee give full power and authority, to be Judges in all Church affaires: according to the Law of God and the Holy Church. What shalbe by them decreed, shalbe of as great force and strength, as if it were determined in any other Consistory whatsoever. . . .

17. And now, in like manner, as all our soldiers have made Oath to be unto us true and obedient: so also shall they observe this following Article, hold up their hands, and sweare as followeth.

The Oath of all Under-Officers of Horse or Foote.

I. N. N. Doe here promise and sweare, that unto the High and mighty King Gustavus, as also unto the Crowne of Sweden, I will be a true and a faithfull servant and soldiour: every manner of way performing my best endeavour for his Majesties service, and the profit of his Kingdome. To my power also shall I hinder all actions prejudiciall unto his Crowne: and if I have tidings of any thing likely to be prejudiciall, I shall give his Majesty present notice thereof; or some one or other of his Councell. Moreover I will doe my best endevour to observe all these his Majesties Articles of warres. Also, I shall behave my selfe manfully in battle, skirmishes, and entryes of breaches, as well by Water as by Land, in all times and places, when and where I shall be commanded. I shall also keepe watch and ward, and doe all other duties willingly, unto the best profit of his Majesty and his Kingdome; wheresoever I shall be commanded, either by Land, or Water. Also, I shall beare my selfe obediently towards my superiour Officers, in all that they command me for his Majesties service. In like manner, as I shall answer it before God and every honest man, I shall not fly from my Colours[127] or Token whatsoever, that I am commanded to follow; so long as I am able to goe after them: and I shall be willing to doe this at all times; and by no means absent my selfe from them at any time. I shall lay downe my life and goods for the advancing of his Majesties service, [and shall bear] all miseries that can possibly fall out in the warres: [fighting manfully] to the very last; so farre forth as I am able, or that any true soldiour ought to doe. Furthermore, if hereafter I be put into any place of charged by his Majesty; I shall doe my best endevour fairely to discharge my duty therein: so as I ought to doe according to my place. This Oath shall I well and truely keepe, as the Lord of Heaven and Earth shall helpe my soule at the last Judgement.

18. All at this time present, or hereafter to come into our service, shalbe bound to keepe these following Articles: aswell in the Field, as in any Fort or Worke[128] whatsoever, where they shalbe commanded.

19. For that no Goverment can stand firmely, unlesse it be first rightly grounded; and that the lawes be rightly observed: Wee the King of Sweden doe hereby make knowne unto all our soldiours and subjects, noble and others; that in our presence they presume not to doe any unseemely thing: but that every one give Us our due honor, as wee ought to receive. Who presumes to doe the contrary, shalbe punished at our pleasure.

20. Next, shall our Officers and soldiers be obedient unto our Generall and Feild-Marshal, with other our Officers next under them, in whatsoever they shall command, belonging unto our service: Upon paine of punishment as followeth.

21. Whosoever behaves not himselfe obediently unto our great Generall or our Ambassador commanding in our absence, as well as if wee our selves were there in person present; shalbe kept in Irons or in prison, untill such time as he shalbe brought to his answer before a Councell of warre: where being found guilty; whether it were wilfully done, or not; he shall stand to the Order of the Court, to lay what punishment upon him they shall thinke convenient, according as the person and fact is.

---

127. Colors were the banners under which the different regiments marched, so to "fly from my Colours" meant to flee the battlefield.

128. Military fieldwork or structure.

22. And if any shall offer to discredit these great offices by word of mouth or otherwise and not be able by proofes to make it good, he shalbe put to death without mercy.

23. Whosoever offers to lift up any manner of Armes against them, whether he does them hurt or not, shalbe punisht by death. . . .

29. If any Colonell, Leiftenant-Colonell, Sergeant Major, or Quarter Maister, shall command any thing not belonging unto our service; he shall answer to the complaint before the Court. . . .

31. If any Inferiour officer either of Horse or Foote, does challenge any [common] soldiour to be guilty of any dishonest action; the soldiour finding himselfe guiltlesse, may lawfully call the said officer to make proofe of his words before the Court, as his equall.

32. If any soldiour either of Horse or Foote, shall offer to strike his officer, that shall command him any duty for our service; he shall first loose his hand, and be then turned out of the Quarter. And if it be done in any Fort or beleaguered place, after the watch is set, he shall loose his life for it.

33. And if he does hurt to any of them, whither it be in the field, or not, he shall be shot to death. . . .

35. He, who in the presence of our Generall shall draw his sword, with purpose to doe mischiefe with it; shall lose his hand for it. . . .

37. He who shall once presume to draw his sword upon the place where any Court of Justice is holden, while it is holden, shall lose his life for it. . . .

44. Whatsoever is to be published or generally made knowne, shalbe proclaimed by sound of Drumme and trumpet; that no man may pretend ignorance in it: they who after that shall be found disobedient, shalbe punished according to the quality of the fact.

45. No soldiour shall think himselfe too good to worke upon any peice of Fortification, or other place, where they shalbe commanded for our service; upon paine of punishment

46. Whosoever shall doe his Majesties businesse slightly or lazily; shall first ride the wooden Horse,[129] and lye in prison after that with Bread and Water: according as the fact shalbe adjudged more or lesse heynous.

47. All Officers shall diligently see that the soldiers ply their worke, when they are commanded so to doe: he that neglects his duty therein, shalbe punished according to the discretion of the Court.

129. A punishment in which the culprit was forced to sit for an extended period straddling a narrow board suspended above ground (sometimes elaborately designed to resemble a wooden horse), so that his feet dangled below him. Serious injuries could occur.

48. All soldiours ought duely to honor and obey their Officers; and especially, being by them commanded upon our service: but if at any time they can on the contrary discover, that they are commanded upon a service which is to our prejudice any manner of way: then shall that soldiour not obey him, what charge soever he receives from him: but presently give notice of it.

49. No Colonell nor Captaine shall command his soldiours to doe any unlawfull thing: which who so does, shalbe punisht according to the discretion of the Judges. Also, if any Colonell or Captaine, or other Officer whatsoever, shall by rigor take any thing away from any common soldiour, hee shall answer for it before the Court. . . .

51. No man shall presume to make any Alarme in the Quarter, or to shoot off his Musket in the night time, upon paine of Death.

52. He that when warning is given for the setting of the watch by sound of Drumme, Fife, or Trumpet, shall wilfully absent himselfe without some lawfull excuse; shall be punisht with the woodden Horse, and be put to Bread and Water, or other pennance, as the matter is of importance.

53. He that is taken sleeper upon the watch, either in any strength,[130] Trench, or the like; shall be shot to Death.

54. He that comes off his watch where he is commanded to keepe his Guard; or drinkes himselfe drunke upon his watch, or place of Sentinell, shalbe shot to Death. . . .

56. When any march is to be made, every man that is sworne shall follow his Colours: who ever presumes without leave to stay behind, shall bee punisht.

57. And if it be upon mutiny that they doe it, be they many, or be they few; they shall die for it. . . .

60. He that runnes from his Colours in the field, shall die for it: and if any of his Comrades kill him in the meane time, hee shall be free.[131] . . .

62. And if the thing be occasioned by any Officer; hee shall bee publikely disgraced for it, and then turnd out of the Leaguer.

63. But if both Officers and Soldiers be found faulty alike; then shall the Officers be punished as aforesaid: If it be in the Souldiers alone, then shall every tenth man be hanged: The rest shal be condemned to carry all the filth out of the Leaguer, untill such time as they performe some exploit, that is worthy to procure their pardon: after which time they shall be cleere of the former disgrace. But if at the first, any man can by the testimonie of ten men prove himselfe not guilty of the Cowardise, he shall goe free. . . .

130. A fortification.

131. In other words, there is no punishment for killing a deserter.

65. If any occasion be to enter any Castle, Towne, or Sconce[132] by assault or breach, he who retyres from the place before he hath beene at handy-blowes with the enemy and hath used his sword, so farre as it is possible for him to doe service with it & before he be by maine strength beaten off by the enemy shalbe so punisht as the Court shall censure him. . . .

68. Whatsoever Regiment, Troope, or Company refuses to advance forward to charge the Enemie: but out of feare and cowardise stayes behind their fellowes, shalbe punisht, as before. . . .

70. Whatsoever Regiment, Troope, or Company, shall treate with the Enemie, or enter into any conditions with them whatsoever, (without our leave, or our Generalls, or chiefe Commander in his absence) whatsoever officer shall doe the same, shalbe put to death for it, and all his goods shalbe confiscated. Of the Soldiers every tenth man shalbe hanged; and the rest punished, as is aforesaid. . . .

81. Every man shalbe contented with that Quarter that shalbe given him, either in the towne or Leaguer: the contrary doer, to be reckoned for a mutinier.

82. Who ever flings away his Armes, either in the Field or other where; shalbe scourged through the Quarter; and then be lodged without it: be enforced to make the streets cleane: until they redeeme themselves by some worthy exploit doing.

83. He that sells or empawnes his Armes, or any kind of Ammunition whatsoever; or any hatchets, spades, shovells, pickaxes, or other the like necessary implements used in the Field; shalbe for the first and second time, beaten through the quarter: and for the third time punisht, as for other theft. He also that buyes or takes them upon pawne, be he soldiour, or be he victualler: he shall first loose his money, and then be punished like him that sold them. . . .

88. He that forces any Woman to abuse her;[133] and the matter be proved, he shall dye for it.

89. No Whore shall be suffered in the Leaguer: but if any will have his owne wife with him, he may. If any unmaried woman be found, he that keepes her may have leave lawfully to marry her; or els be forced to put her away.

90. No man shall presume to set fire on any Towne or Village in our land: If any does, he shall be punisht according to the importancy of the matter, so as the Judges shall sentence him.

132. Fortification.
133. Rapes a woman.

91. No Soldiour shall set fire upon any Towne or Village in the enemies land; without he be commanded by his Captaine. Neither shall any Captaine give any such command, unlesse hee hath first received it from Us, or our Generall: who so does the contrary, he shall answer it in the Generals counsayle of Warre, according to the importance of the matter. And if it be proved to be prejudiciall unto us, and advantageous for the enemie; he shall suffer death for it.

92. No soldier shall pillage any thing from our subjects upon any march, strength, leaguer, or otherwise howsoever, upon paine of death.

93. He that beates his Host[134] or his houshold servants, the first and second time he shalbe put in Irons, and made to fast with bread and water, according as the wrong is that he hath done: if the harme be great hee shall bee punisht thereafter, according to the discretion of the Court.

94. None shall presume to doe wrong to any that bring necessaries into our Leaguer, Castle, or strength whatsoever, or to cast their goods downe off their horses, and take away their horses perforce: which who so does, shall die for it.

95. They that pillage or steale eyther in our land or in the enemies, or from any of them that come to furnish our Leaguer or strength, without leave; shalbe punisht as for other theft.

96. If it so pleases God that we beate the enemy, eyther in the field, or in his Leaguer, then shall every man follow the chace of the enemies, and no man give himselfe to fall upon the pillage, so long as it is possible to follow the Enemy, and untill such time as he be assuredly beaten. Which done, then may their quarters be fallen upon, every man taking what he findeth his owne quarter. Neyther shall any man fall to plunder one anothers quarters, but rest himselfe contented with that which is assigned him.

97. If any man gives himselfe to fall upon the pillage, before leave be given him so to doe, then may any of his Officers freely kill him. Moreover, if any misfortune ensue upon their greedinesse after the spoyle, then shall all of them suffer death for it. And notwithstanding there comes no damage thereupon, yet shall they lye in Irons for one Moneth, living all that while upon bread and water: giving all the pillage so gotten, unto the next hospitall. He that plunders another quarter, shall also have the same punishment.

98. When any Fort or place of strength is taken in, no man shall fall upon the spoyle, before that all the places in which the enemy is there lodged, be also taken in, and that the soldiers and Burgers have layd downe their Armes, and that the quarters be dealt out and assigned to every body. Who so does the contrary, shall be punished as before.

---

134. The person in whose house he has been lodged.

99. No man shall presume to pillage any Church or Hospitall, although the strength be taken by assault, except hee bee first commanded; or that the soldiers and Burgers be fled thereinto and doe harme from thence. Who does the contrary, shall be punished as aforesaid.

100. No man shall set fire upon any Church, Hospitall, Schoole, or Mill, or spoyle them any way, except hee bee commanded. Neyther shall any tyrannize over any Churchman, or aged people, Men or Women, Maydes or Children, unlesse they first take Armes against them, under paine of punishment at the discretion of the Judges.

101. If any soldier happens to get freeboot, in any Castle, City, Towne, Fort, strength, or Leaguer; and moreover, whatsoever Ordnance, Munition for warre, & victuals is found there, shall be left for Our use; the rest shall be the Soldiours: onely the tenth part therof, shall they give to the sicke and maymed Soldiours in the hospitals. All prisoners shall first be presented unto Us; amongst which if there be any man of note, whom We desire to have unto Our selves; we promise in lieu thereof, honestly to recompence the taker of him, according to the quality of the person. Other prisoners of inferior ranke, may the takers keepe unto themselves; whom by Our leave or Our Generals, they may put to their ransome, and take it to themselves: but without leave they may not ransome them, upon paine of death.

102. If any be found drunken in the enemies Leaguer, Castle or Towne, before the enemy hath wholly yeilded himselfe up to our mercy, and laide downe his armes; whosoever shall kill the said drunken Soldiour shall be free for it: always provided, that good proofe be brought that he was drunken. And if that soldiour escapes for that time with his life, and that it can appeare that some damage or hinderance hath come unto Our Service, by his drunkennesse; then wheresoever he be apprehended, he shall die for it. But if no hurt ensued thereof; yet shall he be put in Irons for the space of one month, living upon his pittance of bread and water. . . .

111. If any soldiour Our native Subjects desires to be discharged from the warres, he shall give notice therof unto the Mustermaisters; who, if they find him to be sicke, or maimed, or that he hath served 20. yeares in our warres; or hath beene tenne severall times[135] before the enemy; and can bring good witnesse thereof; he shall be discharged. . . .

117. If upon necessity the case sometimes so falls out in the leaguer, that Pay be not alwayes made at the due time mentioned in the Commissions; yet shall every man in the meane time be willing to further Our service; seeing they have victuals sufficient for the present: and that they shall so soone as may be receive the rest of their meanes, as is mentioned in their Commission.

135. Many times.

118. Very requisite it is, that good Justice be holden amongst our Soldiers, as well as amongst other our subjects.

119. For the same reason was a King ordained by God, to be the soveraigne Judge in the Field, as well as at home.

120. Now therefore, in respect of many occasions which may fall out, his single Judgment alone may be to weake to discerne every particular circumstance; therfore it is requisite, that in the leaguer as well as other where, there be some Court of Justice erected, for the deciding of all controversies: and to be carefull in like manner, that Our Articles of warres be of all persons observed and obeyed, so farre forth as is possible.

121. Wee ordeine therefore, that there be 2. Courts in our leaguer, an Higher Court, and a Lower.

122. The Lower Court shall be among the Regiments both of Horse and Foote; whereof every Regiment shall have one among themselves. . . .

125. In our Highest Martiall Court, shall Our Generall be President: in his absence, Our Field Marshall. When Our Generall is present, his Associates shall be, our Field-Marshall first, next him. Our Generall of the Ordnance, Sergeant-Maior generall, Generall of the Horse, Quarter-Maister generall. Next to them shall sit Our Muster-Masters, and all Our Colonels; and in their absence, their Leiftenant-Colonels. All these shall sit togither, whenever there is any matter of greater importance in controversie. . . .

127. All these Judges both of our Higher and lower Courts, shall under the blew Skies thus sweare before Almighty God, that they will inviolably keepe this following Oath unto Us. I N. N. doe here promise before God upon his holy Gospell, that I both will and shall Judge uprightly in all things according to the Law of God, of the Swedens, and these Articles of warres; so farre forth as it pleases Almighty God to give mee understanding. Neyther will I for favour or for hatred, for goodwill, feare, ill will, anger, or any guift or bribe whatsoever, judge wrongfully: but judge him free, that ought to bee free, and doome him guilty, that I finde guilty; as the Lord of Heaven and Earth shall helpe my Soule and Body at the last day, I shall hold this Oath truly. . . .

133. Our highest Court shall be carefull also to heare and Judge all criminall actions: and especially, cases of Conspiracie or Treason practised or plotted against us, either in word or deed. Secondly, If any gives out dishonourable speeches against our Majesty. Thirdly, or consulteth with the Enemy to betray our Leaguer, Castle, Towne, Souldiers, Fleete, any way whatsoever. Fourthly, Also if any there bee partakers of such Treachery, and reveale it not. Fiftly, or any that hath held correspondency and intelligence with the Enemy. Sixtly, If any hath a spite or malice against us or our Country. Seaventhly, if any speakes disgracefully, eyther of our person or endeav-

ours. Eightly, if lastly intendeth treachery against our Generall, or his under-Officers, or that speaketh disgracefully of them. . . .

138. Any Criminall action that is adjudged in our lower Court, wee command that the sentence bee presented unto our Generall. Wee will not have it presently put in execution, untill hee gives command for it in our absence. But Our selves being in person there present, will first take notice of it, and dispose afterwards of it, as wee shall thinke expedient. . . .

149. Whosoever is minded to serve Us in these warres, shall be obliged to the keeping of these Articles. If any out of presumption, upon any Strength, in any Leaguer, in the Feild, or upon any Worke shall doe the contrary; be he native, or be he Stranger, Gentleman or other: Processe shall be made out against him for every time, so long as he serves Us in these warres, in the quality of a soldiour.

150. These Articles of warres wee have made and ordeined, for the welfare of our native Country: and doe commaund, that they be reade every month publikely before every Regiment: to the end, that no man shall pretend ignorance. Wee further will and commaund all whatsoever officers, higher and lower, and all our common soldiours; and all other that come into our Leaguer among the Soldiours; that none presume to doe the contrary hereof, upon paine of rebellion, and the incurring of our high displeasure. For the firmer confirmation whereof, we have hereunto set Our hand and Seale.

Signed, Gustavus Adolphus

These above written Articles, are the standing and generall Orders and Politie, whereby his Majesties Army is directed. They were in use, I perceive Anno 1621. when He went to conquer Riga in Leiffland: for I finde them written in a Journall book of that expedition, by a Scottish Gentleman then in that service: the copy whereof was communicated unto me, by the Right Honorable the Lord Reay: which I have since also compared with another Copy. To these, upon occasion hath his Majesty sometimes made addition of some others; as the last yeare, 1631. he did: when upon the unrulinesse of his soldiours in the New Marke of Brandenburg (of which his Majesty, as wee told you in our former booke, much complained) He caused these new Articles to be published, which I find in the booke called *Arma Suecica.*

1. No Soldiour shall abuse any Churches, Colledges, Schooles, or Hospitals, or offer any kind of violence to Ecclesiasticall persons nor any wayes be troublesome with pitching or enquartering, upon them: or with exacting of contribution, from them. No soldiour shall give disturbance or offence to any person excercising his sacred function, or ministery; upon payne of death.

2. Let the Billets and Lodging in every City, be assigned to the soldiours by the Burgo-maisters; and let noe Commaunder presume to meddle with that office. No Commaunder or Common soldiour shall eyther exact or receive of the Citizens, any thing besides what the King hath appointed to be received.

3. No Citizens nor Countrey Boores[136] shall be bound to allow unto eyther soldiour or officer, any thing but what is contained in the Kings orders for Contributions & Enquarterings, that is to say, nothing besides House-roome, fire-wood, candles, vineger and salt: which yet is so to be understood, that the inferior officers, as Sergeants and Corporals, and those under them, as also all common soldiours; shall make shift with the common fire and candle of the house where they lie, and doe their businesse by them. . . .

8. Nothing is to be allowed the soldiours in any house, but in the same where he is billetted: if they take any thing otherwhere by force, they are to make it good.

9. If eyther officers, soldiours, or Sutlers, be to travaile thorough any Country; the people are not to furnish them with wagons, Post-horse, or victuals, but for their ready money, unlesse they bring a warrant, eyther from the King, or theyr Generall.

10. No Soldiour is to forsake his Colours, and to put himselfe into entertainement under any other Colonell or Garrison, or to ramble about the Country, without he hath his Colonels passe, or his that is in his steade: who so does; it shall be lawfull for the Boores or any other to apprehend him, and to send him prisoner to Stetin,[137] or the next garrison of the Kings: where he shall be examined, and punished accordingly.

11. Whosoever have any lawfull Passes, ought by no meanes to abuse the benefit of them; or practise any cheates under pretence of them. If any be found with any pilfery, or to have taken any mans cattell or goods: it shall be lawfull for the Country people to lay hands upon them; and to bring them to Stetin or other the next garrison: speciall care being allwayes had, that if the prisoner hath any letters of moment about him, they be speedily and safely delivered. . . .

13. The houses of the Princes or nobility, which have no neede to borrow our guard to defend them from the enemy, shall not be pressed with soldiours.

---

136. Peasant farmers.

137. A city in western Pomerania that was taken and fortified by the Swedes soon after their arrival in the empire. Now Szczecin, Poland.

14. Moreover, under a great Penalty it is provided, that neyther officers nor soldiers, shall make stay of, or arrest, the Princes Commissaries or Officers, or any Gentlemen, Councellors of state, Senators or Burgers of any Cities, or other Country people; nor shall give offence to them by any fact of violence.

15. Travailers or other Passengers going about their businesse into any garrisons or places of muster; shall by no meanes bee stayed, injured, or have any contribution laide upon them.

16. Our Commaunders shall defend the Countrey people and ploughmen that follow their husbandries, and shall suffer none to hinder them in it. . . .

19. Whatsoever is not conteined in these Articles, and is repugnant to Military discipline; or wherby the miserable and innocent Country, may against all right and reason be burdened withall: whatsoever offence finally, shalbe committed against these Orders; that shall the severall Commaunders make good, or see severally punished; unlesse themselves will stand bound to give further satisfaction for it.

20. According to these Articles, let every man governe his businesse and actions and learne by them to take heede, of comming into the lurch or danger.

> Signed in our Leaguer Royall, Anno, 1632.
> Gustavus Adolphus.

20. Memorandum of Hoë von Hoënegg (January 30, 1634)[138]

[On April 23, 1633, princes from the Rhenish, Swabian, and Franconian imperial circles joined together under the leadership of Sweden and France to form the Heilbronn League, which was designed to defend the German Liberties and to fight to regain Protestant territories from the imperialists. The elector of Saxony, however, refused to join the league and, although remaining an official ally of Sweden, spent a great deal of time in separate peace negotiations with General Wallenstein. In preparation for further discussions in 1634, the elector asked his court preacher, the Lutheran theologian Matthias Hoë von

138. Matthias Hoë von Hoënegg memorandum (own hand copy), Loc. 8113 1, Buch, fol. 43–9, another copy fol. 50–9, in Katherin Bierther, ed., *Die Politik Maximilians I. von Bayern und seiner Verbündeten 1618-1651*, T. 2, Bd. 10, *Der Präger Frieden von 1635*, T. 2 *Korrespondenzen* (Munich and Vienna: Oldenbourg, 1997), 403–9.

Hoënegg (1580–1645), to provide his opinion on the religious implications of possible peace terms. Hoë von Hoënegg is famous for his fervent hatred of Calvinism, but after the 1629 Edict of Restitution, he had begun to argue that the Habsburgs were an even greater threat, and so Protestants needed to unite to defeat their common Catholic enemy. His militant inflexibility toward compromise with the Catholics can be seen below, for Hoë von Hoënegg advised the elector that there should be no concessions at all in religious matters, even in the case of seeming catastrophic military defeat, for God's hand would influence the ultimate outcome of events. Such religious justification for continued war and inflexibility in peace negotiations influenced many political leaders of the time, Protestants and Catholics alike.]

In the name of Jesus.

I have understood Your Serene Electoral Highness of Saxony's gracious request, as it was presented to me by my lords the privy councilors, for there has now, once again, appeared a means to promote and obtain a Christian, good, and secure universal peace. And I recall the kinds of points that were previously drawn up and proposed to our opponents, which would yield the desired satisfaction in both religious and secular matters for Evangelicals[139] and Protestants. However, I sincerely advise His Princely Grace the landgrave George of Hesse,[140] as well as His Excellency the lieutenant general,[141] to contrive the points in such a way that they would not be far too hard, lest the opponents be forced to upset the entire negotiations right at the beginning, preferring to do everything in the world rather than agree amicably to such intolerable things.

So I shall once again reexamine the points and unhesitatingly disclose my Christian theological considerations on how far one could, in the most extreme case, yield and step back in one and another point without damage to the conscience, giving complete advice on how extremely necessary it would be to bring back the noble peace and, failing this, how impossible it would be for Your Serene Electoral Highness to conduct and continue the war any longer out of your own pocket.

Although I now acknowledge that, by Your Serene Electoral Highness' gracious order, I am responsible most humbly to obey and especially to inform your scruples and conscience (which have currently been committed

---

139. Lutherans.

140. Landgrave George of Hesse-Darmstadt (1605–1661) was the elector of Saxony's son-in-law and close ally, and was leading the negotiations with the imperialists.

141. Hans Georg von Arnim-Boitzenburg (1583–1641), the elector of Saxony's field marshal.

and entrusted to me, though without my being worthy), yet I find this work to be of such splendid, high, and great importance that I would wish most fervently and ask most humbly that Your Serene Electoral Highness would deign to hear from further religious scholars, pure and zealous theologians, on this matter, so that no presumptuousness would be attributed to me in the future, as if I dared to take upon myself alone such an extremely great matter. For I would much, much prefer and wish from my heart to be relieved of this, rather than participate in it. Because of the most humble respect that I bear for Your Serene Electoral Highness, however, and because of my present office, for which I am unworthy, I shall reveal my thoughts, though they are entirely unassuming and non-authoritative, and I most humbly ask that Your Serene Electoral Highness will graciously deign to take note of them.

To begin with, it is holy and right that Your Serene Electoral Highness is desirous and ready for peace. That is the sign of a true child of God. Blessed are the peacemakers: for they shall be called the children of God, says the Lord Jesus Himself (Matt. 5:9). The pious king Hezekiah wished, from the depths of his soul, that there would be only peace and truth in his days (2 Kings 20:19). And God said, pursue peace (2 Tim. 2:22, 1 Pet. 3:11). To the counselors of peace is joy (Prov. 12:20). During your entire, lengthy electoral reign, Your Serene Electoral Highness has been no disturber of the peace; you never bore a desire for discord and disquiet; you warned unutterably often of the emerging destruction of the empire, foresaw and prophesied all of the misfortune that followed, and diligently prayed that the emperor and the Catholic League would not let it come to this. On your part, you were forced against your will to take up arms and were pulled by your hair into the war. You had as legitimate a cause for war as ever did Abraham or David or anyone else, because in return for the greatest loyalty and good deeds, Your Serene Electoral Highness was shown the most extreme ingratitude and disloyalty. And one can read of no similar example of a Christian potentate being shown such inequity to such a great degree by those whom he had so powerfully served with the sacrifice of life and limb, property and blood, land and people, as has befallen our most laudable elector, whom they can thank, next to God alone, that they either gained or recovered their crowns and scepters, their kingdoms and lands. Yet they now seek to eradicate and exterminate His Serene Electoral Highness and his entire electoral house. God, who is just, has already handsomely punished this universally known disloyalty, in part, but He will also punish it in the future with eternal hellfire.

It redounds to the immortal fame of Your Serene Electoral Highness that you have given not the slightest cause for the general discord in Germany, but it is also most praiseworthy that during the still-ongoing war you have allowed your readiness for peace to come to light. And if Your Serene Electoral Highness wishes to get involved in peace negotiations, I have no doubt, according to your various previous Christian declarations, that you will endeavor to conclude a general, reputable, secure, and God-pleasing peace.

The bloody war has cost the Evangelicals many millions in gold, the war has cost them their land and people; it has cost many thousands of people, who have perished by the sword, pestilence, hunger, frost, affliction, anguish, and hardship. Thus it would be forever a shame and unjustifiable if one should or would now, benevolently or willfully, surrender something from the true Church of God that could still be preserved for its benefit.

God handsomely chastened the arrogant Babylonian whore and, per His word (Rev. 17:16),[142] stripped her naked. He is eternally to thank for this, and no Evangelical Christian, of whatever rank he might be, can in good conscience aid the great whore, as she is called by the Holy Spirit—the Roman anti-Christian papacy[143]—so that she might once again acquire her previous clothes, pride, splendor, and wantonness. And it is the just, holy people of God, here and there, who have previously helped to disrobe the Babylonian whore and have brought about this result through their valor and Christian zeal. May blessings and mercy cover them all from eternity to eternity.

God should be asked with penitent hearts that He graciously protect Your Serene Electoral Highness from the cunning snakes, the papists, with whom you must negotiate, so that you are not further deceived by them. . . .

The Almighty, who is to be praised and thanked for it, has until now conferred such good luck, well-being, grace, victory, and blessings on His people—and especially on the most praiseworthy House of Saxony and its fellow religionists and military allies—that one justly has cause to exert every possible human diligence so that the proposed salutary peace is a peace imposed on the enemy, rather than one gained from the enemy by request. Therefore for the impending peace negotiations Your Serene Electoral Highness has cause to call upon your Lord and God to preserve the heroic, joyful, unflinching valor that you have displayed up to now, and not to allow you to be moved to faintheartedness by the boasting and defiance of the enemy, so that what has fortunately been constructed up to now will not be torn down once again.

---

142. "And the ten horns that thou sawest upon the beast, these shall hate the whore, and shall make her desolate and naked, and shall eat her flesh, and burn her with fire" (Rev. 17:16).

143. Protestants in this period regularly referred to the Catholic Church or the pope as the great whore of Babylon.

God, who previously put a hook in the nose of the papist Sennacherib[144] and a bridle in his mouth (Isa. 37:29)[145] can do so still. And although there appears to human eyes to be no possibility to confront the powerful braggart further, yet God can find a thousand ways to make it possible. His reach remains uncurtailed. If Your Serene Electoral Highness does not abandon your God, in return He will also certainly not abandon you. Just as He has been with you up to now, so He can and will also be with you in the future. And this is something one can hope for all the sooner and more when good, loyal consistency with your military allies, whose handiwork God has also powerfully blessed up to now, is continued—at least until, through the cooperation of both sides, the good, predetermined objective is attained.

In no way, however, do I wish to suggest by all of this that Your Serene Electoral Highness could not, in good conscience, allow any negotiations of the peace, nor any dealings with the enemy. That would be far from my intent. Instead, my only aim is that Your Serene Electoral Highness be assured of the correct foundation of such negotiations, that they are securely based and allow no fear of deception, and that one knows what kind of peace one should negotiate and how joyful and unabashed one should remain when things turn out just as God wishes. For if the time and hour appointed by the Lord for the return of the golden peace have not yet arrived,[146] everything that men do or intend in this case is to no purpose. And should someone act precipitously and let himself have a peace that was distasteful to God, he not only would gain discord in his heart and conscience over it, but would also have to fear and expect greater discord from God, instead of the temporal peace he had desired. . . .

I know quite well that some secular people, and especially military people, do not think much of such theological opinions. Yet these will be proclaimed. For a theologian cannot fail to speak and judge affairs according to similar things from the Holy Book.

Concerning the above-mentioned points, I recall that these were partially communicated two years ago at Torgau,[147] and partially communicated here

144. The king of Assyria (c. 745–681 BC) who attacked the rebellious Judah and besieged Jerusalem. Here, Hoë von Hoënegg equates this historical king with the current pope by calling him a "papist."

145. "Because thy rage against me, and thy tumult, is come up into mine ears, therefore will I put my hook in thy nose, and my bridle in thy lips, and I will turn thee back by the way by which thou camest" (Isa. 37:29).

146. In the margin, Hoë von Hoënegg writes: "'Peace has its time' (Eccles. 3:8)." He is referring to the passage: "A time to love, and a time to hate; a time of war, and a time of peace."

147. A town in Saxony where the elector of Saxony and the elector of Brandenburg

to me (unworthily) a year ago;[148] and both times I advised on one and another point in writing, most humbly and completely non-authoritatively, according to my knowledge and conscience.

These points were composed most intelligently and most rationally, thoroughly deliberated, and so constructed according to the opportunity of that time and that circumstance, that I think one should now propose much bolder and more virile points to the opposition, and not retreat from them so easily and soon. For although some of these points might seem to them to be very unjust, yet the iniquities and oppressions inflicted by them against the Evangelical electors, princes, and estates have been thousands and tens of thousands of times greater than those incited against them by this side. And should all things be treated equally, one would certainly not insist that something unjust be demanded of them. They might consider, however, whether even more might not be wrung from them by our Lord and God through means that are pleasing to Him.

For now, I have obtained only the first nine points for my reexamination. . . . so I cannot deliver the entirety of my report. I will, however, disclose my simple thoughts one way or another on those points that have presently been transcribed.

Concerning the first point [which grants Protestants all territories they held as of January 1, 1612],[149] I really do not know that one could mitigate or compromise on its contents in good conscience. I would very much prefer that the words: "or to those who gained possession [of these lands] since then [1552] through election and request" be replaced with these words: "through election, request, or in another way" (certainly by right of combat), so that those archbishoprics and other dioceses that were captured since [1552] would not have to be offered back right away and voluntarily evacuated. As for the marginalia,[150] however, in my humble opinion this would be more damaging than beneficial to the essence of the religion, and can only be seen as benefiting the damned Calvinists.[151]

---

met in 1632 to discuss their thoughts on the terms they would expect and require for a peace.

148. In January 1633 the elector of Brandenburg, the landgrave of Hesse-Darmstadt, and the elector of Saxony all sent delegates to meet with the imperialists for peace negotiations. At that point, however, the imperialists were unwilling to modify their demands enough to suit the Protestants.

149. This would cement Lutheran territorial gains since the 1555 Peace of Augsburg.

150. Suggestions about this point that were written in the margins.

151. The elector of Brandenburg and other Calvinists objected to a cutoff date of

To concede anything in the second point [which gives Protestant princes legal rights in the empire because of the Catholic lands they had seized since 1552] would only make the peace doubtful and uncertain. . . .

The third point [which protects Protestant worship in Catholic territories where it had previously been allowed] is the proper core of a peace that is Christian, God-pleasing, and beneficial to the true Church. Posterity will learn from this how zealously those in the praiseworthy privy council of electoral Saxony have concerned themselves with the honor of God and the maintenance of the pure, divine, Evangelical doctrine. . . .

It is a matter for mature consideration and contemplation whether one should not include those places where the Evangelical doctrine was introduced and taught during the ongoing common war, so that in the future the same should be left to them, unhindered alongside the papists, and they should be allowed the free exercise of our true religion, unperturbed, forever. For it is said, the gates open wide to the king of glory (Ps. 24). That is, expand the kingdom of God and spread His holy word.

The fourth point [which grants to Protestant princes any Catholic property or goods within their borders] appears to be completely political. It proceeds by logical consequence, however, to concern very much the advantage of the Church, and probably several of the Evangelical estates of the empire will not disregard it so easily. Also, by rights, the papists should not forcefully refuse to accept such a point, because in one hundred and more years, the many Evangelical estates could not expect to gain as much benefit from such goods as what they have already suffered from the war damage caused and extorted by the anti-Christian Papist League.[152] Time and negotiations will tell, however, whether to moderate this point without fail, such that a distinction is made between that which the Evangelicals have, up to now, honestly gained possession of by right of combat and by spilling their own Christian blood, and that which is still in the hands and in the power of the papists; or whether, when otherwise we gain good satisfaction in other essential points, this fourth issue could be entirely left out of the ongoing negotiations.

Concerning the fifth, sixth, seventh, eighth, and ninth points: if one wishes to conclude and erect a fair, reputable, genuine, abiding, eternal, and secure peace that is conducive to the true Evangelical Church and doctrine, one can give way on nothing for each and every one of the said points. Should one be forced by means of a greater power[153] (God forbid) to tolerate and suffer

---

1612, since many Calvinist territorial gains occurred after that date—and at the expense of the Lutherans.

152. The Catholic League of princes who supported the emperor.

153. In other words, in case of a military victory by the Catholics.

something else, yet a God-loving, conscientious, and Christian potentate or his loyal councilors cannot, without offense to the conscience, condone something repugnant and empower it with their consent and agreement.

In the year 1555, the Evangelicals could not prevent the Ecclesiastical Reservation[154] from being inserted into the Religious Peace.[155] To save their consciences, however, they strongly protested against it again and again, as imperial records demonstrate. And should one allow oneself to be overcome by the papists on this point, it would then have been a thousand times better if one had never wielded a sword than for one to have waged a war, justly and with good conscience, for the honor and doctrine of the Lord. . . .

All of which I have, as commanded, most humbly advised and suggested in haste, praying to the Almighty daily from my heart and wishing that He establish and grant divine courage, good advice, and just deeds to the entire proposed work; that He lead the directors of the same through His Holy Ghost; and that He turn everything so that His name is hallowed, His empire expanded, His most holy of wills is given the greatest observance and fulfilled, many thousands of souls are both given the golden freedom of conscience and helped to eternal salvation and blessedness, and that our gracious lord's Christian diligence and effort is rewarded with millions of heavenly blessings and many thousands of good deeds. Amen, amen.

Dresden, January 20/30, 1634

21. The Assassination of General Wallenstein (February 25, 1634)[156]

[Wallenstein's enormous and unchecked power in the empire led to increasing complaints and bitterness among the other princes. After the death of Gustavus Adolphus in November 1632, Wallenstein also became increasingly arrogant, signing unauthorized armistices and undertaking independent negotiations

---

154. The stipulation that any ecclesiastic who converted to Protestantism must renounce and lose his territories, which would thus remain Catholic. The 1629 Edict of Restitution (see Document 14) was issued by the emperor principally to regain those territories in which the Protestants had disregarded this Ecclesiastical Reservation.

155. The Peace of Augsburg.

156. *The Relation Of the death of that great Generaliſimo (of his Imperiall Majesie) the Duke of Meckleburg, Fridland, Sagan, and great Glogaw, &c. Together with the cause thereof . . . Printed by Tho. Harper, for Nathaniel Butter and Nicholas Bourne, 1634* (Tho. Harper, 1634). A copy can be found at the University of Illinois, Urbana-Champaign.

with the Saxons, among others. By the beginning of 1634, the emperor had begun to plot secretly to have Wallenstein removed, arranging the matter with some of Wallenstein's closest officers. Then, in February 1634, the emperor is-sued a public order that Wallenstein was henceforth deposed and a traitor. The emperor's own son, Ferdinand, king of Hungary, was to take Wallenstein's place as head of the imperial armies, with Count Matthias Gallas[157] *as his second. As the emperor had hoped, Wallenstein's leading generals abandoned him, as did most of his army. Wallenstein then fled to Eger in Bohemia, where he planned to join up with contingents from the Swedes (under the command of Bernard of Saxe-Weimar) and Saxons (under the command of Arnim)*[158] *and turn against the emperor. What Wallenstein did not expect, however, was that some of his own officers had conspired to kill him. The following ac-counts of the assassination of Wallenstein and some of his few remaining loyal officers appeared in an English broadsheet that was published soon afterward in London.]*

The True Relation of the Duke of Fridlands death, and the Cause thereof.

What Reputation Albert Duke of Fridland (commonly called Wallenstein, which is the name of his Family) hath acquired in the possession of armes, during these long and yet lasting warres in Germany, is knowne to all men; and with what a lamentable end all his actions have lately beene concluded, We do here present unto the Reader, without any alteration or addition, onely as wee have received the same, and translated out of Germane and other letters. . . .

From Ratisbone[159] Letters written the 20. of February old stile,[160] doe say thus much;

Although the Duke of Friedland (having full knowledge that both himselfe and the Earles of Tertzky and Kinsky,[161] and others had beene declared

---

157. Matthias Gallas (1584–1647), an imperial officer under Wallenstein and a party in the secret conspiracy to unseat him. Gallas later took supreme command of Wallenstein's army.

158. Hans Georg von Arnim-Boitzenburg (1583–1641).

159. Regensburg.

160. According to the old Julian calendar. By the new Gregorian calendar, this was March 2, 1634.

161. Wallenstein's loyal officers Adam Erdman Trčka (1599–1634) and Wilhelm Kinsky (1574–1634).

Rebeles) had by many severall Letters written by the Fieldmarshall Llaw[162] from Egra, visited and advised Duke Bernhard of Saxen, and with many particular circumstances and instances prayd him, to march and come without delay with his troupes in good order, to joyne with him against the Emperour: and although Duke Bernhard was informed that over all Austria the Emperour had caused Patents to bee published and Proclamations made, whereby the Duke of Friedland, with all his Complices were declared to bee Rebels and enemies to the Emperour, and commanded to be persecuted by the sword and all possible hostilitie; and also that a young Lord Walstein and divers superior Officers with him, had been taken prisoners at Lintz: Yet neverthelesse the said Duke Bernhard remembring how often, and how many the Duke of Friedland had formerly deceived, would never trust, but drew onely such troupes of his as he thought best for his turne together, and kept them in good order, fashion and readinesse for any opportunitie and service; untill on the 20. day of February old stile, he did receive the true and horrible advise, that Collonel Lieutenant Gorden[163] (who commanded at Egra) having received commandement from the Emperor, to bring or send the Duke of Friedland either alive or dead to Vienna. There on Saturday last when the principall Officers were together at supper in the Castle, were most cruelly slaine (with muskets and otherwise) the Field-Marshall Llaw, the Earle of Tertzky, the Earle of Kinsky, Collonel Newman[164] and some other persons: & that from thence the said Lieutenant Gordon did runne downe into the Duke of Friedlands lodging (being the house of Alexander Bacholm) and having taken a partisan out of the hands of one of the Guard, he went into the Chamber, and therewith thrust the Duke through his body, saying to him, Thus shall dye all that doe rebell against the Emperour. And afterwards caused the bloudie body of the Duke to bee drayled downe the staires, cast upon a dung cart, and be carried up to the other corpses.

At that very time Duke Henry Tules of Saxen Lawenburg was without the Towne with Friedlands troopes, otherwise hee should (without doubt) have beene forced to drinke the same health at supper: And there is now a great distrust and dissention amongst the troopes, some being called Imperialists, and others Friedlandists.

162. Wallenstein's loyal officer Christian von Llow (1585–1634), imperial field marshal.

163. John Gorden (d. 1649) was an imperial colonel and a Scottish Calvinist. He served as commander of the fortress of Eger and was loyal to the emperor, not to Wallenstein.

164. Wallenstein's loyal cavalry captain, Neumann.

The next day (being Sunday, and the 16/26 of February) Duke Francis Albert[165] passed from Weyden towards Egra, and being come halfe league beyond Turshenried, hee found himselfe assaulted by a troope of Crabats and Dragons,[166] who tooke all from him and from his men, and carried him prisoner to Egra, as a Page of his related who by flight did escape.

On the 19. of February Duke Bernhard of Saxen parted with his forces from Ratisbone towards Weyden or Bohemia, and it is hoped, that such troopes as remaine Friedlandish, and intend to revenge their Generalissimo's death, will willingly joyne with him.

BY OTHER LETTERS WRITTEN BOTH FROM WEYDEN AND FROM EGRA, OF THE 20 AND 21 OF FEBRUARY OLD STILE, THE FORE-SAYD THINGS ARE AVERRED IN THIS MANNER.

The Duke of Friedlands death and execution happened in this sort. The Duke being arrived at Egra with about 800. men, he did lodge them in the Villages, and himselfe, being fetched and conducted by Collonel Butler, (a man of whom as likewise of Collonel Lieutenant Gordon, Friedland had not the least suspition of any ill will) went into the Towne: There the Earle of Tertzky, the Earle of Kinsky, Marshall Lllaw, and Collonel Newman were invited, and very willingly went up into the Castle; and being on their way, as also againe at the table, there was some speech amongst them of the last conclusion and resolution taken and signed at Pilsen. Now when they sate merry at supper, and when the day was spent that it was somewhat darke, ther was commanded & brought into the parlour or stove, a company of Dragons, who with their muskets, shot and slew without any more adoe the said foure Lords: And from thence they speedily were led downe to Friedlands lodging, and there killed before the house the Guard, a Page, and one that waited on the Duke in his Chamber: At the noyse the Duke opened the doore, and there the Commander Gordon thrust him presently through the bodie: And when the Duke, being by such a salutation roused to looke and reach for his sword, thought to defend himself, he gave him two other thrusts through, So that the Duke fell to the ground in his blood; And then they lapped him in a coverlet, and so drew him down the staires, to be carried up into the Castle to the other bodies: there was found much wealth in his lodging.

On the 19/29 of February at evening, Francis Albert of Saxen-Lawenburg, was carried with 9 dead corpses, accompanied with a strong convoy from Egra towards Pilsen. The said Duke made offer of 2000 dollars unto a

165. Duke Francis Albert of Saxe-Lauenberg was a friend of Wallenstein and a commander in Saxon service.

166. Croatian soldiers and imperial dragoons.

souldier to kill him with a shot: And therefore hee is now more strictly kept and guarded. He hath beene forced to write to Duke Bernhard that the Duke of Friedland did earnestly long and expect for him, that all things, hee knew off, were in good estate, and all in readinesse for him. But Duke Bernhard was sufficiently advised and assured of the contrary and of all that was past.

Piccolomini[167] hath plaid also his part for the Emperour at Pilsen, killing the Governor there by a pistoll shot through his head and so preserving that place in the Emperors devotion. The Imperiall forces are marching to and gathering at a place called Weissenberg there to keepe a Rendezvous. The Gates at Egra have still beene kept close, except now and then for halfe an houre they were opended; the cause was thought to bee, that the Imperialists did hope to catch also Generall Arnheim, if he should come with an intention to conclude what was begun with Friedland.

On the 20. of February at evening, Duke Bernard of Saxen, arrived at Weyden, with three thousand horses: Himselfe and his principall Officers tooke their lodgings within the Towne, and his horse in the suburbs: One day before him a Collonel of his, named Rose past here with some 3000 horse towards Turshenried, to discover the enemies posture; And the foote is expected tomorrow. Order is taken both to fortifie this towne and to make preparations for the keeping of a garrison, as like wise for tilling and sowing of the ploughland. On the 22 there came newes from severall parts, that on Friday last, there were againe slaine many Collonels, Officers, and soldiers, both Imperiallists and Friedlanders at Egra, so that there is a great confussion: There is also a report, that the Dutchesse of Friedland (Walsteins widdow) with her daughter and much treasure, is arrived at Dresden: And that also all Fridlands Chancery, or his letters, writings and papers are safely brought to Plassenburg, a strong place belonging to the Marquis of Brandenburg Cullembach; whereof nevertheleesse more assurance must be expected. . . .

This was the tragicall end of this great Generalissimo, the Duke of Fridland, what effects will yet follow, time will shortly discover.

22. The Battle of Nördlingen and Its Aftermath (September 6, 1634)[168]

[In August 1634 the army of the Swedes, led jointly by Bernard of Saxe-Weimar and Gustav Horn, came to relieve the city of Nördlingen, which was

---

167. Prince Octavio Piccolomini, 1st duke of Amalfi (1599–1656), an officer under Wallenstein who was part of the conspiracy against him.

168. "Die Bieberauer Chronik (1579–1654) des Pfarrers Johann Daniel Minck," in

being besieged by the imperial army under Ferdinand, king of Hungary. On September 6 the Swedes attacked, unaware that while they had delayed, Ferdinand, cardinal-infante of Spain, had arrived with Spanish reinforcements to aid his Habsburg cousin. The result was a disaster for the Swedes. After being utterly defeated, the Swedish troops fled into the countryside with the imperial-Spanish army in hot pursuit, and with both armies looting the populace indiscriminately. The following description of the battle and its aftermath appears in the chronicle written by the pastor of the Hessian town Groß-Bieberau, Johann Daniel Minck.[169]

Anno 1634. This was an extremely dangerous year, and a grievous and very injurious year for all Evangelicals.[170] In it there occurred such a battle at Nördlingen as will never be forgotten as long as the world exists. . . .

What happened during this great battle can be found amply published in many other histories. Here I aim only to show what irrevocable injuries our dear fatherland suffered in the process.

After both armies, imperial and Swedish, had arrived at Nördlingen, the imperialists gained strong reinforcements from well-equipped Spaniards and placed themselves in an advantageous position. Duke Bernard of Saxe-Weimar, however, who had been named lieutenant general after the death of the king [of Sweden], had not received word of the Spanish reinforcement, and so took a risk and attacked the imperialists before his own reinforcements, who were already in the vicinity, had arrived. He was, however, attacked with great seriousness by his enemy, and although he and his followers battled with bravery and chivalry—including Landgrave Johann,[171] a colonel and our gracious prince and lord's next-eldest brother, who also gained great honor with his swordplay—he was nevertheless forced to abandon the infantry entirely and flee with a portion of the cavalry, to the ruin of the best portion of the army.

Then those [Swedish soldiers] who had survived made their retreat into the upper county [of Hesse-Darmstadt], our fatherland, and to Mainz, and although our gracious prince and lord was neutral and His Princely Grace's brother, Landgrave Johann, was himself in Swedish service, nevertheless they

Rudolf Kunz and Willy Lizalek, eds., *Südhessische Chroniken aus der Zeit des Dreissigjährigen Krieges*, 4 (Lorsch: Verlad Laurissa, 1983), 252–3.

169. See also Document 38 for another account of the aftermath of this battle.

170. Protestants.

171. Johann von Hesse-Braubach (1609–1651) was the brother of Landgrave George II of Hesse-Darmstadt (1605–1661) and commanded a regiment of cavalry in the Swedish army.

thoroughly plundered the entire land. Soon thereafter, in order to seek out their enemy, the imperialists followed and chased the Swedes over the Rhine. Then they stole and destroyed everything in our land that the Swedes had left, to such an extent that neither cattle nor horses, pigs nor fowl, nor anything of the sort remained in either cities or villages. Soon the Swedes plunged back across the Rhine and chased the imperialists out of their quarters, but were then themselves soon chased out once again. As a result, the entire land between the Main and Rhine rivers was totally spent, and no man could dare to be spotted in the countryside, lest he be hunted down like game; were he captured, he would be mercilessly battered and bound—worse than the methods used by the Turks—until he disclosed money or cattle or a horse; he would be tied up naked in a hot oven, suspended, and steamed with smoke; he would be saturated with water and dirty water by the people who poured it down his throat using a tube and then jumped on his engorged stomach with their feet. This barbarous saturation was called "the Swedish drink"—not because it was used by the Swedes alone, but much more because the imperialists treated their prisoners or those partial to the Swedes in this evil way.

Due to such tyranny, and because there was no more food in the country, all villages, without any exception, were abandoned by all of their inhabitants. Reinheim and Zwingenberg stood completely empty and vacant for two years, and in this year the suburb of Reinheim was burned by the Swedes, except for about three or four houses.

Darmstadt was heavily burdened by the French, yet there the burghers stayed in their houses.

Lichtenberg, Rüsselsheim, and Otzberg—which at that time were still held by our gracious prince and lord—were all spared; yet for this reason they were pillaged and pressed by both parties so that they had to hand over all of their reserves.

Many hid and concealed themselves in woods, hollows, crags, etc., but were spied out, for the soldiers had man-hunting dogs with them that, when they came upon men and animals, betrayed the people with their loud barking and so gave the robbers notice.

For this reason everyone fled to the castles. There all the alleys, courtyards, and squares were full of people, especially at Lichtenberg, which was of little help. And therefore many people also lay out under the open sky in rain, snow, and cold, while others lay in barrels and tubs. In the wintertime, heated rooms were so packed that no one could sit because of the crowd, but people had to stand tightly packed against each other. It was a great misery and distress to behold, not to mention that I myself was included among them.

23. Advice of Cardinal Richelieu of France (after September 6, 1634)[172]

[The defeat at Nördlingen on September 6, 1634 was not just a military disaster for the Swedes; it was also an existential blow to the entire anti-Habsburg alliance. As imperial forces advanced behind the fleeing remnants of the Swedish army, frightened German Protestant princes quickly began to abandon what now seemed to be a lost cause. They were led in this by the example of the elector of Saxony, who rebuffed the appeals for aid made by the Swedish Chancellor Axel Oxenstierna, and entered instead into peace negotiations with the emperor at Pirna. This turn of affairs appalled the French prime minister, Cardinal Richelieu, who wrote to King Louis XIII of France, giving the following advice.]

It is certain that if the [Protestant] party[173] is entirely ruined, the brunt of the power of the House of Austria[174] will fall on France.

It is also certain that after the recent setback, the party cannot subsist if it is not sustained by present and notable help and by greater hope of a powerful name—it being certain that without such help, all the imperial cities would disarm, Saxony would come to terms, and each one would think of his own affairs so that this great party would soon become a shadow of its former self.

It is certain, moreover, that even if France did not declare herself on this occasion, the House of Austria would be no less hostile to her, because it would conclude that she had only failed to do so out of imprudence, weakness, or fear.

It is also certain that the worst thing that France can do is to conduct herself in such a manner that she would remain alone to bear the brunt of the emperor and Spain, which will be inevitable if she does not gather up the remainder of this great party that has been subsisting for a while in Germany. By such means, the worst that could happen to her would be to sustain for a while the expense of the war in Germany, and this along with princes who would be interested in adhering to the party. Otherwise, it would

---

172. "Advis donné au Roy Sur le Sujet de la bataille de Nordlingen perdue par les Suedois six heures apres en avoir receu la nouvelle par le Sr de Mire," n.d., but shortly after September 6, 1634, Archives des Affaires Étrangères, Correspondance Politique Suède 3, fol. 265–6. Translated with Paul Sonnino.

173. The Swedes and their German allies.

174. The Habsburgs.

be necessary to sustain the war in the heart of France without the assistance of the princes in whose states it would otherwise be waged.

Hence there seems to be no doubt that it is necessary to help this party, but the only question is how to do it.

To make a good decision in such a difficult and important matter, it is necessary to be well informed, to wait for news from the losers, [and to hear] the entreaties and the offers that they would make to the king, in the meantime encouraging them and letting them know the willingness of His Majesty to help them, if they demonstrate to him that they can maintain themselves with his assistance.

Meanwhile, it is necessary to recruit soldiers and be in a condition to execute what prudence and necessity oblige.

If one considers the expense on this occasion and wants to reduce it so that it can be afforded for a long time, it should be replied that great emergencies have no rule; that it is not a question of an expense that will last for many years; but that if, in order to remedy the present evil, one fails to make an extraordinary expenditure now, it will be necessary to make one in the future—though it would then not produce any result, nor prevent our ruin.

III

THE LONG WAR (1635–1648)

Since its beginning, the balance of the war had shifted continuously, with princes of the empire stepping forward or dropping out, entering leagues with and against each other, and maneuvering for advantage. The intervention of the foreign crowns had also radically changed, enlarged, and prolonged the war. Without the assistance of Spain, the emperor would surely have been defeated, but without the assistance of Denmark, Sweden, and France, so too would his Protestant enemies. The decisive role of the foreign powers as counterweights in this conflict became particularly evident, however, in 1635. At this time the Protestant party was desperate for peace, and the emperor was ready to compromise in order to cement the gains he had already made. On May 30, 1635, therefore, the leader of the Protestant party in the empire, Elector John George of Saxony, concluded a peace with the emperor at Prague (see Document 24).

Though made solely between the elector and the emperor, the Peace of Prague was intended as an empirewide settlement, and its most striking feature was its compromise on the religious question. Despite complaints by the emperor's theologians and leading Catholic princes, including the duke of Bavaria, the emperor now agreed to set aside the Edict of Restitution[1] for forty years, during which time a new normal year of 1627 would be in effect for all ecclesiastical properties. Any ecclesiastical properties seized and secularized before that date would be left in the hands of the Protestants; any properties seized after that date would have to be returned. This date was a careful compromise selected by the elector of Saxony and the emperor, and, not coincidentally, it represented a point in the war that benefited the elector far more than it did many other Protestant princes—who would lose large territories to the Catholic Church. The peace also directly rewarded the elector with the territory of Lusatia, which he had desired since the beginning of the war, and left the bishoprics of Halberstadt and Bremen in the hands of one of the emperor's sons.

By setting aside the difficult question of the religious makeup of the imperial courts to another day, the peace left in place their existing bias in favor of Catholics and imperial power. The power of the emperor was also bolstered by other terms of the peace, including the stipulation that signatory princes were barred from all existing or future alliances or leagues among themselves or with foreign powers, and that they must subsume their

1. Document 14.

armies and forces into that of the emperor. The new combined imperial army, which would proceed under the command of the emperor's son Ferdinand of Hungary, would be supported by contributions voluntarily paid by each prince and estate.

The Peace of Prague was thus a diplomatic triumph for the emperor and imperial power. Though Ferdinand had been forced to postpone the victory of Catholicism for forty years, in a single blow he had removed almost all internal military opposition, crippled the Swedish war effort in the empire, enlarged his own army considerably, and ensured its financial support. Some princes had to be browbeaten into signing the peace; some had to be coaxed. The elector of Brandenburg, in particular, insisted on an imperial guarantee of his lands in Pomerania, knowing that the Swedes would never voluntarily give them up. But most princes of the empire were simply tired of war, broke, and discouraged, and the peace was also cleverly crafted to appeal to their prejudices against foreign interference in the affairs of the empire. For whatever reason, then, most princes and estates of the empire signed on to the Peace of Prague within days or months.

It seemed to many in the empire that the war might finally be over. In the Protestant city of Ulm, for example, "all the bells were tolled together and salvos or shots of joy were fired from great cannons around the entire city and from every bastion."[2] Others across the empire celebrated as well, eager to put the long years of conflict behind them. But such festivities were premature, for the peace was fatally flawed. First, it did not resolve many of the empire's structural problems, which had spurred or aggravated so much of the internal conflict. The still-broken imperial court system was one such difficulty, but the most serious structural problem was Calvinism, which the peace excluded by omission—just as the 1555 Peace of Augsburg had done. In addition, since some imperial estates were not included, either explicitly or by choice, the Peace of Prague was not actually empirewide. Some princes, such as the heirs of Frederick of the Palatinate (who had died in 1632), the margrave of Baden-Durlach, and the duke of Württemberg, had been explicitly excluded by the emperor. They were, the emperor had complained to his delegates to the negotiations, "so tightly bound to Sweden and France . . . that they have made themselves into vassals of the crowns."[3] Others, such as the duke of Saxe-Weimar and the landgrave of Hesse-Cassel, were not completely excluded, but were only offered amnesty on conditions they found

2. Document 38.

3. Ferdinand II's Instructions for His Delegates, March 12, 1635, in *Die Politik Maximilians I. Von Bayern und seiner Verbündeten 1618–1651,* Teil 2, Bd. 10: *Der Prager Frieden von 1635* (Munich and Vienna: R. Oldenbourg Verlag, 1997), 241–89 [246].

intolerable, and so refused. Threats had merely made these princes more stubborn, not more tractable. The peace also had excluded the foreign powers. Sweden's horrible defeat at Nördlingen had most likely left it too weak to fight on alone, but there now appeared a new foreign threat to the emperor's plan for peace: France. Fearing that a fully triumphant emperor could fall upon France like a wave, and provoked even further by the Spanish kidnapping of the pro-French elector of Trier, France declared war on Spain on May 26, 1635, only days before the final agreement at Prague.[4]

The year 1635, therefore, marked one of the war's most dramatic shifts; yet the intervention of France meant the two sides' balance of power, which had already allowed the conflict to stretch on for seventeen years, was once again preserved. Many players had now swapped sides, however—a change made most evident in October 1635, when the elector of Saxony declared war against his former ally, Sweden, and led a portion of the new imperial army against it. Pushed back to the Baltic coast, the Swedes began to think of coming to terms with the emperor. The French army, meanwhile, was both inexperienced and disorganized, and the French had to struggle to defend Lorraine against an invasion by the elector of Bavaria.[5] To rescue their new and floundering war effort, the French allied with Duke Bernard of Saxe-Weimar, who promised to maintain an army of almost twenty thousand men in return for French subsidies. The Swedes also managed to regroup somewhat, repulsing the Saxon army and maintaining their position in Pomerania and Mecklenburg.

The elector of Saxony soon began to suspect that the Peace of Prague had failed. Not only had the emperor—despite the terms of the peace and his promises—continued to re-Catholicize portions of the empire, but the peace also had not united the empire against the foreign powers. Instead, the nonsignatory princes and estates had stubbornly refused to lay down their arms, and the elector informed the emperor that the Swedes seemed determined not to abandon their remaining German allies without first seeing them included in the Peace of Prague (see Document 25). Then, on March 20, 1636, only days after the elector's warning to the emperor, the Swedes and the French agreed to the Treaty of Wismar, by which they vowed to fight together to defeat the Habsburgs. The Swedish army, bolstered by French subsidies, would attack Habsburg territories in the east, while the French army would fight along the Rhine.

This grand plan was only slowly put into effect, for the French first had to repulse a vigorous invasion by the Spanish which, with the aid of the imperial cavalry under Johann von Werth, briefly led to the capture of Corbie,

---

4. See Document 23.
5. See Document 37 for a description of this campaign.

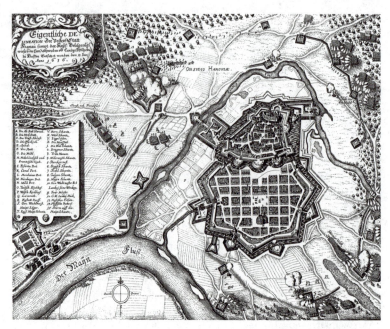

Siege of Hanau, 1636 (*Theatrum Europaeum,* III, p. 663+, Universitätsbibliothek Augsburg, Sign. 02/IV.13.2.26-3)

frighteningly close to Paris.[6] On October 4, however, the Swedes dealt a serious defeat to the Saxon and imperial army at the battle of Wittstock in Brandenburg. The allies were also joined in their renewed efforts by the Calvinist Landgrave Wilhelm of Hesse-Cassel, who rushed with his army to relieve another nonsignatory of the peace, Hanau,[7] and who also threw himself against his Lutheran cousin George of Hesse-Darmstadt.

Rather than enjoying peace, therefore, people across the empire continued to suffer the unpredictable brutality of war. William Crown, a member of an English embassy traveling to the Imperial Court in early 1636, recorded in his diary the patchwork of destruction he witnessed during his journey (see Document 26). As his ship traveled along the Rhine he saw battles and abandoned villages, evidence of plague and abject poverty. At Mainz, a city that had recently endured a long siege, his ship stopped for the night. "We cast Anchor and lay on ship-board," he wrote,

6. See Document 37.

7. For an eyewitness mention of the siege of Hanau, see Document 26.

for there was nothing in the Towne to relieve us. . . . heere likewise the poore people were almost starved, and those that could relieve others before, now humbly begged to bee relieved, and after supper all had reliefe, sent from the Ship ashore, at the sight of which they strove so violently, that some of them fell into the Rhine and were like to have bin drowned.[8]

The English party quickly moved through, but witnessed many further horrors before their eventual arrival in Vienna.

In February 1637 Emperor Ferdinand II died, leaving his son Ferdinand of Hungary as his designated heir. That same year the imperial armies, under General Götz, invaded both Hesse-Cassel and its territorial holdings in Westphalia, forcing the landgrave to flee with his family as a declared enemy of the empire. Still master of a huge army, however, and managing to keep control of key fortresses in both Hesse and Westphalia, the landgrave moved to the far northern reaches of the empire, invading the neutral county of East Frisia and putting it under contribution. But he was dead of natural causes by the end of the year, leaving a regency government under his widow, Amalia Elisabeth, who faced serious opposition from both her late husband's generals and her own Hessian estates (see Document 27). Hesse-Cassel was now, at least temporarily, out of the war, and the landgravine entered into negotiations with the imperialists.

Bernard of Saxe-Weimar, however, fought on, and after victories along the Rhine in late 1637, he advanced again in 1638, taking the city of Rheinfelden in March and capturing Johann von Werth and other officers. "This business could have amazing consequences," wrote one overly excited Protestant observer, "since having almost all the imperial officers killed and captured is something that has never happened during this war."[9] Bernard continued his string of successes with a victory over the army of Götz, and then moved toward the mighty fortress of Breisach, which he besieged. In December the fortress surrendered. The Swedes, strengthened by large subsidies from a new treaty with the French,[10] also advanced in 1638 against the imperial army of General Gallas,[11] who was forced to fall back into Bohemia and Silesia.

8. Document 26.

9. Extract of a Letter from Frankfurt, March 1/11, 1638, Hessische Staatsarchiv Marburg, 4d Nr. 93, fol. 17.

10. The Treaty of Hamburg, March 5, 1638, confirmed the earlier agreement made at Wismar.

11. Matthias, count of Gallas (1584–1647), imperial field marshal.

"Of Bloodshed and Killing" (*The Lamentations of Germany,* p. 27, Vincent Philip, 1638, Beinecke Rare Book and Manuscript Library, Yale University)

The constant back-and-forth of the two sides was due to the continuing military balance between them. In late 1638, however, yet another diplomatic maneuver threatened to upset this delicate equilibrium. The elector of Mainz, who was Emperor Ferdinand III's negotiator with Amalia Elisabeth, had now come to terms with the landgravine. This meant her large and experienced army might soon fall into the hands of the imperialists, and so tilt the balance heavily in the new emperor's favor. But at the last minute, Ferdinand issued a signing statement changing the religious terms worked out by the elector of Mainz. Despite the enormous benefits of bringing the Hessian army to his side, he waged the entire war on his refusal to allow Calvinists the same legal recognition in the empire as Lutherans (see Document 28). The landgravine, a fervent Calvinist, backed out of the treaty and accepted instead the frantic offers of alliance and large subsidies from the French. Furthermore, although Bernard of Saxe-Weimar died in July 1639, his army agreed to keep fighting for the Protestant cause; with these "Bernadines," joined now by the full power of the army of Hesse-Cassel and the assistance of George of Brunswick-Lüneburg, the foreign crowns and their German allies enjoyed excellent campaigns in 1639 and 1640. The war was now ever so slightly, but significantly, tilted in their favor.

As 1640 dragged on with still no end to the war in sight, the emperor and the electors agreed to call a full meeting of the imperial diet, the first since before the war began. In September, representatives of most German princes assembled in Regensburg. There the delegates agreed to the emperor's demand that they proceed from the basis of the Peace of Prague, while the emperor, concerned both by his recent defeats in the empire and by his Spanish cousin's troubles with revolutions in Catalonia and Portugal, expressed himself willing to renounce entirely the Edict of Restitution and the forty-year

expiry of the normal year of 1627. The question of amnesty for the excluded princes also seemed to be close to resolution, for the princes of the
empire were fully determined, in the landgravine of Hesse's words, to "set
aside the divisions and misunderstandings that have occurred in the Holy
Roman Empire between the head and members, and also among the members themselves."[12]

The negotiations were disturbed briefly by a daring raid across the frozen
Danube River to Regensburg by the Swedish General Banér in January
1641; but, in the end, the success of the diet was defeated not by weapons,
but by the resurgence of the issue of the German Liberties. The question had
been decided firmly in the emperor's favor in the Peace of Prague, and it had
seemed likely that the princes at the Regensburg diet would similarly let the
issue die. In 1640, however, a pamphlet (pseudonymously written by the
Swedish historian Bogislav Philipp von Chemnitz) began to circulate among
the princes and their advisors. Titled *Dissertatio de ratione status in Imperio
nostro Romano-Germanico,* it was both a devastating critique of the Habsburg attempt to strengthen the emperor's power at the expense of the
princes, and a well-argued scholarly analysis of the empire as being fundamentally an aristocratic republic, not a monarchy. This enormously popular
work helped to remind the imperial estates of their earlier claims and demands against the emperor. It also led some princes to eye his propositions
with greater suspicion.

One such prince was the new elector of Brandenburg, Frederick William.[13]
Brandenburg had served as the battleground for years of destructive warfare
between the Swedes and imperialists, and Frederick William noted that, if
anything, his territories were now in even worse shape than they had been
when his father had been coaxed to sign the Peace of Prague. A new peace
with the emperor on those terms would be similarly fruitless, he decided,
and so he not only publicly rejected the Peace of Prague as the basis for any
future agreement, he also concluded a separate truce with Sweden. The Regensburg diet now had no hope of creating an empirewide peace, and the
emperor finally dissolved it in November 1641. New, more limited negotiations were planned for a later meeting at Frankfurt.

Representatives of the Swedes and French, meanwhile, had been meeting
with the imperialists in the city of Hamburg, where they struggled to find
some general solution to the international aspect of war. Finally, on December 25, 1641, the three parties agreed to a general framework for a peace

12. Copy of a Letter to the Most Praiseworthy Electoral College, 1640, Universitätsbibliothek Augsburg, Sign. 02/IV.13.4.185angeb.08.

13. Frederick William, elector of Brandenburg (1620–1688), later called "the Great
Elector."

congress. To speed the resolution of the different issues involved, they would split the negotiations in two. The French and the emperor would meet in the Westphalian city of Münster, while the Swedes and the emperor would meet approximately thirty miles away in Osnabrück. Both cities would be declared neutral zones for the duration of the negotiations. The planned international peace congress, which soon grew to include both Spain and the United Provinces, was initially set to begin on March 25, 1642, a start date that was later moved to July 11, 1643.

Meanwhile, the long war went on. Under General Lennart Torstensson[14] (who had replaced Banér after his death in May 1641), the Swedish army rolled through Saxony in early 1642, and then on into the Habsburg hereditary lands, and almost as far as Vienna. Repulsed by the emperor's army, led by Archduke Leopold Wilhelm and General Piccolomini,[15] the Swedes then retreated back to Saxony, where they besieged the city of Leipzig. The imperial army followed, and on October 23, 1642, the two armies met at the second great battle of Breitenfeld.[16] Like the first, the second battle of Breitenfeld was a great victory for the Swedes and a disaster for the imperial army. The people of nearby Catholic territories panicked at the thought of a new Swedish advance to match the one that had terrorized them ten years earlier. In Bavaria, Elector Maximilian hurriedly tried to prepare for a possible invasion. "Our elector once again did everything that he could do," the abbot of Andechs wrote. "He once again newly equipped his army, called up the territorial militia, convened the hunters and marksmen, who came together in great number at Munich, at Ingolstadt, and at Landshut; and advertised in all places for horses for hauling and for the cannons" (Document 29). The shock of the battle of Breitenfeld and the subsequent fall of Leipzig spurred Catholic princes across the empire to consider peace even more seriously. The electors of Bavaria, Mainz, and Cologne, for example, made concerted efforts to seek a separate peace with France in case the general peace congress fell through.

In February 1643 the Frankfurt diet got underway, and difficult negotiations began among the imperial deputies on the issues of the amnesty, the reform of the imperial court system, and other pressing matters. Some princes, however, began to suspect that the diet was designed merely to sep-

---

14. Lennart Torstensson (1603–1651).

15. Archduke Leopold Wilhelm of Austria (1614–1662), the emperor's brother; and Octavio Piccolomini, duke of Amalfi (1599–1656), an Italian-born general in the imperial army.

16. The first battle of Breitenfeld occurred on September 17, 1631; King Gustavus Adolphus and Elector John George of Saxony defeated the imperial General Johann Tserclaes, count von Tilly.

arate them from their foreign allies, and so block their ability to coordinate their demands. This was especially troubling to the elector of Brandenburg and Amalia Elisabeth of Hesse-Cassel, both of whom distrusted the emperor enormously and supported an expansive interpretation of the extent of the German Liberties. The emperor's plan to represent the entire empire in the negotiations with the foreign crowns, they argued, was yet another attempt to impose a monarchical structure on the empire, and to deny the princes their sovereign right to make war and peace. Amalia Elisabeth thus appealed to the French and Swedish to demand the inclusion of the imperial princes as a precondition for the Westphalian negotiations. The two crowns "must quickly be vigilant," she warned them, "on account of their own great interests as well as those of the collected princes and estates of the empire, which are interconnected with their own" (Document 30).

The French had, in the meantime, been somewhat distracted by their own problems. First came the December 1642 death of Cardinal Richelieu, followed in May 1643 by that of King Louis XIII. The French government— now in the hands of Richelieu's successor, Cardinal Jules Mazarin, and Louis XIII's widow, Anne of Austria—continued the war and enjoyed great successes in the 1643 campaign. Among these were their victory over the Spanish at the battle of Rocroi on May 19, and their capture of the city of Rottweil on November 19. Their satisfaction over such advances was short-lived, however, for on November 24, as the French Marshal Rantzau basked in his recent victory outside the nearby town of Tuttlingen, the Bavarian General Franz von Mercy[17] sprung upon him in a surprise attack. The French army, decimated, fled back across the Rhine to Alsace, and Rottweil fell once again into the hands of the imperialists.[18]

Then, to add to the troubles of the French crown, at the end of 1643, Oxenstierna ordered Torstensson to abandon his winning efforts in the Habsburg hereditary territories and to attack instead the Danes in Jutland. This new Danish–Swedish war had been sparked by existing rivalries between the two Scandinavian powers, rumors of a planned Danish intervention in the war on the side of the imperialists, and perhaps also the desire of the Swedes to capture new territories to support their troops. Its timing, coinciding with the great victory of the imperialists at Tuttlingen, threw the allied cause into confusion and put the outcome of the approaching campaign season in great doubt (see Document 31). Yet the Swedes had arranged a countermeasure to keep the emperor and his allies busy in Torstensson's absence. As the emperor dispatched General Gallas to come to the aid of Denmark, Prince György Rákóczi of Transylvania attacked the Habsburgs in Hungary (see

17. Freiherr Franz von Mercy (c. 1598–1645).

18. See Document 29 for the Bavarian take on this battle.

Document 32). Gallas, outmaneuvered by Torstensson and needed on the new eastern front, eventually turned back, returning to Bohemia with no more than a third of his previous forces.

The uncertainties of the allied cause in late 1643 were soon forgotten in light of their tremendous victories in 1644 and early 1645. The French redeemed themselves from the loss at Tuttlingen by advancing into the Lower Palatinate and seizing fortresses along the Rhine. Then, joining with the army of Hesse-Cassel, they moved into Bavaria, where they defeated and killed the imperial General Mercy at the battle of Allerheim.[19] At the same time, a portion of the Swedish army under General Königsmarck[20] advanced into Saxony, forcing the elector to drop out of the war and putting his lands under contribution. Torstensson, meanwhile, having quickly defeated Christian IV of Denmark, advanced once again into the Habsburg heartland of Bohemia. On March 6, 1645, he met the emperor's forces under Götz at Jankov, just south of Prague, and crushed them. Then, with the aid of the prince of Transylvania, the Swedes advanced to besiege Vienna itself. Only the defection of Rákóczi saved the city.

The Congress of Westphalia had been scheduled to begin in June 1643, and although the imperial plenipotentiaries arrived in time, others only slowly trickled in over the course of the next year. Early negotiations were consumed with questions of precedence and terms of address, and only in mid-1645 did the major issues of religion, the imperial constitution, and the satisfaction of the foreign powers even begin to be discussed seriously. The emperor acquiesced to the foreign powers' demand for the inclusion of the imperial estates, and by the end of the year the Frankfurt diet disbanded and its members moved to Westphalia. Yet in other matters, the emperor was not yet ready to admit defeat. Secretly instructing his plenipotentiary and close advisor, Count von Trauttmansdorff, to concede almost anything in order to bring about peace, the emperor publicly pronounced himself firmly opposed to anything more than he had already conceded at the Peace of Prague (see Document 33).

If the emperor's defeats had left him reeling and depressed, at least in private, they had filled the French, Swedes, and Hessians with extraordinary optimism and greed. Amalia Elisabeth of Hesse-Cassel launched a full invasion of Hesse-Darmstadt and seized the contested territory of Marburg, while the French and Swedes issued sweeping demands at Westphalia for their own financial and territorial compensation. Cardinal Mazarin, for example, not only demanded Alsace and areas on the right bank of the Rhine, including the fortresses of Philippsburg and Breisach, he also tried to gain

19. A battle also known as second Nördlingen.
20. Count Hans Christoff von Königsmarck (1600–1663).

the entire Spanish Netherlands (see Document 34). But as the parties negotiated in 1646 and 1647, the war raged on, constantly complicating the discussions. On March 15, 1647, for example, the elector of Bavaria signed the
separate Peace of Ulm, dropping out of the war; but after only a few months,
he returned again to aid the emperor. The situation was even more frustrat-
ing and frightening for the residents of the empire, since Swedish, French,
Hessian, Bavarian, Spanish, and imperial armies still ranged freely and seemed
to devastate everything in their path.

Yet, over the course of 1647, the diplomats slowly, slowly began to resolve
their remaining differences over the Swedish and French satisfactions and
the complaints of the imperial estates. These moves toward peace were aided
by a combination of different factors. The emperor, unwilling and unable to
fight for much longer, put enormous pressure on his allies to give way; the
Protestants princes were willing to compromise in order to end the war and
get rid of the Swedes; and the Swedes themselves were eager to collect their
spoils and return home. The French, whose greed for the Spanish Netherlands had helped to prolong the negotiations for so long, were also now in
a much weaker position. Not only did French armies suffer a disastrous
campaign season in 1647, but Cardinal Mazarin was also facing plots and
tax revolts at home. Even worse, on January 30, 1648, the Spanish and
Dutch plenipotentiaries at Münster agreed to a separate peace. The Peace of
Münster ended their eighty-year conflict and officially recognized the independence of the United Provinces from the Spanish monarchy. It also un-
pleasantly surprised and further weakened the French, who had counted on
their alliance with the Dutch to help them force the Habsburgs into further
concessions.

The momentum was now shifting toward peace in the empire, but the
combatants were not quite yet ready to stop. On May 17, 1648, the imperial army of General Melander[21] was defeated at the battle of Zusmarshausen,
outside Augsburg; and Swedish and French troops under Generals Wrangel
and Turenne[22] advanced deep into Bavaria, blocked only by the efforts of
Piccolomini from overrunning it completely. The troops looted with abandon, and the people of Franconia and Bavaria could do nothing but flee for
their lives. The nun Clara Staiger, who, along with many of her fellow sisters, fled to the fortified castle at Eichstätt, described seeing "three hundred

21. Peter Melander, count of Holzappel (1589–1648), formerly general of the armies
of Hesse-Cassel, imperial officer since 1645, and commander of the imperial army
after the death of Gallas in 1647.

22. Karl Gustav Wrangel (1613–1676), Swedish field marshal who succeeded
Torstensson, and Henri de la Tour d'Auvergne, Viscount de Turenne (1611–1675),
commander in the French army of Germany.

fires" in the area below the fortress, and soldiers so unrestrained and enraged in their looting that they killed what livestock they could not carry away. They "stripped everything that was in the cloister," she wrote, "from grain, flour, vegetables, and fowl, to bedding, pillows, and feather comforters. Whatever had been hidden, such as copper, tin, and brass, they found, seized, and took. In short, whatever they could haul and carry, they took away" (Document 35).

On October 24, 1648, the plenipotentiaries at Münster and Osnabrück finally reached a general peace (see Document 36). The war was over.[23] The result of the Thirty Years War was an empire much like the one of 1618, but smaller, poorer, and with millions fewer people. Territories to the north, in Pomerania, were granted to Sweden, while the French gained Alsace and control of some areas along the Rhine. Purposely vague wording in these latter terms, however, would make control of this area the source of numerous further conflicts between France and the empire, both during the reign of Louis XIV and into the twentieth century. The Swiss Confederation, long independent of the empire in practice, gained official recognition of that fact in the treaty, while the United Provinces, also long independent, was simply accepted as such after January 1648 without anyone in the empire actually having to say so. The costs to the empire in blood and treasure are much harder to determine than the territorial costs, and historians have argued over the numbers for years. Seven or eight million were dead, many agree, but there is no way to estimate the number of wounded or the number whose lives or minds were shattered. Whatever the final score, no one doubts that the price was extraordinarily high.

In return, the empire gained a solution both to most of the larger structural problems that had been bedeviling it since the sixteenth century, and to a number of other smaller flashpoints. Calvinism was legalized and its adherents given the same rights as Catholics and Lutherans, and all three gave up for good their dream of a total conversion of the empire and of a united Christendom. Residents of the empire gained freedom of conscience, and the rights of some religious minorities were protected. This, then, was the end of the Reformation and of religious wars in Central Europe.

The constitutional problems of the empire were finally resolved as well. The princes gained their German Liberties and sovereign rights to make war and peace, and the emperor was blocked from converting the empire into a tightly centralized state (something many of his European colleagues soon attempted within their own lands). The princes were not fully sovereign, however, for they still lived within the federal imperial structure and were barred from converting their territories to any faith not practiced there as of

---

23. France and Spain continued to fight until the 1659 Peace of the Pyrenees.

January 1, 1624, the new normal year. The imperial legal and legislative systems were also revised, giving Protestants and Catholics legal parity, or equal treatment, so no one group could ever again overrule the other in matters of religion.

Dynastic and territorial squabbles, which had been a constant source of conflict during the war, were also addressed in the peace. The internal map of the empire changed considerably, with numerous territories swapping hands. Many transfers were caused by the requirement that princes use the new normal year to determine who should own ecclesiastical properties; but other transfers had been painstakingly worked out over months or years of negotiation and were thus carefully stipulated by the treaty. The elector of Bavaria, for example, was allowed to keep the Upper Palatinate and the Palatine electorate, while Frederick of the Palatinate's heir was given back the Lower Palatinate and a new, eighth electorate. The Austrian Habsburgs were allowed to ignore the normal year within their hereditary territories, and over subsequent years these lands would become the base of their growing power as territorial princes.

The people of the empire were simply glad the long war was finally over. "We celebrated the festival as formally and with such a will as ever we had Christmas Day, and God be praised and thanked," wrote the shoemaker Hans Heberle. "Because of this, we cannot sufficiently praise and laud God for the noble peace that we have lived to see."[24]

24. The Peace of Prague (June 12, 1635)[25]

[In 1635 the emperor managed an enormous diplomatic triumph, the Peace of Prague. By this treaty, which the emperor negotiated with the elector of Saxony, he agreed to abandon his long insistence on full re-Catholicization of the empire by suspending for forty years the Edict of Restitution. This would be modified in part, however, by the establishment of a so-called normal year of November 1627; only those lands held by Protestants as of that date would remain in their hands, and whatever the Catholics had managed to reclaim prior to that date must be returned. This normal year worked well for the

---

24. Document 38.

25. *Copia Deß zwischen der Kayserlichen Mayestaet und der Churfuerstl. Durchleucht in Sachsen beschlossenen und publicierten Friedens und deßwegen den 12. Junii Anno 1635. ergangener Keyserlichen Patenten [. . .] also nachgedruckt zu Heybronn den 10. Julij Anno 1635. Durch Christoff Krausen* (Heilbronn: Christoff Krausen, 1635). Copies can be found at the Universitätsbibliothek Augsburg, Sign. 02/IV.13.4.183angeb.06 and 02/IV.13.4.183angeb.07.

elector of Saxony (who also gained other territories by this agreement), but was less advantageous to those Protestant princes in the south who had already lost lands by that point in the war. In addition to settling the important questions of territory, this treaty also allowed for a full amnesty for any prince who agreed to adhere to the peace (though a few key princes were specifically excluded). In return for the emperor's concessions, the treaty stated that the elector of Saxony and other signatory princes must end their rebellion against the emperor and turn instead to resist the foreign powers. They must place all of their military forces under the control of the emperor and agree to cede their right to form independent military alliances among themselves or with foreign powers.]

Let it hereby be known to all, that our most gracious lord the Roman Imperial Majesty, who is also king of Bohemia and Hungary, etc., most zealously endeavored, with the faithful cooperation of His Serene Highness the elector of Saxony, etc., who is one of the preeminent pillars of the Holy Roman Empire, to find out how and to what extent a Christian, general, reputable, just, and secure peace might once again be erected in the Holy Roman Empire; and he endeavored that this same empire might, after so many long-lasting wars and their ensuing distress, misery, and destruction, be revitalized, that the bloodletting be ended once and for all, and that the beloved fatherland, the most noble German Nation, be rescued from final ruin.

Yet because of this trying and evil situation, and especially on account of those foreign nations and warring parties that are still present on imperial ground, one could not securely convoke a general imperial assembly or other common meeting to achieve this purpose, which is both holy and in the common interest. Thus both sides sent their advisors and plenipotentiaries first to Leutmaritz,[26] then to Pirna, and finally to Prague. And then, for the advantage and honor of the empire and the German Nation, for the consolation and salvation of the royal and electoral land and people of both respective parties, and for the benefit of the commonwealth, they have settled on and agreed to the following common peace.

First: as for those mediate dioceses,[27] cloisters, other ecclesiastical properties, and their collected belongings, which the ancestors of the electors, princes, and estates of the Holy Roman Empire who were adherents of the Augsburg Confession[28] confiscated and possessed before the establishment

---

26. Litoměřice, the Czech Republic.

27. Mediate territories were those subject to at least one legal overlord below the emperor. Territories directly below the emperor were called immediate territories.

28. Lutherans.

of the Treaty (or Religious Peace) of Passau,[29] these shall thoroughly and absolutely remain by the clear letter and decree of the said Religious Peace, which is strongly affirmed.

As, however, for what concerns the immediate dioceses and ecclesiastical properties that were confiscated before the Treaty (or Religious Peace) of Passau, as well as those dioceses and ecclesiastical properties that came under the power of adherents of the Augsburg Confession after the Treaty (or Religious Peace) of Augsburg, whether mediate or immediate (and including also the free secular dioceses, as well as the lands under the sovereignty and command of the high-ranking imperial knights), it has finally been agreed that these electors, princes, and estates shall for forty years, to be reckoned from the date of this concluded accommodation, hold in tranquillity whatever they possessed, held, and used in the year 1627, on the 12th of November (new style),[30] with no exceptions of whatever name; and also without any claim or assertion of whatever pretext, appearance, pretense, or claim as could or might occur; and whatever one or the other party confiscated or removed from such possessions after that date shall be restored fully and completely, yet without any reimbursement for any usage, damages, or expenses that one party might claim of another. . . .

For those dioceses and ecclesiastical properties that are regulated by the above paragraph (beginning "As, however, for what concerns . . . " etc.), during the allowed forty years, they shall absolutely remain in ecclesiastical and secular affairs as they were on the 12th of November (new style) 1627. . . .

Concerning those seats and votes in the imperial and deputation diets,[31] as well as in the sessions of the Imperial Chamber dedicated to inspection and appeals, that the estates that are adherents of the Augsburg Confession might wish to use because of the rights included with their possessions, or because of those immediate dioceses they attained by the power of this peace agreement, it shall remain thus, that these seats and votes be set aside for the whole of the forty years. . . .

So that posterity, after the lapsing of the oft-mentioned forty years, is not once again caught up in upheaval and complications because of disputes begun so very long before, but instead is maintained in good love and unity, peace-loving estates of both religions in equal numbers (or their empowered

29. The 1555 Peace of Augsburg had legalized the loss of all Church property confiscated by Lutherans before the 1552 Peace of Passau, but had barred any future secularization.

30. According to the new Gregorian calendar, not the older Julian calendar that many in the empire still used and that was ten days behind the new one.

31. A deputation diet was like a diet of electors, but somewhat larger, as it included deputies from several other great princes and prince-bishops.

advisors, ambassadors, and envoys) shall meet before the expiry of the approved forty years and shall expend the utmost effort, concern, and diligence in order to determine if the matter of the ecclesiastical property could one day completely be settled to the satisfaction of both sides.

However, so that this accommodation is not saved until too late or until the very last minute, it should at the latest be taken up and, as far as is humanly possible, concluded within ten years from this date. . . .

Should this, however, not happen, after the expiry of the forty years each party shall possess those rights that it had on the 12th of November (new style) 1627—however strong or weak they may have been at that time—and may employ them amicably or legally. And no party may, on account of this, take up arms against another's unrecognized legal rights, nor is it permitted that the Roman Imperial Majesty do such a thing, nor for the estates to complain about it.

Yet in case there is no accommodation or there are further disputes, His Imperial Majesty retains for himself and for his successors, as supreme heads of the empire, the proper sovereign power and jurisdiction to judge disputes in every case between parties, both through the Imperial Aulic Council and through the Imperial Chamber Court,[32] though always after a sufficient preceding examination and by means of the legal process; and, since he carries the high imperial office, he shall also maintain the Religious (and Secular) Peace [of Augsburg] and shall justly enforce it according to the designations of the imperial recesses[33] and the imperial election capitulation.[34]

The Catholics shall neither be opposed nor dispossessed, in the least, of their archbishoprics, cloisters, and other ecclesiastical property that they possessed on the 12th of November (new style) 1627, or that they should once again recover by dint of this peace agreement. Instead, should something further be taken from them or struck down, they shall immediately, and without delay, have it restored to them. . . .

Likewise, adherents of the Augsburg Confession shall be maintained in the same way, namely that they shall not in the least be oppressed contrary to the terms of the Religious (and Secular) Peace, or of this peace, or of any other imperial ordinances and statutes; nor shall they be dispossessed of that diocesan and ecclesiastical property which they possessed in the past and which, according to the stipulations of this peace agreement, they should retain.

As to the archbishopric of Magdeburg, for the sake of peace a decision has been reached that His Princely Grace Duke August of Saxony, Jülich, Cleves,

32. The two supreme courts of the empire.
33. The resolutions of the imperial diet.
34. Emperors had to agree to certain limitations on their power (such as swearing to protect and respect the rights of the princes) as a prerequisite for taking office.

and Berg,[35] the beloved son of His Serene Highness the elector of Saxony, may possess and enjoy [Magdeburg] during the remaining days of his life, and His Princely Grace shall neither be perturbed nor hindered therein. . . .

As for what has been approved for the adherents of the Augsburg Confession in the Passau agreement, as stated above, His Imperial Majesty expressly stipulates that this shall not be understood to abolish or change the 1629 peace agreement of Lübeck[36] erected between His Imperial Majesty and His Royal Majesty of Denmark, Norway, etc.; rather the contents of that peace shall be absolutely untouched.

As, then, for His Imperial Majesty's beloved lord son, Archduke Leopold Wilhelm,[37] Most Princely Serene Highness, he shall retain, among other things, the bishopric of Halberstadt . . . and in the archdiocese of Bremen, he shall maintain the Catholic religion and the Augsburg Confession, and their free exercise, for the entire forty years in the state in which they were on the 12th of November (new style) 1627. . . .

The free imperial knights shall be left in peace in their exercise of the Augsburg Confession, as allowed by the Religious Peace, and there shall be no injury made against them because of this; rather, insofar as some might sometime occur, they would receive restitution for it.

For those imperial cities with which His Imperial Majesty has already made a separate accord during this war, such accords shall remain in force. For all other imperial cities, however, things shall remain, through and through, by the terms of the Religious Peace. . . .

As to the Roman Imperial Majesty's hereditary kingdom of Bohemia and the rest of the Austrian hereditary lands, His Serene Highness the elector of Saxony most imploringly, most strongly, and most diligently insisted that His Most Highly Esteemed Imperial Majesty allow the free exercise of the unaltered Augsburg Confession[38] in those places and locations where it existed in the year 1627, and that it also remain free and unmolested; and he also fervently urged such a thing by presenting numerous different reasons, and he refused to weaken from this in any way. Yet no matter how often and

---

35. The family of the elector of Saxony had long claimed the title of "dukes of Saxony, Jülich, Cleves, and Berg," but did not actually hold the territories.

36. The Treaty of Lübeck was the peace made between the emperor and Christian IV, king of Denmark, after Christian's failed intervention in the war.

37. Archduke Leopold Wilhelm von Habsburg (1614–1662), the youngest son of Ferdinand II and his wife Maria-Anna of Bavaria, served as a general during the war. The emperor had granted him the bishoprics of Magdeburg and Halberstadt in 1627, in reward for his service.

38. Lutheranism. By including the word "unaltered," the phrase makes it clear that Calvinism is specifically excluded.

in how many ways His Imperial Majesty was appealed to on this matter, he would not be moved; rather, he became much more opposed, raising all kinds of objections and, among many others, pointing out that one would then appear to be willing to dispossess His Imperial Majesty, for estates that were adherents of the Augsburg Confession had argued, using numerous appeals and demands, that the right to establish their own regulation of religion and its exercise was dependent on their princely territorial sovereignty. What is just for one estate of the empire must then not be unjust, nor forbidden, for another—especially for His Imperial Majesty himself. His Serene Electoral Highness was displeased to learn that His Imperial Majesty was not willing to allow this, and he wished that things might be otherwise, but as His Imperial Majesty so firmly stood by this position, it remained absolutely as it was. As for Silesia, His Imperial Majesty has made a special resolution,[39] and as for Lusatia, it shall remain with the particular agreement it reached with His Serene Highness the elector.[40]

His Serene Highness the elector of Saxony also sought and desired that a greater equity of religion on the Imperial Chamber Court be introduced, and that after the current Catholic judge,[41] an adherent of the Augsburg Confession be named, and then after his retirement, once again a Catholic, and so on and so on, alternating; also that four presidents,[42] among which two would be Catholic and two adherents of the Augsburg Confession, be appointed; and that the number of assessors[43] who were adherents of the Augsburg Confession be made exactly equal to the number of Catholic assessors. . . .

Yet this article is deferred until the soonest meeting of the estates of the empire, including adherents of both religions, and as soon as they might come together, this matter shall be taken up. In the meantime, however, and until this is resolved, the previous general arrangement of the Chamber Court shall remain unchanged. . . .

As to the Imperial Aulic Council, His Imperial Majesty and his ambassadors once again declared that, by virtue of the contents of the imperial capitulation, at the first imperial assembly the matter of the Aulic Council's composition be given to the assembled lord electors for their determina-

---

39. The emperor, through the mediation of the elector of Saxony, had reached a separate religious accommodation with Silesia in 1621, allowing the free exercise of Lutheranism. This older assurance of religious freedom was now affirmed.

40. The elector had gained the territory of Lusatia by this agreement. He had long desired Lusatia, and the possibility of its acquisition had been at the heart of his initial support for the emperor against Frederick of the Palatinate, the "Winter King."

41. The chief justice, appointed by the emperor.

42. The presidents would serve under and assist the chief justice.

43. The assessors were the judges. Most were appointed by the imperial estates.

tion. . . . However, His Serene Highness the elector of Saxony thereby further sought that the Aulic Council be occupied in an even manner by an equal number from each religion. Yet the imperial ambassadors opposed this, arguing that the appointment of Aulic councilors in equal numbers from adherents of both religions would not occur within the Roman Empire, and that, furthermore, His Imperial Majesty would not do such a thing. . . .

In the Palatine matter, from which a great deal of gruesome commotion, unrest, and hardship have proceeded in the past years, His Serene Highness the elector of Saxony, etc., urgently insisted that this matter, in terms of both the electoral title and lands, be entirely and fundamentally settled and agreed.

As is universally known, however, and also as the most praiseworthy electoral college determined at Mühlhausen in 1627, the proscribed Count Palatine Frederick was a main instigator and originator of all of the disasters that took place in His Imperial Majesty's hereditary kingdom of Bohemia and subsequently in the Roman Empire, and His Imperial Majesty, along with his most highly honored house, incurred many millions in debts and other great losses and was also forced to give up part of his hereditary lands on account of expending such war costs. And therefore, no matter how strongly and zealously His Serene Highness the elector of Saxony endeavored on this matter, the emperor would not budge from his resolution.

Namely, that things would remain entirely with what His Imperial Majesty had arranged elsewhere—giving the prince Palatine's electoral title and lands to His Serene Highness the elector of Bavaria and to the Wilhelmine line[44]— as well as with what His Imperial Majesty had ordained on account of several existing Palatine servants and properties. Yet the surviving, widowed wife of the deceased Elector Frederick IV, count Palatine of the Rhine, should be given a lifetime annuity . . . and, as long as they dutifully humble themselves before His Imperial Majesty, the proscribed children should be provided a princely pension—though this would be out of imperial graciousness, not out of indebtedness. . . .

As to the restitution, the estates that are adherents of the Augsburg Confession shall, without fail, restore and withdraw from whatever and however much they still hold of the electoral lands, principalities, counties and domains, lands and peoples, castles, passes, fortresses, agricultural properties, and all associated rents, revenues, uses, income, and all places that, after the

44. Bavaria and the Upper and Lower Palatinate had once belonged to a single member of the Wittelsbach family; but in the fourteenth century, the territories were split between two branches of the family. The elder or Rudolphine branch of the family held the two Palatinates and the electoral dignity, while the younger or Wilhelmine branch held Bavaria.

disorder caused by King Gustavus Adolphus of Sweden's arrival onto imperial territory in the year 1630, they took from the Roman Imperial Majesty, his archducal house, and all of those electors, princes, and estates who assisted him, as well as all of their confederates and their advisors, servants, estates, and subjects . . . and specifically from the duke of Lorraine and his affiliates, and also whatever His Imperial Majesty and those who assisted him had in their possession at the said time, or whatever is otherwise due to them by dint of this agreement (whether they had it in their possession in the year 1630 or not). . . .

Yet this point should always be understood not to mean or include that ecclesiastical or secular property that was in the hands of the Catholic estates in 1630, but that by force of various points of this peace agreement should belong to the adherents of the Augsburg Confession.

Likewise, His Imperial Majesty and the collected Catholic estates and their confederates shall and will restore everything and withdraw [from all property] belonging to all electors, princes, and estates of the empire that are adherents of the Augsburg Confession, as well as their advisors, servants, estates, and subjects, and, in general, each and every one of their affiliates, excluding no one (except for those who are excluded from the amnesty), and which His Most Highly Esteemed Imperial Majesty, those electors, princes, and estates who assisted him, and their confederates occupied during the turbulence that resulted after the arrival of the king of Sweden onto imperial territory in the year 1630, and shall also [restore] everything that should, by dint of this peace agreement, remain with the adherents of the Augsburg Confession. . . .

Above and beyond this, for the sake of peace, His Roman Imperial Majesty has also conceded that whatever was occupied in the Lower Saxon Circle[45] during the turbulence that arose in the year 1625—including in particular the fortresses of Wolffenbüttel and Nienburg—shall be restored without fail to its legal lords, along with whatever cities and fortresses of these places His Imperial Majesty and those who assisted him have in their hands. . . .

Whatever His Serene Highness the elector of Saxony still possesses in the kingdom of Bohemia and in the duchy of Silesia, he shall restore without any delay within seven days after the acceptance of this peace . . . and on the same day that Bohemia and Silesia are restored to His Imperial Majesty, His Imperial Majesty shall likewise restore and withdraw from all parts of electoral Saxony or other lands belonging to His Serene Highness the elector of Saxony that His Imperial Majesty or those military officers assisting him have then in their possession.

45. A circle was an administrative region of the empire.

Furthermore, His Serene Highness the elector shall and will, along with the newly raised imperial army, also help to ensure the withdrawal from that property which, according to this treaty and peace agreement, belongs to the Catholics of the empire, whether or not the other electors, princes, and estates that are adherents of the Augsburg Confession recognize and adhere to this accord.

On the other hand, His Imperial Majesty and the Catholics shall, with united effort and assistance, harmoniously provide and offer help, rescue, and the reacquisition of those possessions that, according to the stipulations of this peace agreement, are due to the adherents of the Augsburg Confession.

It shall also hereby be expressly stipulated that His Serene Highness the elector of Brandenburg,[46] if he agrees to this pacification and brings himself to abide by all of it, shall then absolutely keep the entitlement to and enfeoffment of the Pomeranian lands, and this shall be protected by His Imperial Majesty.

Not only on account of the Pomeranian lands, but also in general, all men shall join together to endeavor that the Upper and Lower Saxon Circles are liberated from foreigners (especially the Swedes) and other troops that are situated there but refuse to abide by this peace agreement, and that such are driven from imperial territory. And should they not be willing to retreat, they shall be met by a united force; the places that they possess shall be freed and shall, without fail, once again be withdrawn from and returned to their former lords or to those to whom the lands belong by dint of this peace agreement.

This shall also happen in the same way in the Westphalian or Lower Rhenish Circle, and especially along the Weser River. . . .

As for the duke of Lorraine, it is hereby expressly stipulated and agreed that he be everywhere restored to all of his lands and people, castles, passes, fortresses, agricultural properties, usages, revenues and incomes, dignities, titles, and rights, as they were in the year 1630, with no exceptions. . . .

There shall be a complete amnesty between, on the one side, His Roman Imperial Majesty and the collected Catholics, the electors, princes, and estates of the empire who assisted them, and all of their confederates; and on the other side, His Serene Highness the elector of Saxony, as well as all of those warring parties who have been with him until now and who are estates that adhere to the Augsburg Confession, as long as all of them absolutely agree to and bind themselves by this peace agreement, and truly bring themselves to abide by and take up its entire execution and implementation, immediately after its publication. . . . In such a way, one may try to abolish entirely everything that occurred between the two sides since 1630, during

46. George William, elector of Brandenburg (1595–1640).

this last military operation in the Holy Roman Empire after the king of Sweden's arrival onto imperial territory, whatever cause was given, established, or erected for this; and all disagreements, ill humor, and antipathy that emerged from this, however it may have happened.

His Imperial Majesty, however, expressly excludes from this amnesty the Bohemian and Palatine negotiations and matters, and whatever depends upon them. . . .

Furthermore, His Imperial Majesty also excludes from this amnesty some persons and property for which His Imperial Majesty and His Serene Highness the elector of Saxony have made a special written communication.[47] . . .

For because His Imperial Majesty most graciously insisted on this separate extract, and because His Serene Highness the elector of Saxony also did not wish that, on account of such a reservation, the beneficial pacification of the empire be hindered for a single hour, thus His Serene Highness the elector finally, for the sake of peace, allowed it to remain; and this reservation and its specifications, which are drawn up in a supplementary settlement under today's date, shall have the same force and validity, and shall be held to as if they were incorporated exactly, word by word, into this treaty.

Yet His Imperial Majesty has, aside from this, most graciously declared that when, after the publication of this specification, one or another of the excluded persons should, unsolicited, apply for and desire mercy, then, depending on the situation, the path to the seat of imperial mercy shall not be blocked for them.

For this peace was made for the purpose that the esteemed German Nation be brought back to its former integrity, tranquillity, liberty, and security, and the Roman Imperial Majesty and his high archducal house, as well as all electors, princes, and estates of the empire (that are not excluded and that declare themselves for it), without distinction between those of the Catholic religion and the Augsburg Confession, are restored to their possessions and maintained in them; but until and inasmuch as this is put into effect, there shall be no rest nor celebration.

For the real and final execution and implementation of all of this, His Imperial Majesty, as the head in the empire, remains armed, and the troops of His Serene Highness the elector of Saxony and of all other electors, princes, and estates (excluding those troops they shall keep . . . for the occupation of their fortresses) shall join with him and perform their duty for His Imperial

---

47. Among those specifically excluded from the peace or its amnesty were the heirs of Frederick of the Palatinate, the margrave of Baden-Durlach, and the duke of Württemberg. Other princes, such as the duke of Saxe-Weimar and the landgrave of Hesse-Cassel, were given separate terms that they found intolerable, and so refused to sign.

Majesty and the empire for the execution and implementation of this peace. And so, from all the armies, there shall be made one main army that shall be called and named the grand army of His Roman Imperial Majesty and of the Holy Roman Empire. From this grand army, His Imperial Majesty leaves a considerable body under the high general command of His Serene Highness the elector of Saxony. The remaining troops, altogether, shall be and remain immediately under the highest general command of His Imperial Majesty's beloved son, the king of Hungary and Bohemia.[48] . . .

The armies, as well as all of their generals, general lieutenants, field marshals, and each and every one of their allied persons, from the highest to the lowest, shall be faithful, well disposed, loyal, and attentive to His Roman Imperial Majesty and the Holy Empire. . . .

And because it is impossible at this time to achieve general assemblies of the imperial circles and deputation diets—and yet an arrangement must be made for the support of still so many troops, even if we soon reach a complete peace (may God graciously grant this)—thus one anticipates that immediately along with and beside their acceptance of this peace agreement, no elector, prince, or estate of the empire, nor any of the free imperial knights or Hansa cities,[49] will hesitate to grant 120 months, according to the simple Roman month,[50] and to pay this, without fail, in six equal payments: namely on September 1 and December 1 of this year, and March 1, June 1, September 1, and December 1 of next year, 1636. . . .

No estate shall then be responsible for contributing and also having to bear the burden of military quartering or the support of the soldiery for free; rather, His Imperial Majesty and the imperial commissaries, who will be appointed specially to this task after the conclusion of this agreement, shall take care to make and keep ordinances of support that are just and equal, so that whatever an estate or its subjects supplies in terms of provisions or animal feed will be subtracted from its contributions. . . .

There shall be no single military alliance made in the Holy Roman Empire, either by the head or the members, that goes against the imperial election capitulation, the imperial recesses, or the constitutions of the circles.

48. Ferdinand von Habsburg (1608–1657), the eldest son of the emperor and his successor. He had served as commander of the imperial army since Wallenstein's death in 1634.

49. Cities belonging to the Hanseatic League.

50. The Roman month, or *Römerzug,* was originally a trip made by a new emperor, accompanied by his feudal vassals, to Rome to be crowned by the pope. Once emperors no longer participated in this ceremony, the Roman month became a fixed tax or rate of tax granted by the imperial estates for emergencies or extraordinary circumstances.

It shall also not be allowed that any foreign military power come onto imperial territory on account of any matter—whether addressed in this treaty or not, and especially not on account of the Palatine matter—that is in opposition to the imperial concession, enfeoffment, or decree. . . .

Furthermore, by and with the erecting of this peace agreement and its publication, each and every union, league, federation, and similar agreement, as well as those oaths and duties that apply to them, shall be entirely abolished and shall instead be directed solely and alone toward the constitutions of the empire and the circles, and toward this present peace. . . .

> Made at Prague the 30th of May in the year of our Savior and
> Redeemer 1635.

25. Complaint of Elector John George of Saxony (March 15, 1636)[51]

[By March 1636 the elector of Saxony, John George, began to think that the 1635 Peace of Prague, which he had been instrumental in bringing to fruition, had failed. Rather than producing a lasting peace in the empire that would quickly lead to the expulsion of foreign armies, it had instead only sown the seeds of further conflict. The explicit exclusion from the peace of key princes of the empire who had maintained their alliance with the Swedes (including the duke of Saxe-Weimar, the landgrave of Hesse-Cassel, the duke of Württemberg, the margrave of Baden-Durlach, and the heirs of Frederick of the Palatinate) had left these princes with no option but to keep fighting and had also encouraged the Swedes to intervene further on their behalf. Furthermore, despite his assurances, the emperor had continued to push the process of re-Catholicization. This violated the promises that John George had made to his fellow Lutherans—that their religious liberty would be preserved—and, he feared, had begun to make him look like a fool.

Most Serene Highness, etc.

I, along with the army I command, have been continually in the field and engaged in military campaigns since the month of August in the recently past year [1635], with all of my thoughts and deeds directed toward the quickest return of the most highly needed peace within the poor frightened

---

51. John George, Elector of Saxony (letter sent) to the Emperor, Hall, March 15, 1636, presented April 6, 1636, Haus-, Hof- und Staatsarchiv, Wien, Friedensakten 17a, fol. 78–83.

fatherland of the German Nation, and hereby not sparing my own life and limb, nor having the least dread for any danger, adversity, or difficulty. As for myself, after the issuance of the peace, I greatly strove to eject the officers of the crown of Sweden from the empire, first through the use of kindness, next through force of arms. To some extent, I also, with numerous well-meaning warnings and most humble intercessions, appealed to Your Majesty for a rebuttal of the pretexts by which the foreign troops justify their persistent residence and evil start in the Empire of the German Nation. For it is not only the common man who is uncertain at times, but many leading men and potentates are also thrown into confusion. All of this is known within and outside the empire, but it is especially apparent to Your Most Gracious Imperial Majesty.

I now affirm from my heart and consider it to be my greatest misfortune, that the care, effort, and exertion that I have employed and the troubles that I have willingly borne have, as of yet, not been able to reach my goals. Instead, my lands and people and those of neighboring electors and princes have been irrevocably ruined, and almost more than half of the army entrusted to me has been lost. Thus the evil increases from day to day. Nevertheless, I shall not fail to appeal to Your Imperial Majesty further with the most humble good intentions (because of the love that I bear for the fatherland and for my electoral duties, such that Your Imperial Majesty and the Holy Empire know that I am tightly bound to you), and to point out that from the letters exchanged between the duke of Mecklenburg and the Swedish imperial chancellor[52] in Stralsund, which Your Imperial Majesty sent out on February 29, we can see that the chancellor principally intends to obscure his activities [with these negotiations], for many of the estates in Germany that are allied with the crown of Sweden are excluded from the amnesty, or rather are suspended so far away from a grant of amnesty that the crown of Sweden would not, out of honor and conscience, abandon them before they gained a reliable certainty, nor would it retreat from the empire before their inclusion in the amnesty.

On the other hand, and although I have now referred various times to what we understood among ourselves in the negotiations of the Peace of Prague, at that time Your Imperial Majesty most graciously offered—not only in the published peace agreement, but also in the side agreement—to agree with me that the peace should not be infringed due to this [issue of amnesty]; and you have also, since then, often written in reply that you would graciously extend the point of amnesty so that none ought have any cause to continue the war any longer in Germany because of it. Yet Your Imperial Majesty can see from the Stralsund documents how very badly all of

52. Axel Oxenstierna.

this is being received on the part of the Swedes, and that the longer this goes on, the more firmly they make every effort to challenge the point.

And perhaps one should again attempt to bring the neighboring crowns of Denmark and England to see our viewpoint, as all hopes of a further reconciliation with the remaining [German] estates are completely gone and lost.

Only out of German sincerity, I must acknowledge that the constant reproach makes me not a little aggrieved and saddened. For weapons are now being wielded against my own fellow religionists, loyal to Your Imperial Majesty, who trusted the words of the published peace agreement, accommodated themselves to it in a timely manner and without hesitation, and—rejecting all foreign help that was offered, and with great patience—partially maintained themselves through misery. And yet their churches were taken from them, the Roman Catholic religion was imposed, reconciliation was kept from them day after day, that which they had specifically been promised was not afforded to them, and the religion and administration of their communities were practically abolished through unbearable quartering of troops and exorbitant, forced contributions. Thus my electoral dignity, given by Your Imperial Majesty's commission and subsequent confirmation, has been made worthless, and I am regarded with ignominious contempt almost everywhere.

Examples of such disapproval come from the duke of Württemberg,[53] the city of Augsburg, and other oppressed imperial estates and cities, and also from the territory of Silesia[54]—especially from the cities in the principalities of Schweidnitz, Jauer, Groß-Glogau, and Münsterberg, as well as the nobility in the bishopric of Neisse. Your Imperial Majesty can most graciously rest assured that until my earthly life shall vanish and fall away from me, according to God's gracious will, I will be obliged to heed Your Imperial Majesty and observe the peace agreement. Yet at the same time, I maintain the humble certainty and immutable confidence that Your Imperial Majesty will not leave me open to any disgrace; and I also advise and humbly ask, following the guidance of the peace agreement, the side agreements, and the various and most gracious clarifications that have appeared since then, that, first of all, you would not endanger the duke of Württemberg any longer in his possession of those lands, people, and religious status that he had in the

---

53. Eberhard III, duke of Württemberg (1614–1674). Many of his territories were re-Catholicized after the 1629 Edict of Restitution, and even more after his devastating loss at the 1634 battle of Nördlingen.

54. Silesia is an area in the east of the empire, attached to the Bohemian crown (the region is now divided among Germany, the Czech Republic, and Poland). The vast majority of Silesians were Lutheran, and they initially opposed the Habsburgs during the Bohemian uprising. The people of Silesia suffered particularly grave losses during the war.

year 1627;[55] that you would grant, in the same way, the city of Augsburg justice; that you would most graciously leave the Silesian cities and nobles with the assurance that was given by me and affirmed by Your Imperial Majesty, as they never, neither in general nor in particular, committed a crime against Your Imperial Majesty; and that you would thereby deflect the objections of the foreigners and give all the world to know that Your Imperial Majesty, with innate archducal leniency, does not allow an innocent and loyal subject to be driven out. (But that is not to say that Your Imperial Majesty's dignity ought to submit to a threatened adversary.)

I once again return to my above humble declaration that these, my warnings and requests, benevolently, faithfully, and earnestly spring from the dear obligations by which I stand attached to Your Imperial Majesty and the Holy Empire, and from love for the aggrieved fatherland. And I am undoubtedly convinced that as soon as Your Imperial Majesty shall allow the amnesty and previous practice of religion to those who will humble themselves to you and obediently appeal to you on their own or through my offered intercession, the above-mentioned and other potentates will themselves recognize this and will thus oppose and help to impede the threatened advance of the Swedish military officers and others. I will also willingly, and with so much the more joyfulness, undertake all the difficulty, concern, and danger that may occur in the service of Your Imperial Majesty and the Holy Empire. And in addition to this, I would especially rejoice should Your Imperial Majesty not move to involve a foreign power and league[56] in such a resolution and directive as I have sought for the oppressed obedient estates who are my fellow religionists; but rather that you would only use Your Imperial Majesty's inherent and universally recognized benevolence, clemency, and great love for the oppressed poor fatherland. I also trust that you firmly and most graciously intend to support my word, which was given as an elector, and that you will uphold for posterity the lofty names and laudable honor of those who have made peace and of the fatherland, which will be delivered from final collapse.

I now, most patiently and without misgivings, await Your Imperial Majesty's most gracious resolution. Thus I remain always willing and ready to serve you most humbly and loyally.

Dated in my headquarters at Hall, the 15th of March 1636

Your Roman Imperial Majesty's most humble, loyal, etc.
John George, duke of Saxony, Jülich, Cleves, and Berg, elector.

55. In that year, foreshadowing the empirewide Edict of Restitution, the emperor ordered the duke to return to the Church some significant ecclesiastical properties, including the priory of Reichenbach.
56. Spain.

26. Voyage of William Crowne (April–June 1636)[57]

*[By the mid-1630s the war had involved most European powers and spread
across Central Europe. Plague and famine raged in many places, battles and
sieges in many others. Some areas, however, remained relatively untouched, as
did one major power, England, which had resisted all appeals for it to enter
the fray. In 1636 the English ambassador to the emperor, Thomas Howard,
the earl of Arundel, traveled to the continent to visit the emperor at Prague.
One of his young servants, William Crowne (c. 1617–1682), recorded a jour-
nal of their trip from England to the Dutch Republic and then across the
breadth of the empire. It provides an interesting account of the state of the empire through the eyes of an outside observer.]*

Relation by Way of Journall, etc.

THE seventh of April being Thursday, 1636. His Excellency departed from
Greenwich for Germanie,[58] tooke Barge about three of the clocke in the
morning, and landed at Gravesend, from thence by Coach to Canterbury to
bed, the next day to Margate where wee dined, and about three of the clocke
in the afternoone, hee tooke shipping in one of the Kings Ships called the
Happy Entrance, and landed the tenth day being Sunday at Helver-sluce,[59]
and from thence to the Brill,[60] there sailing over a lake into Masanssluce,[61]
and so on by waggons to Delph,[62] and to the Hage:[63] but a mile before wee
came thither, there met us some of the Queene of Bohemia's[64] Coaches,

---

57. William Crowne, *A True relation of all the Remarkable Places and Passages Observed in the Travels of the right honorable Thomas Lord Howard, Earle of Arundell and
Surrey, Primer Earle, and Earle Marshall of England, Ambassador Extraordinary to his
sacred Majesty Ferdinando the second, Emperour of Germanie, Anno Domini 1636, By
William Crowne Gentleman, London, Printed for Henry Seile and are to be sold in Fleet-
street, at the Signe of the Tygress-head betweene the Bridge and the Conduit* (London:
Henry Seile, 1637). A copy can be found at the Huntington Library.

58. A map may be helpful for those who wish to follow along with Crowne's voyage.

59. Hellevoetsluis.

60. Brielle.

61. Maassluis.

62. Delft.

63. The Hague.

64. Elizabeth Stuart, queen of Bohemia, was the daughter of King James I of England and the widow of Frederick V, elector Palatine. She had lived in the Dutch Republic since she and her husband had fled Bohemia at the beginning of the war.

which her Majesty sent for his Excellency, and in one of them his Excellency went to her Majesty that night, the time we staid there, was spent in visits betweene the Prince of Orange,[65] his Excellency and the States,[66] with some other Ambassadours, that were then there, as the French, Venetian, and the Swedish, heere we staid three daies, and departed the fourteenth day by wagons, passing through Leiden to Woerden, and then entred the Bishopricke of Utrecht, and so to the City it selfe where wee lay, the Princes being there at schoole, his Excellency went to see them that night, the next day thence to Rhenem[67] to dine, where the Queene hath an house adjacent to the Rhine, on the left side, which wee viewed, having faire roomes and gardens belonging to it, after diner, wee entered into Gelder-land, so through Wagening[68] to Arnheim[69] to bed, passing that afternoone through much danger, by reason of Out-lyers from the Army at Schenckenschans,[70] which was not farre off, the Prince of Brandeburgh being heere in Towne, visited his Excellency the next day, and the day after his Excellency visited him, who was shewed by him, the ashes of some Romanes preserved in pots, that were found in a Mountaine called Zanten,[71] which wee afterward passed by, heere wee lay Easter-day and the Munday following, and did see the smoake and fire out of the great Peeces[72] from the Sconce,[73] as they were in skirmish, thether his Excellency sent the Steward and a Trumpeter to demand passage of the Spanyard in the Schans, and Grave William[74] for the Hollander, but the Spaniard would not grant it, without order from Brussels, Grave William hearing their answer, sent his Excellency word, hee made no doubt, but to give him free passage the next day, for he resolved to make an assault that night upon the Sconce, upon the assault, the Spaniards yeelded it up on conditions,[75] and heere his Excellency published certaine orders, to be generally

65. Frederick Henry, prince of Orange (1584–1647).

66. The States-General was the governing body of the Dutch Republic.

67. Rhenen.

68. Wageningen.

69. Arnhem.

70. Schenkenschanz was a heavily fortified island in the middle of the Rhine.

71. Xanten, a city in modern North Rhine–Westphalia (Germany), was the site of a large Roman settlement.

72. Cannons.

73. A small defensive fortification.

74. Count William, a commander in Frederick Henry's army.

75. The capture of Schenkenschanz by Frederick Henry's army at the end of April would be a huge strategic victory for the Dutch against the Spanish.

observed amongst us, one reason was, the sickenesse,[76] being heere very much, wee staid heere three daies and departed the nineteenth in waggons for Schans, first crossed over the Rhine just by the towne on to the right side into Cleveland,[77] and so to the Tolhouse, a Castle where the Hollanders take toll at,[78] adjoyning to the Rhine on the same side, then passing through all their workes and Army, leaving the Schans at a distance which was miserably battered, untill wee came to Grave William his Tent, where some of the Spaniards were sealing of their agreements what quarter they should have, who instantly left them, to bring his Excellency over the Rhine on a Bridge of flat bottom'd Boates, guarded with all his Troopes of Horse, untill wee came at the Barke wherein his Excellency lay that night, then returned and sent a Company of English Souldiers to guard it, the next day earely wee weighed Anchor and sailed up the Rhine, having a Guard of Souldiers along the shore, by reason the Enemy went out of the Schans that morning, so passing by Emmerick and Rees, Townes with strong sconces adjoyning to the Rhine on the left side, then in sight of the Mountaine Zanten on the other side, so by Burick,[79] on the same side, to Wesell a Towne on the left side of the Rhine, against which wee cast Anchor, and lay on ship-board all night, for they died there of the sickenesse more than thirty a day, neverthelesse the next morning we tooke waggons in number eighteen and displaied our English colours in three severall wagons, passing over a little River in Boats call'd Lipp, then by Rheinbergh on the right hand being the last Towne of the States,[80] then by Dinslacken, on the same side to Duisburgh to dinner, where none of our carriage might enter in, for as his Excellency entered the gate, one of the watch discharged his peece neere unto the horses breast, the rest being instantly commanded to the contrary, but the Gates were shut up, and wee kept out, until the Towne were satisfied, wee were no Enemy, our carriage and Company being great, frightened them at the first, after diner we past through a long Wood in much danger, and in the view of Rogues, who did not set upon us because our Company was great, yet we fearing the worst, had sent for a Convoy of Musketiers to the next Towne before, who met us not untill we were out of the Wood.

Then wee entered into Bergish-land,[81] and went by Keiserswert to Dus-

76. Plague.
77. The duchy of Cleves.
78. Where they have a customs house that collects tolls from passing ships.
79. Perrich.
80. The Dutch Republic.
81. The Bergisches Land was the territory traditionally controlled by the duke of Berg, now a part of the German state of North Rhine–Westphalia.

seldorp[82] to bed, which adjoynes to the Rhine on the left side, where the Duke of Neiuburgh[83] lay, who was with his Dutchesse abroad taking the aire, but espying us comming, returned backe into the Towne with speed, and sent to have the Ports shut up, thinking wee had beene some Enemy, but hearing it was his Excellency was very joyfull, and sent Coaches for him, to come and suppe with him, and to make his house his lodging the time he staid, but the next morning after breake-fast, perceiving his Excellency would goe away, had three Coaches waiting at the doore, into one hee put his Excellency, and us into the rest, and brought us out of Towne, with a Company of Horsemen and Foote in Armes, and a Troope of Lances going before, and Trumpets sounding about the Coach, his owne Guard; being thus brought without the Gates, hee tooke his leave of his Excellency and returned, and as wee were departing, there went off great peeces of Ordnance.

Thence neere Neusse, and then crossed over the Rhine at a little Dorpe[84] called Hittorpe,[85] into the Territory of Collein,[86] and then to the City where we lay. It is seated on the right side of the Rhine, where the Bishop of Mentz[87] was, who sent one of his Privie Counsell to invite his Excellency the next day to diner, he then sent three of his Coaches for us, and gave his Excellency very noble entertainement; the first night his Excellency came, were presented unto him twenty foure Flaggons of severall kindes of Wine, the next day twenty eight, and at every Present, there was a long speech made to his Excellency in Latine by one that came with the Wine, which came all from the Magistrates of the City in Flaggons with the City Armes on them, the Jesuits there have built them a very stately Church and richly adorned it with gildings and erected an Altar one of the stateliest, I ever saw, in the City likewise there is a great Church called the Dome,[88] wherein lye the Bodies of three Kings, called The three Kings of Collein, which went to worship our Saviour, then is there another Church called Saint Ursulas, in which lyeth the bones of 11000. Virgins in places locked up, and Saint Ursula in a faire Tombe by them, which came all thither with her for their Devotion, there is besides a Nunnery and some English Nunnes there.

Heere we staid a weeke, and the twenty eighth day wee tooke a Boate drawne with nine horses and went up the Rhine, by many Villages pillaged

82. Kaiserswerth to Düsseldorf.
83. Wolfgang Wilhelm, count Palatine of Neuburg. His capitol was at Düsseldorf.
84. Village.
85. Hitdorf.
86. Cologne.
87. Mainz.
88. Cologne cathedral, or *Kölner Dom* in German.

and shot downe, and many brave Vineyards on Mountaines, along the Rivers side, passing by Bonn on the right side, and seven high Burghens with old Castles on them, seated on the other side of the River, and to Drachenfels Castle on the left side of the Rhine, against which wee cast Anchor and lay that night on ship-board, the next morning earely weighed Anchor, passing by an Island in which is a Monastery of Nunnes called Nonenwerther, so on by Hammerstein Castle by Keigrmagen Andernach and Ormus[89] three Townes on the right side of the Rhine, against Ormus wee cast Anchor and lay on ship-board.

The next day earely weighed Anchor and went by Engers on the left side, and there begunne Trierischlandt,[90] and so to Coblentz[91] a Towne adjoyning to the Rhine on the right side, which the French lately lost, being driven out by the Emperours Forces into a Castle seated on a very high Rocke, opposite to the Towne called Hermanstein, which commandeth the Towne, who were then skirmishing when wee came, wherefore wee cast Anchor about halfe an English mile before, and sent a Trumpeter desiring passage, which they willingly granted, ceasing their fight on both sides, the Generall in the Towne[92] making the preparation to entertaine his Excellency, did but open the Gate, thinking to cleare the passage for his Excellencies entrance, presently they in the Castle[93] let flye a Cannon and were like to have slaine some of them, wherefore they withdrew from shewing of themselves, untill his Excellency came against the Gate, and then came forth and intreated his Excellency to dine with him, but hee staid not having a long way to goe that night; they in the Castle are besieged on every side, before them are Cannons placed just by the Rivers side, behinde them are a great company of Horsemen called Crabbats,[94] beyond them in a plaine great field, are other Horsemen and Footemen, and likewise in Islands in the Rhine, all watching that they cannot be relieved, they in the Towne, if they doe but looke out of their windowes, have a bullet presently presented at their heads, yet the Towne is somewhat the stronger for a River called the Mosell,[95] which runneth along one side of the Towne into the Rhine, over which there did stand a faire Bridge, though part of it now be beaten downe, that there is no passage over, but have made a little lower on the Mossell a passage on Boates,

89. Remagen (possibly), Andernach, and Urmitz.

90. The land of Trier.

91. Koblenz.

92. Of Koblenz.

93. The French troops were besieged within the castle of Hermanstein above the town of Koblenz.

94. Croatians.

95. Mosel River.

to relieve the Towne, under the Castle there is a very beautifull house, which the Emperour gave to the Elector of Tryer, and hee resigned it to the French, whereupon the Spaniard besieged him, when he lay in a faire Castle on the Mossell called Tryer, and tooke him prisoner, and is prisoner now: as wee were departing from hence, the French gave us a brave vollie of shot as hath beene heard, with foure or five peeces of Ordnance, from hence up the Rhine, by Lonstein and Branbach[96] two Townes on the left side, to Boppart a Towne on the same side, against which wee cast Anchor and lay aboard.

The first of May being Sunday, and their Whitsunday, we departed, passing by Villages shot downe, and by many pictures of our Saviour and the Virgin Mary, set up at the turnings of the water, until we entered the Land of Hesse, where we still viewed pleasant Vines on the Mountaines, so by Saint Goware,[97] and by Rhinefilds Castle both on the right side, to Catzenelbogen Castle on the other side, then by Oberwesell on the right side; then begins the Lower Palatinate, so by Caub[98] on the left side, which is the first Towne in the Pfaltz,[99] and so to Pfaltz Castle, seated in a little Island in the River, from hence to Bacharach, a Towne where we landed, it is seated on the right side of the Rhine, having a Castle on a high Rocke within the walls, and under that a Church, which is from the plaine ground 100. steps before one can come into it, heere the poore people are found dead with grasse in their mouthes: from hence by a Village on the same side, in which none but Leapers[100] are, being not farre off the Towne, and so to Hambach on the same side, by Drechshausen on the other side, to Armanshausen,[101] a Towne on the left side of the Rhine, against which we cast Anchor and lay on Ship-board.

The next morning departed hence, and then begun Momtzistzland,[102] so by a little Tower in the water, called Mouse Thour, which one Otto a Bishoppe of Mentz,[103] having lived not well, being much troubled with Mice, built this, and lived in it, thinking there to be secure, but even thither they pursued him also, and eate him up:[104] then by Bingen, a faire Towne on the

---

96. Lahnstein and Braubach.

97. Sankt Goar.

98. Kaub.

99. The Palatinate.

100. Lepers.

101. Trechtingshausen and Assmannshausen.

102. The archbishopric of Mainz.

103. Mainz.

104. The Mäuseturm, or Mouse Tower, is on an island in the Rhine. The legend tells that the bishop of Bingen, Hatto II, who was also the archbishop of Mainz, was eaten alive by mice there after brutally murdering his hungry peasants.

right side, and by Ehrenfels Castle on the other side to Rudeshein, a Towne on the left side of the Rhine, into which I entered, and did see poore people praying where dead bones were in a little old house, and here his Excellencie gave some reliefe to the poore which were almost starved as it appeared by the violence they used to get it from another: from hence by Geisenhem, Elfeld, and Wallaff,[105] three Townes on the left side of the River, and then we crossed over the Rhine, unto the other side.

Then to Mentz a great City seated close by the Rhine on the right side against which we cast Anchor and lay on ship-board, for there was nothing in the Towne to relieve us, since it was taken by the King of Sweden,[106] and miserably battered, there the King of Bohemia[107] dyed, in a faire corner house towards the Rivers side, heere likewise the poore people were almost starved, and those that could relieve others before, now humbly begged to bee relieved, and after supper all had reliefe, sent from the Ship ashore, at the sight of which they strove so violently, that some of them fell into the Rhine and were like to have bin drowned.

The next day being the third of May, from hence we departed, leaving the Rhine halfe a league above the City on our right hand, and entered into a shallow River called the Maine,[108] passing by a place which the King of Sweden was building for a Fort, but could not finish it, then by Cassell, on the left side, thence by Flersheim[109] on the left side to Russelsheim on the right side of the Maine, and then to the stately City of Francfurt,[110] adjacent to the Maine on the left side, where we landed and lay; from Collein hither, all the Townes, Villages, and Castles bee battered, pillaged or burnt, and every place wee lay at on the Rhine on ship-board, we watched, taking every man his turne; heere wee staid foure daies, untill our carriages were made ready: where we saw the place wherein they keepe the Dyet,[111] afterward entered into the Church called Saint Bartholmews, where the Emperours use to bee crowned and take their oath; the City is inhabited with Lutherans and Jewes, for in the Jewes Synagogue, I entered in to see the manner of their service, which is an undecent way, making a hideous noise, having on their heads and about their neckes things called Capouchins,[112] the women are not ad-

---

105. Geisenheim, Eltville am Rhein, and Walluf.

106. King Gustavus Adolphus of Sweden (1594–1632).

107. Frederick V, elector Palatine and, briefly, king of Bohemia (1596–1632).

108. Main.

109. Flörsheim am Main.

110. Frankfurt am Main.

111. The imperial diet, which met at Frankfurt.

112. *Kippahs,* or yarmulkes.

mitted into their Synagogue, but in places about. And on Sunday the seventh of May, by waggons through the City over two Bridges which are alwaies guarded with Souldiers, leaving the Maine on our left hand, from hence we tooke a Convoy of Musketiers along, being wee went through much danger, by Offenbach, Selgenstat, seated betweene us and the Maine, passing thus along through a great Forest in much danger, hearing the great Peeces so swiftly discharge off at Hannaw,[113] which the Swedes subdu'd, and now besieged by the Emperors Forces, being not above three English miles off, then by a very great Mountaine two English miles long, all beset with Vines, untill we came at a poore little Village where wee staid and dined with provision of our owne, and after dinner departed, passing through Plaines untill wee came at the Maine, and there ferried over into a towne called Klingenberg, passing through this, we came to a very high hill the way up being all stone & 2. English miles up to the top, and then through a Wood, after we were past this, we came to a poore little Village called Neunkirchen, where we found one house a burning when we came and not any body in the Village, heere we were constrained to tarry all night, for it grew very late, and no Towne neere by 4. English miles, spending the night in walking up and downe in feare, with Carrabines[114] in our hands, because we heard Peeces discharg'd off in Woods about us, and with part of the coles[115] of the consumed house his Excellency had his meat rosted for supper, the next morning earely, his Excellency went to view the Church, which we found rifled with the pictures and Altars abused, in the Church-yard, we saw a dead body scraped out of the grave, in another place out of the Churchyard, there lay another dead body, into many of the houses wee entered, and found them all empty. From this miserable place we departed, and heard after, that they in the Village fled by reason of the sicknesse, and set that house on fire at their departure, that Passengers might not be infected.

Then came we into Wÿrtzburg-land,[116] and descended downe another steep hill and there crossed over a little River call'd Tauber, and through Keichelsheim,[117] to Neubruim[118] a poore Village where wee dined, after dinner passing by the side of the Maine, and through Woods and Plaines, untill we came to Wÿrtzburg,[119] a faire City passing over a bridge first, standing

113. Hanau.
114. Carbines are similar to rifles, but smaller.
115. Coals.
116. Würzburg is a region north of Bavaria.
117. Reicholzheim.
118. Neubrunn.
119. Würzburg.

over the Maine[120] into the Towne, seated on the left side of the River, and a faire Castle opposite to the Towne on the other side, in which the Towne put all their riches when they heard the king of Sweden was coming, thinking there it would not be gain'd, but they hearing of it, surprised and pillaged it in 3. daies, and it was 3. or 4. moneths before the Emperors forces could regaine it, the next day earely departed being the 10. of May, and entered the Marggrafen-land,[121] and to Kitteingen[122] to diner, after diner, thence through Ipza a City, and so to Marckbibrach,[123] where we lay all night on the plancher,[124] for the Village was pillaged but the day before, earely the next morning wee went away and passed through Neustadt,[125] which hath beene a faire City, though now pillaged and burnt miserably, heere we saw poore children sitting at their doores almost starv'd to death, to whom his Excellency gave order for to relieve them with meat and money to their Parents, from hence we went to Eilfkirchen a poore Village where wee dined, with some reserv'd meat of our owne, for there was not any thing to be found, after diner, thence we passed by many Villages pillag'd and burnt down, and so into Nurnberger-land[126] passing through the place where the King of Swedens Leaguer[127] lay, when the King of Bohemia was with him and my Lord Craven,[128] and in sight of the place the Emperors Army had intrenched themselves by the side of a great wood, here the King of Sweden set upon poles alive three of his souldiers, for killing 2. of their Commanders, and flying presently to his Enemy, and at the end of a Battaile that was then fought, he tooke them prisoners, and so executed them. . . .

From thence we departed May 22. being Sunday, for Regenspurgh, thinking there to meete with the Emperor, first passing through a part of the upper Palatinate to Newmark,[129] where we lay, seated in a plaine where the king of Bohemia had a house, which his Excellency viewed, adjoyning to the wall within the Towne, fortified with bulwarkes and pallizadoes, having spa-

120. The Main River.

121. The territory of the margrave of Brandenburg-Ansbach.

122. Kitzingen.

123. Iphofen and Markt Bibart.

124. A wooden floor.

125. Neustadt an der Aisch.

126. Nuremberg.

127. Camp.

128. William Craven, earl of Craven (1608–1697), an English officer who had fought for Frederick of the Palatinate and Gustavus Adolphus in the hope that he might help Elizabeth Stuart, the queen of Bohemia, regain her throne.

129. Neumarkt in der Oberpfalz.

cious roomes and a faire Armory: early the next morning, from hence, by Churches demolished to the ground, and through Woods in danger, understanding that Crabbats were lying heere about, untill we came at a poore little Village called Hemmaw[130] where we staied and dined, which hath beene pillaged eight and twenty times in two yeeres, and twice in one day, and they have there no water but that which they save when it raineth: after dinner, to Ettershausen a poore Village where we crossed over a little River in Boates, the Bridge being burnt downe by the Swedes forces; from hence wee ascended up a high hill, being descended downe, wee passed a long on an high banke, having the River Danubius[131] on our right hand, and high Mountaines with Vines on our left, passing thus through severall Villages beaten downe or burnt, untill we came at a round Fort before the Bridge which a guard kept, and so over it through a Tower in the middle standing over the Danuby, which runneth with as swift a current as at London Bridge, dividing it selfe into several Ilands[132] which had howses on them, but now burnt, and also houses on the Arches which were demolished likewise, then into the Citie Regenspurg to his Excellencies lodging, the Citie hath bin taken by the Swedish forces, and regained by the King of Hungary. . . .

The sixth of June, being the second day after wee came, his Excellence had audience of the Emperour and Empresse, who sent their coaches for us; being come to his palace, which is seated on a hill, we went up foure ascents of staires, the Guard standing on each side of us, with halberds and carrabines in their hands, passing thus thorow roomes, untill wee came at the doore of the chamber in which the Emperour was, and when his Excellence came at the doore, out came the little Count of Kezell, high Chamberlaine to his Majestie, and brought in his Excellence, and then withdrew and shut the doore after him, that none might enter in: after his Excellence had beene within a while, we were all admitted, and kissed his Majesties hand, and then withdrew, and passed thorow other roomes and a gallerie, where the Guard stood in like manner, to the Empresses chamber, where none might enter neither, stealing a sight of her as wee stood, and then returned.

The eighth day his Excellence had his second audience of the Emperour, as private as the first: and the tenth day audience againe of the Empresse, and then wee were admitted to kisse her hand: the same day there were seven men beheaded which were Rebels, for rising up in armes with foure hundred other Boores[133] against the Emperour: the first that was executed, was

130. Hemau.
131. Danube River.
132. Islands.
133. Peasants.

said to be one that had inchanted himselfe, that no bullet could hurt him,[134] and the onely seducer of the others: after he was upon the scaffold and his face covered, two men held him fast to the blocke, then came the Executioner with a red hot paire of pincers, and violently clape hold of both his brests, that done, nailed his right hand fast to the blocke, and chopt it off, then presently whipt out his sword from his side, and cut off his head, one of the hangmen presently tooke it up, and cryed at the eares of the head, Jesus, Jesus; then the Jesuite which came a long with him admonishing of him, desired everie one to joyne in prayers with him for him; then came the other, and a Boy which was beheaded likewise, all making private confessions to Priests, at the foot of the scaffold, having a Crucifix in their hand, kissing their hands & feet at the end of everie prayer: After all those men were beheaded, and quartered, there went two of their confederates a foot to bee hanged about an English mile off, to a place where a Priest of theirs hung upon a pole, and his head on the top which taken in a Church a yeere before called Ering, which we afterward passed by.

27. The Trial of Ludwig Schmalhausen (February 1638)[135]

[During the war princes faced numerous threats, from economic chaos to peasant uprisings to enemy armies overrunning their territories. Yet princes also had to worry about preserving what they saw as their traditional sovereign and dynastic rights. Thus protecting the so-called German Liberties (or the rights of princes to control their own territories without interference by the emperor) was one of the key war aims of many imperial princes. Yet these rights were challenged not just by the emperor, but also by the princes' own nobles—struggling to protect their own rights and privileges—and by their fellow princes, who were competing with them for territories or honors. These local conflicts frequently became intertwined with each other and with the larger war, which they helped to drive. The following documents illustrate this interrelationship and show how religious difference could even further complicate local politics. They are a portion of the trial records for Cavalry Captain Ludwig Schmalhausen, a member of the Hessian lower nobility who was taken into arrest after his drunken admission that he had contemplated the treasonous act of handing over the fortress of Ziegenhain to a besieging Bavarian army. Schmalhausen ar-

134. Witchcraft was a constant fear during the war and was closely tied with fears of treason and rebellion.

135. Vice Chancellor and Council (letter sent) to Amalia Elisabeth, Cassel, February 16/26, 1638, rec. Groningen, March 1/11, 1638, Hessische Staatsarchiv Marburg, 4d Nr. 90.

gued that his rulers, the landgraves of Hesse-Cassel, had prosecuted an unjust and dishonorable war against the emperor and so had caused the people of Hesse great suffering. This was a frequent and increasing complaint of the Hessian nobility, especially from Lutherans (like Schmalhausen), who resented the landgraves' conversion to Calvinism and hated Calvinism in general. The Lutheran nobility tended to favor the neighboring Lutheran prince, Landgrave George of Hesse-Darmstadt, who claimed portions of Hesse-Cassel for himself and had taken the opposite side in the war. Thus in Schmalhausen's trial two separate events—one being his discussion of the fortress of Ziegenhain over drinks on November 22, 1637, and one a criticism of Lutheranism at a baptism the previous day—are brought together by the (clearly nervous) authorities to demonstrate a pattern of treasonous thoughts.

I. Introductory Letter by the Hessian Council to the Landgravine of Hesse-Cassel[136]

Most serene, gracious princess and lady:

We do not wish to fail to inform Your Highness of how Cavalry Captain Schmalhausen expressed several thoughts concerning the fortress of Ziegenhain, but also contrary and derogatory statements against our dearly departed prince, Landgrave Wilhelm of Hesse, most highly blessed and of Christ-mild memory, who rests with God. These have all been verified in depth by the inquiry made by the officials of Ziegenhain, which is hereby attached as a copy so that Your Highness might be graciously pleased to receive this most humble report.

As we now, not unjustly, have been deeply offended by such outrageous talk, and especially pained on account of His Princely Highness of Christ-mild and well-regarded memory, we have not failed to issue an immediate order that the said Schmalhausen be taken into arrest at Ziegenhain and furthermore be made to speak and respond, as has also occurred. Although he responded to us with a letter (which can also be found here as a copy), arguing that these matters should be excused and he should be freed from his arrest, yet since it is very clear that he is not completely innocent in this, and since we think that he is not ultimately exonerated by his excuse of a pretended and feigned drunkenness . . . it would be, in our opinion, not unjust that he be required to pay a considerable financial fine of about five hundred *reichsthalers*. Nevertheless, in the end, on account of his lack of wealth, the same could be reduced to two hundred *reichsthalers,* and he could

136. Landgravine Amalia Elisabeth was the widow of the former landgrave, Wilhelm V, and served as regent of Hesse-Cassel from the time of his death in September 1637 to the end of the war.

be released from his arrest upon payment of the same. Thereby others could take from this an example and so know to abstain from similar loose talk.

All of this we humbly present for Your Highness' gracious pleasure and command. We hereby faithfully and humbly hope that Your Highness gains from the Almighty the strongest protection and the greatest prosperity and well-being that Your Highness may desire, and we recommend ourselves to your constant grace.

Dated Cassel the 16th of February 1638.

II. Questions Put to the Witnesses

INTERROGATION OF THE MAGISTRATE OF SCHWARTZENBORN, MAGISTRATE OF NEUKIRCHEN, LOWER MAGISTRATE HENRICH BAUER OF OTTRAU, AND TOWN CLERK HENRICH CAULIUS

1. Is it not true that Cavalry Captain Ludwig Schmalhausen, on the 22nd of November in Neukirchen, said at the clerk's office that he'd wrench off his own head and hand it to someone if he hadn't tried to deliver Ziegenhain to the enemy one night three years ago, if only the enemy had desired that he do so?

2. And when he was asked how such a thing would be done and could have happened, did he not answer that he knew well, once again grasping his throat with his hand, saying he'd give it away if it had not happened?

3. Is it not true that the magistrate of Neukirchen said that the enemy must not have known of all this, and asked him to explain: and he answered that before midnight [the water] had become so deeply frozen that, after midnight, it would have held thousands and even more thousands [of men], such that [taking the fortress] would not have cost the enemy more than two hundred men, and the magistrate of Neukirchen once again answered that the enemy must not have known of all this?

4. Did Schmalhausen declare that His Princely Grace, Landgrave Wilhelm of most praiseworthy memory, had perjured himself toward the emperor, and had not fulfilled what he had sworn to His Majesty?[137]

5. That Landgrave Moritz[138] of most praiseworthy memory had also, as punishment, had to live in exile from the land several times in the past?

---

137. Landgrave Wilhelm had risen up in revolt against the emperor and allied with Gustavus Adolphus.

138. Landgrave Moritz was Wilhelm's father and predecessor and had also opposed the emperor until the Hessian estates forced him to abdicate in favor of his son.

6. That His Princely Grace Landgrave Wilhelm of most praiseworthy memory had abandoned his poor people, marched out of the land, and so, as punishment, had been forced to die outside the land?[139]

In sum, that His Princely Grace Landgrave George was justified, and it was completely legitimate for him to seize the Lower Principality [of Hesse-Cassel]?[140]

7. And seventh, was it not true, as Mr. Johann Pistorem, pastor of Lower Creutzbach, testified, that on the 21st of November in the house of Philip Lucken, he [Schmalhausen] stated that "It will soon happen that you priests[141] will be driven out; things will soon change;"[142] and that, in sum, he glorified the Lutheran religion and the Darmstadter administration?

III. Witness Statements Taken by the Colonel of the Fortress of Ziegenhain

RECORD MADE AT ZIEGENHAIN, THE 4TH OF DECEMBER 1637

Testimony of Heinrich Bauer Heinrich Bauer, forest warden and lower magistrate of Ottrau, was asked what he had heard from Cavalry Captain Schmalhausen at the clerk's office at Neukirchen on the 22nd of November, with enough certainty that in the future he could affirm his knowledge of it with a solemn oath. He replied that Ludwig Schmalhausen, in the presence of the magistrate of Neukirchen, the town clerk, and the magistrate of Schwartzenborn, had said that when the army of the enemy was in the land, had [the enemy] wanted to bring two thousand men into the fortress of Ziegenhain, then suffering a frost, he wouldn't have lost more than two hundred men doing so, and that [Schmalhausen] would have delivered [the

---

139. In 1637 imperial armies had overrun much of Hesse-Cassel and Wilhelm had marched north with his army, his wife, and his sons, and occupied the neutral territory of East Frisia, leaving behind his infant daughters and much of his council within the fortresses, which the imperial armies did not manage to take. The people of Hesse suffered horribly at the hands of the imperial troops, however, and Wilhelm had died in exile soon after.

140. On the death of Wilhelm, his Lutheran cousin, Landgrave George of Hesse-Darmstadt, claimed supreme rulership over Hesse-Cassel and was backed in this by his ally, the emperor.

141. The Lutheran Schmalhausen accuses the Calvinist pastor of being a priest—that is, of being the same as a Catholic, i.e., a heretic.

142. In other words, George of Hesse-Darmstadt would soon eject all Calvinist pastors.

fortress] if the enemy had desired. He had also indicated, with his right hand on wood, that he would hope to lose the same [were this not true]. And when the magistrate of Neukirchen said to him that the enemy must not have known this, Schmalhausen had indeed answered with something, but that [Bauer] had not properly heard it.

He said further that Schmalhausen had said that both of Their Highnesses, Landgrave Moritz and Landgrave Wilhelm, of Christ-mild memory, had not kept the promises they had made to the emperor, and that, for this reason, both of Their Highnesses had been pulled from their land and people. [Bauer] did not hear what else Schmalhausen had said about Landgrave George, but it had pained him deeply that Schmalhausen had so ignominiously spoken of the fortress and other things.

Testimony of Heinrich Caulius   Heinrich Caulius, town clerk of Neukirchen, similarly asked about the above points and of what he could testify to in court in the future, said that on the 22nd of November Cavalry Captain Schmalhausen had said in the clerk's office at Neukirchen that when the army had lain before Herzfeld, he had wished to deliver the fortress to them, or he would lose his head [if it wasn't true]. How and in what way Schmalhausen had hoped to arrange this, [Caulius] had not heard. Whether and what Schmalhausen had discussed about Their Highnesses Landgrave Moritz and Landgrave Wilhelm, both of Christ-blessed memory, and if he thought the best or worst of them, [Caulius] had not heard, for as soon as Schmalhausen had spoken thusly about the fortress, [Caulius] had left and gone to the little room by the stove, and so had not heard this discussion. He thus knew nothing to report of the remaining points.

Testimony of Victor Lindeborn, 14th of December   Victor Lindeborn, magistrate of Schwartzenborn, was asked to say under oath if it was not true that Cavalry Captain Schmalhausen, in the little meeting room of the town council,[143] had at that time said about the fortress of Ziegenhain that from the Bavarian camp one could, as the ground became frozen, make for and conquer the fortress with only a few regiments. But [Lindeborn] knew nothing much about this point, nor did he have anything further to report at that time. He did have some thought, however, that the town clerk and Schmalhausen had indeed exchanged some words with each other on this topic. But because [Lindeborn] had gotten somewhat drunk, he had soon left and had not observed anything further about this point. As for the other points, however, Schmalhausen had said that His Highness Landgrave Wilhelm had opposed the emperor, and it would have

---

143. The clerk's office also served as the town council's smaller meeting room.

been better if such had not occurred. The witness also thought that some-thing had been said about His Highness Landgrave Moritz, but he did not actually know what. He wished he could better remember whether and what Schmalhausen had said about His Highness Landgrave George, but did not actually know what had been said. He wished to think about it more.[144]

Testimony of Pastor Johann Pistorem   Honorable Johann Pistorem, pastor of Lower Creutzebach, questioned, said in an affidavit concerning the words that Schmalhausen had said in the house of Philip Lucken, during the baptism, that Cavalry Captain Schmalhausen had desired that he, the wit-ness, would press the party to sing a Lutheran song, "Lord, Keep Us in Thy Word and Work," which had then happened.[145] Yet as the words "Restrain the murderous pope and Turks" were sung, Schmalhausen had sung instead "Restrain the murderous Turks and Calvinists."[146] At which he, the witness, had spoken to him, saying that when [Schmalhausen] sang such a thing, he was not acting as an honorable man. Schmalhausen had then asked if he, the witness, was a Calvinist. [Pistorem] had answered no, he was a Christian.[147] Schmalhausen had then gone on to say: "You are the kind of Christian who does not believe God and His word;" so he, the witness, had denied this and demanded proof. Schmalhausen had answered: "From the words of the Holy Eucharist, in which Christ said, This is His body and His blood, but the Calvinists do not believe this, but instead reject it and interpret it." At this the witness had answered, "No, we believe sincerely that we eat and drink the true body and blood of Christ," and he had thereupon made a public avowal [of his faith].[148] At which Schmalhausen had answered, when such a confession was actually [Pistorem's] heartfelt opinion, then the Devil would take him and offer him a toast, and God would punish him for it. Furthermore, and when [Schmalhausen] could proceed no further, he had

144. In a subsequent letter Lindeborn replied that even after considerable thought he still could not recall anything else about that night, because of the large quanti-ties of brandy he had consumed.

145. Luther's hymns were also extremely popular among Calvinists and even Cath-olics (though sometimes with different wording).

146. The song's words should be: "Lord, keep us in thy word and work / Restrain the murderous Pope and Turks / Who fain would tear from off thy throne / Christ Jesus, thy beloved Son."

147. The pastor was here not denying he was a Calvinist, merely stressing that he saw himself as a true Christian, not merely as a follower of a single reformer.

148. The question of the Eucharist's meaning was a serious point of contention be-tween Lutherans and Calvinists.

finally said: "You papists[149] will soon, and within four weeks, have to run away." He [the witness] doesn't know any more than this.

IV. Schmalhausen's Written Defense to the Hessian Council

A short time ago I was told by the colonel and paymaster of Ziegenhain that I supposedly acted against our gracious territorial lords of most blessed memory with several crude and irresponsible words. Supposedly I made it known that during the military occupation I hoped to have been able to deliver the fortress of Ziegenhain to the enemy with only a few troops, and there had also supposedly been some similar talk exchanged with the pastor of Lower Creutzebach; for such reasons I was put under arrest in the fortress.

Now I am, not unjustly, dismayed beyond all measure by such impertinences; but I have no memory of such a thing nor of how I should have come to it, for I am Their Highnesses' subject; and although I had plenty of good opportunities to live elsewhere and take up other vocations, yet I never once thought to relocate my domicile—even during this ongoing and wretched situation—but along with other true patriots, I accepted and tolerated both fortune and misfortune, but mostly misfortune. Anyway, if such words as have been attributed to me were indeed spoken against the territorial princes and against the fortress, then they were doubtless provoked for another reason, namely drink, for each and every person who was at the clerk's office at Neukirchen on the 22nd of November 1637 can attest that I was completely drunk, so that on my own I couldn't put one foot in front of the other. I recall that in the beginning the fortress was mentioned, and I explained that, during the military occupation, the ice was constantly submerging and soon thereafter once again breaking through, and then quickly freezing once again, such that one would then be able to travel over it after midnight. If I had ever contemplated and thought to put into effect such a plan, no one would excuse me. But the result demonstrates my innocence, and should I have wanted something like this, I would not have set it aside until now. I would have also, it seems to me, not publicly discussed it and made it commonly known. Indeed, I would have thereby forfeited all of my cash and personal possessions, which I had saved in the fortress, and so condemned myself and my wife and little children to ruin. The defect [in our defenses] that I saw at that time, because of the ice, I told in confidence to my then-

---

149. Here Schmalhausen accuses the Calvinist pastor of being like a Catholic, or "papist." Since the Calvinist understanding of the Eucharist was not the same as the Catholic understanding, Schmalhausen is probably merely lumping Calvinists in with Catholics as both being heretics.

colonel, who immediately changed it so that the ice was forced to split the water and could no longer be submerged under it. This I recall, as I said before, and nothing more, and I cannot believe that I supposedly said that I wanted to have delivered it to the enemy. Should it, however, actually have happened, it was due to drunkenness during a drinking bout, and not meant seriously, and perhaps it happened that my drinking buddies tried to convince me of the impossibility of it. For you surely know well how, when one is well along in boozing, one goes from one marvelous topic to another, and if one wants to rush to accuse another man of treachery because of it, then perhaps many others would also have their great rage [while drinking] turned into great heartache and misery.

Your lords will, for the above reasons, not believe the remaining words that I supposedly said against Their Highnesses' persons. If, however, despite my hopes, they were spoken out of drunkenness, your lords will this time pardon and excuse me for this, for I am beyond all treachery and have demonstrated up to now my steadfast, upright disposition toward Their Highnesses with my service both in and out of war. . . .

Concerning the disputation that occurred between me and the pastor on the 21st of November in Philip Lucken's house, I recall how it started: that it was not I, but the pastor who began it, and as we, in our discussion, finally came to the question of the Lord's Supper, he had avowed that he believed he received the true body and blood of our Lord Jesus Christ, who had suffered and died on the cross; and when I then asked if he believed that he received the true material body and blood of our Lord Christ, he answered that if he were to believe this, he would be like a rogue and a thief and would believe himself into the most extreme perdition. At which point I answered that this was harshly spoken, for many very honest people believe such a thing, people of both high and low station, who are neither rogues nor thieves because of this belief. If I then said that they must soon leave, which I, however, know nothing about and also do not wish, then it would similarly have happened while I was drinking and without doubt, as mentioned above, at the pastor's instigation. Indeed, no one would pay any attention to such curses and drunken talk, nor wring from it a serious disposition; the pastor himself counted it as merely hot air, and so we parted from each other peacefully and nicely, as I was told. And thus because of all of this, I humbly ask you not to believe any of this that I am accused of; or, should one or another thing have been said—since I was beyond all treachery, completely drunk, and, so to speak, crazy, provoked and prompted by another, and spoke as a joke and for amusement, and my upright, well-affectionate disposition has certainly been already demonstrated—this time generously pardon and excuse me, and release me from my arrest so that my poor, small household—which, as almost everyone can attest, is almost completely destroyed—is not fully ruined and neglected. Should, however, despite my hopes, I be denied and am to be further afflicted, then I undertake to give to the court as a bond all my possessions to permit me to be freed. I ask that your lords might allow me to do this and to relax the arranged arrest, and also commend to you my petition to proceed concerning the fee against me, and await your firm resolution.

Written at Ziegenhain on the 14th of February 1638

28. Religious Security and War
(November 1638–January 1639)

[Landgrave Wilhelm of Hesse-Cassel had been one of the few princes excluded from the 1635 Peace of Prague, and so had continued to fight as an ally of Sweden and France. After his death in 1637, however, his widow, Amalia Elisabeth (1602–1651), began new negotiations with the emperor. These negotiations were conducted under the mediation of the elector of Mainz, and they produced a treaty that Amalia Elisabeth signed. Yet the emperor's ratification of the treaty included a signing statement that rewrote the key point of religion, returning it to the wording proposed during prior negotiations at Marburg. This change, which weakened the protections granted to Calvinism, caused great consternation both at the Hessian court (which was operating from the safety of Hessian-occupied East Frisia) and back at Cassel, where the majority of the Hessian council remained under constant threat from imperial forces. The following three letters provide a look at the reaction of both the Hessian council and Amalia Elisabeth to this turn of events, illustrating some significant points: first, the difference in attitudes between the Hessian council, which had to field daily complaints from the Hessian people about the horrible burdens of war, and Amalia Elisabeth, who was concerned more with her principles and reputation; second, Amalia Elisabeth's argument that religious security had been the driving cause behind the Hessian war effort from the beginning; and third, the French ambassador's extreme interest in acquiring the Hessian army, which was one of the most experienced and largest then in service in the empire. It would have been truly disastrous for France had this army fallen into the hands of the emperor, but they need not have worried; the emperor's stubborn insistence on the point of religion soon pushed Amalia Elisabeth to ally again with France and Sweden and, despite the firm opposition of her council and people, bring Hesse-Cassel back into the war.]

Letter from the Hessian Vice Chancellor and Privy Council to Amalia Elisabeth, November 20/30, 1638[150]

Most Serene Highness and distinguished princess, [etc.]:

We have no doubt that you will have already, long ago, successfully received our newest, most humble report to you, dated the 14th/24th of this month and concerning the Mainz negotiations. Since the letters of the elector of Mainz that were mentioned in that report, one to Your Highness and the other to us, arrived here on Wednesday the 18th of this month, we opened up both to gain better information. We most humbly ask that Your Highness not take this with bad grace, and that you graciously receive both letters, which we have hereby attached as copies, along with what we wrote and replied in response to His Electoral Grace of Mainz.

Because we see that the entire work of peace rests solely and alone on the point of religion (for, in our opinion, the remaining failings are quite easy to remedy), we delivered to the ministry here this same point as it was composed and found in the current imperial confirmation, so that they might then present their thoughts and opinion on it. We also assembled ourselves, along with the local colonel and commander Johann Geyso,[151] and brought it to a vote whether, if indeed nothing more could be obtained in regard to religion, Your Highness could then accept in good conscience this point as it had been previously formulated at Marburg and was then inserted into the imperial confirmation, and so finally conclude the long-ongoing peace negotiations and thereby be assured in your religion. We then, for many serious reasons and factors for and against, which Commissioner Horn's[152] detailed oral relation will lay out, unanimously agreed that in case one could indeed not gain anything more on account of religion (something that should still hereafter be sought zealously and with proper respectability and modesty), Your Highness could accept, in God's name and in sound conscience, this point as it is now inserted in the imperial confirmation. You might and could thereby bring to an end the work of peace, which is so

150. Vice Chancellor and Privy Council (letter sent) to Amalia Elisabeth, Cassel, November 20/30, 1638, rec. Groningen, December 9/19, 1638, Hessische Staatsarchiv Marburg [HStAM] 4d Nr. 38.

151. Johann Geyso (1593–1661), a Hessian officer and councilor with long and varied military experience.

152. Commissioner Horn was a Hessian officer who had attended the negotiations at Mainz and who had been tasked by the council to report to Amalia Elisabeth in East Frisia. The Hessian Commissary was in charge of such matters as supplying the troops and fortresses, and territorial defense.

deeply desired by every man, and so somewhat soothe the poor ruined land and the few remaining subjects who still reside in it, fulfilling their confidence and hope. We were then even further reinforced in this opinion by the local ministry, since it completely agreed with us in its consideration (which it disclosed to us, in this regard, not only on the 22nd of January of this year, but also now in written form—a copy of which is hereby being sent to Your Highness), and argued that one must leave remaining matters to God, whose affair it is, and who will never abandon His word and the true religion. We also called on the theological faculty here to deliver their expert opinion on this point (which Your Highness will similarly find attached here as a copy), and although the faculty argues that we would be insufficiently assured on account of religion by this article,[153] yet we cannot deviate from our opinion, given the nature of the times and the situation of our land, and for other reasons we find compelling. Instead, when nothing more stands to be gained, it would be appropriate to leave things at that.

Your Highness shall carefully consider this matter—not only by yourself, but also with your councilors who are present there, and with other people who are sensible and dispassionate and who understand the situation here. And graciously let us know, as swiftly as possible, how we should proceed.

We humbly make this matter known to Your Highness, faithfully commending the same to the Almighty, to His powerful protection and shield, and humbly commending ourselves to His persevering grace. Dated Cassel the 20th of November 1638.

> To Your Highness,
> From your humble and obedient vice chancellor and privy
>   councilors who were left at home

Letter from Amalia Elisabeth to the Hessian Vice Chancellor and Privy Council, December 26, 1638/January 5, 1639[154]

Our noble, steadfast, very learned, and especially dear ones:

We have heard in depth not only from Commissioner Horn, who presented a detailed oral report of what occurred during his and the count of Solms'[155]

---

153. The theological faculty at the University of Cassel argued that the wording used by the emperor was filled with hidden loopholes that would allow Calvinists to be suppressed or pursued in future years.

154. Amalia Elisabeth (minute, Sixtinus hand corrections) to the Vice Chancellor and Privy Council, Dorsten, December 26, 1638/January 5, 1639, HStAM 4d Nr. 38.

155. Count Albrecht Otto II von Solms-Laubach (1610–1639), Amalia Elisabeth's brother-in-law.

recent trip to Mainz—information that you had humbly entrusted and charged him to bring back to me—but also from the letters you sent to us—especially that of the 30th of November, which described your and the ministry's, along with the theological faculty at Cassel's, humble opinions concerning the point of religion (though these were varied and not altogether consistent with each other), which His Roman Imperial Majesty did not care to confirm in the manner in which it was laid out in the accord and recess reached at Mainz.

Now, because the Mainz accord was approved by the elector of Mainz himself, as was, among other points incorporated into the accord, also that [point] which was formulated concerning religion, we had anticipated nothing more than that it would remain absolutely fixed (even though before Commissioner Horn's arrival, some indication had reached us from one and another place that some difficulties still existed). After, however, the contrary came to light in such a way that one could quite plainly sense how we and our co-religionists were regarded on account of our religion, we justly had all the more reason to keep our eyes wide open. We also had to consider carefully and pursue zealously, with a fervent prayer to God, how we might then not only save our conscience and rescue so many thousand souls, but also free ourselves from such an enormously heavy responsibility and from the critical judgment that we must be prepared to withstand from God, all the world, and dear posterity, both during our life and after our death.

This had been the sole principal work with which our most honored, dearly beloved lord and spouse, of most praiseworthy memory, concerned himself from the beginning of this war up until his blessed final end. For this reason he took up and bore arms, withstood so much trouble, effort, and danger, and finally lost his life. Furthermore, the land incurred the most extreme ruin and irrecoverable damage, and the subjects spent their lives, limbs, and property in order to assure freedom of thought and the free exercise of their traditional religion, and to preserve the same for their children and descendents. So should one now consider this matter so negligently, and not even get out of it an assurance in mere words that one ought to be allowed, quietly and untroubled, the public free exercise of religion?

It is, to be sure, the opinion of the ministry at Cassel, as far as we can see from the concerns they have raised, that the Marburg project brings with it sufficient assurance in this point, which they also endorse. But just as before, when the Marburg concept was first communicated to us and the delegates from the estates remonstrated to us about one and another aspect of it, we could in no way agree with such a thing; and other dispassionate, foreign, leading political and theological people whom we have consulted on this have also equally had to recognize and acknowledge the same thing: namely, that one is not thereby secured in the conduct of religion. Thus we shall also set it aside.

And hence, to apply in this matter the written formulation proposed previously by Doctor Crocius,[156] intelligently and with good reasons—not only
for himself, but also with and alongside the other members of the theological faculty of Cassel (and which is in accord with the thoughts of the lieutenant general[157] and the privy councilors who are present here)—if the
oft-mentioned religious point were to remain merely as it was formulated at
Marburg, it could not be approved. If, however, some clearer words were inserted—namely that we should be left unperturbed in our religion and in its
public, free exercise—or were this point taken care of by another assured
means (and Commissioner Horn shall explain our opinion in this matter to
you in depth), then it will not fail to gain our approval.

Now, in order to attain this with greater respectability, we find it to be not
of low priority that intercessions with His Royal Imperial Majesty and the elector of Mainz be solicited from various places (provided that you have not already been supplied with a different and better resolution from the Imperial
Court). And to this end, we have had produced here various letters and blank
forms and given them, along with a measured instruction, to Commissioner
Horn, with the hope and expectation that everything will be negotiated on all
sides with good dexterity and discretion, so that something fruitful will come
of it and one will yet achieve the desired objective through God's grace.

Commissioner Horn will provide you with a more complete oral report
on one and the other point, as I have instructed him, and we thus hereby refer ourselves to you and remain yours.

Dated Dorsten the 26th of December 1638
To the vice chancellor and privy councilors at Cassel

Letter from Amalia Elisabeth to Her Councilor Johann Vultejus, January 7/17, 1639[158]

Just as we, thank God, have arrived here safely with our beloved son and our
entire train, we also hope that you have no less successfully completed your
trip to Hamburg,[159] from where we now daily await letters from you. We

---

156. Dr. Johannes Crocius (1590–1659) was head of the University of Cassel and a
leading theologian. He had proposed an alternate wording for the point of religion
that he and the other faculty members thought more sound.

157. Lieutenant General Peter Melander, count von Holzappel, was the landgravine's principal military general at this time.

158. Amalia Elisabeth (letter sent) to Vultejus, Dorsten, January 7/17, 1639, rec.
Hamburg, January 19/29, 1639, HStAM 4d Nr. 50, fol. 32–3.

159. The free imperial city of Hamburg served as a neutral diplomatic center during the war.

forward to you hereby, in written form, what Lieutenant Müller asked of us on November 27/December 7, and also what we gave him to understand in response. Ambassador Wolf[160] has also written to us, as the attached extract shows, which we have similarly communicated to you for your information. And along with this, we do not wish to leave out how Ambassador d'Estampes,[161] after our departure from Groningen, betook himself to Wesel. Both he and others thought that, because we had gotten underway with the princely corpse,[162] this must certainly mean that our peace was now concluded and we would soon proceed to the next step of disbanding the troops. He thus came with the intention of using money to gain these troops for himself. However, when he realized that it had not yet come to this point (something that many of his officers who were with him confirmed), he then finally rode back to The Hague after first visiting us here along with Monsieur de la Boderie.[163] He gave us all kinds of remonstrations as to why we should set aside our separate peace and await the universal peace instead. We, however, remonstrated to the contrary about our situation and what had required us to take up the separate negotiations, such that he was indeed forced to recognize our reasons on many points. Yet still, he maintained and asserted one way or another that we were doing the wrong thing and that, in the end, time would yield the right effect. He then disclosed to us one and another thing about the strong preparations for war that were newly in the process of being realized—not only on the part of the crowns of France and Sweden, but also by others—and he particularly strongly mentioned Duke Bernard of Saxe's successful progress.

Commissioner Horn is still present here, but he is now going to ride back to Cassel and will then also proceed with Count von Solms back to Mainz, where he will then, if possible, bring to an end our now so long-awaited peace treaty. Yet many think it very much in doubt whether His Imperial Majesty will agree to concede more than he already has in the point of religion, which many—among them also the theological faculty of Cassel—think would not secure members of our religion.

---

160. Hermann Wolff (1596–1645), a Hessian jurist and councilor who served as Swedish ambassador to Hesse-Cassel from 1631.

161. Jean d'Estampes de Valençay (1595–1671), the French ambassador to Holland and royal councilor.

162. Amalia Elisabeth still had with her the body of her husband, who had died in exile at the Hessian military headquarters in East Frisia on September 21/October 1, 1637. She wished to have him buried in his capital city of Cassel when she was finally able to return home.

163. The resident French ambassador to the landgravine's court.

In the end, the Almighty will tip the scales in this matter; and we, for ourselves and our minor son, as widow and orphan, leave and commend it to Him in the Christian hope and confidence that He can and will powerfully rescue us from all need and turn everything to our benefit.

In the meantime, we would very much like to be thoroughly informed about what is happening with the universal negotiations, if there is some hope, and how soon we might be able to proceed with them; whether we also might thereby hope and expect something good to come of them, and how things are going with our safe conduct. You can give us the best information about it, as well as about His Royal Highness of Denmark's interposition and what proceeds from it, and also how things proceed with the Lower Saxon Circle diet, all of which we shall eagerly await. Meanwhile, we shall remain here or in Wesel with our beloved son for a bit longer; but all the same, for the sake of hope, which is more difficult to maintain the longer this lasts, we shall remove some of our people and horses and send them to Cassel.

So we hereby make this known to you, along with our wish that you have a very happy New Year, and we remain well devoted and with favorable goodwill toward you.

Dated Dorsten the 7/17th of January 1639

29. Diary of Abbot Maurus Friesenegger (1641–1643)[164]

[Maurus Friesenegger (1595–1655) spent the Thirty Years War in the Upper Bavarian Benedictine abbey of Andechs, a famous pilgrimage site since the tenth century. Due to its fame and its possession of famous relics, including three sacred hosts said to be consecrated by Popes Gregory I and Leo IX, the abbey's hilltop location was popularly known as "der heilige Berg" (the Holy Mountain). From 1627 to 1648 Friesenegger, who became abbot of Andechs in 1640, kept a diary of the wartime experiences of the abbey and its monks. Following are his entries for the years 1641 through 1643, which began with tremendous successes by the armies of the French and Swedes (and their daring winter attack on Regensburg), but ended with these allies' crushing surprise defeat at the battle of Tuttlingen on November 24, 1643. Also interesting in this account are the descriptions of some of the difficulties of everyday life in these later years of the war. For example, Friesenegger writes about the wartime return of wild animals (such as wild swine and wolves) to civilized

---

164. Maurus Friesenegger, *Tagebuch aus dem 30jährigen Krieg, Nach einer Handschrift im Kloster Andechs,* P. Willibald Mathäser, ed. (Munich: Süddeutscher Verlag, 1974).

areas, the ongoing demands for war taxes and contributions from the government, and the effects on agriculture of the so-called Little Ice Age, which was a period of significantly colder and more unsettled and volatile weather in Europe during the early modern era, and especially during the sixteenth and seventeenth centuries. The Little Ice Age saw the rapid and destructive advance of glaciers in the Alps, on whose northern foothills Andechs is located; heavier snows, shorter and wetter growing seasons, and more violent storms and flooding. Such climatic shifts only exacerbated the economic and agricultural problems brought about by the war, and so contributed to periods of increased famine and disease throughout Europe.]

1641

The year 1641 quickly ushered in some wartime disturbances. Already in January, during a very bitter winter, the Swedish tyrant Banér[165] invaded the Upper Palatinate and devastated multiple places with fire and sword. In his rage, he also went as far as Regensburg, which he fired on with several cannons and where the emperor was, at that very moment, together with his household and all the princes of the empire.[166] And Banér was not pleased that the emperor and, even more, the empress, were not captured when returning from a hunt,[167] though the falcons and hunting horses fell into his hands. Banér kept the horses and sent back the falcons with the taunt that he waged war using horses, not falcons. This unexpected incident admittedly frightened all the great men, but no one took steps to oppose him—except for our elector[168] alone. Without delay, he brought the army out of its winter quarters, called up horses for hauling from every market town, city, and cloister (the Holy Mountain provided two horses and one groom), and had all cannons and munitions conducted to Ingolstadt. On the 20th of January it snowed so much that almost every road and street became impassable, and the old ones said that they had never seen such snow.

Nevertheless, the enemy crossed the Danube on the ice and invaded Lower Bavaria, where he inflicted immense damages, took immense booty, and led away many captives.

165. Johan Banér (1596–1641), Swedish field marshal. He undertook this attack in conjunction with the French General Guébriant.

166. The imperial diet had been meeting at Regensburg since September 1640. Its goal was to end the war among the states of the empire by expanding amnesty to those princes excluded by the Peace of Prague, including the prince Palatine, the landgrave of Hesse-Cassel, and the duke of Brunswick-Lüneburg.

167. The emperor and his wife had planned to attend the hunting party, but had been delayed.

168. Maximilian I of Bavaria (1573–1651).

Meanwhile our troops also gathered near Regensburg from their winter quarters, but during their march they did little to improve things. Our abbey of Paring[169] alone incurred damages of 1,000 fl.[170] from seized horses, cattle, and plundered possessions. Or at any rate, people think that it was the imperialists who did such things. During all of this turmoil and these affairs, the elector did not forget the Holy Mountain. The 24th of January I received an electoral letter and a command to pack up the sacred treasure at once and to carry it to Munich.[171] What a fright for us, for we did not know what would come to pass and what would happen! The treasure was indeed packed up, but due to the snow and bad weather, it was impossible to take it away.

The 28th of January the territorial militia was most urgently called up and commanded to go to Ingolstadt in a hurry. But all at once, and completely unexpectedly, there came a warm wind that melted the ice on the Danube; so now the robbing Swedish hordes had their retreat cut off, and not a few who still entrusted themselves to the ice as their sole way of escape, drowned with their booty in the Danube.

Around this same time, the enemy took the city of Cham from our side, who fled like rabbits, and he tyrannized the surrounding region as only tyrants like him do.[172]

The 13th of February our treasure was taken to Munich, and on the very next day I followed with the three sacred hosts, among so many tears from our people that I can more easily bemoan than describe it. The sacred relics and the sacred hosts were kept in our vault, and the rest was kept in the mint. . . .

Meanwhile, horses were called up from the subjects toward payment for the cavalry, which the authorities had to manage. They were also strongly bidden to identify all hunters and marksmen and order them to go to Munich, where their names would be recorded and they would be allowed to return home, with instructions to appear again at the first call.

As then the enemy evilly and wretchedly punished the Palatinate and threatened Bavaria with additional trouble, we had to live with constant fear and in more fearful anticipation.

Meanwhile the emperor and elector collected their troops at Regensburg,[173] crossed the Danube, and attacked in complete silence, which had

---

169. Paring Abbey was a Benedictine abbey in Lower Bavaria.

170. Fl. is the abbreviation for *gulden,* a common coin also known as a *florin.*

171. The capital of Bavaria.

172. Cham is a city in the Upper Palatinate about thirty-five miles northeast from Regensburg. Banér had chosen the area of Cham as winter quarters for his army.

173. The Imperial-Bavarian army was led by Archduke Leopold and Piccolomini.

never been done before, and for which we must thank God and the intercession of Mary alone. [The troops] overpowered the city of Neunburg in the height of winter and the most horrible weather, and took the entire garrison prisoner, including the famous General Schlang,[174] who had long since made a name for himself. The booty was likewise not small. As soon as word reached Cham, Banér left the city, abandoning it to our side with open gates, and fled with his army back to Bohemia, where he soon died the death of a tyrant out of displeasure, they say, over his rout and flight (for he lived by pride).[175] And so we once again enjoyed our lives free of fear, and celebrated Easter with joy.

The 9th of April the transport groom, who had been sent from the abbey with two horses for military hauling, returned without horses and only half alive. He explained that, due to the lack of provisions and fodder, many horses and men had sickened and died. He was provided with better fare for fourteen days, and payment for the horses followed without delay from Munich according to the appraisal.

On the 18th of April our sacred treasure was brought back to the abbey from Munich with the greatest and universal joy.

Ascension Day solemnities saw frequent pilgrims. But we had hardly ushered in those from Augsburg and Munich when the wind began to storm with snow and rain, and it stormed for three full days. . . .

The 14th of May the emperor Ferdinand III traveled from Regensburg to the city of Munich, where he was entertained in true imperial style.

The past spring was very wintery, and now summer began very stormily. A flood that was worse than any in human memory did the greatest damage everywhere, and a frightening downpour flattened everything from Ulm to Straubing. Wild swine in unbelievable numbers caused the greatest damage to our fields and to those of all the surrounding areas, causing the greatest difficulty for the peasants.

On St. Bartholomew's Day[176] eve, the highest sovereigns, the elector and electress, came to the Holy Mountain and spent their time mostly in prayer and devotion, and on Sunday, they also attended the procession of the three sacred hosts around the church. And they only departed three days later, after vespers.[177]

---

174. Major General Erich Schlang (c. 1600–1642) defended Neunburg against a vastly larger imperial army, delaying it and so allowing the army of Banér to escape.

175. Banér died in May 1641 in the Saxon city of Halberstadt, after a frantic but successful retreat through Bohemia.

176. The festival in honor of St. Bartholomew, one of the twelve apostles, occurs on August 24.

177. The evening prayer service.

The 18th of August the harvest began for us and was more fruitful than one could have expected when looking back at the very cold spring, the wet summer, and the damages caused by game. . . .

1642

The first evil that appeared with the year 1642 was, once again, the wolves, of which there were scores, and which made the roads and paths of all places unsafe.

The 14th of February it snowed, and around seven o'clock in the morning there was terrible lightning, during which our house of worship stood as if in a fire; and immediately following there was a frightening clap of thunder, which, however, left behind it nothing but an evil smell in the church and in the tower.

The 5th of April our most highly treasured hero, Johann von Werth,[178] was released from his imprisonment by the French, which had lasted over four years and from which he was ransomed in exchange for General Horn,[179] and he arrived in Munich with the greatest joy and hope for the future.

After the coldest wind and hoarfrost, which lasted up into the middle of May and which caused great damage to the crops and especially to the fruit trees, there followed a protracted drought, during which one could neither cultivate, nor sprout, nor germinate the fields. What a sad outlook for the summer cultivation!

Only on the 5th of June did it begin to rain, and our fields began to grow.

The 8th of June, on the festival of Whitsunday, showery weather developed, which, among other things, dropped hail weighing up to a pound and caused the greatest damages to the fields, livestock, and houses in many areas. We, God be praised, were spared.

On the 11th of June our fields were covered with hoarfrost, as if with snow; what luck that the rye had not yet come into bloom! Still, the hoarfrost caused some damage.

In the middle of August two butchers came from Munich with the request that their guild might be accepted and enrolled permanently into our Holy Trinity confraternity, so that they could join in an annual procession to the Holy Mountain. This was quite easily allowed and affirmed in writing.

---

178. Johann von Werth (c. 1595–1652), a cavalry general of the imperial and Bavarian army. He had been captured in 1638 by Bernard of Saxe-Weimar, the French-paid military entrepreneur, and had then been handed over to the French. He was held in Paris in grand style.

179. Swedish Field Marshal Gustav Horn, count of Pori (1592–1657), was taken prisoner by the Austrians after the battle of Nördlingen in 1634.

The 27th of August lightning struck our tower three times—or rather, three strikes repeated one after another—yet each time without damage; but we fear that this tower, which has already had this bad luck seven times in only a few years, but has not yet caught fire, might one day do so and cause us the worst bad luck.[180]

One has to be amazed at how the wolves multiply and get out of control. They mauled eight lambs and one sheep from the abbey flock, and calves and colts from others. Small wild game is no longer anywhere to be seen, and it is hard to know if [the wolves] dispersed them or completely ate them up.

These wild carnivores might well have given a government treasurer the idea of the meat-pennies. The butchers have long since been ordered to collect one penny for the treasury for every pound of meat that they weigh out. Now this order is being extended to all cloisters and dominions, ecclesiastic and secular, to pay one penny per pound of every type of meat that they slaughter for their own use and from their own herds. Whether it will be implemented remains to be seen.

Our army having been badly beaten and weakened at Leipzig in past days,[181] there once again arose a general terror and fear that the enemy might use our weakness and, as ten years ago, move and rush here straight away and plunge us into the now long-threatened distress.

Our elector once again did everything that he could do. He once again newly equipped his army; called up the territorial militia; convened the hunters and marksmen, who came together in great number at Munich, at Ingolstadt, and at Landshut; and advertised in all places for horses for hauling and for the cannons, which he later had brought to Donauwörth. The Holy Mountain was again required to send two equipped horses and one groom. And so we remained in peace for this year, but anxiously, and uncertain of what new events the future would yield.

1643

The 2nd of January I received the highest command to send my two required horses to Munich for the team hauling the cannons. But I had the greatest difficulty finding a transport groom for this. The old one wanted nothing to

---

180. A lightning strike in 1669 burned down the tower, church, and monastery, though the chapel survived. Rebuilding, including a new slate roof for the church, lasted until 1676.

181. The second battle of Breitenfeld, outside Leipzig in Saxony, took place on November 2. The imperial army was crushed by a smaller Swedish army under General Torstensson.

do with it and would prefer to face the Turks, he said, rather than go against these fiends once more, and everyone else said the same thing. Finally, a young married man stepped forth, which pleased me greatly, and I gave him seven *gulden* in travel money to take with him.

The peasants had great trouble in hunting the wolves, for which they were called up to diverse and often distant places.

On January 3 there came yet another electoral request for contributions, by which every dominion should pay only what its subjects would give altogether, whereby an entire farm would give two *gulden,* a half [farm][182] one *gulden,* and so forth, as was arranged three years ago. The sum I assembled was 136 fl., 52 kr.[183] How gladly would everyone give the same again, if he could thereby buy peace.

The 7th of January Father Georg Strohschneider drowned in the upper pond, for he too boldly risked going on the ice, and all the others who went walking with him failed to save him.

The 19th our wagoner, who had recently been sent with two horses for the cannons, returned to us on foot and explained that his and other abbey horses had been appraised and marked and handed over to others. The grooms, however, were all told to return back home.

The 3rd of February the territorial militia from the jurisdiction of Weilheim was called up in order to reinforce the territorial troops of Landsberg and Schongau,[184] because the enemy was supposedly coming very close. They soon turned back, however, and received only half pay; according to the highest decree, the other half had to be paid to them by the village commune.

In these days, the most enormous, raging winds were once again everywhere and did great damage. They took from us a large part of the church roof.

The 7th of February the hunters were called to Rain;[185] but contrary to all expectations, these too soon turned back, and complained about the pay.

Since the French–Swedish army had already besieged Württemberg in large part, and had already made many sorties into Swabia, we could think of nothing but our utter fear of having to flee, and were especially anxious about our sacred treasure, all the more as it had been forbidden at the highest levels to flee with anything.

I wrote, therefore, in this regard to the elector, and received the answer to remove nothing from its place. He sent along, however, the key to the sacred

---

182. In Bavaria, for tax purposes, a farm of a certain size was known as a whole farm, and smaller farms were designated as halves, quarters, eighths, and so on.

183. 136 *gulden,* 52 *kreuzer.* One *gulden* was equal to sixty *kreuzer.*

184. All towns in Upper Bavaria.

185. A town in Lower Bavaria.

treasure, so as not to cause any delay if worse came to worse. And hereby our anxiety and fear were not at all alleviated.

Only our adored Johann von Werth, to whom, after God and Mary, we are the most thankful, delivered us from our anxious fear. He attacked the enemy repeatedly in his winter quarters, killed many, chased him out of all of Württemberg, and gained a great deal of booty.

On the 24th of February I once again had to deliver an equipped horse with groom to Munich, though three days later they came back again to me by means of a good intercession.

On the 1st of March the same assessment was once again issued as in previous years: namely, that every dominion should collect as much as their subjects would give altogether, whereby a farm would give 2 fl., and so on downward in proportion.

The 16th and 17th of May we had very damaging hoarfrost, especially for the fruit trees.

The 11th of June lightning struck through the window just as we were singing vespers; yet from this barely one or two panes were broken in the choir. It came like a flaming ball into the middle of the choir, where it then split into multiple parts; it blackened the gilding in large part, and powerfully spun a brass candlestick around. Many of our fathers fell unconscious to the ground. May God be infinitely thanked for preventing greater evil!

The 4th of July our Most Serene Lady Highness[186] came from Ettal and Peissenberg,[187] where she visited the reliquaries, and also went to the Holy Mountain and traveled the next day to Starnberg.[188]

The harvest this year was, contrary to all expectations, well blessed, and the hay was in greater quantities than we had seen in quite some time.

Toward the end of November, our enemies, the French Swedes or the Swedish French, arranged for the downfall of Bavaria. After they had conquered Rottweil, although with effort and many losses,[189] nothing more stood in the way of their invading Bavaria through the already entirely devastated and plundered Swabia, to despoil it and to murder. At least this was what was decided at Tuttlingen, where, at an assembly, the French Colonel Rantzau moistened his collar with red wine and said to those around him, who laughed at this: "Thus will my hands soon be colored with the blood of Bavaria." However another man, Rosen by name, who was himself no

---

186. Maria Anna of Austria (1610–1665), wife of Elector Maximilian I of Bavaria.

187. Places in Upper Bavaria with well-known pilgrimage churches.

188. Another town in Upper Bavaria.

189. The French general Jean-Baptiste Budes, count of Guébriant (1602–1643), died from his wounds soon after the battle.

better than Rantzau, replied to him: "But you didn't say, 'if God wills it.' You don't know the Bavarians, but you will get to know them!"

Then the enemy army, more than twenty thousand cavalry and infantry, assembled near Tuttlingen, and the generals feasted and enjoyed good days and celebrations with their commander Rantzau over the capture of Rott-weil and the booty of Bavaria, of which they were as assured as that the sun would rise tomorrow. But look! All at once, the Bavarian army appeared, at-tacked the unwary—who never even dreamed of an enemy in the area—slaughtered more than a thousand, and also took many thousands prisoner; they turned the enemy cannons against the city and surrounded it, and on the second day, the 24th of November, they took the city and captured all of the high officers within. The booty was similarly great.

Three French officers fell at the feet of our commander, Wolf, who was the first on the scene and who brought down many of the enemy with his own hand, and they promised never again to cross over the Rhine, and also to convince other French of the same thing, and were in such a manner set free. Johann von Werth let go five hundred French altogether with the ad-monition that they never again have anything to do on this side of the Rhine. Captain Rosen, who reconnoitered even on the day of the attack and who amazingly managed to evade our troops, was denounced as a traitor and taken prisoner. And it was he who previously had made the admonition to Rantzau that he did not know the Bavarians, but that he would get to know them.

30. Preparations for a General Peace Congress (January 6, 1644)[190]

[Years of complicated negotiations among the imperial princes and among the foreign powers had led, by the end of 1643, to a peculiar tripartite peace congress. Since February, deputies from most of the German princes had been assembled in Frankfurt am Main to discuss peace within the empire. Mean-while, representatives from the foreign powers began to trickle into their own peace congress in Westphalia, though tensions between Protestants and Catholics resulted in them each meeting in a separate city: Catholics in Mün-ster, Protestants in nearby Osnabrück. The emperor's plan was to resolve the peace in the empire first, and then represent the entire empire at the negotia-

---

190. "Memorandum of what Krosigk should discuss with the French legates dele-gated to Münster concerning the general peace treaty," Cassel, December 27, 1643/ January 6, 1644, Hessische Staatsarchiv Marburg, 4h Nr. 2116, fol. 13–6.

tions in Westphalia. This would allow him to separate the imperial estates from their foreign allies, and so increase his bargaining power against both groups. Some German princes, especially Protestants, objected strenuously to this scheme to exclude them. Leading the opposition were the elector of Brandenburg and Landgravine Amalia Elisabeth of Hesse-Cassel, who, as a declared enemy of the empire, had been barred from participating in the Frankfurt assembly. They argued that the right to make war and peace (ius belli ac pacis) was not the special possession of the emperor and electors alone, but was a fundamental German liberty belonging to all the princes and estates of the empire. Yet their complaints had little support among the Catholic princes. Thus, as we see in the document below, Amalia Elisabeth turned to her allies, the French and Swedes, and tried to convince them that it would be in their own interests to help. This appeal would be successful.]

Memorandum of What Krosigk[191] Should Discuss with the French Legates Delegated to Münster Concerning the General Peace Treaty

Both crowns of France and Sweden should endeavor that the princes and estates of the empire are included in the universal negotiations and, indeed, with the right to vote, for the emperor wishes to exclude them and to allow no one but the electors to attend. It is unnecessary to explain in copious detail how beneficial it would be to the foreign potentates for the right of war and peace in the Roman Empire not to lie solely under the power, will, and decision of the emperor and the few electors, and that instead all the princes and estates should be included in the now-imminent general peace negotiations. Indeed, the crowns can easily appreciate this on their own. . . .

Necessity demands, therefore, that above all things this is put forth by the illustrious crowns of France and Sweden as the foundation and sine qua non for their participation in the negotiations. For, as is well known, the princes and estates of the empire have the right of peace and war in common with the emperor. So [the crowns] neither could nor would negotiate nor enter into a treaty with the emperor alone, without the consultation, advice, and approval of the estates; but they would instead take up arms, as they have wielded them until now and still wield them, to ensure the maintenance and retention of [the estates'] liberties. Nor would they allow any weakening or discontinuation of these, especially of the right of peace and war, without which the remaining rights of the princes and estates cannot be maintained, but which is always thrown into disarray by those who would arrogate to themselves alone such a decision or would proceed by themselves. Indeed,

191. Adolf Wilhelm von Krosigk (1610–1657), one of the landgravine's closest advisors.

for the crowns' own reasons of state, or at their own discretion and consent, a newer war could be announced or decided upon sooner or later.

Whereby it should also be pointed out, that if the said illustrious crowns do indeed enter into the general peace negotiations without the estates of the empire and finally make an agreement, it would not be binding. Nor would it give the crowns any security (something they, above all things, must nevertheless have as their concern in such negotiations). For those who belonged with them and were their partners, and whose interests were also conjoined with theirs, would not be included, nor would they be heard concerning [the peace].

One has, unfortunately, more than enough evidence of what kind of calamity has already accrued to the entire Roman Empire and its members, and what kind of misery and fundamentally ruinous situation the estates have already encountered, because, contrary to the ancient convention and imperial constitution, in the past and again recently in the year 1630 in Germany, the electors and the emperor alone concluded and proceeded against the crown of Sweden without consulting the princes and estates of the empire (who would not have given their approval, but would have brought forth their considerable reasons against it, or would have offered loyal, well-intentioned proposals for mediation). The crowns may not have been able to understand previously that they should be careful in this regard, but if the remaining estates are not able to give advice and agreement in the future, there might be more similarly dangerous, adverse, and fundamentally ruinous resolutions and declarations of war from the emperor and the electors. Thus they must quickly be vigilant on account of their own great interests as well as those of the collected princes and estates of the empire, which are interconnected with their own. And as much as possible, they should control these inconveniences by having as a precondition the admission of all estates to the site of the peace negotiations.

There is no doubt that the imperialists will raise one and another objection to it and will do their utmost to hinder such an admission, especially with the right to vote. Also, should they finally acquiesce and give the princes and estates, like the electors, the right of suffrage, yet they would still not allow it during the negotiations themselves, nor at the site of the negotiations. They would use the pretense that few examples or documents could be found that indicated that the collected estates ever appeared at the site of negotiations when the emperor negotiated either peace or war with foreign potentates. So if His Imperial Majesty and the electors were now to allow the princes and estates to be heard at the impending peace negotiations, and also with right of suffrage, then [he would argue that] they should be in another site instead, and perhaps at Frankfurt, for people have already assembled there. Yet if this were the case, the crowns would find that Frankfurt was too far distant from Osnabrück and Münster, and, with sending things back and forth, a lot of time would be wasted uselessly. One would also not know beforehand whether those estates assembled at Frankfurt would be duly, elaborately, and faithfully informed of everything that proceeded and was negotiated at the site of the negotiations. Nor if, third—due to the authority of the emperor, intimidation, or awe—the same would be able to vote freely. And then, fourth, it would be inconvenient for the crowns always to fetch or await the votes and conclusions from Frankfurt. And so for these and other reasons, there could be no more useful means of accelerating and promoting a lasting and secure peace, than to allow all the imperial estates to assemble in person at the site of the negotiations.

If this were seriously the intent on the part of His Imperial Majesty and the electors, and if one seriously had as one's objective a concise, secure, and speedy peace, then indeed one would also not be opposed to the nearest and strongest means to accomplish this, without digression and loss of time; all the more, because the deputies currently present at Frankfurt are also not actually instructed for the general peace negotiations and therefore could not in this case duly legitimize it. Not to mention that there are only a few of the deputies themselves, and not all are appropriately a part of this peace business; and also there are many other princes and estates remaining who must be included just as much as the deputies.[192] And furthermore, in regard to the admission of the collected estates to the site of the negotiations, it could be considered that the imperialists might undertake to raise discussions at Münster and Osnabrück before the negotiations begin. So it would be necessary and useful that as soon as the French legates arrive at Münster they let all the princes and estates know this, invite them to the peace negotiations, and, at the same time, send out necessary passports. As it is, such has already been done by the Swedish legates—though, for evident reasons, they only wrote to Evangelicals,[193] and also because they were concerned that it would be badly interpreted by many Catholics.

Her Highness the landgravine, however, would humbly approve that the crown of France, or those legates and plenipotentiaries it sends to the general peace negotiations, behaves differently and disseminates everything, directing its letters to both Catholic and Protestant estates alike. For in these common affairs concerning German liberty, the adherents of both religions must stand as one man. And just as the House of Austria[194] has until now gained some advantage by making and fomenting division between the Catholics and Evangelicals, in order thereby to gain absolute dominion all

192. Including herself.

193. Protestants.

194. The Austrian Habsburgs.

the sooner (which would not otherwise be possible), so one must strive all the more and in all ways, so that the adherents of both religions set aside, as much as possible, all umbrage and unequal thoughts, and that first and foremost their minds be disposed and brought again toward unity and good understanding.

The above-mentioned letter of invitation, however, should not only be sent to the collected electors, princes, and estates, but also, so that notice reaches every man and is not held back, a copy of it should be communicated to the leading estates of every circle, who might then notify others.

Likewise, one ought to arrange for it to go to the deputies present at Frankfurt all together and, in case the elector of Mainz withholds the general letter, then to send out a copy of it to every deputy individually.

The subject matter of such a letter will be determined during the first private meeting and conference of the French, Swedish, and Hessian deputies.

The crown of Sweden would then also still be able to have a letter sent out to the collected Catholic and Evangelical electors, princes, and estates, so that from this they would sense how both allied crowns, unanimously and without distinction for religion, take an interest in their liberty.

In what way one could most reasonably negotiate about the Peace of Prague,[195] whether to annul the same through direct or indirect ways, and whether and in what way to raise an amnesty during the ongoing negotiations, all this one should likewise consider carefully in the above-mentioned first meeting and discussions, and agree upon a certain conclusion. As soon as she is advised of the French legates' trip to Münster, the landgravine will not fail to empower her people with sufficient instructions.

>   Signed Cassel the 27th of December 1643[196]
>   Amalia Elisabeth

31. Military Contributions and French Subsidies (Early 1644)

[By the end of 1643 the dramatic allied rally against the imperialists was in disarray. In November 1643 the French army, encamped at Tuttlingen, in Swabia, was routed by a surprise attack from the Bavarian General Franz von Mercy, and what remained of the French Army of Germany fled back across the Rhine. Meanwhile, the Swedes chose just this moment to enter into war

---

195. The 1635 Peace of Prague was made between the elector of Saxony and the emperor, but was later signed by most other princes of the empire. See Document 24.
196. Old style. By the new Gregorian calendar, the date was January 6, 1644.

*with their Baltic rivals, the Danes, by invading their lands in Jutland. With
the French army driven from the empire and the Swedes distracted, the coming
campaign season looked extremely promising for the imperialists and Spanish.
Only Landgravine Amalia Elisabeth of Hesse-Cassel, the strongest remaining
German ally of the French and Swedes, seemed to be in a position to meet the
oncoming threat. The following three letters focus on the grim situation of the
allies in early 1644. The first is from Joachim de Wicquefort (1600–1670), a
Dutch merchant serving as the landgravine's resident at The Hague, and was
sent to the French superintendent of finances, Nicolas de Bailleul (1586–
1652). The following two are from the landgravine's close advisor, Adolf Wilhelm von Krosigk (1610–1657), to the prime minister of France, Cardinal
Jules Mazarin (1602–1661). These letters are interesting not just because they
demonstrate the troubles of France and its allies in this period, but also because
they focus on one of the key issues driving this war: money. Though most military leaders of this period tried as much as possible to maintain and support
their troops off the lands (or "quarters") they occupied, after decades of economic degradation, these lands could yield only so much tax revenue, food,
and fodder, and so could sustain only a finite number of troops. Thus, in addition to the forced military "contributions" continually extracted from local
populaces by occupying armies, external funds would also be necessary to allow
the warring parties to continue to raise, maintain, and pay thousands more
troops than the land alone could support. The Hessian army, which was one of
the largest in the war, lived off of quarters throughout the northwestern portion of the empire. Yet these quarters were not enough to allow the Hessians to
build up a significantly larger force than they already possessed. In the following letters, one can see, therefore, the Hessians' efforts to gain additional financial assistance from France, as well as their concern that any new troops raised
on the landgravine's behalf be supported not through her existing contributions, but through new extraordinary subsidies.]*

Letter of Joachim de Wicquefort, Resident of Hesse-Cassel, to Nicolas de Bailleul, Superintendent of Finances, January 25, 1644[197]

My lord,

The joy of the enemies over this new war of the Swedes shows well enough
that they intend to make their profit out of it, as well as of the misfortune
that occurred at Tuttlingen. Their preparations are great and can only give
great apprehension to Her Highness, Madame the landgravine of Hesse, all

---

197. J. Wicquefort (own hand letter sent) to Bailleul, Superintendent of Finances,
The Hague, January 25, 1644, Archives du Ministère des Affaires Etrangères, Correspondance politique [AAECP] Hollande 30, fol. 106–7.

the more as she sees herself exposed to their discretion and to her total ruin—
unless we do something quickly and powerfully for her conservation. Her
Highness is entirely abandoned by the Swedes. The States-General[198] [of the
Netherlands] have indeed encouraged her, due to the persuasion of the ambassadors [of France];[199] but far from expecting any assistance from this
country, she has reason to believe that they will not do the least thing in
her favor against the imperialists. Only France remains that can contribute
to her support, and the importance of the affair is such, my lord, that Her
Highness should be assisted with both vigor and promptitude. If the extraordinary subsidy for which she is asking from Their Majesties is not in
any way proportional to her necessity, one will shortly see the ruin of her
armies and the loss of her state. This is what has obliged Her Highness to
send Mr. Krosigk here to inform the ambassadors of the danger she is in, as
well as of remedies to prevent it. By the attached writing, it is clear enough
that the plan of the emperor is to render the Circle of Westphalia[200] to his
devotion, and quickly, considering the forces that Hatzfeld[201] will put on
foot and the weakness of our troops and strongholds. There is no other remedy, my lord, than to reinforce the troops and supply the strongholds, which
lack everything—measures that cannot be taken without a lot of money. Our
treasury is so exhausted that I do not know how to pay the expenditures that
Her Highness has approved, some of which even concern the pension of my
lord the landgrave,[202] something Her Highness had considered so assured,
because it is a point of the alliance, that she assigned it below some others
that she thought to pay promptly. She has been very saddened to learn of
the delay [of the subsidies] after the promise that the queen,[203] as well as His
Eminence,[204] made, nevertheless trusting, my lord, to the effects of the
goodwill that it has pleased you to show her in your letters. She hopes to be
favored soon with satisfaction. I would not have touched on this point, my

198. The highest governing body of the Dutch Republic.

199. The French ambassadors to the general peace treaty in Westphalia, Claude de
Mesmes, count d'Avaux (1595–1650), and Abel Servien (1593–1659), stopped at
The Hague on the way to the conference.

200. The Lower Rhenish–Westphalian Circle was one of the ten administrative regions of the empire and encompassed numerous states in the northwest portion of
the empire.

201. Imperial General Melchior Hatzfeld (1593–1658).

202. The landgravine's son, Wilhelm, received a regular personal pension from the
French as a part of the French-Hessian military alliance.

203. The queen of France, Anne of Austria, who served as regent for her young son
Louis XIV.

204. Cardinal Mazarin.

lord, if I did not know the urgency in her state, and how wrongly some have wanted to make [the queen's] ministers think that Her Highness is seeing to her own particular affairs and not distributing the money that she received from France for the needs of the war. I can say, my lord, in truth, that Her Highness has not received a single penny of the extraordinary subsidies that has not been paid to a treasurer of war, who has rendered account to the commissioner general. Of the ordinary subsidies, I do not think she has received, in all, twenty thousand *reichsthalers* during the time the alliance has lasted. Since Mr. de Polhelm[205] will be able to draw up a rather exact account, I have avoided bothering you, my lord, with a longer discussion.

According to the most recent letters from Hamburg, we have had the march of General Torstensson[206] in Jutland, and that of Königsmarck[207] toward the bishopric of Verden. The king of Denmark has sent eight thousand men for the defense of Jutland, and twelve ships for that of the seaports. He has also given patents to raise new troops so that the Swedes will meet resistance, considering the assistance that Denmark might also have in the spring from the king of Poland, the grand duke of Muscovy, and even the emperor. We have had confirmation of six ships richly loaded with copper and cannons [that were headed] for Amsterdam and stopped at the Sound[208] [by the Danes]. I even believe that there are some eight or ten pieces of brass and thirty or forty of small cannons inside [the ships] that the queen of Sweden has given to Madame the landgravine. The rumor that has spread of the treaties between the two crowns does not continue. The States of Holland[209] are consulting presently about what they must do or not do during this war. And I have learned from a member of the States-General that those of Amsterdam would be disposed to undertake something on the Sound on this favorable occasion. The letters from Cologne have brought us confirmation of the capture of Zittau[210] by Gallas[211] on conditions very bad for the besieged. The principal army is going to take winter quarters in Bohemia and Austria, and it is believed that the count of Traun[212] is coming to Cologne to procure here, so as not to burden the hereditary lands [of the emperor]. The emperor

205. The landgravine's resident at Paris.

206. Swedish Field Marshal Lennart Torstensson (1603–1651).

207. Swedish Major General Hans Christoff von Königsmarck (1600–1663).

208. The Sound, or *Øresund,* is the narrow strait between Sweden and Denmark. Conflict over control this waterway was partially behind the new Danish–Swedish war.

209. The parliament of the province of Holland in the Dutch Republic.

210. A city in Upper Lusatia.

211. Matthias Gallas (1584–1647), an imperial general.

212. Ernst, count of Abensberg and Traun (1608–1668).

has sent to Prague to encourage the estates to offer a contribution of eight hundred thousand *florins*. About Rákóczi[213] we know nothing, since there are some who speak affirmatively of the alliance made with the Swedes and others inform us from Constantinople that the sultan[214] wants to punish the princes of Transylvania and Wallachia in case they stir. On the 20th of this month an assembly of the deputies of the emperor, of Spain, and of Bavaria, is to be held at Passante on important affairs. The duke of Bavaria,[215] it is said, will make some great levies. The duke of Lorraine[216] is descending toward the country of Jülich, having left some hideous marks wherever he passed. It is believed that they are going to look for quarters in Liège. I am, my lord, your very humble, obedient, and faithful servant

> J. de Wicquefort
> The Hague, this January 25, 1644

Letter of Adolf Wilhelm von Krosigk, Hessian Councilor, to Cardinal Jules Mazarin, Prime Minister of France, January 25, 1644[217]

My lord,

It was only on my arrival in this country that I happily received the letter of December 3 that Your Eminence gave me the honor of writing to me, and that commended me to represent to Her Highness the landgravine, and to all those who put some belief in my words, the cares and efforts that were being used in France to repair the breach that the last disgrace made to the arms of the king, and to support powerfully the affairs of Germany. In this, the commandment of Your Eminence will be so faithfully executed that there will remain not the least doubt that, under your generous conduct, all things will be handled with the same prudence and vigilance that have accompanied and felicitated all of your actions up to the present. On this subject, my lord, I venture to say a word to Your Eminence on the passion that Madame the landgravine displays for disappointing neither the king nor the public in a situation in which the quarrel is getting hotter, and numerous new incidents make matters all the more dangerous. It was for this purpose, my lord, that Her Highness had sent me to the ambassadors of France and

213. Prince György Rákóczi of Transylvania.

214. Ottoman Sultan Ibrahim I (1615–1648).

215. Duke Maximilian I, elector of Bavaria (1573–1651).

216. Charles IV (1604–1675), duke of Lorraine, served as an officer in the imperial army.

217. "To repair the loss of the defeat of Tuttlingen," Krosigk (secretary hand letter sent) to Mazarin, The Hague, January 25, 1644, AAECP Hollande 30, fol. 108–9.

to this republic,[218] to see how we could prepare and coordinate affairs to make war against those who are making a trophy of this last defeat, and of the liberty that the unexpected engagement of the arms of Sweden gives them, so as to vomit and discharge all their rage on Madame the landgravine and her armies. And although I am persuaded that the ambassadors will have sent to the court the details of our conference, and even though I have sent a copy to Mr. de Polhelm of what, on behalf of Her Highness, I have been obliged to add by a memoir, I have nevertheless believed it to be not improper and indeed my duty to repeat it to Your Eminence, and so to exhaust the remedy from its source.

It is certain, my lord, that General Hatzfeld already has a considerable body of troops, and that he is going to give to the elector of Cologne[219] all the strongholds that are between the Weser and the Rhine, and then draw from them and put in campaign all the imperial garrisons, so that this army alone could amount to fourteen or fifteen thousand men. . . . Your Eminence will easily judge that, since the army of the king [of France] has to face that of Bavaria (which this duke puts more diligence into reinforcing than he has ever done before), the army of Hatzfeld will have free hand to attack Madame the landgravine. I do not want to go along with the surge of common fear that the crown of Sweden will engage itself so much with its new enemies that it will not be able to face those it has usually been diverting in Germany. If this were the case, the emperor would employ all the more easily his other forces against us. Thus it is absolutely necessary that Madame the landgravine be in a position to sustain the shock; to position herself, with the assistance of her allies, against the roused forces [of the enemies]; and to begin therefore to reinforce her army by good levies. . . . Nevertheless, it requires a lot of time before they can be finished, or be in a condition to serve, and in the meantime, we will have a lot to do. The levies alone, my lord, consume a lot of money, for the least amount one could pay for them would be a thousand *reichsthalers* for a company of cavalry, and half as much for one of infantry. Moreover, it is a truth that does not suffer any contradiction that the quarters of Her Highness cannot maintain the troops, as weak as they are now, and that they would be all the less capable were the number to increase. So the assistance and the expense that the king wishes to make for this purpose have to be considerable if they are to produce a good effect.

I have noticed, my lord—and, in passing, take the liberty to fight this error—that there are those who suspect that Her Highness or her lieutenant

218. The Dutch Republic.

219. The elector of Cologne, Ferdinand of Bavaria (1577–1650), was the brother of Duke Maximilian of Bavaria.

general,[220] instead of employing the extraordinary subsidies for war, make their own conveniences out of them. And some talk that has come to my ears has made me understand that there is some doubt about the handling of the French money. As for Madame the landgravine, I can assure you on my faith and my honor, Your Eminence, to whom I will never tell a lie, that this judgment wounds the sincerity of Her Highness, and that I can vouch for the fact and maintain that she does not even possess any small reserve to use in case of need, since the war can produce diverse accidents. All the less has she made use of the subsidies other than for the things necessary for the war. As for the lieutenant general, it is true that he has received the money and all the extraordinary subsidies, but everything is passed through the hands of one of the paymasters of Her Highness' army, who has kept track penny for penny; and when one will consider the money required to maintain the garrisons of [Düren] and Kempen,[221] which have not drawn any subsistence from the countryside and which have been sustained by distributed bread and from our money, and also consider what was given to the troops that are in the army of the king, and which have only had the single payment for two months, then the reckoning will be easy to make. Your Eminence knows that war requires diverse expenditures, and that the fortification and provisioning of the strongholds consume a lot. And even though ours are not such as they should be, it has been necessary to begin to lay the foundations and beginnings, there not being the least fortification or provision at the moment. I would not have touched on this matter if I did not believe that these bad impressions could be harmful, and I do not think it proper to bother Her Highness by telling her about them. But Your Eminence would do something worthy of truth if you would get rid of this opinion and conclude that it is but false imaginings and bad offices that some have tried to make, for lack of bigger news and to render themselves important. Your Eminence recalls that the principal purpose of my voyage in France was to present the inevitable necessity of the increase of the subsidies, and to gain the favorable declaration that the queen has now given, which states positively that she will increase them above what they have been all these years. And if, in that period of time, the danger was not as evident as it is now, nor was the interest of the king in preserving Her Highness as strong, there is, my lord, now a remedy that can eliminate this general evil.[222]

220. Count Caspar of Eberstein served at this time as lieutenant general of the Hessian army, the highest Hessian military office.

221. Towns in Westphalia that the Hessians took in 1643.

222. In other words, by increasing the subsidies, they can avoid any damage to the common cause.

In addition, Her Highness has ordered me to ask this republic to assist Her Highness in case she needs some troops, whether it is a question of helping some stronghold or for the execution of some good enterprise. I have had the honor of talking particularly with the prince of Orange,[223] who understands very well the importance of this. His Highness has informed me that he will have trouble disposing of affairs in this manner, since, on their side, it will be a question of making a good campaign;[224] but it seems to me, and some of those in the States-General have fortified me in this opinion, that it is possible that they might be able to do both one and the other; and the intervention of France can do a lot, as well, which is a point that I have strongly recommended to the plenipotentiaries, not doubting that they will work it out as best as possible. . . . Besides, my lord, His Highness [the prince of Orange] is also of the opinion that the actions of the coming campaign would be greatly aided if the king would send an army to the Mosel, and if one would press the Swedes to arrange things such that they can make the ordinary diversion in Germany and leave some troops on the Weser. Your Eminence will remember, no doubt, what the count of Eberstein[225] had put on the table some time ago: namely, that the king would do well to raise two regiments of cavalry and two of infantry, to keep them in his pay, and to put them with the core of Her Highness' army so as to make it all the more capable of executing the things that might be asked of us. It seems to me that, if this can be worked out, there is more reason to consider it now than there ever was. Whatever the case, it is a task that takes time, and we are in a conjuncture at which promptitude goes right along with the necessity of putting everything in order. Finally, my lord, one can easily infer and then fool himself if one does not measure the affair with this truth: that if Her Highness lacks the above-mentioned means, she will be obliged to act simply in the defensive, to make a reduction of her troops, and to lower the number of the officers through whom the levies and recruits are, of necessity, raised—even though, by this means, the small number of troops that Her Highness will keep will not be secure. Another inconvenience is that the army of Hatzfeld, having nothing to fear, could turn against the armies of France, leading Her Highness to see herself sacrificed to the discretion of the enemies on the eve of a universal treaty. She has ordered me not to forget anything that can demonstrate her zeal and the pain in which she finds herself, and it is for this reason

223. The prince of Orange, Frederick Henry (1584–1647), was military leader of the Dutch Republic and Amalia Elisabeth's uncle.

224. They were concerned to have sufficient troops to wage their own campaign against the Spanish.

225. The Hessian lieutenant general.

that I am more prolific than should be permitted by a consideration of the quantity of important matters occupying Your Eminence.

I shall finish with the very humble prayer that you do me the grace of believing that my intention and my ambition are to serve the king on this occasion and in all those of my life, with as much passion and fidelity as the most faithful of his subjects could do, indeed the most zealous for his service. I would also, my lord, be carried beyond all satisfaction if, by my very humble obeisance and respect, I could deserve the happiness that Your Eminence would deign to, and would, dispose toward me as one who is perfectly,

> My lord,
> At The Hague, this January 15/25, 1644
> Of Your Eminence, the very humble very faithful and very obedient
> servant,
> Krosigk

Letter of Adolf Wilhelm von Krosigk, Hessian Councilor, to Cardinal Jules Mazarin, Prime Minister of France, February 15, 1644[226]

My lord,

I will not fail to console Madame the landgravine, given the disorder of her affairs, with the assurances that Your Eminence has given me of the affection with which you want to support her interests and honor her person. It is also in this goodwill, my lord, that Her Highness has lodged her greatest hopes, and it is to this that I dare refer back on her behalf, so as to beg Your Eminence to excuse the liberty that I take in telling you that I have had the honor of talking with the [French] ambassadors and plenipotentiaries, who have declared to me that the queen would assist Madame the landgravine with fifty thousand *reichsthalers* of extraordinary [subsidy], and would send the aid [of a contingent of troops] destined for her army if Her Highness would let it subsist on equal footing with her own troops, although the king would pay these auxiliaries the same as those of Her Highness. And Your Eminence used terms similar to these in that [letter] that you did me the honor of writing to me. To this, my lord, I cannot keep from representing to Your Eminence that Madame the landgravine will always receive, with respect and a great sense of gratitude, the graces and assistance that Her Majesty gives to her. But this does not come near to Her Highness' need to reinforce her army in the present conjuncture. Fifty thousand *reichsthalers* cannot suffice for the recruiting that Her Highness desires and will be able

---

226. Krosigk (secretary hand letter sent) to Mazarin, The Hague, February 15, 1644, AAECP Hollande 30, fol. 214–6.

to make. She could not add to it any of the ordinary subsidies, which are already employed for the subsistence of the troops that Her Highness has on foot, and which cannot be drawn from her quarters; no less can Her Highness use the money that she is obliged to spend for the maintenance of the artillery of her fortifications and the provision of the strongholds. She cannot do more, my lord, than to repeat, once and for all, this truth, which had brought the queen to promise to Her Highness some assistance more considerable than this, if we stop here.

Although it is beyond what can be expressed in the soul of Her Highness—who has great veneration for everything that comes from Her Majesty [the queen]—if, my lord, the queen does not respond to a necessity as urgent as the one that is enveloping Her Highness, and which regards the entire public, Her Highness begs Her Majesty and her ministers, among whom Your Eminence occupies the first rank, to consider the consequences of this affair, which will be dangerous in one way or another. For it will happen that if Her Highness is not able to put her troops in good condition (which is a pure impossibility without more help, and at least double fifty thousand *reichsthalers*), then her army will act with so much weakness that the enemies will do everything they please or will turn, without hindrance, against our allies. Your Eminence will learn from all those who know what is happening with the levies in Germany, what fifty thousand *reichsthalers* will buy, and I am sure that our officers would perform their duty better than any others, and that one hundred thousand *reichsthalers* distributed to Madame the landgravine would produce more effect than two hundred thousand elsewhere. As to the auxiliary troops that Her Majesty wants to put with the army of Her Highness, she recognizes sufficiently the infinite obligation that she has to Her Majesty, and also the effects of Her Majesty's great prudence, which lets her judge well that, where there are a lot of enemies, there are also people needed to occupy them; and that since an army of such a great size as Hatzfeld's (which is twelve thousand men effective strength now, without counting the reinforcements on which it is relying) will fall on Her Highness or will have to be diverted by her arms so as not to disturb other plans, it would be just, also, if one gave her the counterweight. Her Highness would be obligated to Her Majesty for this, but the interest is equal, and I dare say even greater, for Her Majesty. For nothing is more certain than that, if there is no considerable body [of troops] in Westphalia or around it, the imperial army will make itself master, to the great prejudice of the public; or, also likely, if it does not see an army that can act with deliberation and if the forces of Her Highness die little by little, it will fall entirely on the armies of France.

But, my lord, as happy as is this decision to form a good body of troops in the places above stated, so it will be impossible for Her Highness to

furnish the subsistence to additional troops. And it is reasonable that one
adjust oneself when one makes progress or new conquests; but when an ally
enters into another's lands and quarters, which are the sole sinews of war, the
maintenance that you want to extract will run to the destruction of this state,
and the alliance that Her Highness has with the king has limits. Her Highness, however, would happily pass by all this if there were any appearance of
being able to find some arrangement. But the new troops would quickly go
up in smoke if they could only get what ours receive while in the field (as
ours also become ruined for this very reason), because all our subsidies would
hardly account for one *montre*.[227] Ours, however, are more accustomed to
the ordinary discomforts. We try to give them some assignations[228] and
some small amount of money, and when they are in garrison, we mix the
contributions with the subsidies, and each one is paid the best that is possible, and usually very badly, which the ruin of our companies demonstrates,
and which is something we would not have before us if we could extort more
revenue from our quarters. We would have no grounds at all to importune
France for extraordinary assistance if we could get it elsewhere and at the expense of our enemies. From this, it is easy to infer that to lead troops into
the lands of the landgravine without paying them would be to put them upside down instead of helping her, and to take away from her the last means
of making war. Also, the troops that found themselves in the countryside
would disband immediately, for they would not be able to subsist for long.
So it would be necessary to expect to regulate the payment of the auxiliary
troops according to their needs, principally in view of the fact that their
number would not be so great and that they could not be treated as ours are,
Her Highness not being able to accommodate them with any quarters nor
assignations, not having enough for her own and being constrained to employ a good part of the subsidies for this. On her part, Her Highness does
not fail, either in duty or in obedience, to relieve the coffers of Her Majesty;
but the naked impossibility (which is entirely apparent) will act as her excuse and will dispose Her Majesty to advise how to maintain the above-
mentioned troops so that the expense of the levy will not become entirely
useless. There is reason to hope that, with the diversions made by the allies,
and with the actions of this army, we will see some daylight and will discharge the king from this expense—but this is something we cannot assume
at the beginning.[229] These are two points, my lord, that are not very agree-

227. Originally a month's wages, but, in practice, usually given more infrequently.

228. An assignment of revenue from a certain place or source (i.e., taxation, fees, or
rents owed from a piece of land or institution), usually lasting for a fixed duration.

229. In other words, if they manage to conquer enemy territories, they could use

able, but they are inseparable from the matter of maintaining our affairs, and I have orders to make this necessity understood at the court. I have not wanted to dwell upon the great displeasure that I have in being a perpetual petitioner, but I must follow up on the importance of this matter to beg Your Eminence, by all the prayers through which Her Highness the landgravine can touch you, to make an effort of your goodness and of your power to aid the demands that Her Highness cannot avoid repeating. I have talked in detail with the plenipotentiaries, who I believe will not pass over in silence what I have told them. The representations that Her Highness makes are worthy of belief and reflection now, or they never will be. God do me the grace that Your Eminence deems to give me, by the passion with which I revere you, and that my very humble and true services can maintain you with the zeal that makes me be,

My lord,
From The Hague, February 5/15, 1644
Of Your Eminence, the very humble and very obedient servant,
Krosigk

To His Eminence
My lord the Cardinal Mazarin
Paris

32. Declaration of György Rákóczi, Prince of Transylvania (February 17, 1644)[230]

[In 1630 György Rákóczi succeeded Bethlen Gábor as prince of Transylvania. A Calvinist, Gábor had entered the war on the side of the Protestants in 1620, but after the defeat at White Mountain, he had abandoned his allies in return for land grants in Hungary from the emperor. In subsequent years, however, the Habsburg emperors continued to try to re-Catholicize the area and increase their power over the Hungarian and Transylvanian nobility. The growing

---

them to extract additional contributions, but this is not something on which one can count.

230. György Rákóczi, *The Declaration or, Manifesto of George Racokzkie, Prince of Transylvania, to the States and Peeres of Hungarie; Together With the reasons added thereunto of his modern taking up of Armes the 17. of February, Anno 1644. George Racokzkie by the Grace of God, Prince of Transylvania, Lord of a part of the Kingdome of Hungarie, and Count of Zekella, London: Printed for Edward Blackmore, and are to be sold in Pauls Church-yard at the signe of the Angell, May 28. 1644* (London: Edward Blackmore, 1644). A copy can be found at the Huntington Library, Rare Books 57701.

conflict between the Transylvanian Prince Rákóczi and the emperor was fol-
lowed with great interest in the rest of Europe, for the prince's intervention in
the war might shift the delicate balance of opposing forces. Therefore, when
Rákóczi finally reentered the war as an ally of Sweden on February 17, 1644,
versions of his declaration—including the following English translation—
appeared in pamphlet form throughout Europe. One can see here that, while
religious issues are important in his justification for war, he also stresses the is-
sue of political power and control. Thus the combination of "the liberty of the
soule and body" is as key to his argument for war as it was for the Bohemian
rebels, for King Christian IV and King Gustavus Adolphus, and for many
others throughout this conflict.]

The Declaration or Manifesto of George Racokzkie, Prince of Transylvania, to the States and Peeres of Hungarie:

George Racokzkie by the grace of God, Prince of Transylvania, Lord of a part of the Kingdome of Hungarie, and Count of Zekella: To the right Honourable and right Worshipfull; Our well-beloved Lords and Gentry, Greeting.

How precious, and of what high esteeme there be with every one the lib-erty of the soule and body, hereof we need not to seeke afar off many exam-ples, nor to write thereof to your Lordships in many words. The modern state & condition of the Occidentall Provinces,[231] doth sufficiently testifie it; which, to reduce the aforesaid inestimable good to its ancient State and con-dition,[232] have counted for nothing all other Temporall and precious goods; yea with hazarding, and quite losing their own lives, doe not cease as yet to fight for it. How seriously also the Countreyes of Portugall and Catalonia, who sate under the Spanish power, and taken up Armes not in defence of the liberty of their soules, but only in defence of their temporall liberty do labour and endeavour to settle the same in the former condition of liberty:[233] is not unknown to your Lordships, especially my Countrymen, the Hungarians, how much blood they have shed for it, yes how many of them have suffered death for it, We have sufficient examples thereof. What troubles and miseries Our Nation, especially from the years 1619. hath suffered in this case, hereof whole bundles of letters full of complaints are to be found with us. How of-ten also We have not only been admonished, but also quite forced, as well by

231. The territories and estates of the empire.

232. In other words, in order to bring back their ancient liberty.

233. Both Portugal and Catalonia revolted against the Spanish monarchy in 1640 to defend their local liberties against the power of the central state.

the Protestants, as by the Roman Catholicks, that Wee at last would awaken, and remedie the grievances, because otherwise, if the oppression of the priviledges and liberties should further encrease and enlarge itself, Our Children and Posterity would be forced to possesse a Kingdome hereafter, that had lost all Liberty. We have been desired also by some of the high Officers and Ministers of the Crown which have discovered unto Us, that the Clergie intends to make the Kingdom of Hungarie hereditarie Subject to the House of Austria, and withal strives to domineer both Spiritually and Temporally over the fellow Members of their Religion, & to keep them under. It is not unknown to your Lordships, how many complaints there have bin made against those last Wils and Testament, that have bin forced from some, and thereby the lands and goods of the right natuall heir been alienated? The Clergy hath begun also to impropriate unto it selfe the chiefest Offices and places in the Frontier Townes of the Kingdome, and thus to pull fully out of the hands of the Temporall States and Peeres, that small Prerogative which they had left unto them: But what shall I say of the washing of the common Revenues of the whole Kingdom, and then the ruine following thereupon, which however must concern also the Clergie it selfe.

With what swiftnesse or tricks also the Jesuits are crept into the Kingdome to the utmost ruine of the libertie thereof, & of the Protestant Religion (which by all meanes and wayes is expressed) and with what unjustnesse also in the Frontier Townes themselves, those, that have Iura Patronatus in the Churches,[234] are troubled: hereof your Lordships have sufficiently been enformed.

One of the Spirituall Prelates also, who is yet living with His Imperial majesties knowledge, hath desired Us also by a confiding person, and in His Imperiall Majesties name, promised unto Us to turne over also all Our lands and goods situated in the Kingdom of Hungarie, to Our Heirs and Successors (which are as yet pawned to Us till they are redeemed) and to shew unto Us yet greater and more graces and favour, if We would only give Our assent unto it, that Hungarie might be an Hereditary Kingdome to the house of Austria, but whereas neither Our Conscience nor also the zeale and love we beare to Our Hungarian nation could give way to it, We returned unto him that answer, as hath been seeming to an Hungarian Prince loving his native Countrey, and desiring the liberty of his Countrey.

234. The right of patronage over the administration of a church benefice, which includes the right of presentation (or the proposing of a suitable person to fill a church vacancy), honorary rights (such as special privileges in processions and seating within the church), and the right to have a say in the disposal or alteration of the benefice's property.

Concerning the authority of the Palatine,[235] it was laid thus, that nothing but the mear name was left to that office; though He do sollicite something for the good of the Countrey, yet he labours in vaine, yea withall is prohibited to do it. How zealous the Protestant States and Peeres as well in particulare as in generall have been in the Dyet, Anno 1638.[236] to sollicite that their grievances might be redressed, but what effect after divers great charges and expences your Lordships have seen thereof, and enjoyed indeed, is sufficiently manifest unto every one.

The decree which His Imperiall Majesty caused to be imparted to the Protestant States and Peeres, is in Specie[237] in Our hands, but that notwithstanding hereupon divers Churches and Ministers houses have bin taken away, and the Ministers driven out of them; to repeat all would require a great deale more of time.

If we now consider the violation of Our corporall liberties, We finde it, that the offices and places are conferred upon no Protestant fellow-Member of the Countrey, neither are they preferred to any higher dignity, and if by chance one or other attains thereunto, yet he hath no honour, trust and credit with them. Moreover also though the Protestants have good right or claime to some requisition, yet they labour to hinder therein in one or other way: Yea it happened also, that one that pretended a just cause to his Lands, notwithstanding by reason of a pretended contradiction, went in extream danger of his life about it.

When the 13 Counties in Generall in the yeare 1640, [1]641, [1]643, petitioned his Imperiall Majestie and the Lord Palatine for the redressing of their Grievances, what benefit & profit got your Lordships by it? yea what unkind entertainment your Lordships Deputies had for demanding of their just cause, and with what sharp and bitter words they have beene sent away againe, your Lordships have still in fresh memory; all which, how justly We took it to heart, so as well Our conscience, as also our duty to the glory and service of God, and the love and zeale to the Libertie of Our native Country and Nation required Us, yea by some of the Protestant States and Peeres also, and not lesse by some of the Roman Catholiques, We have beene exhorted upon Our soules salvation, and in a manner beene forced, that for defence of their Liberties We would rule.

235. The palatine was the highest officer of the land under the king of Hungary. Over time, the local Hungarian nobility had seized control of this office and used it as a means to increase their own authority compared with that of the king.

236. The Hungarian Diet met in 1638 at Dés in order to resolve existing religious problems. A major result of this diet was the Accord of Dés, which tried to suppress growing anti-Trinitarianism within Hungary.

237. In appearance.

Wherefore We could suffer this no longer, nor see the apparant ruine and perdition of Our native Country and the oppression of Our Nation, which before had tryed all meanes how these inconveniences by faire meanes might have beene remedied. . . .

We take God the Lord the searcher of all hearts to Our witnesse, and We dare write it also to your Lordships in very truth, that We have taken up Arms not for Our own profit, nor out of a desire of revenge, neither also for those manifold wrongs and injuries done unto Us, nor lastly out of an intention to reforme or presecute Religion, much lesse to extirpate the same: But that We onely intend to Erect againe the Statutes and Laws of the Kingdome, to Reestablish the same, and to proceed according to the same, insomuch that every one without feare, trouble, let or hinderance openly may professe and exercise that same wherein his conscience is appeased, and thereby also safely to enjoy the corporall Liberty, because to Domineere and Rule over Consciences doth not belong to men, but to God alone.

But being our dear God hath already graciously turned off from us many hinderances, such herein principally have hitherto stood in our way, yea also drawne to Us the Outlandish hearts; We must needs conceive thereby that it is Gods will and providence that to the service of his glory We shall protect the Liberty of Our Native Country, whereof the glory will be rendered to God and not to men. And We beleeve therefore firmely that his divine Majestie without all doubt will grace this Designe with a happy desired issue, and Crowne it with a joyfull end.

Wherefore We deme and exhort your Lordships friendly, that you will be pleased in a zealous consideration, that for your Lordships good, and upon the desire and request of many amongst you We are risen from Our peaceable Government and wholly quiet Native Country, and taken up Armes, to afford your helping hands to the furtherance of this Worke, being in it selfe well pleasing to God Almighty, that will tend to the benefit and profit not onely of your Lordships, but also of the whole Country, and of all the grieved Inhabitants thereof. And withall in this case to shew their love and zeale as well towards God, as towards the Protestant Religion and the Liberty of their Native Country; and as soone as you have received these letters, to send unto Us one of your good Friends and Fellow-Brethren, and thus to joyne with us unanimously in the commendable furtherance and expedition of this worke.

We assure all persons, of what degree or qualitie soever they be, by Our true Christian Faith and Truth, that in no way We will disturbe or opresse Religion, nor also that We have any intention to offend or trouble in the least way Our deare Native Country and Nation, and so all and every one of you in Generall either now or in future time in all Right, Libertie, or Immunitie, but rather that your Lordships according to your pleasure may safely live, and yet further rejoyce in those precious Priviledges which have beene obtained long agoe with much blood.

No man shall also thinke, that if perhaps one or other hath done and shewed here before any wrong to Us, or committed any thing against Us whatsoever it bee, We would revenge Our selfe on him, and thus beare an ill will in Our heart for a future punishment; but rather that all and every the like wrong shall be buried in a perpetuall oblivion as if it had never happened or been done. We admonish therefore all and every one of what degree or qualitie soever he be, that no man retire out of the Country to another place, or forsake his Lands or Goods: for if by chance such (which We doe not hope) should be found, and We should bee forced to seize upon their Goods, they may attribute the fault and losse which thereby they may receive to no man else, but to themselves.

But in case your Lordships (against all hope and expection) should offer to doe contrary to that which hath beene said above, We will protest hereby before God and his holy Angels, that We are not the cause of the ruine and destruction which thereby will fall upon them; for otherwise We should be forced also to draw to Us so much the more stronger Ayde, and the greater number of Souldiers from Our High and Mighty Emperour, if your Lordships should oppose Us in the defence of Our Native Country, and not accommodate yourselves unto Us, which Wee will not hope.

The God Almighty who rules and governes all the hearts, doe thus rule and direct the hearts and minds of your Lordships that you doe unanimously every one, putting in the meane time out of his mind all other respects, afford unto us your helping hands, for the obtaining of that wherein consists every ones true proper benefit and profit, that, after that We have finished this happy worke, and every one of Us attained to His intention, both you and your whole Posterity may safely and peaceably enjoy both spirituall and corporall liberty till unto the end of the World, Amen. Given at Our Castle Calow the 17th of February, Anno 1644.

Georgius Racokzkio

33. Imperial Instructions for the Peace Congress (October 16, 1645)[238]

[The brutal defeats suffered by Emperor Ferdinand III in the campaign season of 1645 and the rapid defection of important allies convinced him that peace was now necessary at almost any cost. To accomplish this task, he fixed upon his most trusted confidant, friend, and chief minister of state, Maximilian, count von Trauttmansdorff,[239] whom he decided to send to the general peace negotiations already underway at the two Westphalian cities of Münster and Osnabrück. The following document, written from the emperor's castle in the Austrian city of Linz on October 16, 1645, contains the emperor's secret instructions for Trauttmansdorff on how to negotiate this peace.]

After I considered the lengthiness of the current war; the ruin of the Holy Roman Empire and especially of my hereditary kingdom and lands that ensued from it; the ever-increasing growth of the enemy's arms and forces and, on the contrary, the ebbing of mine and my allies'; the almost complete lack of resources; the general longing for peace; and, for all these reasons, the necessity of this peace; and also thereby considering the good qualities, the long experience in the job, and the zealousness toward my and the general benefit constantly displayed by the count von Trauttmansdorff, my high steward, I have resolved (according to the advice obtained from my privy council, but especially from my dear, most beloved noble consort[240] and my most beloved princely brother[241]) to dispatch the above-mentioned Count von Trauttmansdorff to the peace negotiations at Münster and Osnabrück (as my plenipotentiary), and to give him, to take with him, the following secret instruction, by which he should direct himself and have the power to conclude the peace (in the last resort and when nothing else can be obtained).

238. Emperor Ferdinand III (own hand) Instructions for Trauttmansdorff, Haus-, Hof-, und Staatsarchiv, Staatskanzlei, Friedensakten, Kart. 1, fol. 210–7, in Fritz Dickmann et al., eds, *Acta Pacis Westphalicae*, S. 1: *Instruktionen*, Bd. 1 (Münster, Westfalen: Aschendorffsche Verlagsbuchhandlung, 1962), 440–52.

239. Maximilian, count von and zu Trauttmansdorff and Weinsberg (1585–1650).

240. Ferdinand III's wife, the Spanish infanta Maria Anna (1606–1646).

241. Ferdinand III's brother, Archduke Leopold Wilhelm of Austria (1614–1662), who served as one of the emperor's principal generals.

242. France and Sweden.

1. And first, he shall take pains (besides seeing that the negotiations with the foreign crowns[242] are extremely and zealously promoted, so that no time is lost) so that the estates of the empire are united as limbs, with me as the head and father to them; the disconcerted imperial harmony is brought back into tune; the good old trust is reestablished; the proper composition of all the estates is restrengthened; and, thereby, the foreign enemy crowns are brought to a just peace—or, failing this, that one might be so much more able to resist them. This accommodation or union of the [imperial] estates will consist principally of two parts: namely, the point of amnesty[243] and the point of grievances.[244]

2. Now as to what concerns the point of amnesty, stay with the answer already given to the foreign crowns on this point.[245] Because, however, one could likely assume that the estates will not be contented with this, the amnesty could be extended back to the year 1627 in the empire alone; and finally, in the last resort (when otherwise the peace or the union of the estates would not be obtainable), it could also be conceded back to the year 1618 (though also only in the empire alone), expressly excluding in all ways my hereditary kingdoms and provinces[246] and the Palatine business[247] (which should be rediscussed). In my provinces, however, the following limitations could (when it really could not be otherwise) still be conceded: that those whose property must be restored in my hereditary lands (by force of the amnesty back to the year [16]30 or [16]27), be tolerated in the use and possession of the same, or at least (like other persons of quality found in my lands)

---

243. The point of amnesty included forgiveness for all acts performed during the war. This point was also closely tied into the question of who would control numerous contested territories within the empire. Rather than resolve all such disagreements on a case-by-case basis, the point of amnesty created a general, empirewide solution that reverted everything back to the situation as it was on a specific date, a so-called normal year. The choice of date was thus quite important, since some dates would greatly benefit the Catholics, while others were more favorable for the Protestants. Certain especially contentious territorial conflicts were still handled separately.

244. The grievances (*gravamina*) were the imperial estates' complaints against the emperor. These principally concerned the empire's internal religious and constitutional affairs.

245. The emperor's offer had been not much more than what he had already conceded at the 1635 Peace of Prague—that is, an amnesty date of 1630 for all who had taken up arms against the emperor.

246. The emperor's hereditary lands included Austria, Hungary, Styria, Bohemia, Moravia, Silesia, Carinthia, Carniola, and a number of other smaller territories.

247. The negotiations over what to do about the dispossessed elector Palatine and his territories.

not be rushed with short deadlines of emigration; and furthermore, that the discharge of such deadlines be gently indicated and not very strictly punished.

3. Concerning the grievances [of the imperial estates], these will be based especially on the Ecclesiastical Reservation,[248] on the possession of ecclesiastical property,[249] and on parity in the Chamber and Aulic Council.[250] The above-mentioned von Trauttmansdorff should trouble himself only in general on this point, for, since the grievances are held mostly among the estates themselves, they should also be settled among themselves and, where possible, done so in perpetuity or at least for a specific time, which should only require my assent or confirmation.

4. To be specific, however, there must be no concessions made about the Ecclesiastical Reservation; rather, it should remain in favor of Catholics. Ecclesiastical property should remain in its present condition, or, if the amnesty is extended to the year [16]18 in the empire, it should remain as it previously was, with reciprocal assurances that nothing shall be changed in the future.

5. Concerning the parity of religion, the Chamber should remain as it is now.[251] In the Aulic Council, however, three or four persons of the Lutheran religion could be conceded.[252] Should the union of the estates or the peace depend on this point alone, however, parity of religion could also be conceded—yet only after first establishing definite standards and rules that would have to be followed in the case of religious matters.[253]

6. The count should first strive to conclude the Hessian matter in accordance with the final treaties of Mainz and Cologne.[254] However, since things

---

248. The Ecclesiastical Reservation was an article of the Religious Peace of Augsburg (1555) that prohibited future transfers of imperial ecclesiastical territories (like archbishoprics) to Protestant control. See Document 14 for more information.

249. The possession of Catholic property by Protestants.

250. The Imperial Chamber (*Reichskammergericht*) and the Aulic Council (*Reichshofrat*) were the two supreme courts of the empire. Members of the Chamber were chosen mostly by the princes, and members of the Aulic Council were appointed by the emperor alone. Both had large Catholic majorities at this time. Religious parity meant that each religion would be given equal treatment (such that judges of one religion could not outvote those of the other), not that there would necessarily be the same number of judges from each religion.

251. With a majority of Catholics who could outvote the Protestants.

252. A small minority. Also, the emperor here allows for Lutheran representatives in the Aulic Council, but not Calvinist ones.

253. The emperor is here offering to discard the principle of majority rule in favor of parity for those cases concerning religion that came before the court.

254. This was the agreement between the landgravine of Hesse-Cassel, Amalia

may still stick on the Marburg matter,[255] one should strive to settle the matter in favor of the Darmstadt line, especially because justice is on their side. In the end, however, one should endeavor so that both sides set something aside and the affair is settled.

7. As to the Palatine matter, since it was the start of this war, it must also be attended to before the end of the war and must, by necessity, be settled in these negotiations. This matter does not rest, as the opposition claims, only on the complete restitution of the Palatinate, but rests as much on dignity as it does on provinces.[256] Concerning dignity, an alternation[257] must always be insisted upon and, except in extremity, not be conceded. In the end, however, when nothing else is obtainable and the electors and estates also consent to it and deem it to be good, then an eighth electorate could also be agreed to—yet, in this case, one should lean toward having a ninth also be created from our house.[258] In the end, however, when this is not obtainable, one can also retreat from it.

8. As to what concerns the lands [of the Palatinate], stay with what has already been negotiated up to this date for the Lower Palatinate. For the Upper Palatinate, however, one's work should be focused so that a piece of land from the Palatinate is left in the hands of Bavaria.[259] In this case, Bavaria should waive several millions; the empire, England, and the friends and supporters of the prince Palatine should pay several [millions]; and I likewise [should pay] (though my sum should not exceed three million and should be paid within six or eight years); and meanwhile, Bavaria would keep in its hands as security a proportional amount of land in the Upper Palatinate. When it comes to the restitution of the lands, however, the Catholic religion must always be reserved in its present state. And this concerns equally the estates of the empire and their union.

Elisabeth, and the elector of Mainz, Anselm Kasimir, made on July 25, 1639, and later partially ratified (excluding the terms of religion) by Emperor Ferdinand III. See Document 28 for more information.

255. The two branches of the Hessian dynasty, Hesse-Cassel and Hesse-Darmstadt, were fighting over the territory of Marburg. Hesse-Darmstadt was an ally of the emperor.

256. In other words, on both the question of the lands that had formerly belonged to the prince Palatine and his electoral rank. The seven electors were the greatest princes of the empire, since they alone could elect the Holy Roman Emperor.

257. Such that the electorship would be held alternately by the prince Palatine and the duke of Bavaria.

258. From the family of the Austrian Habsburgs.

259. Bavaria had occupied the Upper Palatinate since 1621 and was demanding fifteen million *reichsthalers* for its return.

9. Second, as to the foreign crowns, there the count should first be intent that all obstructions are cleared out of the way and that the negotiations are not delayed any further. Then, second, he should take pains so that one could conclude first with both crowns (because undoubtedly they will not negotiate separately, much less want to conclude thusly). Third, however, should he notice an opportunity to negotiate and conclude with one or the other crown separately, he should go off with the one with whom he thinks he could reach a conclusion sooner, and with more just, easy, and secure terms. And when it happens that Sweden gives an occasion for some separate negotiations, then he shall seize on it, or, failing this, seek on his own for some opportunity to come into negotiations with them and endeavor to make a conclusion with this crown first. For both crowns, however, it will mostly depend on their own points of satisfaction[260] (for as to those that concern the estates, this is mostly a pretext and has already been discussed above).

10. Namely, as to what concerns Sweden, there he should initially adhere to the Schönbeck negotiations.[261] Because we have already offered them half of Pomerania in secret, however, it can be assumed that they will not only refuse to retreat from this, but will also not be satisfied with it. Thus, finally, all of Pomerania could also be conceded to them, and, when it could not be otherwise, something from the archdiocese of Bremen could also be added on, and Stralsund, Wismar, and Rostock[262] could also be conceded up to a fixed year, or even in perpetuity. But these should be understood as being in fief to the present queen and her masculine line, or even, finally, to the feminine as well, and, at the end, even in fief to the crown itself. It goes without saying, however, that all this should be entered into gradually and in turn, and should not be gone into except in the utmost necessity.

11. Because, however, it can be assumed that those who will leave behind these lands will want to have some compensation for them,[263] the elector of Brandenburg could be offered, in addition to the ceding of my rights over the duchy of Crossen,[264] a sum of money, and so be delayed as long as possible with that. If, however, he did not want to be satisfied with this, Halberstadt

260. The question of satisfaction (*satisfactio*) concerned the demands by Sweden and France for financial and territorial recompense for their war costs.

261. The Schönbeck negotiations occurred between the representatives of the Swedes and the Saxons in late 1635, shortly after the latter had joined the imperial side. On the urgings of the imperial representative, the Saxons had offered the Swedes only a full amnesty and two million *reichsthalers* in compensation.

262. Important Baltic seaports in Western Pomerania.

263. The Swedish demands for territorial compensation meant that numerous estates—particularly Brandenburg, which owned Pomerania—would lose their lands and so also have to be compensated somehow by the treaty.

264. The duchy of Crossen belonged to the elector of Brandenburg as a fief of the

and, finally, several districts in Magdeburg could also be given to him. On the contrary, however, the owners of the archdiocese of Magdeburg, as well as of Bremen and Mecklenburg, are to be contented with money. The imperial estates would have to advance this money instead of providing that which they would have given to Sweden by the treaty of Schönbeck.

12. Third, to come now to the French and to consider their satisfaction, there the count will first adhere to what was conceived in the letter I sent to the elector of Bavaria on the 3rd of April of this year,[265] and will insist on it as long as possible, but finally concede to them Alsace[266] on the other [west] side of the Rhine in return for the transference to us of the fortress of Breisach.[267] If that is not obtainable, also add Breisach; and if the peace should stick on the Breisgau[268] alone, finally let it go as well—yet this last only in the most desperate case, especially because it is to be hoped that France would not desire it or, at the very least, would not insist on it, because to this date she claims nothing but Alsace (which lies on the other side of the Rhine). This point, however, will necessarily have to be settled with the archducal representatives.[269] If, however, they would not want to consent to this, in the last resort they would have to be forestalled.

13. Because, however, the ruling line of Innsbruck[270] will undoubtedly not want to let go of this [territory] for nothing, in order to satisfy them, a certain amount of money could be agreed to; and toward this, a piece of land from Carinthia[271] could be given them as a bond or, in the end, be let go completely. For it is better to gain a peace by this land being given over to my house, although of another line, than it is to continue the war (the outcome of which is still doubtful) and have the county of Gerz sold to the Venetians.[272] Count von Trauttmansdorff ought, however, to endeavor that

---

Bohemian crown. The emperor (as king of Bohemia) is offering here to release the elector from the duchy's feudal dues.

265. At this point, the emperor proposed only that the imperialists relinquish to the French the fortress of Pinerolo and, in the last resort, the fortress of Breisach.

266. An imperial province on the west side of the Rhine River (today, part of eastern France).

267. A strategic fortress on the eastern bank of the Rhine River.

268. The Breisgau is the area around Breisach, east of the Rhine River.

269. Archduke Ferdinand Karl of Austria (1628–1663), the emperor's cousin, ruled the Habsburg territories in southern Alsace (the Sundgau), the Breisgau, Swabia, and Tyrol.

270. The house of Archduke Ferdinand Karl.

271. A duchy in southern Austria belonging to the emperor.

272. The republic of Venice was on the southern border of Carinthia and was offering to buy the area.

the ruling Innsbruck line, where possible, claim nothing from me, but bite into this sour apple out of a love of peace.

14. It can also be assumed that France will want to claim and assert a seat and a vote in the empire,[273] but this claim should be totally rejected and most forcefully opposed. If, however, she does not wish to retreat from it, this should be deferred until the end; and if everything else is settled and things are stuck on this alone, and should the electors and estates of the empire also consent to this, then the count, depending on his own expert opinion, will dispatch a speedy courier and await my resolution about it.

15. Fourth, things will also mostly stick on the Spanish interests. Now it is known that all of our enemies' designs, intentions, efforts, and work go toward separating the German and Spanish lines[274] from each other and, after that, dividing and conquering, oppressing one or the other or, if you will, both successively. Thus Count von Trauttmansdorff shall, above all things, see to it that this separation does not occur, and better for everything to go awry than that he should let it come to this. In order to escape this danger, however, one must work so that peace is also concluded with Spain. The count will thus constantly remain in good confidence and correspondence with the Spanish plenipotentiaries; represent to them the danger, the impossibility of continuing the war, and the necessity for peace; admonish them to make a speedy conclusion; and also learn from them what kind of conditions they would consider in order finally to conclude the peace. Should they refuse this, however, or declare that they have no instructions on what to concede, then in this case he should indicate to them that I really cannot set aside this work, but rather I would try to present to the king of Spain—my most beloved cousin, brother-in-law, and brother—something with a fixed time limit attached, within which he would be able to accept the conclusion, or, if he did not wish to do so, would not then consider me wicked if I could not assist him. And thereupon, in the last resort, [Trauttmansdorff] should concede Roussillon[275] and an agreed-upon place in the Netherlands to the French, so long as thereby the peace would be concluded with them and they would renounce all alliances that they have with Portugal, Breganza, and Catalonia, and would offer their former allies no help under whatever pretext. And a time limit of six months for acceptance on the part of the king of Spain could be affixed, and in the meantime there would be an armistice between the two crowns.

273. A voting seat in the imperial diet, which France could claim because of its gain of Alsace, then part of the Holy Roman Empire.

274. German and Spanish branches of the Habsburg family.

275. Roussillon was a county in northern Catalonia, an area that, aided by the French, had revolted against the Spanish crown in 1641. The French finally gained Roussillon in the 1659 Peace of the Pyrenees.

16. Fifth, it can be assumed that negotiations will begin before a general armistice. Then, in such case, the count shall follow the same instruction that I previously gave to my ministerial envoys,[276] and, in addition, he should also find out about the report on the travels of my dear, most beloved brother.[277] And finally, after considering the state of the war, my weapons and lands, and also the attending danger, he should make an armistice or exclusion or inclusion (if time does not allow him first to get a decision from me) with all the best conditions possible. Also, if an armistice is entered into, it should be understood to be only for a short time and a few months.

17. Sixth, concerning the disbanding of the troops, it would be best to direct matters so that every party adopts the same fixed time limit [in which to disband], which would be so much the easier for the enemy crowns because they have raised immense treasures from the empire. Finally, however, if it could not be otherwise, the empire must just come together to give money for it.[278]

18. Seventh, because my house and I have done and suffered so much on account of the empire, it would be just also to consider some compensation from it. The count should thus endeavor so that, at some point, a considerable tax is raised and granted to my house, or, instead, a considerable sum of money is conceded by the empire.

19. Eighth and last, concerning the point of security,[279] I will always be satisfied with whatever will be considered the most secure, but only when equality is thereby observed on all sides.

And this is what I give to von Trauttmansdorff as instructions, but with the full understanding that he should give way in everything gradually: not agree prematurely to one thing or another, but rather, direct himself according to the shape and course of time, and give up the final step only in the end, and at the point of extreme necessity, and when there is no hope that something more might be obtained. My most gracious confidence is placed in his prudence, adroitness, experience, and loyalty, that he will always correctly observe the pace and proceed neither too soon nor too late; as I will then always hold him and his in the imperial grace and will remain his most gracious emperor and lord. Given in my castle at Linz, the 16th of October 1645.

Ferdinand

276. It is unclear which instruction he is referring to here.

277. Since Ferdinand III's brother, Archduke Leopold Wilhelm, was one of the leading generals of the imperial army.

278. Troops would refuse to disband without being paid their (usually considerable) back pay.

279. The point of security (*assecuratio*) concerned a guarantee that estates' territorial integrity and sovereignty would be preserved in the future.

34. Letter of Cardinal Mazarin to the French Plenipotentiaries at Münster (January 20, 1646)[280]

[By 1646 the emperor was willing to concede almost everything and even abandon his Spanish cousins if necessary. The possibility of peace was closer than ever before. But rather than push for an immediate conclusion, which Mazarin himself argued could be accomplished "in one day," the cardinal saw an opportunity to strengthen France. This document, a secret letter that he wrote to the French plenipotentiaries at Münster (Henri d'Orleans, Claude d'Avaux, and Abel Servien),[281] shows the extent of his confidence, for in it he makes a number of incredible assumptions: first, that his acquisition of the Spanish Netherlands, which would be undeniably and enormously advantageous to France, would be accepted by her enemies (though he admits that the Spanish would oppose it if they thought France wanted it); and second, that the Dutch (whom Mazarin refers to as "the States") would tamely allow a meddlesome France to replace an overbearing Spain as their southern neighbor. This document is also noteworthy as it represents the first mention by Mazarin of the possibility that France might someday try to claim the succession to the Spanish crown.]

I had promised you gentlemen by my previous letters to indicate to you the particular reasons why it seems to me that it would be very advantageous to this crown to consent to withdraw our arms from Catalonia, and even from the county of Roussillon,[282] provided that the king of Spain cede to us the Netherlands[283] and the county of Burgundy, whether through a marriage or, without one, by exchange, assuming that everything possible be done for the

280. "Mémoire [Lionne minute] de Son Em^ce a M^rs les Plenipotentiaires," January 20, 1646, Archives du Ministère des Affaires Étrangères, Correspondance politique, Allemagne 59, fol. 82–7, copies in Allemagne 63, fol. 180–8, and Allemagne 75, fol. 112–6. A published copy can also be found in Fritz Dickmann et al., eds, *Acta Pacis Westphalicae*, S. 2, Bd. 3/1 (Münster, Westfalen: Aschendorffsche Verlagsbuchhandlung, 1985), 266–73. Translated with Paul Sonnino.

281. Prince Henri d'Orleans, duke de Longueville (1595–1663); Claude de Mesmes, count d'Avaux (1595–1650); and Abel Servien, count de la Roche (1593–1659).

282. The county of Roussillon was a region of northern Spain in the Pyrenees Mountains. The territory, which is also known as Northern or French Catalonia, was ceded to the French by the 1659 Peace of the Pyrenees and now corresponds roughly to the French *département* (province) of Pyrénées-Orientales. The French were aiding Catalonia's revolt against the Spanish crown.

283. The Spanish Netherlands.

advantage and the security of the Catalans, in keeping with the statements made in various dispatches.

I shall keep my word now that I have a little more leisure than I had last week, and I will give you my reflections on this, asking you to send me your considerations as well.

First, the acquisition of the Netherlands would form an impregnable bulwark for the city of Paris, which could only then be called the heart of France and find itself in the most secure location in the kingdom. The frontiers would be extended up to Holland, in the direction of Germany, where there is also much to be feared, and up to the Rhine through the retention of Lorraine and Alsace, and by the possession of Luxembourg and the county of Burgundy.

In the second place, this would bring us out of the present war with so many gains that the most malicious would have little to complain about. When the old kingdom of Austrasia,[284] and entire provinces whose princes were in a position not only to resist France, but also to trouble her, are seen annexed to France, even the most critical will not be able to deny that all the bloodshed and the money spent have been well employed.

Third, the guilty, the malcontents, and the fractious would lose by this means the facility of withdrawing and the convenience of forming cabals with the assistance of our enemies, it being easy to see that all the plots and conspiracies against the state have usually been hatched in the Netherlands, Lorraine, or Sedan.[285]

In the fourth place, the power of France would become awesome to all its neighbors and particularly to the English, who are naturally jealous of its greatness and who would not let any opportunity escape to procure its disadvantage and its diminution—unless such a great acquisition deprived them of all hope of succeeding. Thus one can be assured that if they had any knowledge of such a negotiation, and if their internal dissentions were not as preoccupying to them as they now are, they would stop at nothing to prevent its success.

The States would also be more respectful of us and would become more tractable, and the Catholic religion would do much better in their country, since the Catholics there are persecuted not so much out of hatred for their religion as out of suspicion, with good reason, of their being pro-Spanish.[286]

---

284. The kingdom of Austrasia was an old Frankish kingdom that flourished under the Merovingians in the sixth and seventh centuries. It encompassed the areas of modern Belgium, Luxembourg, the Netherlands, and parts of western Germany and eastern France.

285. The principality of Sedan was controlled by the La Tour d'Auvergne family. It is today part of the *département* of Ardennes in northeastern France.

286. The United Provinces, or Dutch Republic, was a union of seven provinces that

If things are conducted properly, there should be no fear that the States would obstruct this kind of settlement, because it is in their own interest as well as ours, in that they could forever be assured of a lasting peace without being obliged to pay the excessive expenses that they must now sustain, since there would be no more talk of a truce and, if the Spanish ceded Flanders to His Majesty, there would be no more cause for war.

Besides, if the Spanish were to cede the Netherlands to us, they would, at the same time, be ceding to the States all their rights and claims in the United Provinces; and since France would consent to this and ratify it most solemnly, the States would be able to enjoy a durable peace with all the advantages of a complete freedom of commerce, all the more so because the lay of their land is such, and it is so well fortified, that it would be useless to attempt to attack them and imprudent to embark upon such designs.

It is only the internal dissensions that often increase or begin during a peace that are capable of disturbing it. And this is still another reason for France to prefer acquisitions in this direction, since, without failing in its friendship or alliance, it could eventually profit from their divisions.

And whoever will examine the affairs of the States according to the best rules of politics, will no doubt recognize that they can hardly survive unless, after the peace, they establish another form of government than their current one.

Moreover, the prince of Orange, whose authority will be extremely important in order to bring about this decision, is not only old, but so ill that everyone is concerned about his health, especially when it becomes known that he is so threatened with dropsy that, in the consultations that have been held in Paris by his order, it has been concluded that he will have trouble avoiding death.[287]

This is all the more reason for settling with Spain, because the death of this prince can only be prejudicial to this crown, since his wife is so hated

---

declared independence from the Spanish crown in 1581. The United Provinces were loosely governed by an assembly called the States-General.

287. In times of war the States-General and the individual provinces of the United Provinces deferred greatly to their military leader, the captain-general. Since 1625 this leadership had been exercised by Frederick Henry (1584–1647), prince of Orange, whose wife, Amalia von Solms (1602–1675), exercised considerable influence over him. Even though the provinces and the prince needed each other, and Frederick Henry was an extremely skillful politician, there were always tensions in the republic between the "States" party, led by the province of Holland, and the "Orangist" party, strong in the outlying provinces. The 1641 marriage of Frederick Henry's son William II to Mary Stuart, daughter of King Charles I of England, also raised suspicions that the House of Orange had secret designs to increase its power in the republic with the aid of foreign monarchs.

that they may even get rid of her; and since Prince William [II] is still young and, from what we hear, more given to his pleasures than to his affairs and, in consequence, less fitted to assume the mantle of his father. The States will work initially to diminish his authority, not only because they chafe under that of the prince, but because of their jealousy over the marriage in England and over his close contact with France since the death of Cardinal Richelieu.[288]

Sixth, if France has anything to fear from the House of Austria,[289] it can only come from the direction of Flanders and Germany, both because they can unite their forces (these countries being contiguous) and because, whatever advantage we may have over them, a single success of theirs—whether by surprising some strongholds on the Somme, winning some battle, or otherwise—can immediately cause as much terror in Paris, which is so close, as there was with the capture of Corbie[290] and the loss of the battle of Honnecourt, and so oblige us to withdraw or at least weaken the forces employed at a distance, as in Catalonia and Italy, and leave these places unguarded as was done for Corbie—which caused the raising of the siege of Dôle, which was about to surrender even though we had no war in the direction of Spain.[291]

The acquisition of the Netherlands would free us from these two fears forever. There would be no more junction of enemy troops, since Spain would not possess anything in that direction; and, having extended our frontiers up to the Rhine everywhere, far from our having to fear anything from the direction of the emperor, his fear of us would oblige him to conserve his good relations with this kingdom, all of which would contribute, in no small part, to the separation that France has so much reason to desire between the House of Austria in Spain and that in Germany.

Seventh, it seems to me that prudence requires us to leave to our enemies what they are likely to reconquer. It is certain that, since it is only necessity and fear of greater evil through the continuation of the war that oblige them to make peace, whenever they feel that they can reestablish themselves with the appearance of success (which the long minority of the king gives them great hope of doing), they will not lack pretexts by which to engage them-

---

288. Mazarin, like many others, was completely underestimating William, who, shortly after his father's death, staged a successful coup d'état against the States party before dying prematurely of smallpox.

289. The Habsburgs.

290. See Document 37.

291. France's war against Spain (declared in May 1635) had gone badly, with the Spanish immediately invading France, taking the stronghold of Corbie in 1636, and even threatening Paris. The French suffered numerous other military reverses before the tide of war began to turn around 1640.

selves again, whatever precautions may have been taken.[292] And in this case, even though by the peace we remain masters of everything that we presently possess in Catalonia and the Netherlands, it is much more possible for our enemies, by making great preparations of men and money and by cultivating their connections in Catalonia (where our best stronghold is the love of the people, on which it is not possible to rely), to be able to recover this principality (whether by force, connections, or other advantages that their arms would gain in the direction of Flanders), than it is for them to recover the Netherlands after being displaced or to make any progress in Languedoc, since they would initially have to confront all the forces of the most powerful France that there ever has been, and that would no longer be diverted by those of Flanders who threaten Paris.

Eighth, and this, in my opinion, would be the true security for the duration of the peace, which we would find through our own forces. For under these circumstances, our enemies would have to be out of their minds ever to resolve to break with this kingdom, since—whether by the advantages of our establishment in Germany or by the old friendships and alliances that we would conserve there and the new ones that we could acquire, or by the weakening of the emperor through the conclusion of peace—not only would we have nothing to fear from that direction, but it is to be believed that even if we did not restrain the emperor from helping the Spanish, which we will do by the peace, his own interest and his fear of our forces would prevent him from taking part in any commotions that the Spanish would like to cause. And thus, having nothing in the direction of either Flanders or Germany that could occupy our forces, one could only imagine what they would then be capable of doing if we were only obliged to employ them in Spain and in Italy, especially given the progress that they are making today in these two provinces (even though the king of Spain is only acting in the first on the defensive), and since we are making our principal efforts and incredible expenditures in the direction of Flanders and Germany, where the best troops of our kingdom ordinarily serve.

One of the reasons that the most sensible ministers of Spain use to advise their master to get out, at any cost, of the embarrassment in which he finds himself, is the hope with which they flatter themselves: that, since the peace would prevent us from purging France's ill humors, internal dissentions will soon arise from which [the Spanish] hope to profit. Now, it is evident, however, that the Spanish would only be able to give considerable assistance to any faction that would be formed in this state from the direction of Flanders, where their forces have always been ready for this and are more to be feared because they are better trained. When the Spanish formerly persuaded

292. Louis XIV was not yet five when his father, Louis XIII, died in 1643.

the duke d'Orléans to bring the war into Languedoc, even though this was a province contiguous to Spain, they could not furnish him with any assistance from that direction, but they gave it to him from Flanders instead; and in the last treaty by the late Grand Equerry, as everyone knows, all assistance was to come from the Netherlands.[293]

The people of Flanders, who suffer from incredible oppression since their country has, for so long, been the theater of war, would find such a change in their condition that it cannot be doubted that we would quickly gain their affection when they saw themselves with no more fear of invasion, forevermore enjoying all the advantages of a profound tranquillity under the domination of this crown.

And far from our expenses increasing from the acquisition of so many strongholds, aside from receiving notable assistance from the people without taxing them in any way, we could also save a lot in maintenance for the garrisons of Picardy, where most of the strongholds would need to be razed and the others could be maintained at little expense—since, with the States on our border, there would be no fear that they would ever undertake to attack us, nor attempt any surprises, because they would not alienate a power so much greater than theirs and that would have so many means to react.

It would take me too long to go into detail about the commercial and other advantages of such an important acquisition, and even of the fortresses of Mardyck and Dunkirk,[294] which are the most beautiful and convenient that exist on the ocean and the most important for us in getting closer to the States and putting them in our sights (just as they are in those of England).

The only difficulty that I see in this affair is not so much in the thing itself—since the Spanish also have their reasons to desire it, as is seen in the attached *mémoire*[295]—but in the form of the negotiation. For if they learned

293. The king's brother Gaston, duke d'Orleans (1608–1660), conspired unsuccessfully for years to unseat Cardinal Richelieu as prime minister, even joining an abortive rebellion in Languedoc in 1632 (for which he was pardoned). The "late Grand Equerry" refers to Henri Coiffier de Ruzé (1620–1642), marquis de Cinq-Mars, a favorite of Louis XIII who held this court office (which supervised, among other things, the royal stables). In 1642 Cinq-Mars led another conspiracy against Richelieu, and though he initially managed to gain some support among the nobility, the conspiracy failed and Cinq-Mars was executed.

294. The port cities of Mardyck and Dunkirk were part of the Spanish Netherlands just north of the French border. Today they belong to the French *département* of Nord.

295. There was originally an additional *mémoire* (memorandum) attached to this letter, in which Mazarin gave the plenipotentiaries a more thorough discussion of his analysis of Spanish goals.

that we wish it, this would certainly be enough to make them believe that they must never go along with it. This is why I feel that it is necessary for you gentlemen to dedicate yourselves, with your customary prudence and dexterity, to seeing if you can arrange that someone who does not know our intention makes a similar proposition with the consent of our enemy, and that, with the same skill with which you have made them desire a truce, you display your reluctance over the considerations contained in the other *mémoire,* which can be presented so as to make our opponents more eager.

And even though I know very well that your great intelligence will furnish you with a thousand better means than those that I can suggest to you from here, I cannot help telling you that if I were conducting this thing, I would casually drop some hint to the ministers of the emperor or of Bavaria, or to someone else who could report it to those of Spain, that we are well aware of the pressing reasons that the Spanish have to get back into Catalonia, and that this makes us all the more astonished that, since there is no way they can expect, in the present state of affairs, that we would ever allow this, they would themselves not seek some proportionate expedients and terms on which one could negotiate and reduce things to a mutual satisfaction.

I don't know if there isn't some person there, with access to the ministers of Spain or of the emperor, in whom one could have full confidence and who would know just enough about this affair to make the proposition on his own.

You might also consider if it wouldn't be good if one of you gentlemen, either acting as if it is without the knowledge of the others, or indicating that it is with their participation, slipped something confidentially to Saavedra or to Brun[296] in response to what one of them has said lately about letting the violins play.

I have not mentioned the mediators because, since they are badly disposed toward us, I consider them the least proper for this affair—for if they recognized its very real advantages for France, they would doubtless have more intention of ruining it than of making it succeed.[297]

Perhaps Trauttmansdorff[298] would be the best instrument who could be used for this, because this option would solve everything for everyone in a moment by means of his intercession, which would give him the glory not only of having restored the peace of the empire, but of having concluded the

---

296. Diego de Saavedra Fajardo and Antoine Brun were Spanish ambassadors to the congress at Münster.

297. The mediators were Fabio Chigi (the papal nuncio) and Alvise Contarini (the ambassador for the Republic of Venice), and Mazarin neither liked nor trusted them.

298. Count Maximilian von and zu Trauttmansdorff was the emperor's chief minister of state and imperial ambassador to the peace negotiations.

general peace. And he might well believe that he had rendered a considerable service to Spain by having her regain Catalonia and Roussillon, and having put her in condition to put an end to Portugal, just by ceding a country that, at the height of her power, she has often thought of abandoning, and that we could become the masters of in one campaign if the war continues.

What is to be feared in Trauttmansdorff's intentions is the great passion of the emperor and the empress to marry their son to the infanta of Spain,[299] and perhaps their desire to give their daughter to the king. But if one does not speak to him of a marriage or, in speaking to him, finds him opposed to the Spanish one and desiring the other, think about giving him satisfaction on this in return for the exchange and for according us our claims in Germany.

Unless I am mistaken, I venture to say that the Spanish would rather consent to leaving the Netherlands and Burgundy to us in order to resume possession of Catalonia and Roussillon, with the hope of also recovering Portugal without concluding the marriage with the king [of France] when their truce expires, rather than concluding it and constituting the greatest part of what they would be ceding to us as a dowry. My reasoning is that the only advantage that they would presently derive from this alliance would be to satisfy their vanity by appearing to leave us our conquests in the form of a dowry. But since this would only be capable of salvaging a little bit of their reputation with the vulgar, it would be found that we had all the substance; and with the infanta married to His Majesty we could aspire to the succession of the kingdoms of Spain, whatever renunciation she signed; and this could not be too far-fetched an expectation, since only the life of the prince, her brother, stands in her way.[300]

What must, in my opinion, principally be considered, is that even though the peace can be concluded in one day by this means, the ratification that must come from Spain and the execution of the contents could take a lot of time, during which, all hostilities ceasing and consequently our preparations for this year becoming useless, the Spanish might well change their minds once they were out of danger. This is why, in my opinion, in arranging for the truce for the execution of the treaty, precaution must be taken to insert very exact articles; or there should be separate acts in good form to oblige

299. Maria Theresa (1638–1683) was the daughter of Philip IV of Spain and thus held the title of infanta, or daughter of the king. The Austrian Habsburgs and the French were competing for the diplomatic and territorial advantages that a marriage alliance with the Spanish would win for their side.

300. Here Mazarin first mentions the possibility that France might someday try to claim the succession to the Spanish crown through the marriage of Louis XIV to the infanta.

the emperor, Bavaria, and the other electors and princes of that party to give sufficient guarantee and security for the good faith of the Spanish, so that if they made some difficulties, these would all be expected to join their forces to ours in order to force them to execute their agreements.

35. Diary of Clara Staiger (Spring 1648)[301]

[In spring 1648, in the last campaign of the war, the combined Swedish–French army under Generals Wrangel and Turenne pushed deep into Bavaria, driving back the Bavarian and imperial forces. The following is an account of this period from an Augustinian nun, Clara Staiger (1588–1656), who was the abbess of the convent of Marienstein outside the Bavarian city of Eichstätt.[302] Staiger's diary reinforces the point that the effects of the war varied widely from place to place and over time. Some areas of the empire were continuously occupied or repeatedly sacked and destroyed, some were completely untouched, and others, like Marienstein, fell somewhere in the middle. Eichstätt, its surrounding bishopric, and much of Bavaria and Franconia had been devastated by Swedish armies from 1632 to 1634. Marienstein had been completely plundered and burned, its nuns had been forced to flee, and its then-abbess had died of the shock. Following the retreat of the armies, the nuns, under Clara Staiger's leadership, had returned to their cloister and begun to rebuild. Then, in 1648, the Swedes returned.]

The enemy strengthened himself again this year, and during the winter, he repeatedly crossed the Rhine into the empire and onto German soil. Then there was once again great fear and fleeing from Franconia into the bishopric, and from the upper bishopric here to us.[303] The worthy mother and her sisters at Marienburg[304] were taken by surprise and were chased out of the cloister with nothing but the clothes on their backs, driven into the woods like animals. Some were seized at Schwabach[305] and ransomed, and they lost everything that was left at the cloister: food, livestock, hay, straw, and bed linen—everything was lost.

301. Ortrun Fina, ed., *Klara Staigers Tagebuch: Aufzeichnungen während des Dreißigjährigen Krieges im Kloster Mariastein bei Eichstätt* (Regensburg: Pustet, 1981).

302. Eichstätt is about seventeen miles northwest of Ingolstadt, about sixty miles north of Munich, and about fifty miles south of Nuremberg.

303. The prince bishopric of Eichstätt was split into upper and lower dioceses.

304. An Augustinian cloister near Abenberg, about thirty miles north of Eichstätt.

305. A city just north of Abenberg.

Meanwhile, the vicar[306] commanded us to flee. I explained that we needed to stay together and asked for armed guards, and also purchased a ship for 6 fl.[307] and tethered it to the washhouse,[308] and secured it with a lock. Six armed guards were sent to us from the castle,[309] but four were soon recalled. Two were left with the cloister, and day and night they stood watch, along with our agriculturalist and farmhands, and they climbed up a ladder to the wall and looked down. I sent some of the livestock to the castle mill[310] and the horses to the city, and some of the livestock I had at the cloister; but, as much as possible, I drove them onto the ship and had them transported away.

Sunday, Oculi,[311] they burst into Weiler,[312] smashed doors and gates, carried away hay and straw, blinded the people.[313] There arose an enormous alarm and a hue and cry. The people of Weiler came flooding here into the cloister, and their children, cows, and pigs wove in and out of the rooms of the washhouse, the builder's yard, and the barn, until these and the court-yard were all packed full. . . . To make matters even more miserable, there came such a great cold spell that everyone might have frozen.

On the Friday before Letare[314] the vicar commanded me and those [sis-ters] who were fearful to go to the city of Eichstätt and into the dwelling of the chancellor.[315] I packed up and had brought there the most important necessities: grain, kitchen equipment, larder supplies, fat, salt, and also clothes and bed linen; and I also brought whatever I had at hand of religious implements, images, and chalices. And we set ourselves up there near the fire with the two armed guards who had accompanied us.

On Sunday, Letare,[316] we heard mass in the Jesuit church [in the city]. On Monday, we remained in the house. On Tuesday, the vicar sent us a priest who read us the mass in the house, in the upstairs room. And this occurred from then on, for there were many people from the countryside who had fled to Eichstätt, and yet in the city there was just as much fear, fleeing, and

306. The bishop's representative to the cloister.

307. Fl. is the abbreviation for *gulden,* a common coin also known as a *florin.*

308. The cloister washhouse (which also served as a brewery) was situated at the river's edge.

309. The court of the prince-bishop of Eichstätt.

310. The mill and brewery for the prince-bishop's court.

311. The fourth Sunday before Easter, or March 15, 1648.

312. The village of Weiler at Marienstein.

313. She probably means this literally, not that they took the people by surprise.

314. The Friday before the third Sunday before Easter, or March 20, 1648.

315. Dr. Volpert Motzel, the prince bishop's leading government minister.

316. March 22, 1648.

people hauling and carrying their possessions to the castle.[317] His gracious lord the prelate of Rebdorf[318] came to Eichstätt on the same day as me and went into the castle.

On the last day of March, after twelve o'clock, I was urgently commanded to go to the castle, and when I was only a little way into arranging for us to flee, the coaches arrived, and everyone who was in the house had to get in, and we had to abandon all the food that was in the house, and we left with some of us in a panic. As I came to the Hospital Gate[319] there was a horrible melee of city-dwellers, but they were letting no one through. I had to send our belongings back to the house to be unloaded, but I managed to arrange that they let through our coaches and those people who belonged to us. Just as I was coming out through the gate, I saw the enemy troops swarming the hill in hordes, making bridges and crossing the Altmühl River with their horses, riding horses past the west mill, and hurrying to the cloister. They sought quarters there and climbed in force over the walls and roofs. At the same time that I, on the castle hill, saw the great power of such an enemy, I was also filled with fear and anxiety about the carriage horses,[320] for those manning the castle gate also did not want to open it, and the entire castle road was full of people, and below the castle road there were already enemy troops who took whatever the poor people were hauling and carrying. Thus, out of fear, I got out and began to walk up the hill to the entrance [to the castle]. And as I arrived at the top of the hill with several sisters who I had brought with me from the cloister, the concern I felt for my other twenty sisters in the cloister filled me with such fear that I did not know how I could possibly begin to drag myself to the castle, and I felt that I could not ward off collapse. Meanwhile, our armed guards from Marienstein arrived with the wife of our agriculturalist and her children, for they had also been forced to flee. I was then dragged or carried under the arms more than I walked, until I came to the entrance. Here a melee immediately arose, with screaming and hitting and pushing, for they would let in no one but ecclesiastics and those who were with them. As soon as I came into the castle, there immediately arose lamentations that I had brought neither food nor bedding. We had with us secular and ecclesiastic people, both from the nunnery and from the cloister farmyard, and their children, and also many people who had stuck to us and had said that they belonged to us so that they could get into the castle, and all of us had to make do in a single room. It was a long night, and

---

317. Willibaldsburg Castle was the residence of the prince-bishop and lay outside the city, on top of a hill overlooking the Altmühl River.

318. A nearby monastery.

319. A city gate leading to the road to the castle.

320. That they would bolt.

there was great suffering. And it was thus for three days, going around without eating and drinking. And during this time spent crammed on top of each other, we heard fighting and crashing, and during the night, we could see three hundred fires burning in the cloister courtyard and garden, in Weiler, and in houses. They took thirteen head of cattle from the cloister, stabbed sheep and pigs, took the fish from the water, and stripped everything that was in the cloister: from grain, flour, vegetables, and fowl, to bedding, pillows, and feather comforters. Whatever had been hidden, such as copper, tin, and brass, they found, seized, and took. In short, whatever they could haul and carry, they took away, and there was one fire after another [in the area] stretching from cloister Rebdorf to the new house,[321] and even more followed later.

The 2nd of April at four o'clock in the morning, [the troops] marched out and assembled in the castle fields. Right after this, two soldiers who had asked our sisters for protection showed themselves to be wicked by demanding we give them a lot of money or they would take a sister. . . . I borrowed two ducats and had it given to [the soldiers]. I intended them to split this among themselves, but this did not happen. As soon as I sent away the first, the second appeared and demanded even more. The lord prelate advanced me a loan of a double ducat and Sister Maria Jacobi a *thaler* that she had in safekeeping. In the end, getting rid of the soldiers cost me 14 fl. in cash. And the moving here and there, the loading and unloading, the hauling of so much stuff back and forth, meant we had to pay a great amount in gratuities. Plus, with all the smashing and breakage of all the furniture, doors, and gates in the cloister—the destruction of the hops supports alone cost us 100 fl.—and with everything that they took from us, we suffered damages of 2,000 fl. May God come to our aid like a father and send us some means so we can begin to build again, and so we can compensate for the damage to all of the cloister buildings, along with the great loss in linen, religious implements, tin, and copper.

36. The Peace of Westphalia (October 24, 1648)[322]

[On October 24, 1648 the long negotiations at Münster and Osnabrück[323] finally came to a close, and the Thirty Years War staggered to an end. On that

321. A building in the city of Eichstätt.

322. *Die Westfälischen Friedensverträge vom 24. Oktober 1648. Texte und Übersetzungen* (Acta Pacis Westphalicae. Supplementa electronica, 1). http://www.pax-westphalica.de/. Accessed December 1, 2006.

323. Due to tensions among the parties, the Catholic powers met at Münster, the

date, the plenipotentiaries signed two separate treaties, the Instrumentum
Pacis Osnabrugensis *(IPO) and the* Instrumentum Pacis Monsteriensis
*(IPM), which together made up the Peace of Westphalia. The Peace was a religious, political, and territorial compromise. It granted a general amnesty to all
within the empire, except for those in the Habsburg hereditary lands. It gave
substantial territorial concessions to the Swedes (as fiefs of the empire) and
French (as sovereign territories), and also shuffled numerous other territories,
including lands for the elector of Saxony, the landgravine of Hesse-Cassel, the
elector of Brandenburg (in return for his loss of half of Pomerania to Sweden),
and the duke of Bavaria (who kept the Upper Palatinate). Some also received
financial reparations for lost territories, and the peace also provided financial
satisfaction necessary to disband the large Swedish and Hessian armies. The
various additions and subtractions of lands and monies had been carefully negotiated over the years, but in at least one point, this cleverness led to future
difficulties. This was §87 of the IPM, a contradictory paragraph that seemingly both preserved and took away the liberties and independence of Alsace.
The interpretation of this point later served as a source of considerable conflict
between France and the empire.*

*In addition to territorial and financial transfers, the agreement also adjusted the political structure of the empire by leaving the Palatine electorate in
the hands of the duke of Bavaria, but also establishing an eighth electorate for
Frederick's heir, Karl Ludwig, enshrining certain political liberties that the imperial princes claimed had been theirs all along, such as their sovereign right to
wage war and make alliances, and making the independence of the Swiss cantons official. Many judicial matters were set aside for later discussion, but the
treaty did arrange for an equal number of Protestant and Catholic deputies to
be seated at imperial deputation diets,[324] and it established the principle of
"amicable agreement," rather than majority vote, for any religious matter
brought before the collected diet. The peace also resolved the religious issues
that had been so intertwined with all other issues driving the war, by fixing
the religious makeup of the empire as of the so-called normal year of January
1, 1624. The result of this was to remove the right of princes to set the religion
of their territories (but not to remove their right to regulate such established
territorial religions), to recognize all previously secularized church territories,*

Protestants at Osnabrück, and the mediators traveled back and forth between the
two cities. Some parties had representatives at both cities, since alliances had often
crossed confessional bounds.

324. The deputation diet (*Deputationstag*) was an assembly of the Holy Roman Empire in which only the electors and the most important princes of the empire participated, either personally or through their deputies.

and to revoke the Edict of Restitution.[325] *Furthermore, it gave legal recognition to Calvinists, required toleration of religious minorities (except in the Habsburg hereditary lands) and freedom of conscience, and extended the Ecclesiastical Reservation*[326] *to include Protestants (and fixed it to the normative date).*

The selections given below include most of the key articles, but also offer a few additional sections concerning the city of Augsburg (IPO Art. V, 3–V, 5), to provide some sense of the kind of detailed negotiations required to sort out the empire's religious divisions.]

Instrumentum Pacis Osnabrugensis (IPO)

In the Name of the Most Holy and Indivisible Trinity, Amen.

[**Preamble**]   To each and every one whom it concerns or whom it could in any way concern, let it be known: that once the discord and political disturbance that began many years ago in the Roman Empire had expanded to such a degree that not only all of Germany, but also several bordering kingdoms, especially Sweden and France, were thus enveloped by them, then a lasting and bitter war arose, primarily between the most serene and powerful prince and lord, Ferdinand II of glorious memory, elected Roman Emperor[327] . . . with his confederates and adherents on the one side; and the most serene and most powerful prince and lord, Gustavus Adolphus of glorious memory, king of the Swedes . . . with the kingdom of Sweden and its confederates and adherents on the other side. And then, after their deaths, between the most serene and most powerful prince and lord Ferdinand III, elected emperor of the Romans . . . with his confederates and adherents on the one side; and the most serene and powerful princess and lady, Lady Christina, queen of the Swedes . . . with the kingdom of Sweden and its confederates and adherents on the other side. Through this, much Christian blood was spilled and many provinces devastated, until, finally, divine benevolence made it so that both sides began to think of a universal peace,

---

325. See Document 14.

326. The Ecclesiastical Reservation limited the right of reform granted to imperial princes in the 1555 Peace of Augsburg. It did so by prohibiting future transfers of Catholic Church properties through the conversion of their leaders to Protestantism. This latter article was hotly contested, and subsequently ignored, by Protestants. The Peace of Westphalia extended this idea to include conversions by Protestants to Catholicism.

327. For ease of reading, numerous further titles and honorifics that appear here and throughout the preamble have been trimmed.

and to this end, by a mutual agreement made at Hamburg on December 15/25, 1641,[328] they decided to establish a congress of plenipotentiaries to meet on July 1/11, 1643, at Osnabrück and Münster in Westphalia.

Thus at the established time and place, the lawfully empowered plenipotentiaries appointed by both sides appeared. Representing the emperor were the most illustrious and excellent lords: Maximilian, count von Trauttmansdorff . . . privy councilor and chamberlain to His Holy Imperial Majesty and supreme master of the court, but also Johann Maximilian, count of Lamberg . . . and chamberlain to His Holy Imperial Majesty; and Johannes of Cranen, lawful licentiate, count Palatine, and His Imperial Majesty's Aulic councilor.[329] Representing the queen of Sweden were the most illustrious and excellent lords: Johan Oxenstierna Axelsson, count of Södermöre . . . imperial Swedish senator and chancellery councilor, and Johan Adler Salvius, lord of Adlersberg . . . imperial Swedish senator, privy councilor to Her Majesty, and Aulic chancellor. After they prayed for divine assistance and duly exchanged their full plenipotentiary powers (copies of which have been attached to the end of this document, word for word), they mutually agreed, in the presence and with the approval and consent of the electors, princes, and estates of the Holy Roman Empire, and for the glory of God and the security of Christendom, to the following articles of peace and friendship, which are as follows:

[**Art. I**]   Let there be a Christian, universal, perpetual, true, and sincere peace and friendship between the Holy Imperial Majesty, the House of Austria, all its allies and adherents and their respective heirs and successors, primarily the Catholic King,[330] and the electors, princes, and estates of the empire, on the one side; and Her Holy Royal Majesty and the kingdom of Sweden, all of its allies and adherents and their respective heirs and successors, primarily the Most Christian King,[331] and respective electors, princes, and estates of the empire, on the other side; to be sincerely and seriously preserved and maintained, so that each party promotes the advantage, honor, and benefit of the other, and that faithful neighborliness, real peace, and true friendship might flourish and blossom anew on the part of the entire Roman Empire toward the kingdom of Sweden, as well as on the part of the kingdom of Sweden toward the Roman Empire.

328. Due to an uneven acceptance of the new Gregorian calendar (which corrected the older Julian calendar by adding ten days), official documents often gave the date according to both calendars.

329. The Aulic Council was one of two supreme courts of the Holy Roman Empire.

330. The king of Spain.

331. The king of France.

[**Art. II**]   Let there be a perpetual oblivion and amnesty, on both sides, for all those hostile acts that have been committed since the beginning of these commotions in whatever place or manner, by one or the other party, so that for neither this nor any other reason or pretext is anyone to inflict, cause to be inflicted, or allow any future act of hostility or enmity, nor any kind of trouble or impediment against the persons, condition, property, or security of any other, either by oneself or through others, secretly or openly, directly or indirectly, under color of law or by fiat, either within or outside the empire (notwithstanding any prior pacts to the contrary); but each and every injury, violent act, hostility, damage, and expense inflicted by one against another through words, writings, or deeds, both before and during the war, is, without regard to any person or thing, to be completely disregarded, such that whatever one party could allege toward the other on this account is to be buried in perpetual oblivion. . . .

[**Art. IV, 2**]   Before all else, the assemblies at Osnabrück and Münster addressed the subject of the Palatinate, so that this quarrel, which has been stirring for so long, has now been settled in the following manner:

[**Art. IV, 3**]   First, as to what regards the House of Bavaria, the electoral dignity that formerly belonged to the elector Palatine, with all of its regalia, offices, prerogatives, insignias, and whatever other rights pertain to that dignity, without any exception, and also all of the Upper Palatinate with the county of Cham and all of its appurtenances, regalia, and rights, shall remain in the future with Maximilian, count Palatine of the Rhine, duke of Bavaria, and with his children and the entire Wilhelmine line,[332] as long as there are surviving male heirs.

[**Art. IV, 4**]   In turn, the elector of Bavaria shall entirely renounce for himself and for his heirs and successors the debt owed him of thirteen million, as well as his claims to Upper Austria; and he shall also, after the conclusion of the peace, hand over to His Imperial Majesty all documents issued in this regard, so that they may be voided and annulled.

[**Art. IV, 5**]   As to what regards the House of the Palatinate, the emperor and empire consent, in the interest of public tranquillity, that, by virtue of this present convention, an eighth electorate be instituted, which Karl Ludwig,[333] count Palatine of the Rhine, along with his heirs and agnates[334]

332. The Wittelsbach family included two major family lines: the elder, or Rudolphine, branch of the family was led by the count Palatine, while the younger, or Wilhelmine, branch was led by the duke of Bavaria.

333. Karl Ludwig, known as Charles Lewis in English, was the son of Frederick V of the Palatinate, the "Winter King" of Bohemia.

334. Relations on the father's side.

from the entire Rudolphine line, shall hereafter enjoy in accordance with the order of succession set forth in the Golden Bull.[335] Still, beyond this investiture, neither Karl Ludwig nor his successors shall have any rights over that which has been granted, along with the electoral dignity, to the elector of Bavaria and the entire Wilhelmine line.

[Art. IV, 6]   Furthermore, the entire Lower Palatinate, with each and every ecclesiastical and secular property, right, and appurtenance, shall be fully restored to him to the degree in which it was enjoyed by the electors and princes of the Palatinate before the Bohemian commotions, along with all relevant documents, registers, accounts, and other records, voiding whatever has been transacted to the contrary; and the emperor shall use his authority to ensure that neither the Catholic King[336] nor anyone else who possesses any part of this territory opposes this restitution in any way.[337]

[Art. IV, 51]   Finally, each and every military officer and soldier, counselor and civilian minister, lay and ecclesiastic, of whatever name and condition they may be, who have offered either civil or military service to one or the other party, or to their allies or adherents, from the highest to the lowest, and from the lowest to the highest, and without any distinction or exception, along with their wives, children, heirs, successors, and servants, both their persons and property, shall be restored by both sides to the same state of life, reputation, honor, freedom of conscience, rights, and privileges that they enjoyed or could rightly have enjoyed before the commotions; and nothing shall be done to the prejudice of their persons or property, nor shall any action or accusation threaten them, much less any penalty or forfeiture be imposed on any pretext whatsoever. And all of this shall also apply equally to all those who are not subjects and vassals of His Imperial Majesty and the House of Austria. . . .

[Art. V]   Whereas the grievances that have arisen among the electors, princes, and estates of the empire of both religions[338] have been, in large

---

335. The Golden Bull was a decree issued by Emperor Charles IV in 1356. Among other things, it specified the seven princes who would henceforth serve as electors of the emperor, and fixed their rules of hereditary succession to avoid future constitutional crises. These seven princes were the three prince-archbishops of Mainz, Trier, and Cologne, and four secular princes: the king of Bohemia, the count Palatine of the Rhine, the duke of Saxony, and the margrave of Brandenburg.

336. The king of Spain.

337. This allowed Karl Ludwig to return to the royal residence of Heidelberg, which had been lost since 1622.

338. By "both religions," they mean Protestants and Catholics.

part, the cause and occasion of the present war, the following is agreed and settled:

[**Art. V, 1**]   1. The 1552 Treaty of Passau and the subsequent 1555 Religious Peace,[339] which was confirmed in the year 1566 at Augsburg and later in various diets of the Holy Roman Empire, shall be sacredly and inviolably observed as concluded and agreed to, in all of their provisions, by the unanimous consent of the emperor, electors, princes, and estates of both religions.

Regarding the controversial articles in the present treaty, whatever was agreed to by common consent shall be considered a perpetual declaration of the said peace, to be observed both legally and otherwise until, by the grace of God, there is a religious reconciliation,[340] and this is notwithstanding the opposition or protests raised at any time by anyone, whether ecclesiastic or political, either within or outside of the empire, which are now declared fully null and void.

In all other points, however, there shall be an exact and mutual equality among all the electors, princes, and estates of both religions, in conformity with the laws of the republic, imperial ordinances, and the present agreement, such that whatever is lawful for one party is also lawful for the other, and here, as elsewhere, all violence and use of force between the parties is prohibited forever. . . .

[**Art. V, 2**]   2. The date for the restitution in ecclesiastical affairs, as well as for any associated political changes, shall be January 1, 1624. Therefore, the reinstatement of all electors, princes, and estates of both religions, including the free imperial nobility and the communities and villages immediate to the emperor,[341] shall occur fully and without restriction, whereby all relevant judgments, decrees, settlements, pacts (whether capitulations or otherwise), and executions that were issued, published, and instituted in the meantime are annulled and returned to their state as of the said year and day.

[**Art. V, 3**]   The cities of Augsburg, Dinkelsbühl, Biberach, and Ravensburg shall retain the property, rights, and exercise of religion that they had on the said year and day; but regarding council seats and other public offices, these are to be equally divided among adherents of both religions.

339. The Treaty of Passau (1552) and the Religious Peace of Augsburg (1555) had together formed the basis for religious compromise in the empire. The Peace of Augsburg gave legal recognition to adherents of the Augsburg Confession (Lutherans), gave each prince the right to change and oversee the religion of his territory, and legalized all seizures of ecclesiastical territories made before 1552.

340. This is one of many pro forma expressions in this treaty of a hope for a future reunion of Protestants and Catholics.

341. Under the direct authority of the emperor and free of any other legal overlord.

[**Art. V, 4**]   For the city of Augsburg in particular, however, there are to be seven senators of the privy council chosen from the patrician families: two of these are to be selected as presidents of the republic, commonly called *stadt-pfleger*, one of whom is to be Catholic, the other of the Augsburg Confession, and of the remaining five, three are to be of the Catholic religion and two adherents of the Augsburg Confession. The remaining councilors on what they call the lesser senate, as well as the syndics, city court assessors, and all other officials, are to be of equal number for both religions. There are to be three quaestors[342] of the public monies, two of the one, the third of the other religion, such that in the first year two shall be Catholic, one of the Augsburg Confession; in the next year, two of the Augsburg Confession and the third Catholic, and so on alternating every subsequent year.

[**Art. V, 5**]   In the same way, there are also to be three commanders of the arsenal who are to alternate annually. The same is also to apply to the administration of tax collection, provisions, public buildings, and any other offices that are occupied by three people, so that if in one year, two offices (such as fiscal administration and the administration of provisions and public buildings) are in the hands of two Catholics and one of the Augsburg Confession, then in the same year, two other offices (such as command of the arsenal and tax collection) shall be entrusted to two from the Augsburg Confession and one Catholic; but in the following year, two Catholics will replace two adherents of the Augsburg Confession in these offices, and one Catholic [will replace] one of the Augsburg Confession. . . .

[**Art. V, 14**]   3. In regard to immediate ecclesiastical property, whether archbishoprics, bishoprics, prelatures, abbeys, bailiwicks, provostries, and commendams; whether free secular foundations or otherwise; whether located in or outside the cities; with all their revenues and pensions, of whatever name they might be; whether they were possessed by a Catholic estate or one of the Augsburg Confession on the first day of January of the year 1624: the adherent of that religion that had actual possession at the said time shall, fully and completely and without any exception, possess them peacefully and undisturbed until, by the grace of God, religious dissentions are harmonized; and neither party shall be allowed to disturb the other either in court or otherwise, much less cause any disturbance or hindrance. And if, God forbid, these religious dissentions cannot be agreed upon amicably, this agreement shall be a perpetual one and the peace shall last forever.

[**Art. V, 15**]   If a Catholic archbishop, bishop, or prelate, an adherent of the Augsburg Confession who is elected or nominated to be an archbishop,

---

342. An official who supervises the state treasury and oversees its financial affairs.

bishop, or prelate (whether alone or with some or all of his chapter), or any other ecclesiastic should, in the future, change religions, they shall (without damage to their honor and reputation) immediately forfeit their rights, profits, and income without any delay or exception; and the chapter, or whoever else is legally entitled, shall be free to elect or demand another person of the same religion to whom, by virtue of this settlement, the benefice shall belong; forsaking, however, the profits and revenues collected and consumed in the meantime by the departing archbishop, bishop, prelate, etc.

If, then, any estates, either Catholic or adherents of the Augsburg Confession, have been deprived of their archbishoprics, bishoprics, benefices, or immediate prebendships by either legal or extralegal means after the 1st of January 1624, or if they have been disturbed in any other manner [in their possession of the same], then, by virtue of this treaty, they shall be restored at once both to their ecclesiastical and secular rights, and all innovations shall be abolished; such that whatever immediate ecclesiastical property was managed by a Catholic prelate on the 1st of January 1624 shall once again have a Catholic leader, and in turn, whatever was possessed on the said year and day by adherents of the Augsburg Confession shall be retained by them in the future. Yet whatever one party could claim from the other, such as profits collected in the meantime, damages, or expenses, shall be forgiven.[343] . . .

[**Art. V, 25**]   Whatever monasteries, colleges, bailliages, commendams, churches, foundations, schools, hospitals, and other mediate[344] ecclesiastical property, as well as other revenues and rights of whatever name, that the electors, princes, estates, etc. of the Augsburg Confession possessed on the 1st of January 1624—whether always retained, restituted, or restituted by virtue of this treaty—shall be wholly and singularly possessed by the same until the religious controversies are settled by an amicable universal agreement of the parties, ignoring any objections that they were reformed and occupied either before or after the Treaty of Passau or the Peace of Religion; or that they were not owned by, nor lay within, the territory of the estates of the Augsburg Confession; or that they were exempt or connected to other estates by rights of suffrage or deaconship, or by any other way.

The only and sole foundation of this settlement and restitution, and of its future observation, shall be property held as of the 1st of January 1624, invalidating entirely all exceptions that could be claimed on account of any interim religious exercise introduced anywhere, or on account of either a pre-

---

343. This article reestablishes the Ecclesiastical Reservation, fixes it to the new normal year, and extends it to Protestants, who must now give up an ecclesiastical property if they convert to Catholicism.

344. Mediate properties were those subject to a legal overlord below the emperor.

vious or subsequent general pact or special settlement, either ongoing law-suits or settled cases, or any other decrees, mandates, regulations, issuances, reverses, legal conflicts, or any other pretexts or reasons whatsoever. . . .

[Art. V, 30] As to what pertains to the counts, barons, nobles, vassals, cities, foundations, monasteries, commendams, communities, and subjects of immediate estates of the empire, whether ecclesiastic or secular—because, following the common practice that has been in use up to now throughout the entire empire, such immediate estates have the rights of territorial supremacy and the right of religious reform, and also as it was agreed in the Religious Peace that subjects of such estates who dissent from the religion of their territorial lord be conceded the right of emigration—it has been more-over established that, in order to maintain greater harmony between the estates, care be taken that no one entice the subjects of others to his religion, nor receive them under his protection because of this, nor support them in any manner whatsoever. It is further agreed that this shall be observed by the estates of both religions, and no immediate estate shall, nor may, be hindered in those rights which belong to him in matters of religion, by power of his rights of territorial supremacy.

[Art. V, 31] Nevertheless, the freeholders, vassals, and subjects of any kind who belong to Catholic estates and who had the public or private exercise of the Augsburg Confession during any part of the year 1624, whether by a fixed pact or privilege, whether by long custom, or solely by observance in the said year, are to retain it in the future, along with all of the ancillary rights that they exercised or can prove they exercised in that said year. Included in such ancillary rights are the appointment of consistories and ministries, both scholastic and ecclesiastic, the right of patronage, and other similar rights. Furthermore, they are to remain in possession of those churches, foundations, monasteries, and hospitals, with all their appurtenances, revenues, and accessories that they had in their power at the said time. And all of this is to be observed always and everywhere until something otherwise is agreed concerning the Christian religion, either in general or by mutual consent among the immediate estates and their subjects; and no one is to disturb any other person in any regard or way whatsoever.

[Art. V, 32] Those who have been in any way disturbed or deprived of what they had in the year 1624 are to be restored truly, completely, and without any exceptions.

The same shall be observed for Catholic subjects of estates of the Augsburg Confession where they had the public or private use and exercise of the Catholic religion in the year 1624.

[Art. V, 33] Concerning, however, the compacts, transactions, conventions, or concessions that have been previously initiated, made, and granted between the immediate estates of the empire and their above-mentioned provincial estates and subjects, for the introduction, permitting, and conservation of the public or private exercise of religion, these shall remain in force and valid only insofar as they are not contrary to observed usage as of the year 1624; nor is it allowed to depart from these without mutual consent, regardless of all sentences, reversals, agreements, and transactions that are contrary to the observed usage of 1624, which shall be null and void, and this is to be considered as a rule. Among these are, in particular, what the bishop of Hildesheim and the dukes of Brunswick-Lüneburg agreed in the year 1643 regarding the exercise of religion for the estates and subjects of the bishopric of Hildesheim. An exception to the said term, however, shall be made for the nine monasteries situated in the bishopric of Hildesheim that the dukes of Brunswick ceded in the said year under certain conditions: these shall be reserved for the Catholics.

[Art. V, 34]   It has been further agreed that those adherents of the Augsburg Confession who are subjects of Catholic estates and those Catholics who are subjects of estates of the Augsburg Confession who did not have either public or private exercise of their religion in any part of the year 1624, and who, at some future time after the publication of the peace, shall profess and embrace a religion different from that of their territorial lord, shall be patiently tolerated and have freedom of conscience and private devotion in their homes without investigation or disturbance; and they shall not be prohibited from taking part in the public exercise of religion in their neighborhoods whenever and as often as they wish, nor from sending their children to foreign schools of their religion, nor from having them instructed in their homes by private teachers; yet these freeholders, vassals, and subjects should perform their duty in all other things with due deference and submission, and without giving occasion to any disturbance. . . .

[Art. V, 36]   If, however, a subject who had neither the public nor private exercise of his religion in the year 1624, or who changes his religion after the publication of the peace, shall wish of his own free will to emigrate, or shall be commanded to do so by his territorial lord, then he shall be free to keep or sell his property, to retain it and have it administered by aides, and to visit freely and without obtaining letters of passport, as often as he requires in order to oversee his properties, pursue a lawsuit, or collect debts. . . .

[Art. V, 39]   As to what regards the counts, barons, nobles, and their subjects in the remaining duchies of Silesia who are dependent immediately on the royal chamber, as well as those counts, barons, and nobles presently living in Lower Austria, His Imperial Majesty (although the right of reform belongs to him no less than to all other kings and princes) nevertheless—not because of the disposition of the previous paragraph ("Concerning, however, the compacts," etc.; Art. V, 33) but due to the intervention of Her Royal Majesty of Sweden and out of esteem for the imperial estates of the Augsburg Confession for which she interceded—allowed that these counts, barons, and nobles, as well as all of their subjects who live in the above-mentioned duchies of Silesia, shall not to be required to sell their property or emigrate on account of their confession. Nor shall they be prohibited from the exercise of the said confession in neighboring places outside the land, as long as they otherwise live quietly and peacefully and act appropriately toward their supreme lord. If, however, they wish of their own free will to emigrate and either do not want to sell their property or cannot sell without loss, they shall be allowed free passage to inspect their properties and maintain their businesses.

[**Art. V, 40**]   Besides what has been settled above concerning the duchies of Silesia that are dependent immediately on the royal chamber, His Imperial Majesty further agrees that those adherents of the Augsburg Confession in these duchies shall be allowed to construct, at their own expense, three churches for the exercise of their confession outside the cities of Schweinitz, Jaur, and Glogaw, in convenient places near to the city walls, which shall be designated by His Majesty as soon as the peace is concluded.

[**Art. V, 41**]   And since all the efforts that have been made to negotiate a greater freedom of religious exercise in the above-mentioned lands, as well as in the rest of the kingdoms and provinces of His Imperial Majesty and the House of Austria, have come to naught due to the opposition of the imperial plenipotentiaries, Her Royal Majesty of Sweden and the estates of the Augsburg Confession reserve for themselves the right to intervene amicably and intercede humbly with His Imperial Majesty at the next diet or elsewhere; yet the peace shall always endure, and all violence and hostility shall be prevented.

[**Art. V, 42**]   The right of reform shall not depend on the sole condition of feudatory or subfeudatory,[345] whether it proceeds from the kingdom of

---

345. Imperial territories were classified as either feudal or allodial. A feudal state (fiefdom) was subject to a feudal contract, which gave the vassal (landholder) the right to hold the territory in return for agreeing to certain duties or services toward his overlord. The highest overlord in the feudal system was the emperor himself, but each of his vassals could themselves be overlords for subvassals holding subfiefs. An allodial territory, on the other hand, was not bound by a feudal contract, and so the possessor was free of any contractual duties or services and was subject to the emperor only in his role as sovereign.

Bohemia, or from the electors, princes, and estates of the empire, or from any other; but in matters of religion these fiefs and subfiefs, as well as their vassals, subjects, and ecclesiastical property, and whatever rights that the feudal lord has pretended, introduced, or claimed for himself, will forever be judged according to the situation as of January 1, 1624; and any innovations, whether made through the courts or outside of the courts, shall be abolished and restored to their original state. . . .

[**Art. V, 51**] For the regular imperial deputation diets, the number of deputies for both religions is to be equal. As for the persons or estates of the empire that are to be added to them, this is to be decided at the next general diet. When deputies are sent to such assemblies and to general diets, for whatever occasion and for whatever purpose, and whether there are one, two, or three imperial colleges[346] represented, there is to be an equal number of deputies from both religions.

In the event that extraordinary commissions are to be sent into the empire, if the matter concerns only estates of the Augsburg Confession, only their adherents are to be deputized; similarly, if the matter is between Catholics, only Catholics; if between Catholics and estates of the Augsburg Confession, an equal number of commissioners of both religions are to be named and constituted. It is also approved that the commissioners who are entrusted with these negotiations should report back and give their opinions, rather than making definitive determinations.

[**Art. V, 52**] In religious and all other matters whereby the estates cannot be considered as a single body, and when the Catholic estates and those who are adherents of the Augsburg Confession make up two parties, the dispute is to be decided through amicable agreement alone, and the majority vote is not to be heeded.

Concerning, however, majority vote in the matter of taxation, since this could not be decided at the present congress, it will be deferred to the next diet.

[**Art. V, 53**] Further, because of the changes occasioned by the present war and for other reasons, negotiations over the decision of whether the Imperial Chamber Court[347] should be transferred to another place that would be more convenient for all the estates of the empire; and if the court judges,

346. The imperial colleges included the college of electors (or electoral college), the college of princes, and the college of the cities. Generally, the first two colleges dominated the proceedings.

347. The Imperial Chamber Court, which met in the city of Speyer, was the second of the two supreme courts of the Holy Roman Empire.

the presidents, assessors, and all the judicial officers should be presented in an equal number from both religions; and also what should be done with the remaining matters regarding the Chamber Court, these negotiations could not be completely resolved at the present congress despite their importance; but it has been agreed that all of this will be dealt with and decided at the next diet, and that the deliberations over the reform of the judicial system, which were begun at the imperial deputations diet in Frankfurt, remain in effect, and that if something else should be desired, it is agreed to supplement and amend it.

[Art. VI] Furthermore, whereas His Imperial Majesty, after seeking the opinion and advice of the estates of the empire on the complaints that were made in the presence of those of his plenipotentiaries assigned to the present congress, and in the name of the city of Basel and all of Switzerland, concerning several processes and executive orders issued by the Imperial Chamber Court against the said city and the other united cantons of Switzerland, and against their citizens and subjects, has declared through a singular decree of the 14th of May of last year [1647], that the aforementioned city of Basel and all the other Swiss cantons are in possession, as it were, of full liberty and exemption from the empire, and shall in no way be subject to the tribunals and judgments of the empire; and it has been approved that this same decree shall be inserted into this public treaty of peace and be regarded as valid and enduring; and therefore all related processes, along with those legal decisions that they have at any time occasioned, shall be entirely invalid and void.[348] . . .

[Art. VII, 1] It has also been approved by the unanimous consent of His Imperial Majesty and all the estates of the empire, that whatever rights or benefits are granted to estates and subjects that are either Catholic or adherents of the Augsburg Confession by all other imperial ordinances, as well as the Religious Peace[349] and this public treaty, and especially the resolution of the grievances[350] found herein, these shall also be granted to those who call themselves Reformed;[351] always excepting whatever contracts, pacts, privileges, reverses, and other regulations of religion and its practice (including whatever depends upon it) that the so-called Protestant estates have hitherto provided for among themselves and with their subjects for the

348. This point is an official confirmation of the Swiss cantons' independence from the empire, an independence they had already enjoyed in practice since the late fifteenth century.

349. The 1555 Religious Peace of Augsburg.

350. *Gravamina.*

351. Calvinists.

benefit of the estates and subjects of every place, yet also preserving everyone's freedom of conscience.

Because, however, the religious disputes that have lately come between the Protestants have not yet been resolved, but have been reserved for a future compact, and thus they make up two parties, it is therefore agreed between them with regard to the right of reform,[352] that if a prince or other territorial lord or ecclesiastical patron should, in the future, go over to the religious rites of the other party, or—either through right of succession or by force of the present peace negotiations or by means of any other title—acquire a principality or dominion where the other party's religious rites are publicly exercised, he shall at least be allowed to have court preachers of his confession with him at his residence, though without burdening or disadvantaging his subjects. Yet it shall not be lawful for him to change the public exercise of religion or the ecclesiastical laws or customs accepted there until that time, nor to seize churches, schools, hospitals, or any related revenues, payments, or stipends from their former owners and give them instead to members of his own faith; nor to thrust ministers of another confession onto his subjects by rights of territory, episcopacy, patronage, or any other pretext; nor to cause any other direct or indirect impediment or prejudice toward the others' religious rites. And so that this agreement is more firmly observed, should such a change[353] occur, the communities themselves shall have the right to present[354] suitable teachers and ministers or, if they do not have the right of presentation, the right to nominate them; and these, as long as they are of the same religion as the community that presented or nominated them, shall be examined and ordained by the official consistory and local ministry or, lacking the same, by whatever office the same community should choose, and shall afterward be confirmed by the prince or lord without any dissent.

[Art. VII, 2] If, however, in the event of such a change, some community embraces the religion of its lord and desires, at its own expense, to take up the same exercise of religion to which its prince or lord adheres, he shall be free to grant them such a thing without prejudice to the rest, and this may not be revoked by his successors. On the other hand, members of the consistory, canonical visitors, school and university professors, theologians, and philosophers may only be adherents of the religion that is publicly accepted everywhere in that place at that time. . . .

352. The right to change and oversee the religion of one's territory.
353. Whereby the ruler changes religions.
354. The right to name a suitable person for an ecclesiastical office.

Besides the above-stated religions, none other will be accepted or tolerated in the Holy Roman Empire.[355]

[Art. VIII, 1]   In order to ensure, however, that no future disputes arise over the state of politics, each and every elector, prince, and estate of the Roman Empire shall, by virtue of the present treaty, be established and confirmed in, and enjoy possession of, all their ancient rights, prerogatives, liberties, privileges, dominions, regalia, and free exercise of their territorial rights in both ecclesiastical and political affairs, so that, in fact, they neither can nor shall be molested by anyone at any time, for any pretext whatsoever.

[Art. VIII, 2]   They shall enjoy, without contradiction, the right of suffrage in all deliberations about the affairs of the empire, especially in the consideration or interpretation of laws, the declaration of war, the imposition of taxes, the establishment of levies, the quartering of soldiers, the raising of new fortifications within the sovereign territory of the estates in the name of the public, or the strengthening of old garrisons; as well as when peace or alliances are to be made, or other such business is completed. None of these things, or anything similar, shall ever occur or be permitted in the future without the freely given vote and consent of the diet of all the estates of the empire.

First of all, however, the individual estates shall have the eternal and free right to make alliances among themselves or with foreigners for their conservation and security, yet only where such alliances are not directed against the emperor, the empire, the public peace, or especially this treaty, and where they preserve in all ways the oath by which all are bound to the emperor and empire. . . .

[Art. X, 1]   Furthermore, since the most serene queen of Sweden has demanded that she be compensated for returning those places she occupied during this war, and in order to provide appropriately for the restoration of public peace in the empire, His Imperial Majesty (with the consent of the electors, princes, and estates of the empire, and especially of those directly concerned, and by virtue of the present treaty) relinquishes to the same most serene queen and to her future heirs and successors, the kings and rulers of Sweden, the following dominions, with full rights and as perpetual and immediate fiefs of the empire:

355. Jews were not included in this treaty, yet lived throughout the empire. They had traditionally been under the protection and regulation of the emperor, but in this period their status depended primarily on the whim of the prince in whose territory they lived.

[Art. X, 2]   First, all of Western Pomerania,[356] commonly called *Vorpommern,* that is contained within those boundaries drawn under the last duke of Pomerania, along with the island of Rügen. Also, in Eastern Pomerania[357] the towns of Stettin,[358] Garz, Damm, and Gollnow, and the island of Wolin, along with the Oder River and sea that flows in between, commonly called *das frische Haff,*[359] and its three mouths, the Peene, Swine, and Dievenow,[360] together with the adjacent land on both sides from the beginning of the royal territory[361] to the Baltic Sea; and the exact limits of the width of the eastern coastline and other less important specifications shall be amicably agreed upon by the royal and electoral[362] commissioners.[363]

[Art. XI, 1]   Since, in order to promote the general peace, the elector of Brandenburg, Frederick William, ceded his rights in Western Pomerania and Rügen, and in the attached dominions and places mentioned above, he and his descendents, successors, and heirs, as well as male agnates (but chiefly Christian Wilhelm, marquis and former administrator of the archbishopric of Magdeburg; and also Christian von Kulmbach and Albrecht von Ansbach, with their successors and male heirs), shall, immediately after the conclusion and ratification of the peace between the two crowns and the estates of the empire, be given as an equivalent compensation by His Holy Imperial Majesty (with the consent of the estates of the empire and especially of those directly concerned) the bishopric of Halberstadt, with all of its rights, privileges, regalia, territories, and property, both secular and ecclesiastic, of

356. Pomerania Citeriorem, also known as Hither Pomerania, is now part of the German state of Mecklenburg-Vorpommern. Traditionally, Hither Pomerania included all of Pomerania on the left (west) bank of the Oder River.

357. Pomerania Ulteriori, also known as Further Pomerania, is now part of Poland. Traditionally Further Pomerania included all of Pomerania on the right (east) bank of the Oder River.

358. Modern Szczecin, in Poland.

359. The Stettin Lagoon, also known as the Oder Lagoon or Stettiner Haff, is a large body of water at the mouth of the Oder River, separated from the Baltic Sea by the islands of Usedom and Wolin.

360. These are the three straits, or river mouths, leading from the lagoon to the Baltic Sea.

361. Of Sweden.

362. Of Brandenburg.

363. The Swedes were also granted, among other territories, the town of Wismar, the archbishopric of Bremen, the bishopric of Verden, and the diocese of Hamburg as fiefs of the empire, allowing the cities of Bremen and Hamburg to keep their ancient freedoms and rights as imperial free cities.

whatever name it may be called and without any exception, as a perpetual and immediate fief. Similarly, the lord elector shall immediately be placed in the peaceful and real possession of the same, and shall thus also gain a seat and a vote in imperial diets and in the Lower Saxon Circle.[364] . . .

[Art. XI, 4]   The same lord elector shall, on behalf of himself and his above-mentioned successors, be given by His Holy Imperial Majesty (with the consent of the estates of the empire) the bishopric of Minden as a perpetual fief, with all rights and appurtenances, immediately after the conclusion and ratification of this peace and in a similar method as previously related for the bishopric of Halberstadt; and the lord elector, both for himself and for his successors, shall be placed in peaceful and real possession of the same, and shall thus also gain a seat and vote in general and particular imperial diets, and also in the Westphalian Circle.[365] . . .

[Art. XV, 4]   In addition, it has been agreed that, as restitution and indemnity for places occupied in this war, the lady landgravine and regent of Hesse,[366] her son, and his successors, the princes of Hesse, shall be paid at Cassel[367] the sum of sixty thousand *reichsthalers* (according to the value set by the most recent imperial ordinance) by the archbishoprics of Mainz and Cologne, the bishoprics of Paderborn and Münster, and the abbey of Fulda, within the space of nine months from the time of the ratification of the peace, and at the payers' own risk and expense. No exceptions or pretexts shall be allowed concerning the promised payment, much less shall any seizures be made of the agreed-upon sum. . . .

[Art. XVI, 8]   Finally, as to the disbanding of the Swedish army, each and every elector, prince, and other estate, including free and immediate imperial nobility, that belongs to the seven following circles of the empire: the electorate of the Rhine, Upper Saxony, Franconia, Swabia, the Upper Rhine, Westphalia, and Lower Saxony (preserving, however, the requirements hitherto usual in such cases, and their freedom and exemption in the future), shall be obliged to contribute the amount of five million *reichsthalers* in the common currency of the Roman Empire and in three terms. In the first term

364. The circles of the empire were the ten administrative regions established in the sixteenth century. Each had its own diet.

365. In addition to the bishoprics of Halberstadt and Minden, the elector of Brandenburg also gained the bishopric of Camin, the archbishopric of Magdeburg, and other smaller territories.

366. Amalia Elisabeth of Hesse-Cassel became regent to her young son and ruler of the state of Hesse-Cassel in 1637.

367. The capital city of the landgraves of Hesse-Cassel.

one million eight hundred thousand *reichsthalers* shall be paid (for which each estate shall pay its portion thusly: the Circles of the electorate of the Rhine and of Upper Rhine at Frankfurt am Main, the Circle of Upper Saxony at Leipzig or Brunswick, the Circle of Franconia at Nuremberg, the Circle of Swabia at Ulm, the Circle of Westphalia at Bremen or Münster, and the Circle of Lower Saxony at Hamburg. And in order more easily to obtain the payment of this sum, those subjects who are to be restored by way of the amnesty shall be permitted to pay their contribution not to the actual modern possessors, but to their true lords, who shall be restored by the amnesty; and they shall pay their actual quota and proportion immediately after the conclusion of the peace and even before the restitution occurs, and the modern possessors shall not create any impediment to its collection), and another one million two hundred thousand *thalers* by means of allocations placed on certain estates. For which payment tolerable conditions shall be provided and agreed upon, fairly and honestly, among each estate and the military official assigned to it, between the time of the conclusion and the ratification of the peace.

[**Art. XVI, 9**]   The payment of the said one million eight hundred thousand *thalers* shall occur after the agreement of this treaty and the exchange of ratifications; and the dismissal of the soldiers and the evacuation of the occupied places shall immediately be undertaken and shall not be delayed for any reason. Immediately after the conclusion of the peace, furthermore, all contributions and other forms of exactions shall cease, allowing, however, for the support of the occupying soldiery and other troops, for which a tolerable method shall be agreed upon. Likewise, those estates that have paid their portion (or have amicably agreed to the payment of their portion with the official assigned to them) shall be allowed to demand reimbursement on account of those damages that their fellow estates have caused through a delay of their payment.

The remaining two million shall be paid in good faith by the estates of the seven circles in the above-mentioned places, and to those ministers whom the queen of Sweden has empowered. The first shall be paid at the end of the next year following the dismissal of the troops, and the second at the end of the next year following that one; and both shall be paid in *reichsthalers,* or in other coins or currency customary within the empire. However, the seven circles are responsible solely for the Swedish soldiers and shall not be subject to any other demands; thus each of the electors, princes, and estates shall be obliged to pay only the share that is required by the public roll, the observance of each locality, and the specification presented here of what each one owes. . . .

Instrumentum Pacis Monsteriensis (IPM)[368]

In the Name of the Most Holy and Indivisible Trinity, Amen.

[Preamble] To each and every one whom it concerns or whom it could in any way concern, let it be known: that once the discord and political disturbance that began many years ago in the Roman Empire had expanded to such a degree that not only all of Germany, but also several bordering kingdoms, especially France, were thus enveloped by them, then a lasting and bitter war arose, primarily between the most serene and powerful prince and lord, Ferdinand II of glorious memory, elected Roman Emperor . . . with his confederates and adherents on the one side; and the most serene and powerful prince and lord, Louis XIII of glorious memory, the Most Christian King of France and Navarre, and his confederates and adherents on the other side; and then after their deaths, between the most serene and powerful prince and lord Ferdinand III, elected emperor of the Romans . . . with his confederates and adherents on the one side; and the most serene and powerful prince and lord, Louis XIV, the Most Christian King of France and Navarre, with his confederates and adherents on the other side. Through this, much Christian blood was spilled and many provinces devastated, until finally, through the grace of God—and thanks to the mediation of the most serene Republic of Venice, whose advice for the common welfare and the peace never faltered, even in the most dangerous times for Christendom—both sides began to think of a universal peace; and to this end, by a mutual agreement made at Hamburg on December 15/25, 1641, they decided to establish a congress of plenipotentiaries to meet on July 1/11, 1643, at Osnabrück and Münster in Westphalia.

Thus at the established time and place, the lawfully empowered plenipotentiaries appointed by both sides appeared. Representing the emperor were the most illustrious and excellent lords: Maximilian, count von Trauttmansdorff . . . privy councilor and chamberlain to His Holy Imperial Majesty and supreme master of the court, but also Johann Ludwig, count of Nassau . . . imperial privy councilor and knight of the Golden Fleece; and Isaak Volmar, doctor of law, councilor and chamber president of the serene lord Archduke Ferdinand Karl. Representing the Most Christian King[369] was the most serene prince, Henri d'Orleans, duke de Longueville . . . along with the wellborn and admirable lords, Claude de Mesmes, count d'Avaux . . . and Abel

---

368. Many of the articles of the *Instrumentum Pacis Osnabrugensis* (IPO) were included, verbatim, in the *Instrumentum Pacis Monsteriensis* (IPM). In all such cases, I have included them in the IPO rather than the IPM.

369. The king of France.

Servien, count de la Roche. . . . through the mediation of the high and well-born Venetian ambassador and minister, Alvise Contarini, who performed the office of an impartial mediator without tiring for almost five years. After they prayed for divine assistance and duly exchanged their full plenipotentiary powers (copies of which have been attached to the end of this document, word for word), they mutually agreed, in the presence and with the approval and consent of the electors, princes, and estates of the Holy Roman Empire, and for the glory of God and the security of Christendom, to the following articles of peace and friendship, which are as follows:

[§ 1]   Let there be a Christian, universal, perpetual, true, and sincere peace and friendship between the Holy Imperial Majesty and the holy, Most Christian King, as well as between each and every ally and adherent of the aforementioned Imperial Majesty, the House of Austria, and their heirs and successors, principally the electors, princes, and estates of the empire on the one side; and each and every ally of the aforementioned Most Christian King, and their heirs and successors, principally the most serene queen and the kingdom of Sweden, and the respective electors, princes, and estates of the empire, on the other side; to be sincerely and seriously preserved and maintained, so that each party promotes the advantage, honor, and benefit of the other, and that faithful neighborliness, real peace, and true friendship might flourish and blossom anew on the part of the entire Roman Empire toward the kingdom of France, as well as on the part of the kingdom of France toward the Roman Empire. . . .

[§ 47]   As, in order to establish greater tranquillity in the empire, a certain accord has been reached in the negotiations over the general peace between the emperor, electors, princes, and estates of the empire, concerning the ecclesiastical property and the free exercise of religion, which has been inserted into the peace treaty reached by the plenipotentiaries of the queen and the kingdom of Sweden; it has been decided that this agreement, including what was agreed in regard to those who are called Reformed, is to be included into the present treaty, confirmed and ratified as if it had been inserted, word for word, into the present treaty.[370] . . .

[§ 73]   Third, the emperor cedes for himself, for the entire, most serene House of Austria, and also for the empire, all rights, ownerships, dominions, possessions, and jurisdictions that have, until now, belonged to him, the empire, and the family of Austria, over the town of Breisach, the landgraviate

---

370. This paragraph permits the omission of the entirety of articles V and VII of the IPO, which include concessions to the Protestants that it would have been embarrassing for the French to have spelled out in their treaty.

of Upper and Lower Alsace, the Sundgau, and the provincial prefecture over the ten imperial cities situated in Alsace: namely Hagenau, Colmar, Schlettstadt, Weißenburg, Landau, Obernai, Rosheim, Münster im St. Gregoriental, Kaysersberg, Turckheim, and all the communities and whatever other rights that depend upon the said prefecture. And each and every one of them shall be transferred to the Most Christian King and the kingdom of France, including the town of Breisach with the villages of Hochstatt, Niederrimbsing, Harten, and Acharen (which belong to the community of the city of Breisach), along with the full extent of all of the territory and precincts that they have possessed from antiquity, except, however, for the privileges and immunities previously obtained and procured by the same city from the House of Austria. . . .

[§ 87]   The Most Christian King shall be required to leave not only the bishops of Strassburg and Basel, with the city of Strassburg, but also other immediate estates of the Roman Empire that are in both Upper and Lower Alsace, namely the abbots of Murbach and Lüders, the abbess of Andlau, the Benedictine monastery of St. Gregoriental, the count Palatine of Lützelstein, the count and baron of Nanau, Fleckenstein, Oberstein, and the nobility of all of Lower Alsace; also the aforementioned ten imperial cities that belong to the prefecture of Hagenau, in the same liberty and immediacy to the Roman Empire that they have thus far enjoyed; such that he cannot claim any further royal superiority over them, but shall remain content with whatever rights the House of Austria has observed and that are ceded to the crown of France through this peace treaty. Nevertheless, nothing in this present declaration shall be understood to detract from the right of supreme dominion that was conceded above. . . .

IV
TWO WARTIME LIVES (1618–1648)

The Thirty Years War was so long, widespread, and unpredictable that its effect on the people of the empire varied to an enormous degree. Some lived happy, quiet lives in peace and safety; some died horribly in flames with their entire family and village. In this section are extended selections of two diaries of the war, written by two very different men. The first is by the soldier Peter Hagendorf. His chronicle is incomplete, but the portions still extant follow his life and travels from 1624 to 1649. The second is by Hans Heberle, a shoemaker from the little village of Neenstetten outside the city of Ulm. His chronicle covers his experiences over the years from 1618 to 1672.

Hagendorf, like most soldiers in this war, was a German mercenary. He fought for at least three different armies during the war and walked thousands of miles, from one side of the empire to the other. Over the years he became noticeably hardened and casually brutal. He and his comrades looted the countryside and men like Heberle as a matter of course, and after one victory, he happily reported taking a young girl as part of his spoils. Hagendorf's quality of life was quite varied. Sometimes he lived well, with plenty to eat and nothing to do but laze around and drink. Sometimes things were not as pleasant. Plague and other diseases were rife among early modern armies, and he lost numerous children and his first wife to illness. He also suffered gunshot wounds and other injuries, and had the added danger of regular battles and skirmishes. Food was often a problem, pay was infrequent, conditions in the field could be brutal, and frequent travel meant ever-changing lodgings and constant insecurity. Though his family traveled with

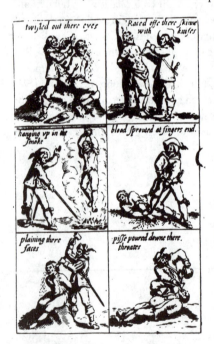

"Of Tortures and Torments" (*The Lamentations of Germany,* p. 9, Vincent Philip, 1638, Beinecke Rare Book and Manuscript Library, Yale University)

him, often they became separated from each other. He seemed quite indifferent to the larger religious and political aspects of the war, though did interest himself in the many different customs, traditions, tourist sites, and foodstuffs of the lands through which he passed.

Heberle was a small craftsman living in a small town, and like many others in the war, he was most often a victim. Over the years he and his family suffered from war taxes, plague, starvation, repeated depredations by soldiers, bad weather, flights to the forest, flights to neighboring lands, and flights to the city of Ulm. Yet Heberle was not a passive victim. He and his fellow villagers fought back when they could, and he also became part of the Ulm citizen militia. He did everything he could to keep his family together and safe, and in some years things were not so bad. He was a good Lutheran and kept himself informed of all the great events going on in the empire, many of which he recorded.

The two men crossed paths at least three times. The first was in April 1627, when Hagendorf came to Ulm after walking over the Alps from Italy to Switzerland and then down into what is now southern Germany. At Ulm he enlisted in the army of the Catholic League, serving under the command of Count Pappenheim. Hagendorf again came to the territory of Ulm in 1634 as part of the Swedish army, stopping at the towns of Günzburg and Langenau, only a few miles from the village of Weidenstetten—where Heberle was then living—and even closer to his birth village of Neenstetten. By Hagendorf's report, it seems an uneventful visit:

> Then we went to Günzburg and over the Danube to Langenau. Günzburg belonged to the city of Ulm. It is a village, but they put three hundred plows to work in the fields. It lies more than an hour from Langenau.[1]

From Heberle's perspective, however, Hagendorf's visit was much more memorable:

> Then they fell upon us in the land and plundered all of us, taking horses and livestock, bread, flour, salt, lard, cloth, canvas, clothes, and all of our poor belongings. They beat the people badly and shot, stabbed, and beat several of them to death. No town was strong enough to fend them off, although several began to do so, but it turned out badly. I also began the same thing at Weidenstetten, but it went awry for us, for we fended them off for two days and drove off many bold groups of riders, and we took all of our livestock and horses into the churchyard and all of our poor belongings into the churches. But it did not help. And because we defended ourselves for a long time, they set fire to the town and burned five houses and five barns.

1. Document 37.

When this happened, our affair was lost. Every man let his weapon
fall and ran to take care of his own.[2]

Hagendorf came to Langenau again in 1638, this time as a captain in the
Catholic League army. Heberle noted in his diary that the soldiers once again
did great damage to his village of Weidenstetten, but Hagendorf found the
visit too ordinary even to describe.

The two diaries are alternately heart-rending and horrifying. Together,
they suggest the awful impact of the war on the empire as a whole, but also
reveal how very different individual experiences of it could be.

37. A Soldier's Life in the Thirty Years War[3]

*[There are numerous accounts by ordinary people and local clergymen of the
effects of the Thirty Years War on civilian populations. Much rarer, however,
are accounts from one of the many soldiers who fought in this war. In 1993
historian Jan Peters discovered just such an account in a Berlin archive. The
diary, which covers the years from 1624 to 1649, had been damaged and was
missing the first and last few pages, so it began in mid-story and its author was
a mystery. Subsequent careful research, however, determined that the anony-
mous soldier was most likely Peter Hagendorf, who may have come from a
family of skilled craftsmen in the area near Magdeburg. Hagendorf's diary indicates how uncertain and unsettled life in a seventeenth-century army must
have been. In addition to the constant concerns of warfare, he had to face bad
weather, illness, food shortages, lack of pay, bandits, and angry civilians, and
also struggled to keep his small family alive as they followed him and the rest
of the army from place to place. One of the most astonishing aspects of his account is the sheer distance he traveled during the war: approximately fifteen
thousand miles, marching back and forth across the empire, from Italy to the
Baltic, from France to Pomerania, and back again.]*

Here the Rhine runs through Lake Constance. From Lindau to Bregenz, to
Maienfeld, over the rise to Graubünden, to Chur, the capital city of Graubünden.[4] There they speak a foreign language[5] and have nothing but mountains and valleys.

2. Document 38.

3. J. Peters, *Ein Söldnerleben im Dreißigjährigen Krieg: Eine Quelle zur Sozial-
geschichte* (Berlin: Akademie Verlag, 1993).

4. Hagendorf is traveling south from Lake Constance (Bodensee) up the Rhine

The Enrollment of Troops (Jacques Callot, 1633, Bibliothèque Municipale de Lyon #F17CAL002511)

Here in the mountains the snow doesn't retreat the whole summer. There is good livestock breeding here, but practically no grain growing, and also no wine growing; a very rough land. At Chur there is a nice warm spa, very healing.

From Chur to Splügen. Here, at this mountain, the Rhine springs forth. The mountain pass is a whole day's journey high.[6] Halfway over the mountain stands an inn, from which point things go back downhill. This mountain is so high that one can only travel in single file, and the snow covers the entire mountain range.

After this to Chiavenna, beneath the mountains, already completely foreign.[7] Here I bought myself a book, half in a foreign language and half in German, and sold my coat for three *thalers*. After this to Riva, in a mighty pass and furnished with a beautiful fortress on the lefthand side of the water, for here Lake Como begins. Here I mounted and then traveled up to Lecco, a day's journey and an area that already belonged to the Venetians. (This is the first city in this region that belongs to the Venetians.) After this to Bergamo, a beautiful city furnished with a beautiful castle. Here the territory of the Venetians truly first begins. After this to Brescia, a beautiful city.

River, into the Alps. Lindau is in modern Germany; Bregenz is about six miles away in western Austria; Maienfeld and Chur are in Graubünden, which was then a free state, but is now a canton in the Swiss Republic. Following Hagendorf's travels with a map in hand may be helpful.

5. The people of Chur spoke a mixture of Swiss German, Romansh, and Italian.

6. The Splügen Pass (elevation 6,932 ft.) connects Graubünden with modern Italy and is approximately ninety miles from Lindau.

7. Chiavenna now belongs to the modern Italian province of Lombardy.

Here I enlisted with the Venetians, joining their service, and they moved us from one city to another where the quarters were. Thus from Brescia to Peschiera on Lake Garda, into an extremely beautiful fortress under which the lake flowed.

Here I became ill, for they have a very fiery wine in this land. I was ill for two months, but the Almighty once again helped me, although many other Germans died.

After three months, we moved with our company to Verona, which was not very well fortified and which lay on the border of Mantua, but it was a very merry place. . . .

From Verona, after three months, to Verolanuova, which lay in the domain of Milan. Everywhere there were vineyards and grain growing.

In this year, 1625, from Verolanuova again to Brescia. Here we decamped and moved to Val Camonica.[8] The headquarters were at Edolo. Here Melander,[9] who had become the field commander, was encamped, and I was put under his command, under captain Wortenburgk.

From Val Camonica we moved to the Valtelline,[10] where the king of Spain was opposing us. When Count Pappenheim[11] arrived, he attacked us mightily with cannons and expelled us from our posts and out of the Valtelline, so that we had to retreat back to Tirano. Then we encamped near Riva and tried to capture its castle. But the pope's troops were encamped within, and negotiations began anew.

In this year, 1625, we were disbanded. Then there were just two of us, me and my comrade, Christian Kresse from Halle. Together we moved to Como, to Milan, to Pavia, to Modena, to Padua, to Parma. Here again we enlisted. We met here a lutemaker, a good German, who paid for quite a few of our drinks. He also managed to get me work, so [every day] after I finished my watch, I worked as a craftsman and earned some nice money.

We stayed here for twelve months. From here, we moved with our company to Piacenza, which also belonged to the duke of Parma and which was

---

8. An alpine valley.

9. Count Peter Holzappel, usually known as Melander, was at this time a colonel in the Venetian army, though he later gained fame as a general for first Hesse-Cassel and then the emperor.

10. A strategic pass through the Alps then belonging to Graubünden, now part of northern Italy.

11. Gottfried Heinrich, count von Pappenheim (1594–1632), who had fought for the Catholic League at the battle of White Mountain and later served in the army of the Spanish in Italy. The Spanish needed to secure the Valtelline and the route north along the Rhine in order to move mercenary troops and supplies from Italy to the Netherlands to fight the Dutch.

also a splendidly beautiful city. In this land Parmesan cheese is made. Here we stayed for six months, then were disbanded. Then we once again returned to Modena, to Bologna, to Pavia, an exceedingly beautiful land. . . .

From Pavia to Milan, a merry path, straight as an arrow. From Milan to Como, etc. Milan is a beautiful city. The fortress lies in front of the city . . . exceedingly well fortified. Here we begged, for our money was gone. From Como to [?], because this land, including Pavia, Milan, and Como, belonged entirely to the king of Spain.

To Bellinzona. This is the first city within Switzerland, and Italy ends here. But everything is foreign here, and the mountains rise up again. The mountain over which one must go is called the Gotthard.[12] It takes an entire day to cross it. Halfway over the mountain stand a chapel and an inn. When one dies up there or freezes to death (for in both winter and summer, there is a cruel cold and lots of snow on the mountain), they toss the body into the chapel. In the inn, however, they give needy people a piece of bread and a half portion of wine and either let them go on or keep them overnight if they are not able to proceed. For one dies the second one sits down on this mountain.

Around midday we arrived at the inn. It was beautiful, clear weather, and we ate the bread that they gave us and were shortly again underway. Then such a storm appeared that no one could see anyone else. So I went in front, always heading down the mountain, until I came to a bridge that they call the Devil's Bridge, which goes from one mountain to another.[13] Under the bridge the water ran, plunging from one rock to another and the height of a church steeple below us. If one were to fall he would be gone, even if he were worth a thousand men. Here I lost my comrade and have no idea what became of him.

At the foot of the mountain lay a town called Urseren.[14] From there to Aldorf, with the linden tree. There I boarded a boat and traveled over the lake. Here one could still see the chapel where William Tell escaped, from which the Swiss had their freedom.[15]

Since we crossed over safely I went to Brugg. Here everything was again German. To Königsfelden, a beautiful cloister, and from there to Schaffhausen. At Schaffhausen I made so much by begging that I was going to buy woolen shoes, but I first went to the inn, and there the wine was so good that I forgot about the shoes. Instead I wrapped my old shoes with willow and then walked as far as Ulm on the Danube.

12. St. Gotthard Pass (elevation 6,916 ft.).

13. The Devil's Bridge crosses the Reuss River.

14. Andermatt. Urseren is the name of the entire valley.

15. William Tell was a fourteenth-century Swiss hero known as an excellent marksman. Legend tells that he helped spark a rebellion against the domination of the Habsburgs and so helped bring about Swiss independence.

In this year, 1627, on April the 3rd, I enlisted with the regiment of Pappenheim[16] at Ulm as a private, for I had become completely down and out. From there we moved out to our muster place in the upper margraviate of Baden. There we lay in our quarters, gorged, and boozed, and it was good.

A week after Whitsunday,[17] on Trinity Sunday,[18] I married the highly virtuous Anna Stadlerin, from Traunstein in Bavaria, and we held our wedding.

On St. Johannes' Day, our [company's] colors were raised and we marched to Rheinbischofsheim.[19] Here we, along with the entire regiment, boarded ships and traveled to Oppenheim, where we disembarked. Underway, however, one ship ran aground, such that it broke into pieces and many drowned.

From Oppenheim to Frankfurt, through the Wetterau[20] and Westphalia, through to Wolffenbüttel in the territory of Brunswick. This we besieged, building entrenchments before it, and fiercely pressed the city by damming up the water and flooding them so that they had to surrender. Here my wife became ill and was sick during the entire siege, for we lay encamped there before the city for eighteen weeks. On Christmas Eve in the year 1627, [the soldiers defending the city] pulled out; but for the most part they enlisted with us.

Then about two hundred wagons came from the Altmark[21] in order to lead out the sick and the wounded. I also brought my wife out, and we moved to the Altmark. Our headquarters were at Gardelegen, and our captain, Hans Hendrick Kelman, lodged with his company at Salzwedel.

Here I became sick, and my wife once again well, and I was laid up for three weeks. Four weeks after my illness, a command came to move to Stade, downriver of Hamburg, and I was commanded to go along.

At this time my wife went into labor, but the child was not yet ready to be born and so shortly died. God grant him a joyous resurrection.

† 1. He was a young son.[22]

We lay before Stade. On Good Friday we had enough bread and meat, but by Holy Easter Day we couldn't get a mouthful of bread. Since [the en-

16. Pappenheim was then back again, serving in the army of the Catholic League.

17. Whitsunday, or Pentecost, is a major Church holiday celebrated fifty days after Easter and commemorating the descent of the Holy Spirit to the Apostles.

18. The day honoring the Holy Trinity and falling on the first Sunday after Whitsunday.

19. A town just north of Strassburg on the Rhine River.

20. A region of Hesse.

21. A region in Brandenburg.

22. Hagendorf marks with a cross each death in his family, and sequentially numbers each dead child.

emy] then, in this year 1628, withdrew, we returned to our quarters and were encamped there without moving for the summer.

After this we moved with our company to Stendal, where we also had good quarters. In this year, 1629, Lieutenant Colonel Gonzaga,[23] prince of Mantua, took two thousand men from the regiment (for it had become three thousand five hundred men strong), moved us to Pomerania, and encamped before Stralsund.[24] But they soon would have shown us the door anyway, had we stayed even a day longer. Our baggage remained in the quarters.

At this time, while I was away, my wife was once again blessed with a young child, a daughter. She was baptized Anna Maria in my absence. She also died while I was away. † 2. God grant her a joyous resurrection.

From Stralsund we all traveled up the river that is called the Swine, crossing the water in two ships and passing into the area of the Kashubians[25]— a very wild land, but splendid livestock breeding of all kinds.

Here we got tired of eating beef[26] and had to have geese, ducks, or chicken instead. Wherever we camped overnight, the head of the household had to give each of us a half *thaler,* but it was for the best, since then we were satisfied with him and let him keep his livestock in peace.

Thus we marched here and there with two thousand men, every day fresh quarters, for seven weeks. At Neustettin,[27] we stayed encamped for two days. Here the officers provided themselves nicely with cows, horses, and sheep, for there were plenty of each.

From there out to Spandau, a mighty gateway where they would not let more than one company at a time go through,[28] and so we returned to the Mark[29] and took our quarters. Soon thereafter in this year, 1629, we decamped with the entire regiment and marched to the Wetterau.

Wiesbaden, downriver of Frankfurt, served as our headquarters under Count Pappenheim. Our captain, with the rest of the company, encamped in the [region of] Vogelsberg.[30] The captain camped in Lauterbach, the company in the countryside. Here we had good quarters for twenty weeks.

---

23. Hannibal Don Luis Gonzaga (1602–1668), imperial field marshal.

24. Stralsund is a city on the Baltic coast.

25. A Slavic ethnic group of Lower Pomerania and modern-day Poland.

26. Because they ate it so often.

27. A town in Pomerania, now known as Szczecinek and belonging to Poland.

28. Spandau, which is now part of Berlin, was the site of a large citadel with extensive walls and fortifications. He may be referring to these.

29. Brandenburg.

30. A region in central Hesse.

Here my wife was once again honored with a young daughter, who was baptized Elisabeth.

After twenty weeks, we decamped and marched to Westphalia. Our quarters were in Lippstadt, and we were encamped there for the winter. In this land there are large, strong people—both men and women—and it is a fruitful land with lots of cattle breeding. In the countryside there are almost entirely only single-owner farms, so they have their cultivated fields, woods, and meadowland all at their houses.

In Lippstadt there was good, old beer and also witches. I saw seven of them burned alive. Among them was even a pretty girl of eighteen, but she too was burned.[31]

In this land they bake bread that is as big as a large grindstone, but square. The bread has to bake in the oven for twenty-four hours. They call it pumpernickel. It is, however, quite a good and tasty bread, completely black.

In the year 1630, we decamped from here and marched to Paderborn. Lippstadt lies on a river full of ships called the Lippe. From Paderborn to Niedermarsberg, which lies on a high mountain. To Goslar in the Harz Mountains, and then to Magdeburg.

We set ourselves up in the local villages and blockaded the city [of Magdeburg] for the entire winter, staying encamped in the villages until the spring of 1631. There we captured several entrenchments in the forest in front of Magdeburg. There our captain, along with many others, was shot dead in front of an entrenchment. One day we captured seven of their entrenchments. Then we moved in close and built up the whole area with our entrenchments and saps,[32] but it cost us a lot of men.

The 22nd of March Johann Galgart was brought in as our captain; the 28th of April he too was shot dead in the saps. The 6th of May Tilge Neuberg was then brought in. He had our company for ten days, after which he resigned.

The 20th of May we attacked and stormed in earnest and also conquered. There I entered the city by storm without incurring any injury. But once in the city, at the Neustadt Gate, I was shot twice through the body—that was my booty.

This happened the 20th of May 1631, in the early morning at nine o'clock.

---

31. Witchcraft trials and executions were a common occurrence throughout Europe in this period. Some scholars have seen a connection between the witch hunts and the war, perhaps due to the increased social disorder, economic disruption, and population mobility that the war engendered. The trials may also have been influenced by religious conflict, greater fears of the Devil, and serious concerns over the imminent Last Days.

32. Trenches used by besieging forces to approach closer to the enemy fort.

Afterward I was taken to the camp and bound up, for I had been shot once through the stomach (shot right through from the front), and a second time through both shoulders, so that the bullet was caught in my shirt. The army doctor bound my hands behind my back so he could use the gouge on me. Thus I was brought back to my tent, half dead.

Nevertheless, I was deeply saddened that the city burned so horribly, both on account of the city's beauty and because it is my fatherland.[33]

As I was now bandaged up, my wife went into the city, even though it was completely on fire, since she wished to fetch a cushion and cloth for me to lie on and for the dressings. I also had our sick child lying with me. But then there came a great outcry in the camp that the houses of the city were all collapsing on top of each other so that many soldiers and their wives who had wanted to loot were trapped. But I was more concerned about my wife on account of the sick child than on account of my own injuries. Yet God protected her. She got out of the city after one and a half hours with an old woman from the city. This woman, who had been the wife of a sailor, had led her out and helped her carry bedding. My wife also brought me a large tankard of four measures[34] of wine and had, in addition, also found two silver belts and clothes, which I later redeemed for twelve *thalers* at Halberstadt. That evening my companions came by, each honoring me by giving me something, a *thaler* or a half *thaler*.

The 24th of May Johan Philipp Schütz was brought in [as our captain]. I and all of the other injured were transported to Halberstadt. There we were lodged in villages. Three hundred [men] of our regiment were lodged in one village, and all recovered there.

I got a very good landlord here. He didn't give me any beef, but only veal, young dove, chicken, and birds. After seven weeks I was once again strong and healthy.

Here also my little daughter, Elisabeth, died. God grant her a joyous resurrection. † 3.

After those seven weeks, we were once again collected into the army. While the Swedish army arrived at Havelberg, we went to Tangermünde and then Werben on the Elbe River.[35] At Havelberg the Swedish army entrenched

33. The total destruction of Magdeburg shocked people across Europe. Contemporary estimates put the number of dead from the attack and subsequent fire, which was most likely set by the attackers, at around twenty thousand. See Document 16.

34. A measure was a specific quantity of liquid, the volume of which was often legally specified by region. Today in Austria and Southern Germany a measure of beer or wine equals one liter.

35. Tangermünde is about twenty-eight miles upriver (south) of Havelberg, and Werben is just downriver of Havelberg.

itself, and it got so horribly hot at that time that a drink of water was expensive.

So because [the enemy] had entrenched himself, we went back to Tangermünde, to Magdeburg, to Eisleben, to Merseburg, to Leipzig.[36] Here we set up camp and immediately built trenches and saps, brought the cannons forward, and fired upon the city. The 7th of September they made an accord and so surrendered both the city and the fortress. . . .

We remained there at camp in good health until the Swedes arrived on the 17th of September. After the conquest of the city, the king [of Sweden] arrived with his entire force, including the Saxon army. We then went out to meet him, fighting for more than two hours.[37]

On this day we were defeated—the entire Bavarian army, all except for four regiments, namely those of Pappenheim, Wahl,[38] Wangler,[39] and young Tilly.[40] For we were situated on the right wing and struck the Saxons, whom we shortly put to flight. Although we then thought that we had won, in the meantime our left wing had been completely defeated, so that we were then also in trouble. Luckily, night came up around us; otherwise we would have been toast.

So by night, we went to Leipzig, and then to Merseburg, to Eisleben, to Mansfeld, all of us fleeing by day and night, then to Aschersleben and Halberstadt. Here stood a fresh regiment that was supposed to come to our aid. From there we went to Franconia and to Aschaffenburg.[41]

Here the count of Rechberg[42] joined us with two regiments and the Lorrainer.[43] Then we installed ourselves in the Taubergrund[44] in the villages, with six or seven or even ten regiments to a single village. Then the king of Sweden arrived and fell upon us during the night, but not the infantry, rather the cavalry. He had already taken Würzburg and its castle.

Then the Lorrainer left us and we moved to Gunzenhausen on the Altmühl [Lake]. Here we installed ourselves in the villages and blockaded the

36. From Werben to Leipzig is a distance of about 143 miles south.

37. This battle is often referred to by contemporaries as the 1631 Battle of Breitenfeld, which was the first major victory of the war for the Protestant forces under the Swedish king Gustavus Adolphus. See Document 17.

38. Count Joachim Christian von Wahl (1590–1644), a Bavarian field marshal.

39. Johann Wangler, an imperial infantry colonel.

40. Werner Tserclaes, count of Tilly and head of an infantry regiment.

41. A journey of more than 280 miles.

42. Heinrich Alexander, count of Rechberg (?–1638).

43. Charles IV, duke of Lorraine (1604–1675).

44. An area to the south of Aschaffenburg, along the Tauber River.

fortress of Wülzburg near Weißenburg,[45] which surrendered after ten days. At this time there came a very great cold. Thereafter, after the conquering of the fortress, we moved into Bavaria to our winter quarters. Our regiment encamped at Kelheim on the Altmühl [River]. We and our company encamped at Riedenburg. Here we once again had good quarters.

But whatever we had devoured in the Altmark, we had been forced to vomit up again before Leipzig.

Here at Riedenburg, in the year 1632, I was made a corporal.

The 16th of April we set out again to Regensburg. At Kelheim on the Altmühl they brewed a splendidly good wheat beer. From Regensburg to Schrobenhausen, to Donauwörth on the Danube. At Donauwörth we once again settled down. Soon the Swedish army was also there and chased us away from Donauwörth. Then to Rain am Lech, a fortress.

Here we settled. The peasantry fought against us, but all in vain. As the king [of Sweden] came against us with force, however, and shot at us with cannons, then several fell, including General Tilly,[46] who was shot by a bullet, and the other soldiers all ran away.

Thus we had to start out during the night and moved to Neuburg and to Ingolstadt. On the second day, the Swedish army was once again at us. Then we went back through Ingolstadt to the other side of the river, for the Danube River runs near Ingolstadt.

The residents of Ingolstadt then fired heavily on the Swedes with cannons, so that the king's horse was shot out from underneath him. The city would soon be taken by treachery, by means of the count of Farensbach, who would, some days later, be judged by the sword at Regensburg at the grain market.[47] So we, the whole army, stayed there at Regensburg on the two islands between the banks of the Danube.

The Swedes went to Bavaria, to Munich and in all directions, and had good quarters.

We, however, were also settled down in cities. Our regiment was settled down in Regensburg in the city. My quarter was near the Market Gate, with Johannes Strobel, a grocer. Good quarters.

Here my wife was once again delivered with a young daughter, with the name Barbara, in the year 1633.

This year the army then came back together near Landshut. Here there is the highest tower that lies on the Isar, which is a river in Bavaria that is also

45. In Bavaria.

46. General Field Marshal Johann Tserclaes, count of Tilly (1559–1632), was wounded and died days later.

47. Colonel Wolmar, count von Farensbach (1586–1633), was arrested for his treachery and executed publicly at Regensburg.

rich in ships. There the Swedish army also came back together and moved
to Augsburg. We divided ourselves, with some going to Landsberg in the Allgäu, but our regiment once again returning to Freising.[48]

My wife, however, not knowing about all of this, followed the army
through to Landsberg am Lech. She became ill, along with the child.

At Freising I, along with my captain and three hundred men, were commanded to go to Straubing. My wife, however, when she learned of this, followed after the regiment, which she met at Munich. The child, however, died
underway, and she, several days later, also died at Munich, at the hospital.

God grant her and the child and all of her children a joyous resurrection,
amen. For in the blessed eternal life we will see each other once again. Thus
now my wife, along with her children, has passed away.

Their names are these:

Anna Stadlerin of Traunstein from Lower Bavaria

Children:

The first did not reach baptism.

The other three, however, all reached blessed Christian baptism.
The mother:

Anna Stadlerin †

The children:

The first (without a name) †
Anna Maria †
Elisabeth †
Barbara †

God give them eternal peace, 1633.

For my part, I went to Straubing on the Danube River. When we arrived,
two regiments of the Swedes were already there before us. They welcomed
us.[49] Of the three hundred men, no more than nine of us escaped, for the
others were all captured and killed. I, however, fell into a hedge, and when
it was all over I went into the city.

---

48. The Allgäu is a region of southwest Bavaria. Landsberg am Lech is about thirty-
seven miles west of Munich. Freising is about twenty-two miles southwest of Landshut and the same distance northeast of Munich.
49. I.e., attacked.

Here my captain made me into a sergeant, for no other corporal but me had returned. We then lay there for four days. Then they sent us almost five hundred men as an occupying force. I had good quarters with the keeper of the inn called "At the Green Fir." I had some pretty good money and also got some more.

After fourteen days the Swedes arrived, besieged the city, and bombarded it. So we had to surrender, because we had no hope of any relief. In the city I supplied myself with a horse, saddle, and gear, including bandolier and pistols, for there were horses enough here. I had thought that they would let us pull out, which is what the accord had specified; but after two hours, it turned into "dismount, give over whatever you have, and you can keep the rest." Thus ended my stint as a cavalryman. We all had to allow ourselves to be enlisted [into the Swedish army].

Then we were led back to Straubing. From Straubing we were led to the Isar River. I was brought in as a sergeant under the Red Regiment. My captain was named Albrecht Stengel, from Sweden.

As we tried to cross the Isar, the current became so strong that our lieutenant colonel drowned. Then we rejoined the army at Straubing.

Because it was so cold, many stayed in the villages and did not follow the regiments. So Sergeant General Kalle[50] came to one of these places, where he then asked which regiments were encamped there. Since they could not answer him, for they were Laplanders,[51] he requested that one man from each regiment escort him. Many then ran up. "Oh no," he said, "I only want one from each regiment." This they arranged. But when he returned to the army with them, he had all seven of them immediately shot dead in front of the regiments. This was their escort payment.

From Straubing to Regensburg. Underway, I once again got two beautiful horses, for I had a good errand boy named Bartelt who managed to bring me both of them.

From Regensburg to Dinkelsbühl. Here I met a cousin named Adam Jeligan, a bell founder.[52] He and I drank away one of the horses.[53] We had ourselves quite a fun time for three full days, though the errand boy cried about the horse.

This all happened in this year 1633. . . .

---

50. It is unclear who this might be. Perhaps he means the Swedish commander Count Lars von Kagge (1595–1661).

51. Lapland is an area of northern Sweden inhabited by the Sami people, who live throughout far-northern Scandinavia and speak their own languages.

52. A bellmaker.

53. They sold the horse for booze.

In the spring of 1634 we broke off with the regiment and moved to Bamberg. Here new colors were raised. . . . We moved to Forchheim and up to Rothenberg. But they showed us the door with cannons, and so we had to leave once again. We moved to Nuremberg, to Donauwörth, to Augsburg, to Friedberg.

Here Duke Bernard[54] advanced to us with his army. We moved to Freising, over the Isar, to Landshut. This we bombarded and took by storm.

Here we stayed for eight days and plundered the city. I got as my booty a pretty little maid, twelve *thalers* in money, and clothes and linen aplenty. When we decamped, I sent it all back to Landshut.

We wished to relieve Regensburg, but then we received news underway that the imperialists and Bavarians had already taken it by an accord. . . .

Thus we returned back to Freising, to Augsburg and Donauwörth. Here we stayed for four days, but then the imperialists came and drove us off. Then we went to Günzburg and over the Danube to Langenau. Günzburg belonged to the city of Ulm. It is a village, but they put three hundred plows to work in the fields. It lies more than an hour from Langenau.[55]

To Aalen, to Bopfingen, which is two hours from Nördlingen. This [Nördlingen] the imperialists besieged and heavily bombarded. Here we lay for fourteen days on the mountain near Bopfingen and waited for troops.

Underway my errand boy became ill and so stayed behind in Aalen. When he was well again and was going to come to me, someone robbed him of everything. For he had with him all of my linen that I had got at Landshut. It was stolen during the night when we were going to attack, so that we were all standing in readiness. They took everything that I had, including my passport.[56] Thus all of my booty was gone, including my passport, which had been the most precious to me. But it was all gone.

On the 7th of September in the year 1634, we moved from the mountain near Bopfingen to Nördlingen and attacked the imperialists.[57] The first day we pressed them, but the second day the battle really began. The Spanish inflicted great losses on us, for on this day the entire Swedish army was de-

---

54. Bernard, duke of Saxe-Weimar (1604–1639), at that time commander in the Swedish army.

55. Here "an hour" means the distance a grown man could travel by foot in that time. The distance from Günzburg to Langenau is about nine miles.

56. Passports in early modern Europe were similar to modern passports, in that they were issued by local governments and stated that the bearer was legally authorized to travel outside his home. Such papers were required for many travelers in Europe at this time, and they helped the bearer pass through numerous customs barriers and checkpoints without being molested as a vagrant or beggar by local officials.

57. See Document 22.

feated, both infantry and cavalry. The Spanish destroyed everything. With your permission; oh knave, ass, fool, cur.[58]

This time the Almighty protected me especially, so that I had to thank the dear Lord greatly for all the days of my life that I had walked away without a scratch, despite the fact that not one other man out of all those who returned to the regiment did so without injury. After the battle all those who had previously been in the Bavarian or imperial armies, but had at some point been captured, now returned to their old regiments.

After an hour, I and my errand boy met up with the company in which I had previously served. The captain, who had also been captured with me at Straubing, gave me back my position of captain.[59]

This happened on the 7th of September in the year 1634.

From Nördlingen we moved after the Swedes. The areas of Lauingen and Kirchheim an der Eck in the land of Württemberg, which were still under siege, willingly surrendered. To Stuttgart, to Pforzheim. Here we stayed.

In the battle the generals Horn and Kratz and many officers were captured.[60]

From Pforzheim to Durlach, where we lay encamped; and with commandeered troops pursued the Swedes, those that were still around, as far as the bridge to Strassburg. . . .

From [Pforzheim] we moved to Heidelberg in the Rhineland Palatinate. We took the city, but not the castle.

This happened the 19th of November 1634.

We had a strength of four infantry regiments and three cavalry. Johann von Werth commanded us.[61] We were too weak, so we had to abandon the city again and then went as far as Pforzheim.

Here an additional nine regiments joined us, along with the count of Gronsfeld.[62] We went back to Heidelberg, took the city once again, and lay there within it for fourteen days. We bombarded the castle and wanted to blow it up. When everything was ready, with twenty-four barrels of powder

---

58. A series of swear words: "*lutrian [Luderer], begfutu [Pech-futter?], Madtza [Matz], hundtzfudt [Hundsfott]*."

59. Thus after the battle of Nördlingen, he changed sides again: from the Swedish and Protestant side to the imperial and Bavarian side.

60. Gustav Horn, count of Pori (1592–1657), Swedish field marshal who had joint command of the Swedish army with the duke of Saxe-Weimar for the battle of Nördlingen. Johann Philipp Kratz, Swedish field marshal and count of Scharfenstein. He escaped but was recaptured and beheaded.

61. Johann von Werth (1591–1652), at this time imperial regimental cavalry commander.

62. Count Maximilian Gronsfeld, Bavarian commander.

placed under the castle, the French army arrived, thirty thousand men strong, and before we were even aware of what was happening, they captured the entrenchments in which seven great cannons stood. For it was then around the time of the changing of the watch, and so our people thought it was the watch relieving them. But the French general allowed us to move out with nine infantry regiments, for the others had already left. We moved to Wimpfen. The cannons he kept, but he let us march out with our whole kit and caboodle.

My errand boy brought out with us a nice cow, which I sold at Wimpfen for eleven *thalers*.

Here flowed a river, the Neckar, which was rich in ships. From there to Pforzheim, where we had the winter quarters for our regiment. This winter I had here wine enough, and for free. . . .

In this year, on January 23, 1635, I was married to the highly virtuous Anna Maria Buchlerin, the daughter of Martin Buchler. Dear God maintain us in lasting health. At Pforzheim I held my wedding, which cost forty-five *gulden*. The father contributed ten *gulden* of it.

I remained here over the winter. The 25th of April we decamped with the entire army to Tübingen, the capital of the land of Württemberg.[63] Here there is a university.[64] . . .

Back again to Colmar. Here we encamped in the field during prime harvest time. We spoiled the entire crop around the city for the residents of Colmar by harvesting it for ourselves, reaping it, riding through it, and burning it. Then they shot bravely out at us from the city with cannons. My wife was almost shot, for she and my errand boy also harvested the crops.

After fourteen days we went to Rufach. Here Leopold[65] had his court when he was in Alsace. A beautiful city and a well-built castle. It has as many windows as there are days in the year.

From there to Sulz, to Thann, a pass in Lorraine. We took Thann. It is a beautiful city, which lies on a mountain and is strongly fortified. Here ends Leopold's land and here begins Lorraine. From there over the rise to St. Amarin, a mighty pass. One man has to go behind the other on account of the swamps. Here springs up the source of the Mosel River.

From there we moved to Remiremònt on the Mosel. Within it were lodged five hundred Frenchmen. We took it by storm. Here we encamped in the field until the 7th of August in the year 1635.

63. It became the second capital, after Stuttgart, in the fifteenth century.

64. Founded in 1477.

65. Archduke Leopold Wilhelm of Austria (1614–1662), younger son of Ferdinand II and a general in the war.

This land is mightily rich in livestock and also has beautiful grain cultivation and vineyards. There a cow is valued at one *gulden,* a sheep for one
kopfstück.[66] There were plenty of each.

The 7th of August we moved to Rambervillers. The 10th of August [the
defenders] came to an accord and pulled out. Then we provided ourselves
well with entrenchments so that the entire army was entrenched. The 15th
of September of this year, the king of France intended to attack with thirty
thousand men; but on account of the many entrenchments, he was unable
to approach us. Then Johann von Werth opposed him with the cavalry, but
he became aware of this and so pitched his camp three hours from us.

At this time there was very little bread for us in the camp. A pound of
bread was forty-five *kreuzer,* but a pound of meat was two *kreuzer.*

The 30th of September the king [of France] returned with his army and
went after Gallas,[67] who bypassed him and went into the countryside. Gallas commanded the imperialists, Johann von Werth the Bavarians. We then
left our entrenchments and came to the aid of Gallas. The 18th of October
the armies, imperial and Bavarian, joined together. Then we made our camp
in the forest. There was no city around for two miles. Our supply house was
at Blâmont.

Here we entrenched day and night with three armies, namely Gallas, Johann von Werth, and Count Gronsfeld. At this time the duke of Lorraine
commanded Johann von Werth and the Bavarians. The entrenchments for
the cavalry and infantry were strong and well provided. They lay along an
entire mile of path on a beautiful mountain a quarter-mile from the enemy.
We had thirty-two entrenchments. There was a sap going all the way around
and from one entrenchment to another. There were, in total, 136 large and
small cannons staged there. The troops in the entrenchments and elsewhere
numbered sixty thousand men strong.

The 25th of October the king [of France] returned with seventy thousand
men. Then our cavalry came out of the entrenchments and lured them back
to the entrenchments where the cannons then fired crosswise at them. They
then retreated, not desiring to attack us because they had seen that we had
so nicely provided for ourselves. We then lay there across from each other
until October 31, when they attacked again. Johann von Werth forayed into
their camp twice during the light of day and had wanted to go against the
enemy with the entire army, but Gallas vetoed this idea.

Our camp was on such soggy ground that the horses often sank down to
their stomachs. Thus we changed our camp and retreated back into the forest.

66. A coin worth twenty-four *kreuzer.*
67. Matthias Gallas (1584–1647), imperial commander.

Here, on account of the many troops, bread and meat were once again something we had little hope of gaining.

Here I still had two horses and also my old errand boy.

The 11th of November my wife gave birth to a child who was immediately baptized. His name was Jürg Martin, and he lived for twenty-four hours. God give him a joyous resurrection. † 1.[68]

Since the enemy had seen that he could accomplish nothing, he returned to Paris and let us sit there in our entrenchments and the woods. The 13th of November we decamped with the entire army and moved to Saarburg and Pfalzburg, both in Lorraine, which was a good land with all kinds of things. It lay completely flat and bordered on France. From there to Saverne. This we also had to capture, for it was the pass. Again out of Lorraine to [the fortress of] Elsasszabern, within which lay six hundred Frenchmen, whom we allowed to pull out.

Here the three armies split up. Johann von Werth commanded the Bavarians, and we moved to Weißenburg, to Landau, to Neustadt an der Haardt, and to Dürkheim an der Haardt, all in Alsace and splendidly good vineyards.

From here out I, in place of a supply master, was commanded to Worms on the Rhine to receive six thousand loaves of bread along with six military provisioners. At Kreuznach I returned to the regiment. The city was captured but not the castle. This happened the 20th of December.

Here the Hunsrück began, a very rough land.[69] At this time there was such a famine within the army that no horse was safe in its stall from the foot soldiers. They would stab a horse with a knife in the chest and then walk away, leaving the horse to bleed to death. Afterward they would eat it. But this meat, however, did not last long, only five days. . . .

In the year 1636, on the 10th of April, we besieged the city of Liège with five infantry regiments and seven cavalry regiments. . . . This bishopric had three hundred churches and cloisters, eighteen cities, eighteen hundred towns. All of these we, for the most part, plundered or robbed.

We lay here before the city until July 26. Then we decamped and moved to Sour and to Charlemont, a beautiful fortress on the Maas River in foreign-speaking Brabant which belonged to the Spanish.

Here I, along with twelve men from the regiment, was commanded to fetch meat for our regiment. Since I came across sheep in the forest we drove them out. As we brought them onto the plain they began to cry and bleat. Then all of the sheep that heard this came running out of the forest so that two thousand sheep congregated, and I was worried to death. Yet we man-

---

68. Hagendorf begins numbering anew for the children of his second wife.

69. The Hunsrück is a mountainous region in the Rhineland Palatinate.

aged to reach the camp, and then the entire camp had sheep enough. I, for my part, took two and slaughtered them. . . .

The 4th of July we came to the French border and moved over to a castle. Within it were seven peasants who resisted the entire army. So we set fire to the castle and burned it up, along with the peasants.

Here also one thousand infantrymen and fifteen hundred cavalrymen were commanded to go before a village. I was also with them. The peasants in the churchyard there resisted so forcefully that we could achieve nothing without cannons. Thus we went back, for there were one thousand peasants in there. Yet we set fire to their village and let it burn. . . .

We then went to Corbie, a mighty fortress on the river [which we besieged]. . . . Within it there was a cannon that we simply called the Bitch. With this [cannon], one day in the early morning they hit the man and wife in the hut next to my tent, shooting off all four of the couple's feet, right below their asses. For they could shoot all of their shots into our camp with this cannon, and they did great damage. The 16th of August they gave up, for we had pressed them mightily and had hurled fire inside. Then they decamped with their whole kit and caboodle, two thousand men.

Here we then rode out after booty, I as well, getting as close as ten hours from Paris. We could see it lying there, like a forest. . . .

The 19th of September we decamped and moved to Doullens, which also lay in Picardy and bordered on Flanders and Artois. From Doullens to Arras, a completely beautiful city, and fortified. This land belongs to the Spanish. Arras is the capital of Artois.

This land is rich in grain, mostly wheat, so that all of Flanders collects its cereal crops from this land. Flanders, on the contrary, is a land of milk and honey. Our regiment lay at Écourt-St. Quentin, three hours from Arras.

Here the mother of my wife died of the plague. We consigned her to the earth on the 30th of September in the year 1636.

God grant her a joyous resurrection.

In this city there are seventy-two churches and cloisters and eighteen abbeys. There are also tons more things to see here; for example, in the marketplace there is a chapel where a candle burns day and night. Supposedly, they say, it has already burned for three hundred years, but the same candle has not yet burned out. I'll leave it at that. Whoever wants to believe it can, but I don't believe it.[70]

In this land there are high church towers. Up above, at the top [of the towers], they have tied a large basket attached to a long rope.

---

70. A candle is still burning and on display today, though now in the church of Notre-Dame des Ardents.

If the sentinel who is on the tower sees something coming, he then lets the basket down. The people then respond to this, and so everyone runs to the church—animals and people—and they leave the rest of the village standing empty. For the French and Spanish have continuously fought over this place, and parties of troops come by all the time. . . .

The 5th of May [1637] we moved with the entire army to Koblenz and to Dungsern.

The 13th of May a ship with one hundred and twenty men sank here in the Rhine. Five men escaped, the others all drowned. Among those who escaped was a priest.

We then besieged the castle of Hermanstein,[71] for there were French lying within. The castle lies high up on a mountain. The Rhine runs between the castle and the city of Koblenz. . . .

We could not get anything out of this fortress of Hermanstein by shooting; rather we approached it with entrenchments and saps until we had come right up to them, all the way into their fortifications. Then they gave in, for they had nothing left to eat and had devoured the horses, dogs, cats, the saddles, everything, so that when we came in, the commander who was lodged there had no more than a quarter-bushel of bran remaining. . . .

The 3rd of March [1638], Duke Bernard assembled his army once again, for he had reconnaissance about us, that we had installed ourselves in villages [near Rheinfelden]. He came in full array early in the morning to the battlefield where we had fought before, and we knew nothing; and before we could bring our troops together, the first were already shot dead. Thus on this day he once again beat us, captured Johann von Werth, and captured all the troops—those that were not killed.

We, with our troop, came to Rheinfelden with three hundred men, and we stayed there until the 24th of March, which was as long as we held the city. But there was no relief, and also no powder or lead, so we had to surrender the city. Rheinfelden is a beautiful fortress. It lies on the Rhine and on a rock.

On the 24th of March [Duke Bernard] let us pull out, but only those who were officers. The rest of the troop, including the foot soldiers but not the troop leaders, were all taken away. I came out with the rest of the officers. . . . They had us escorted as far as Freiburg, where their escort departed.

So we went to Waldkirch, to Haslach, to Wolfach, to Oberkirch, to Baden, to Ettlingen, to Durlach, to Grötzingen. This time a measure of wine cost one *kreutzer*. From there to Bretten, to Heilbronn am Neckar, a beautiful, fortified city with good vineyards and grain cultivation. To Ellwangen, to

---

71. A fortress also known as Ehrenbreitstein or Helfenstein, which lies across the Rhine from the city of Koblenz.

Dinkelsbühl, to Wassertrüdingen, to Gunzenhausen an der Altmühl—which belongs to Ansbach—to Weißenburg, and to Ellingen.

Here was the baggage for the entire regiment, and I was once again reunited with my beloved, in good health. Thank the dear God for this, and may He continue to give His blessings.

From Ellingen to Schwandorf in the area recently taken over by the Palatinate. Here we once again assembled. From Schwandorf to Donauwörth, to Hochstädt an der Donau, to Langenau, two hours from Ulm. Here we lay until August 1, when we once again got our colors, which were raised that same day. . . .

The 12th of September we moved to Herrenberg, to Horb and Rottweil with the entire army; to Villingen, to Donaueschingen, where the source of the Danube is; to Löffingen, to Neustadt in the Black Forest. Here we entrenched ourselves, and our regiment lay alone in the entrenchments by the pass. Here I baked bread and sold it. . . .

The 20th of November we took Laufenburg on one side of the Rhine, for the Rhine ran right through the city. Here they had a beautiful bridge, but Götz had it burned.

Here we camped in the open fields until the 1st of December. It got extremely cold. We had the enemy behind us, before us, and alongside us. There was no crumb of bread to be had for money, but the Swiss crossed the Rhine in order to carry cheese to us. . . .

We returned to Stühlingen, to Blumberg, to Fürstenberg, a beautiful castle. To Geisingen an der Donau, to Pfullendorf. We stayed there for fourteen days and celebrated Christmas by the Danube with not a bite to eat.

Here the winter quarters were allotted. The 10th of December we decamped with our regiment, moved to Sigmaringen, the nearest path to Biberach [where our quarters were]. We moved into the quarters on the 30th of December. My quarter was at Degernau, and I had good quarters there in the village.[72] . . .

My wife gave birth to a young son the 18th of February [1639]. He was called Quirinius. He lived six days and then died. † 2.

God grant him a joyous resurrection. . . .

The 6th of June I decamped with the regiment and moved to Munderkingen an der Donau in the land of Württemberg. To Münsingen, to Reutlingen, where our headquarters were. To Tübingen on the Neckar, where we settled in the villages until July 16. . . .

To Donaueschingen, to Hüfingen, to Fürstenberg and Blumberg, which we took. From there to Engen and Hohentwiel, a totally beautiful fortress

---

72. The village of Degernau is about four miles south of the town of Biberach an der Riß.

which belonged to Württemberg. We besieged the castle (or the fortress), which we showered with cannons and fire, but accomplished nothing, for it lay quite high up. . . .

The 15th of December in the year 1639 we once again left the Rheingau region. . . .

Back to Dinkelsbühl, to Nördlingen, to Donauwörth. Here the winter quarters were allotted. The 30th of January we arrived at Ingolstadt, for our quarters were at Ingolstadt in the year 1640.

My quarter was at the home of Hans Burnner, beer brewer. . . .

To Neustadt an der Saale. Here my wife's father held his wedding.

Here the 22nd of March we settled in the villages. Our quarters were called Haustreu. Here we stayed until July 1, and thereafter we moved to Fladungen and to Vacha. Here we lay in the field, both imperialists and Bavarians.

The 25th of this month my wife lost fourteen ducats and two golden rings. I was then completely broke, having no more than four *thalers.*

Around this time we had such a serious cold spell that we almost froze in our camp. On the streets at this time three people did freeze: a cavalryman, a woman, and a boy. This happened the 7th of August in the year 1640.

At Vacha we decamped and moved to Hersfeld. At Hersfeld the baggage reached us from Ingolstadt. At Ingolstadt my wife had bought a horse; otherwise she would have lost everything all together. So at least I still had the horse.

From Hersfeld we moved to Homberg in Hesse, which we took. This time I was commanded to ride on ahead with the dragoons in the vanguard. From there to Fritzlar in this year on the 21st of August.

Here we began to entrench. From the outset, I supplied myself with feed. I and my wife threshed [from the fields] an entire sackful of barley and rye. This came in handy for us afterward, for Banér, who led the Swedish army, arrived on August 31 and attacked us with a strong escort. Because, however, he saw that we had so strongly entrenched ourselves and that he could not get at us, he established himself on a mountain, and we installed ourselves in the pass so nothing could approach us. So we stayed there until the 30th of September in the year 1640.

In the meantime things went badly for us. A pound of bread went for a *kopfstück,* a measure of salt for three *gulden,* a measure of wine for three *thalers,* a pound of tobacco for six *thalers,* and a pair of shoes for three *gulden.* Peas and beans were our best food at this time. For my part, I and my wife had bread enough. We even sold some, for we made ourselves a mill out of two grindstones, built a baking oven in the ground, and baked bread.

If we wished to forage, every time we would be forced to do so with five or six thousand other cavalrymen, for everyone who could walk, including women and boys, would leave the camp. We brought in apples, pears, beans, and peas, and this was our food. . . .

The 9th of April [1641] my wife gave birth to a young daughter. She was baptized here at Tirschenreuth, which lies in the Upper Palatinate at the Bohemian Forest. Her name is Barbara; God grant her a long life.

The 12th to Waldsassen, to Cham and to Straubing an der Donau. . . .

From Straubing to Paring. At Paring my wife became ill and got such a bad pain in her leg that I could not move her and had to leave her lying at Paring with the judge himself, who was a good acquaintance of mine, while I followed the colonels as far as Ingolstadt. There I had my quarters at a wheat beer tavern.

My wife, along with the child and the horse, remained behind. After fourteen days I returned and fetched her. Since she could move just as little as before, I had to bring her out on the horse. So I moved back [to Ingolstadt] like Joseph traveling to Egypt. The 16th of April I left her there; the 30th of April I fetched her again. She could go no farther than I could carry her.

The 19th of May in the year 1641 my daughter died at Ingolstadt. † 3.

Dear God, grant her a joyous resurrection.

Barbara.

The 24th I had to sell my horse, for which I got twenty-four *gulden*, for I needed the money. The 26th of May I talked to one of the city officials and begged him to take [my wife] in. This took money, for she had become crippled. She went around with two crutches for seven weeks, but the hangman's wife used baths to bring her back to health in those seven weeks. . . .

To Mühlhausen in Thuringia. Here I was commanded, along with my standard-bearer[73] Nordthaff, Hans Adamastus Nordthaff from Weissensten, to go to the sick and injured. . . .

So I remained at Mühlhausen while the regiment lay at Frankenhausen in Thuringia. Here salt is made. From the 12th of November I remained at Mühlhausen and stayed here for the entire winter.

There was a crew of twenty-six men here, and thirty-two were sent back to me when the army decamped and went to the Altmark. I stayed here the whole time. For each foot soldier, I received each day a pound of meat, two pounds of bread, and a measure of beer. I, for my part, had double that.

Here beautiful masses were held, and music. . . .

The 12th of June [1643] to Dierdorf. A very bad land, purely forest and wilderness. Here we received rations, but even the dogs didn't want to eat it.

---

73. The soldier in charge of carrying the company's colors, or standard.

Here one evening I drank a bit too much and in the morning lagged a stone's throw behind the regiment on account of my headache. Three peasants were hiding in the hedge and put up a good fight against me. They took my coat, satchel, and everything. But then, by an act of divine Providence, all at once they sprung off of me as if they were being hunted, and although there was no other person there behind them. So thus I came back to the regiment battered, without a coat, and without a satchel, and they just laughed at me. . . .

The 4th of July [1643] the duke of Lorraine with his troops met up with us, and the 16th we decamped and moved to Pfullendorf, to Heiligenberg. Here the enemy came up to us and fell upon us right in the middle during the light of day as we were marching. But he was soon driven back. . . .

Here a horse could be bought for four *thaler* and twenty-five *kreuzer*. We [two armies] lay side by side with a river between us, for the enemy lay at Walbertsweiler and we at Pfullendorf. The 22nd of July the enemy retreated, and we likewise also retreated, all of us moving next to each other, the enemy to Rottweil and we to Sigmaringen. And then we also went to Rottweil, intending to attack him, for he had besieged Rottweil and had already failed three times to take it by storm. As we arrived, he continued on and marched to Sulz, and we did too. So friend and enemy met at Sulz all at the same hour, and that evening we bravely fired at each other with cannons.

In the night [the enemy army] continued on across the Neckar and to the valley of Kinzig [River]. But we let him go. We remained near Sulz, plundered it, and then moved to Freudenstadt and across the Black Forest to Gernsbach.

Near Pforzheim, while in the field, my wife gave birth to a young son, baptized the 8th of August in the year 1643. His name is Melchert Christoff. . . . God grant him a long life. He was born on the 6th between eight and nine o'clock in the evening. The 8th we decamped and moved to Pforzheim, to Weil der Stadt. Here we stayed until the 19th of August. . . .

The 29th [of August 1643] we took Willstätt, a fortified castle that lies three hours from Strassburg. The 2nd of September we returned to Rastatt. At Rastatt I was once again ordered to tend to the injured. . . .

The 19th of December we moved from Pforzheim to Vaihingen an der Enz. Seven of the sick died.

From Vaihingen to Cannstatt am Neckar, to Hohenasperg, a beautiful fortress. To Schorndorf, also a beautiful fortress, to Schwäbish Gmünd, to Dinkelsbühl.

Here we received our quarters, for the colonel, along with the entire regiment, lay here. My quarter was with Hieronymous Weckerle Schwärtz.

The 3rd of February in the year 1644 we took up our quarters at Dinkelsbühl. The 1st of April I sold to the mayor a horse for sixteen *thalers*. Here
we lay until the 19th of April in the year 1644.

Decamped and moved to Überlingen am Bodensee. The 6th of May we
arrived here. It was fitted out with entrenchments and saps, which we bombarded. We took several entrenchments by storm. When they saw our seriousness, they surrendered. This happened the 12th of May. They pulled out
with four ships to Breisach.

Here we received a ration of wine and got ourselves well and truly drunk.
The 14th of May we decamped and moved to Hohentwiel. . . .

On the 28th, moved to near Freiburg. The enemy also camped there,
General Turenne[74] and his regiment. We besieged and bombarded and
stormed this same city in three places, also taking the outskirts by storm. The
27th of July they surrendered and pulled out.

Here we remained until the 2nd of August. Then the French army arrived
with seventy thousand men, attacked us in our entrenchments, and expelled
us from them. So we, along with the army, moved to a mountain and fought
with the enemy day and night. The enemy kept as many as six thousand men
there, but on our side there were one hundred twenty. The 4th of August he
once again pressed us, but again achieved nothing, so he left once again.

We too left during the night, to St. Peter, to Neustadt. Underway, during
our march, the enemy once again attacked us, but again achieved nothing.
After this we went to Villingen, to Rottweil.

Here I was commanded to tend to the sick and injured, of whom there
seemed to be quite a few, until they once again regained their health. But all
of our baggage had been abandoned and the enemy had gained all of it, excepting only the cannons.

The 26th of September I, along with the men from Rottweil, went to
Balingen, to Hechingen, to Tübingen, to Metzingen, to Göppingen, to
Schwäbish Gmünd, to Schwäbish Hall, to Neuenstadt an der großen Linde.
The linden tree here is so big that beneath it are five hundred columns on
which the branches rest.[75] . . .

---

74. Henri de la Tour d'Auvergne, viscount de Turenne (1611–1675), a marshal of
France who led the remainder of the duke of Saxe-Weimar's troops (the duke had
died in 1639).

75. Neuenstadt is a city in the modern German state of Baden-Württemberg. It is
now usually called Neuenstadt am Kocher, but, as this account mentions, it was previously known for its ancient linden tree, the branches of which were supported by
stone columns decorated with coats of arms. The tree, along with most of the city,
was destroyed by allied bombs in 1945, but many of the columns remain.

At Pappenheim my wife gave birth to a young daughter, the 3rd of November in the year 1645.

God grant her a long life. Her name was Margaretha.

The 6th we moved to Nördlingen. There our regiment lodged in quarters. There I received quarters with Jürg Geiserlerbeck at the Berger Gate. The whole regiment stayed in Nördlingen through to the year 1646.

The 3rd of June [1646] we advanced against the imperialists at Friedberg. Then to Butzbach, to Amöneburg. The 7th of June we took Amöneburg by treaty, the 9th we moved to a mountain, which we entrenched. Here there was very little bread among us, and a bread ration cost six *batzen*.

The enemy lay at Kirchhain, and we watched each other. The 16th we decamped and moved to Grünzberg.

The 19th of June, Holz—Colonel Holz—was appointed as our sergeant general. Here I bought three loaves of bread for one *thaler*.

From there to Hungen, which belonged to Darmstadt.[76] The 28th to Friedberg, and we entrenched ourselves near the cloister.

Here I built a baking oven in the ground and baked bread for the cavalrymen and musketeers. . . .

The 22nd of August my little daughter died.

Margaretha † 4.

God grant her a joyous resurrection. . . .

To Ergoldsbach, to Landshut on the Isar River. Here across the Isar to Vilsbiburg in Lower Bavaria. To Gangkofen, to Eggensfelden, to Brau in Lower Bavaria on the Inn River on the 27th of February in the year 1647.

Here we had quarters with our regiment. Braunau lies right on the Inn River. It is an evil river, though filled with ships, for it quickly overflows its banks if it rains even a little.

With our company we came to [the neighboring town of] Altheim, to the little area of Oberenns. Here we had good quarters, for this winter at Braunau my quarters were with Apollonia, a court clerk who was widowed before I arrived. We arrived here the 26th of February and stayed here until the 15th of September.

When we decamped I left my son, Melchert Christoff, at Altheim with the schoolmaster at [the parish church of] St. Laurenz. I had to give him ten *gulden* a year, plus clothing. . . .

The 27th of September in the year 1647 we arrived at Memmingen. We set up our camp near the cloister of Buxheim. We quickly established entrenchments and saps and laid out two batteries in front. My colonel,

76. Darmstadt is a city in Hesse.

Winterscheid, commanded the larger battery as sergeant general. Within this battery there were two and three-quarter half *kartaune,* four half *kartaune,* and two *schlange.*[17] . . On the other side, on the mountain, we also had two half *kartaune,* which fired only burning cannonballs. We also had four flaming mortars, and we fired them day and night.

The 5th of October they attacked, driving us from the batteries and dumping nails in five of the artillery pieces.[78] They made many further excursions, but we soon chased them back again. We then rallied ourselves and destroyed their walls and batteries with cannons and tunnels,[79] so that they were forced to yield them. We also stormed their entrenchments many times, also the Krug Gate and the Wester Gate, but achieved nothing but a great loss of troops.

The 23rd of November in the year 1647 they surrendered, and the 25th of November they pulled out. There had been three hundred and fifty men within, and Colonel Przyemski had commanded here.[80] They pulled out with their whole kit and caboodle and were escorted as far as Erfurt.

Our colonel, Sergeant General Winterscheid, and his regiment were lodged in the city and took their quarters there.

The 27th of November I moved into my quarters too. My host was David Herman Begk, at the Kalch Gate.

The 5th of January in the year 1648 at three o'clock in the afternoon, my daughter Anna Maria was born. Her godparents were these: Regimental Provost Marshal Christoff Issel, army doctor Melchert Bordt, and Benengel Hessin, the wife of the captain. God grant her a long life, amen.

This city lies in a beautiful location. A half hour away, there arises a river, and it drives the city mills. . . .

It is a beautiful, fruitful land of grain cultivation that lies in Swabia. There are beautiful trout in these waters. The city has two beautiful churches, St. Martin and the Church of Our Lady, and also a beautiful hospital and an Augustinian cloister. But except for the cloister, the city is entirely Lutheran.

In the spring Winterscheid began to rebuild what had been ruined, such as the gates and the walls.

---

77. Cannons with different calibers. *Kartaune* were the larger siege pieces.

78. Nails would make the cannon explode at next firing.

79. In siege warfare tunnels were dug under defensive walls in order to place explosives where they could do the most damage.

80. Colonel Sigismund Przyemski, the Swedish commander of Memmingen, had defended the city against the Bavarian siege for nine weeks with the aid of the local craftsmen, whom he had organized into a militia.

In the year 1648, on the 16th of November, a joyous festival was held by the citizens on account of the peace, as if it were Easter or Whitsunday. In both churches, three sermons were held. The text was from the first book of Moses, chapter eight, in which Noah, after the great flood, came out of the arc, built an altar to the Lord, and offered burnt sacrifices of every clean beast.

The 7th of May in the year 1649 I went from Memmingen to Mindelheim, to Landsberg, to Munich, to Wasserburg, and to Braunau and Altheim. I once again picked up my son, Melchert Christoff. The time in which he had been there, including the daily allowance, which I absorbed, had cost twenty-seven *gulden*. Thus I brought my son out of Egypt.[81]

38. Hans Heberle's *Zeytregister*[82]

[Johannes "Hans" Heberle was a shoemaker from the little town of Neenstetten in the territory belonging to the free imperial city of Ulm. The excerpts below make up only a small part of his Zeytregister, *or chronicle, which covers the years from 1618 to 1672 and includes not only Heberle's own experiences and observations, but also information he gleaned from published reports, histories, and sermons. Heberle was well placed as an observer of these difficult times, for though the territory of Ulm was spared serious damage during the early years of the war, it did not escape the resulting economic upheaval, nor did it fare well in the later years. In addition to the* Zeytregister's *value as a window into the daily lives of ordinary people, it also vividly demonstrates the personal, social, economic, and demographic costs of the war and indicates the ways in which local governments dealt with the challenges of the period. Finally, it allows an analysis of the practical functioning of armies during the Thirty Years War, since Heberle not only records the impact of large invading armies on families and communities, he also provides information by which we can assess the strategic use of territory by both allied and enemy military officers.]*

81. A biblical reference: Hos. 11:1 and Matt. 2:15.

82. Hans Heberle, "Zeytregister," in Gerd Zillhardt, *Der Dreißigjährige Krieg in zeitgenössischer Darstellung. Hans Heberles "Zeytregister" (1618–1672), Aufzeichnungen aus dem Ulmer Territorium: Ein Beitrag zu Geschichtsschreibung und Geschichtsverständnis der Unterschichten* (Ulm and Stuttgart: Kommissionsverlag Kohlhammer, 1975). Zillhardt offers an edited edition of the entire original German text, along with a full discussion of Heberle's life and times.

Foreword[83]

That which has given me cause and occasion to write this little book is as follows. In the year of our Lord 1618, a great comet appeared during the autumn month of November. To see this was terrible and amazing, and moved me such that I began to write, for I thought that it would signify and usher in something great, which has indeed occurred, as the reader will herein find sufficient record. . . .

1618 and 1619

In the year 1619 Ferdinand II became Roman emperor, under whom a great persecution emerged, through war, turmoil, and the spilling of much Christian blood, as examples sufficiently demonstrate. First he began a great war in Bohemia, which he overwhelmed and put under his religion, and thereafter, in the following years, the lands of Brunswick, Mecklenburg, Lüneburg, Friesland, Brandenburg, Pomerania, Gottland, Austria, Moravia, Upper Austria, Silesia, the Electorate of Heidelberg—yes, almost all of Germany, not all of which I can explain and describe.[84]

1620

In the year 1620 many minting houses were established and built, and a great deal of unnecessary money was minted; thereby many burdens emerged.[85] In this year my sister Anna, like the sainted matriarch Rachel, died a painful death during great and difficult childbirth on the sixth day of December.[86] May God the Almighty grant her on Judgment Day a joyful resurrection and eternal life. . . .

In this year a great tumult arose between several estates of the empire and the emperor, as well as the duke of Bavaria, on account of a situation about

83. Heberle first bound together the pages of his chronicle in 1628, at which time he also wrote the foreword. He further edited the chronicle in subsequent years; thus the occasional references to future events.

84. Here he is referring to the events following the Defenestration of Prague and the revolt of Bohemia. Since many of these events happened after 1619, this entry was clearly written at some later date.

85. The great expenses brought on by war (or the fear of war) led many imperial states, including Ulm, to ignore imperial coinage laws and establish their own minting houses.

86. Heberle compares his sister to the biblical figure who was the mother of Joseph and Benjamin, and who died during childbirth (Gen. 35:16–20).

which the common man knew nothing. At that time the margrave of Ansbach, the supreme military general of the empire, had a great camp on the
Danube near Riedheim. With a great army, he also built there many massive entrenchments and bastions, into which all kinds of food and drink were
brought and carried.[87] I myself went in with several companions, and we
drank wine together for a small amount of money. . . .

1621

In the year 1621 the haggling began, and everyone hoped to get rich.[88] One
ran here, the other there, until they had taken the good, old money; and in
its place, the bad, worthless money, which was made of nothing but sheer
copper and bell metal, was brought into our land.[89] Thereby all lands were
ruined, and the cost of all goods rose to the highest level, as we saw in the
subsequent years, particularly in 1622, 1623, and 1624, such that there has
never been such misery, nor has such a thing ever happened with money
from sunrise to sunset, from the beginning of the world to the end, nor will
it ever happen again. In this year spelt reached a price of 20 fl.;[90] rye reached
15 *gulden*. In sum, everything was sold at the highest price. . . .

1622

I will briefly indicate and describe a little of what occurred and took place
with money in this year, with the appearance of all sorts of coins, not all of
which were recognizable. For all emperors and kings, princes and lords,
counts and noblemen, cities and towns, and vagabonds and vagrants minted
and were allowed to mint; so there were many and various kinds of money,
and one had to have a learned tongue and good eyesight in order to be able
to read and see all the engravings. Then a debased and false money arose that

---

87. Joachim Ernst, margrave of Brandenburg-Ansbach, was a general of the Protestant Union. His army faced that of Duke Maximilian of Bavaria and the Catholic
League, which was also camped nearby. Under French mediation, the two sides
signed the Treaty of Ulm on July 3, 1620, to end hostilities and withdraw.

88. Here Heberle is referring to the rush by money changers, known as "kippers,"
to collect old, high-precious metal content coins, which minting houses would melt
down, mix with copper, and reissue as numerous new coins of the same face value.
This widespread practice led to massive inflation and currency manipulation
throughout the empire, especially during the years 1619 to 1625. See Document 8.

89. When Heberle speaks of "our land" or "the land," he is usually referring specifically to the land of Ulm, not to the larger empire.

90. *Gulden,* small coins, were also known as *florins* and so had the abbreviation "fl."

had no substance. For in the beginning, it was pretty, as if it were made of pure silver; but thereafter, in the third, fourth, fifth, or eighth week, it faded away and went red like copper, except for the *thaler* and the old money.[91] But because all the money was so bad and worth nothing, no one wanted to be paid anymore with such awful money, as was only proper and just. As a result it was worth nothing. Then a great misery arose in all lands. . . .

Because such misery and need were caused by the money, several states and cities in the Roman Empire made an agreement with each other about how they might manage the affair and in some way limit the inconvenience. Thus they minted new money and called it land coinage or token money,[92] a bad and contemptible money that one could use nowhere except in the domain in which the lord had minted it. . . .

Because Bohemia was overcome by the emperor and lost all assistance, it also happened to it that all the preachers in the entirety of Bohemia were evicted, although the elector of Saxony pleaded for them.[93] But the emperor stuck firm to his decision, under the pretext that the disorder had arisen out of the religion. Thus we Evangelicals always receive injustice from the Catholics.[94] . . .

1623

Because inflation increased daily, many hundreds of people migrated from their houses and farms to Moravia and Austria, and the majority traveled there on the Danube.[95]

On the fifth day of March it came to pass that several ships at Ulm were again packed full of poor people, in order to travel down to Austria. And as they started off, the sailors ran into a large rock near Thalfingen. Then the ship broke apart and as many as one hundred people drowned.

91. *Thalers,* unlike smaller-denomination coins, were not debased, so they kept their value over time. By "the old money," he means those old coins that had not been melted down, mixed with large amounts of copper, and reissued as if they still had the same value. The copper color was a sure clue that one's coin had been debased.

92. These were greatly debased, small-denomination coins.

93. John George, elector of Saxony, was the most powerful Lutheran prince in the empire. He had sided with the emperor against the Protestant Bohemian rebels, but had asked the emperor to continue to allow Lutheran worship in his territories.

94. The territory of Ulm had converted to Lutheranism in 1531. Heberle uses the term "Evangelicals" loosely throughout his chronicle, meaning either Lutherans in particular or Protestants in general.

95. Ulm was a popular departure point for ships carrying thousands of poor migrants down the Danube River.

On the 15th of March no more than four sacks of grain entered the granary at Ulm, for spelt went for forty-two and rye as much as forty *gulden*. This was caused by the bad money. . . .

During the harvest many drops of blood were found on the stalks as we reaped. Indeed, the stalks became completely bloody, which unfortunately signified the bloody war. . . .

Also during this summer, near Tübingen and Schorndorf in the country of Württemberg, around St. James' Day,[96] fiery balls fell from heaven. On one Sunday, this happened three times: in the morning, afternoon, and evening. A published pamphlet was issued about it, which I myself read. . . .

1624

As far as the money is concerned, the token money has become worthless, for though it previously had worth, later this disappeared. For the lords of Ulm[97] issued a mandate that every man should bring his money to the government office and hand it over to the civil servant. Thereafter, it should be handed over by the civil servant to the lords so that in its place the lords can issue other money that has been newly minted: half *batzen* and *thalers*. For these same coins have been distributed and minted in every land, so that no other money can be seen other than *thalers* and half *batzen*. . . .

1625

On the 24th of March many soldiers fell upon the land of Ulm at Langenau, Öllingen, Setzingen, Nerenstetten, and Wettingen, and they inflicted onto the people great plagues and suffering and all kinds of maliciousness. The men were badly beaten, and many women were raped. This continued for nine days.[98] . . .

In the harvest time around St. James' Day, several hundred cavalrymen fell upon the land. Thus the militia of the land of Ulm had to be called up at Bissingen, Öllingen, Setzingen, Nerenstetten, and Wettingen, for these cavalry were encamped at Langenau, Rammingen, and Elchingen.[99] I myself was posted at Setzingen and Öllingen for twelve days. But the cavalry at Rammingen wreaked havoc, for they set fire to the town such that almost

96. July 25, 1623. Württemberg was a neighboring duchy.

97. The territory of Ulm was governed by a city council, so when Heberle refers to the lords of Ulm he means the members of the city council.

98. The troops belonged to the imperial colonel Pappenheim and were attempting to use the land for temporary military quarters and as a source of plunder.

99. Every town within the territory of Ulm was required by the city council to contribute, when necessary, a certain number of able-bodied men for a defensive militia.

fifty buildings were burned. This continued in the land for fourteen full days, after which they withdrew.

It has been a good autumn, so we could gather all the crops successfully and there was no snow until October 16. There is a great famine among the poor and common people, since no one has any money. Spelt went for 7 and 6 fl., rye for 5 and 4 fl., oats for 24 *batzen*. . . .

1627

In the year 1627, the 2nd of January, a great snow fell and there was cold winter weather. This lasted until Easter, and it was such a harsh winter that no one could remember any winter like it, with snow, frost, and wind; so that on Palm Sunday, yes, even on Easter, one still found an abundance of snow and ice. Only after Easter did the peasants first go to their fields to sow the oats and begin to farm. . . .

In this year, the war reached the farthest reaches of Germany, even as far as the sea in Holstein and the king of Denmark,[100] who provided the emperor with considerable resistance until finally they settled matters. Then the emperor had almost the whole of Germany and the Roman Empire under his power and might, so that no one else can oppose him at this time.

The 9th of October, a Tuesday, I, Hans Heberle, and Anna Buntzen, both from Neenstetten, held our wedding ceremony. I am thirty and she is twenty-four years old.[101]

1628

In the year 1628, although we expected good times and a good year, yet immediately trouble arose, for unexpectedly, a decision came from the authorities at Ulm in the government office that called together the entire community. And when we came together, they commanded, on pain of harsh punishment, that everyone should swiftly and right away set aside all weapons and muskets and bring them to the government office, and that no one should defend himself or shoot. Then everyone straightaway delivered all weapons and hunting guns to the government office, and the entire countryside was completely disarmed.[102]

100. King Christian IV of Denmark.

101. The Ulm city council had decreed that subjects could only marry if they held property worth at least 50 fl., and if the woman had reached the age of twenty-two, the man twenty-four. That same year Heberle moved to the neighboring town of Weidenstetten, where he bought a house and small plot of land.

102. By disarming the peasantry the Ulm city council was attempting to prevent violent confrontations between them and the approaching soldiers.

After this an official commanded us that if anyone had any prized possessions and property, of whatever kind it might be, he should, as far as possible, bring it into the city of Ulm. At this, no one wanted to tarry and so be the last one. Whatever prized possessions and property anyone had, he saw to it that he brought it within, as far as he was able and could.

While we waited in the greatest fear, fright, and worry, there appeared in the land on the 18th of January, near Langenau, the cavalry of Colonel Cronberg.[103] And thereafter they spread themselves out across almost half of the land of Ulm and in further places. The Cronberger cavalry numbered five hundred, or five companies, not counting the rabble that they had brought along: whores and boys and a tremendous number of horses. They roamed around widely for an entire month. The 22nd of January they invaded here at Weidenstetten and in all the neighboring towns.

The 24th of January Colonel Graci[104] fell upon the land with several thousand cavalry and infantry, so that there was no town in Ulm without more than a hundred or two hundred soldiers, according to how small or large the town was. These same thought to take their quarters in the land, and so thought that the Cronbergers should leave. Likewise, the Cronbergers thought that they had quarters here, and so thought the Gracians should leave. Since neither of these colonels would budge, and since both of them wanted to take their quarters here, the affair and the conflict were brought before the emperor and the duke of Bavaria and delayed for four weeks. Then Colonel Graci and his soldiers left on the twenty-fourth day of February.

On top of this, Colonel Guckhele[105] also came with a regiment of cavalry into the region of Geislingen. This same colonel also settled for several weeks in the land and maintained a seemingly good rule, for he secured the streets and kept them safe in order to prevent all robbery and accident. For robbery is extremely rife in the land, so that no one can walk safely unless it is only to the next village. One day, while he maintained his quarters at Geislingen, he had ten men—some of whom were distinguished and high-ranking officers—executed by the sword in the marketplace.

As, however, this misery and disquiet subsided a little and left the land, something that took five weeks (not counting the Cronbergers, who remained in the land for the next three years), so on the 28th of February some

---

103. Colonel Adam Philipp von Cronberg, serving under the command of the duke of Bavaria.

104. Johann Philipp Kratz, aka Graci, was the count of Scharfenstein and a commander of the imperial army.

105. Heberle may mean Count Ernst von Montecucculi, commander of a Cronberger cavalry regiment.

guardsmen came and stayed with us for fourteen days. They cost the community a huge amount.

The 11th of March the Cronberger cavalry captain came to us with several cavalrymen and servants and all of their equipment. We had to put them up here at Weidenstetten and supply them with an unfortunately large amount of provisions, including several barrels of wine, meat, bacon, and all kinds of magnificent things. And if I were to describe the entire business in detail, I would have to write a complete book about it, and a long one at that.

The 6th of May several hundred infantrymen marched through overnight. An impossible burden has now been placed on the peasantry throughout the land wherever the Cronbergers are located, since we have to buy for the soldiers whatever they want to have, including meat, wine, beer, and many other things, whatever they can think of, and the subjects are thus tremendously burdened. Since no one could advise or help any other person, either with money or anything else, we asked the authorities for help and advice on how to handle this. In response an official wrote to Colonel Cronberg, who had his quarters in the land of Hall[106] in the castle of Vellberg. The colonel traveled to Ulm and made an agreement with the lords, which was straightaway posted in the land, that no peasant had to give anything more to the cavalry than wood, straw, hay, candles, and salt, and in return the lords of Ulm had to give to every single cavalry captain fifty *thalers.* And as a cavalry captain received fifty *thalers,* a lieutenant also received twenty-five *thalers,* an ensign twenty *thalers,* a corporal nine *thalers,* a quartermaster [. . .] *thalers,* and every single cavalryman three *thalers.* [The cavalry] had to stick to this agreement firmly and solidly, on pain of life and limb. Yet they only minimally kept to it, and still most horribly tormented and distressed us subjects, and robbed and plundered us on all the streets, so that no one was safe, even riding only a half an hour over the fields. And many of them were hanged for this and judged with the sword, which was only their just desserts. The high court was held at Langenau.[107] . . .

The 25th of August, in the afternoon between one and two o'clock, my dear wife brought into this world my daughter Chatreina, her first child, and on the same day, a Saturday, she was baptized during the vesper sermon. On

---

106. Schwäbish Hall.

107. Invading armies had two principal ways to support themselves in the field. They could simply take what they wanted, or they could follow the newer, more regulated "contribution system," by which set payments in money and in kind were systematically extracted under threat of force from the populace. The agreement struck between the city council and Colonel Cronberg attempted to establish this latter system in Ulm.

that day the sun rose in the morning at five o'clock and twenty-two minutes, and at the end of the day the moon rose in the sign of Scorpio. . . .

Because of the dangerous progress of the war, prayer meetings were set up and begun in the city and country, so that we might ask God the Almighty for forgiveness from the present punishment, and that He might again be good to us. . . .

1629

In the year of our Lord 1629, it has been a damp, warm winter up until the new year, when the first snowfall came, and it has been quite a warm month. But as for the cavalry, they always practice all kinds of maliciousness in every place and location, as is customary with soldiers.

A sad situation took place here at Weidenstetten with a woman, Michael Niblinge's wife. One day, as she was cutting up things for soup at the table, the boy of the cavalryman whom she had quartering there was cleaning his master's, the cavalryman's, pistol, and lifted it unthreateningly toward the good, cheery, and plump woman, and said to her, "I will shoot you," but not knowing that it was loaded; it went off and shot her through the heart so that she died with great pain, the sixteenth day of January at midday. . . .

Lutheranism was now abolished everywhere by the emperor, and [formerly] Catholic property or ecclesiastical property was supposed to be given back to the Catholics. This frightened the Protestant estates while greatly pleasing the Catholics. Then there was a great outcry and lack of trust, and everyone was afraid that his property would be extracted and taken away. . . .

1630

On the 22nd of August the Reformation[108] began in the land of Württemberg, and the prince of Württemberg had all of his cloisters occupied by the emperor, who then installed priests within.[109] They were to remain there for almost twenty years.

The same thing happened in our domain of Ulm, for also on August 22nd the church at Setzingen was occupied by the priests and closed. But through God's help and on the order of our most esteemed lords, the priests were soon magnificently expelled by the governor of Albeck, so that very little that was papist was set up inside.

108. What we would now call the Counter or Catholic Reformation. This attempt to re-Catholicize Protestant areas came after the emperor's 1629 Edict of Restitution, which required the return of all Church lands seized since 1552. See Document 14.

109. By the Edict of Restitution, Duke Eberhard III of Württemberg was required to return as many as fifty secularized monasteries and convents.

The third day of September the priests occupied the great Württemberg cloister of Maulbron, which controlled twenty-four towns. There these ravenous animals once again had good eating.

The 17th of October, by order of the duke of Württemberg, they, the priests, were once again chased out of the cloister and the land. But this did not last long, for they soon settled in again and by force. . . .

At the end of this year, in this difficult, busy, and sad time, it is also good to note that we justly do not forget what God has done for us up to now by His Holy Word, which illuminates us and appears to us so clearly. Thus on the twenty-fourth day of June, Saint John's Day, we Evangelicals held the festival of thanksgiving in all our churches. For this is now the hundredth year since the day on which several princes and estates of the Holy Empire presented at Augsburg the Evangelical confession to the great emperor Charles, the fifth of this name.[110] And we held this festival with lovely church services and prayers and song and communions. In the morning sermon and in the afternoon sermon, the Augsburg Confession was read publicly by the minister from the pulpit, so that everyone now knew what the Confession was and what it contained. . . .

1631

On the twenty-second day of April the militia from the entire countryside had to present themselves on account of the imperial troops, who were coming from the foreign lands and wanted to attack the Evangelical alliance. For the Evangelicals had made an alliance with each other on account of several quarrels with the emperor.[111] The duke of Württemberg also sent to us a troop of infantry, and we camped in the field near Jungingen while the Württembergers camped in the field near Lehr.

The tenth day of June we, as the militia, once again had to come to arms and were called to Ulm to the armory courtyard. And they wanted to make us into real soldiers, for there we had to swear loyalty to the troop, and they read aloud to us in the strongest possible terms all the articles of war. Then we had to stand with our hands raised and promise to comply with them, as is traditional in war. After this we were transferred to the Gänsbau.[112] There several tents were pitched and we were given rations, beer and bread.

110. The Confession of Augsburg was the formal statement of doctrine presented by German Lutherans to the emperor, Charles V of Habsburg, at the 1530 imperial diet of Augsburg.

111. He is referring to the Leipzig alliance made among the Protestant princes in April 1631, which demanded that the emperor repeal the Edict of Restitution.

112. A place in the city.

Then the imperial soldiers made their way close to the city of Ulm, and set up camp near the city, at Gögglingen, and then attacked with force. But the city of Ulm was too strong for them and too well occupied by troops, and also their troop numbers were not really large enough; so they tried to attack in another way and with cunning (but praise God, they did not succeed), for they collaborated with several Catholics in the city on how they might enter and conquer the city. Then the traitors secretly put gunpowder, several small barrels full (and there were supposedly many), into a secret trench that they supposedly made. For they thought to light this same powder so that the city wall and moat would fall into a heap, and the imperialists could then enter and invade the city on the same night.

And this happened on the eighteenth day of June, on a Saturday, while we camped in the city. But the powder was found and removed, and there would have been great misery due to the Catholic perpetrators if our well-intentioned and wise lords had not prevented it.

Still, I cannot fail to mention that [the Catholics] dealt disloyally toward their own city, where they had protection under such a loyal government. For this is truly a fact, since previously, before they set alight such a fire, almost everyone who was Catholic left the city—woman and man, servant and maid—so that few of their belief remained in the city. And they showed themselves to blame for this plan, for I often had to listen to the papists say that something would soon happen to the city of Ulm, so surely almost all of them knew what was up.

As the enemy came close to here, the majority of the populace retreated to the city, although part also fled to the domain of Heidenheim and as far as Steinheim am Albuch,[113] where one was safe. This was the first flight in our land.

Since this attack now failed, [the enemy] fell upon the land and performed all sorts of maliciousness. They robbed, burned, stole, and broke into all the churches, and they chased everyone out into the countryside, with wife and child. Then everyone who was still in the countryside went to the city, except for the best men, the militia. Then our well-intentioned and wise lords suffered enormously and strove to find a way to help this disaster, and so came forward and made an agreement with the imperialists.

As the imperial troops then withdrew on the twenty-third day of June, we [the militia] were immediately released again and on the 25th of this month returned home with complete joy, and once more joined our wives and children. For we had been encamped in the city for sixteen days. And this was called the Cherry War, for during this time the cherries had become ripe; though for us the sweet cherries had become bitter.

---

113. All areas belonging to the duke of Württemberg.

The third day of July an official of Ulm announced to the burghers the state of the war, and why they had to surrender to the imperialists. . . .

The eighth day of July the government set aside our main weapons, since we should not need them any more to use against the imperial troops.

The nineteenth day of July a great number of imperial troops marched through and encamped overnight near and at Weidenstetten. They forced us to pay an enormous ransom of money, such that we at Weidenstetten alone had to give them as much as 320 *gulden.*

And immediately after this, the 21st of July, an additional twelve troops of imperial infantry arrived at Kuchen and Altenstadt. They did great damage to the people.

The fourth day of September the government imposed a war tax on us, so that we from Weidenstetten had to send 13 fl. to Ulm each week. . . .

The twentieth day of October there was once again a tumult with the imperial troops, who invaded at Geislingen. Then the government gave us our main weapons back again so that we could drive the troops out of Geislingen.[114] Thus the twenty-sixth day of October the militia in the land and several officers from Ulm went to Geislingen and should have driven out the imperial soldiers. But because of the terrible leadership that the Ulmer soldiers gave us, the troops that were encamped in the little town manned their weapons and shot boldly out at us.

As four of our number were shot to death—the first from Ballendorf, the second from Bernstadt, and two from Langenau—and as we saw the seriousness of the situation and our officers gave way, then we all ran away and left the people of Geislingen to their soldiers. After this the affair was soon resolved between our lords and the colonel who was encamped at Geislingen, so that he withdrew peacefully. . . .

The eighteenth day of December, thirty-four huntsmen from the militia of the district of Weidenstetten and from almost the entire land were called up to Ulm so that the guard in the city would be strengthened. After this a great flight occurred from the land to the city on account of the imperial soldiers that Tilly[115] had near Donauwörth, so that one feared they would fall upon the land. . . .

1632

In the year of our Lord 1632, several regiments of imperial troops fell upon the land. They took everything that they found.

---

114. The surrender to the imperialists in July clearly did little to improve the condition of the people of Ulm, hence the decision by the city council to rearm the peasantry.

115. Johann Tserclaes, count of Tilly, commander of the Catholic League army.

The fifteenth day of January the huntsmen who had been encamped at Ulm for four weeks came out of the city. And because the Swedish moved ever closer, the imperial colonel, von Ossa,[116] left Schorndorf so that he would not be attacked by the Swedish. . . .

Because the imperial troops were coming through every now and then, the militia was encamped again at Leipheim, for at this time the imperialists were enemies and did damage to the Evangelical alliance wherever they could.

The twenty-fourth day of February the people of Ulm admitted and accepted a Swedish colonel into the city for the first time. And thereafter, the twenty-eighth day of February, the government asked the burghers whether they would want to be Swedish, and this was accepted from the heart with joy.[117]

The fourteenth day of March the young fellows in the land of Ulm were put under the Swedish troops so that resistance could be offered to the enemy. . . .

1634

A distressing year. I should write a happy New Year, but things are upside down and have a sad beginning, for many cavalry entered the land of Ulm, at Langenau and in the region of Heidenheim. There they remained for eleven days and did great damage. The tenth day of January a further two companies of cavalry spent the night. . . .

After gaining Regensburg,[118] the Hungarian king[119] moved up to the Danube River with his soldiers. When Duke Bernard and Colonel Horn[120] learned that Regensburg was lost, they did not delay for long, but left Bavaria, devastating and burning everything before them in their departure, and they came near Lauingen on the Danube. Then they proceeded in great haste, so that the imperialists would not reach the land of Württemberg before them. Duke Bernard moved over the Danube, and since his army had been seriously ruined in Bavaria and the cavalry had almost no horses left, he came with his army to us in the land of Ulm.

116. Wolf Rudolf von Ossa, imperial colonel.

117. The city of Ulm signed a formal treaty of alliance with the Swedes on February 13. On February 28 the burghers agreed to support a garrison of Swedish troops under the command of Colonel Patrick Ruthwen, a Scottish earl in Swedish service.

118. In July 1634.

119. Archduke Ferdinand von Habsburg. He became Emperor Ferdinand III in 1637.

120. Bernard, duke of Saxe-Weimar, at this time a general of the Swedish army; and Gustav Horn, Swedish commander.

Since we considered him to be no enemy, and we were also not warned by the government, we had everything with us: horses and livestock and all of our household equipment, all of our poor belongings. Then they fell upon us in the land and plundered all of us, taking horses and livestock, bread, flour, salt, lard, cloth, canvas, clothes, and all of our poor belongings. They beat the people badly and shot, stabbed, and beat several of them to death. No town was strong enough to fend them off, although several began to do so, but it turned out badly. I also began the same thing at Weidenstetten, but it went awry for us, for we fended them off for two days and drove off many bold groups of riders, and we took all of our livestock and horses into the churchyard and all of our poor belongings into the churches. But it did not help. And because we defended ourselves for a long time, they set fire to the town and burned five houses and five barns. . . .

When this happened our affair was lost. Every man let his weapon fall and ran to take care of his own. Then the cavalry, several hundred, came into the town, plundering, robbing, and taking away everything that they could take and carry, and they took whatever livestock and horses they could catch, so that few horses and livestock remained in the land. And this happened at Weidenstetten the tenth day of August. . . .

After this robbery and plundering that we endured, because it was now the harvest time, we reaped our grain and brought and carried it in as well as we could, since few horses remained. But the summer grain is not yet silken and ripe. . . .

Because [the Swedes] had lost everything [at the battle of Nördlingen] and Gustav Horn was captured and Duke Bernard was wounded,[121] their entire army was ruined and put to flight, so that the fleeing cavalry were already with us at midday. Then as we saw this we did not delay for long. Whoever could run, ran, so that we might still reach Ulm that same day. This was absolutely necessary, since the enemy was at our throats. And we got nothing from the Swedes. Whatever they could grab from us in our flight, that is what they did in their flight, so that we had both at our throats.

Then we had to leave behind everything that we had, and when we could only come from there with our wives and children and our lives, we were happy to let the rest go, so great was the necessity. In the evening we came to the city, many thousand people from all over, and we camped overnight in front of the city, and in the morning of the 28th of August we were let into the city of Ulm. This was the second flight.

While we camped in the city and spent our flight in misery and distress, the soldiers did amazing things. For as soon as the battle was lost, the

121. The Swedes were defeated by the imperialists at the battle of Nördlingen on September 6. See Document 22.

emperor[122] first attacked the city of Nördlingen with force, which had to give up because there was no more help available. . . .

After this the emperor moved off with his soldiers to the land of Württemberg. Then there was a great fright in Ulm, for it was feared that he would also camp in front of the city. Then we and the burghers had to cut down all the beautiful orchard trees in front of the Ladies' Gate,[123] and all of them were brought into the city.

Because, however, the soldiers followed their enemy [the Swedes], they devastated and ruined everything, plundered and completely burned the pretty little town of Giengen, attacked by force and killed several hundred from the little Ulmer town of Geislingen, which defended itself a little, and also cut off the head of their minister and robbed the little town blind; and they did much the same thing in the duchy of Württemberg.

In sum, I cannot sufficiently describe the misery that happened at that time. They marched through our land and set up their bivouac between Neenstetten and Weidenstetten on the Blumenberg. Then our town was badly injured, for the Hungarian king himself camped at Weidenstetten overnight.

The seventeenth day of September we returned home and gathered and brought in our summer crops, whatever the cavalry had left, and sowed a little. The nineteenth day of September my son Bartholomew died, in the morning between seven and eight o'clock, with an age of about four weeks.[124] May God the Almighty grant him on Judgment Day a joyful resurrection and eternal life.

The fourth day of October many imperial troops arrived at Güntzburg and Leipheim, and they constantly prowled around the land and plundered. Then everyone had to retreat to the city again and camp there this entire winter. There we had misery and want, famine and death. There we had to camp on top of each other in great distress. There inflation and famine set in, and, after these, the evil sickness, the plague. There many hundred people died in this year, 1634, and in 1635, as you will also learn hereafter.

The seventh day of October, at Jungingen during the flight, my son Thomas died in the night between eleven and twelve o'clock and was buried on the morning of the same day.[125] May God the Almighty grant him on Judgment Day a joyful resurrection and eternal life. This was the third flight.

122. Here and in the next paragraph Heberle means the king of Hungary, not his father the emperor.

123. One of the five main gates to the city.

124. Bartholomew was Heberle's fifth child.

125. Thomas was Heberle's third child. He was three years old.

The thirtieth day of November my stepmother died in the evening between five and six o'clock. The first day of December, in the morning between four and five o'clock, my sister Barbara died, and immediately afterward, the second day of December, my sister Dorothea died, in the morning between six and seven o'clock. The eighteenth day of December my sister Ursula died, in midday between eleven and twelve o'clock. May God the Almighty grant them all on Judgment Day a joyful resurrection and eternal life.[126] The 29th of December I returned home to Weidenstetten and endured this winter with wife and children, as you will sufficiently read and hear hereafter, in 1635. . . .

1635

In the year of our Lord 1635, the tenth day of January, my brother Bartholomew died, in the morning between seven and eight o'clock.[127] May God the Almighty grant him and all people who believe in Christ on Judgment Day a joyful resurrection and eternal life. Amen. . . .

This entire winter we had no quiet and peace in the land, for imperial cavalry were encamped near Lauingen. They plagued and plundered us almost every day, so that if I wanted to be safe from them, I had to hide us away and conceal us.

Oh, God willed a sorrowful Easter week, but may God grant us a joyful Easter day, and let the sun shine again after this storm.

For at Easter time, during Easter week, an entire regiment of cavalry came again to Lonsee and Urspring. They once again caused the people the greatest fear and fright. They fell upon all towns and villages, took everything that anyone had, drove women and children and every person into the forest and woods, and hunted them like wild animals. Whomever they found, they beat badly or even shot to death, and they took everything from everyone. And they did this for so long that the poor people could no longer survive in the forest, on account of the hunger that they had endured. Then we had to retreat again to the city of Ulm in desperation, with wife and child, so that almost no one remained in the countryside. This was the fourth flight.

The 7th of May, on the day of Christ's Ascension, we returned home again,[128] but an uncomfortable peace lasted only a short time for me. For then, on the 25th and 26th of May, the imperial troops arrived again at

126. These were all victims of the plague.

127. From the plague.

128. After the death of his father in April, Heberle and his family had moved back to Neenstetten.

Lonsee and Urspring. Then they roamed even more widely than they ever had before, so that no person in the entire land was safe. Thus everyone had to run away to wherever he could in order to stay even a little safe.

But one could not stay in the woods and forests because of the great famine, for I could not get my hands on bread, salt, fat, or anything else that I wanted for our sustenance, so that we, including my wife and small children (of which, at that time, we still had many),[129] would not die of hunger and be ruined. We searched everywhere for quiet.

Then I myself, with my wife and small children, along with a great crowd of people, were driven out of the woods. Then we thought that we would find safety in the land of Württemberg, and so we fled to Heuchlingen. But dear God, there we also found no peace, and had to retreat again from there after two days, for troops of cavalry came and plundered everything and took whatever they found. They were at Lonsee and Urspring for up to fourteen days.

The seventh and eighth days of June those at Lonsee took off and moved to Bernstadt. They set fire to and burned Albeck, and at Bernstadt they entrenched themselves and built a bulwark around the village, cut down the trees in the orchard, and used them to keep themselves safe, for they were afraid of the enemy and the Ulmer cavalry.

The twelfth day of June I returned with my wife and my small children to the city. After sunset at eight o'clock I went out from Neenstetten, and in the morning, around five o'clock, I was still not yet to the city with my little embassy, so that the entire night I traveled through hedges and shrubs, over hills and valleys, over thorns and debris, through crops and over ditches, so that I thought I would never reach Ulm. This was the most unpleasant trip I have ever taken from my youth until today.[130] This was the fifth flight.

And as I, during this night of my horrible trip, came near to Beimerstetten, hardly the length of a field away, I saw that the town was full of soldiers and watch fires. Then suddenly a great explosion went off, which greatly startled me and all who were with me, and there was a great brightness, as if it were day. Then we were afraid that the cavalry would seize us and beat us badly.

The twentieth day of June the hamlet of Breitingen was burned. The twenty-first day the pretty and well-built town Altheim in the land of Ulm was burned and put to ashes, so that nothing more remained than two houses, three barns, and the church. There had been more than one hundred and twenty houses there, but all of these were burned by the cavalry. . . .

129. They still had three surviving children: Chatreina, Johannes, and Barbara.

130. Neenstetten was almost twelve miles north of Ulm. What Heberle calls, with some irony, his "little embassy" would have included his wife, children, and whatever livestock and possessions they could manage.

The seventeenth day of July our gracious and commanding lords came home to Ulm and brought with them good news: a peace agreement was accepted by the emperor and Royal Majesty.[131]

Then straightaway, the 19th of July, on Sunday after the sermon, all the bells were tolled together and salvos or shots of joy were fired from great cannons around the entire city and from every bastion.

The twenty-fifth day of July, on St. James' Day, I, with wife and children, moved again from the city to home, as did the entire countryside, after the miserable blockade that we had endured for so long, from Easter until St. James' Day, camped in the city on top of each other, enduring hunger and grief, and to such an extent that I will forbear to write of it, since it would take me far too long to tell. . . .

The twenty-fifth day of August my sister Chatreina died, in the morning between five and six o'clock. May God the Almighty grant her and all of us on Judgment Day a joyful resurrection and eternal life. Amen.

The seventh day of September my first-born child Chatreina blessedly passed on in the Lord. Her age was seven years and fifteen days. May God the most high, who has everything in His hand, who creates mankind and kills them and makes them living again, grant her along with all of us on Judgment Day a joyful resurrection and eternal life.

The 22nd of September my most beloved son Johannes blessedly passed on in the Lord.[132] His age was five years, forty weeks, five days. May God the Almighty grant him and us all on Judgment Day a joyful resurrection and eternal life. Amen. . . .

The twenty-eighth day of October, on the day of Sts. Simon and Jude, we from Neenstetten and Weidenstetten had a huge number of infantry march through, up to a thousand men, who did us great damage with robbing and plundering.

The eleventh day of November many Spanish soldiers fell upon the land, cavalry and dragoons, and they plundered the land almost completely. . . .

Then out of the inflation and famine there arose a misery above all misery, namely a dying-out and pestilence, so that many thousands of people were brought down by famine, war, and pestilence. And because of this famine, many hideous and loathsome things were eaten by the poor people, namely all kinds of things that did not make sense—dogs and cats, mice and dead livestock, horsemeat—so that the knacker and butcher got their meat from dead livestock, such as horse, dog, and other animals, and people scrambled with each other for it and considered it to be delicious.

131. This was news of Ulm's inclusion into the Peace of Prague, made between the elector of Saxony and the emperor on May 30, 1635. See Document 24.

132. Johannes was Heberle's first-born son.

All kinds of weeds from the open country were also considered good: this-
tle, nettle, water hemlock, buttercup, schmerbel, and schertele.[133] In sum,
all kinds of weeds became good, for hunger is a good cook, as one says in
the proverb. Through this hunger, a great dying-out and pestilence arose, so
that many thousands of people died. Then Doctor Conrad Dieterich[134] of
Ulm wrote in his New Year's sermon for the year 1635 that at Ulm more than
fifteen thousand people had died and been carried out of the city. Among
them were 5,672 poor and beggars, 4,033 country people and foreigners,
and 168 foundlings. On many days, 150, 160, or even a maximum of 170
were carried out. Is this not a miserable thing? Yes, I believe it to be a misery above all miseries, and I did not only hear it told, rather I saw and heard
it myself with my own eyes and ears. . . .

1636

In the year of our Lord 1636, the 29th of January I sold a mittle[135] of rye
for 3 fl. 15 kr.[136] at Ulm. The eighth day of February many imperial troops
and cavalry came to the region of Geislingen again. The 11th of February
many imperial troops and cavalry came to the district of Albeck. They almost completely plundered the land and took all tin and copper. No one
had any quiet or peace, so that everyone had to flee and retreat to Ulm on
account of the robbery and famine. This was the sixth flight. . . .

The 14th of March everyone returned home from Ulm. And the lords of
Ulm, our most gracious government, gave the country people grain to seed,
oats and barley. For the country people had become so poor that the land
would have had to lay waste if our lords had not helped. . . .

In the month of April a lot of grain came by water on the Danube, wheat
and rye, so that—God be praised and thanked—there was no shortage of
grain and bread for those who had money. . . .

The eighteenth day of October I sold my house at Weidenstetten for 300
fl., which I bought in the year 1627 for 740 fl.[137] . . .

In those days, because things had gone so miserably and there were practically no horses or livestock, also the fields lay still and waste; the Heidhof
and Zimmerlau forests grew together into an area that, in my time, had all

133. All various types of wild plants.
134. Conrad Dieterich was the ecclesiastical superintendent of Ulm.
135. A unit of measurement equaling about forty-four pounds.
136. There were about sixty *kreuzer* (kr.) to a *gulden* (fl.).
137. Despite steady inflation, large population losses and economic uncertainty
hurt property values. His house may also have suffered some damage over the years.

been open land. Then it had been a common field, on which I myself had harvested crops. Now it has become a forest, so that whoever wants to go to Bernstadt now has to go through a forest that did not exist previously. . . .

1637

The 13th of February [the enemy] spent the entire day robbing and plundering whatever they could get here at Neenstetten.[138] There were only six cows in the entire town, and of these they brought from there and took away four, and the other two were taken and stabbed to death. No one was spared by them, and they even took the shoes off my feet. . . .

1638

This week, the 7th of April, I retreated to the city once again with wife and child. This was the tenth flight. . . .

Today, the 23rd of April, we all fled again to Ulm. For from Lauingen came many wagons and cannons, and then they advanced on the thirtieth day of April, numbering more than one hundred. This was the eleventh flight.

The third day of May, thirty ox-pulled wagons again advanced. On the 5th of May, three companies of Croats[139] came to Langenau, were there for one day, and then came to Weidenstetten and stayed there for two days, spoiling the seeds badly.

The tenth day of May, in Easter week, we found ripe strawberries and put them up for sale. The twenty-seventh day of May, during great warfare, my daughter Chatrina was born into the world, in the early morning between four and five o'clock on a Sunday, and baptized the following Monday—my sixth child.[140]

An unquiet May with warfare, so that no one could live on the land with either horse or livestock.

The fifth day of June everyone, with horse and livestock, wife and child, once again moved out of the city and returned home with great joy. For until now we had spent the entire spring with each other in the city, and each one gave up his poor belongings. We would have been able to get over all of this, if only we could have sowed the summer grains. For neither oats nor peas were sowed before this time, when it was already too late. This was the twelfth flight. . . .

138. Imperial troops under the command of Ottavio Piccolomini.

139. The Croatian companies were part of the imperial armies.

140. Chatrina was Heberle's sixth child, but only one other, Barbara, was still alive at this time.

1639

Since all trades (the farmer with his field and wagon, the smith, wagon builder, cobbler, tailor, and, in sum, all sorts of craftsmen and tradesmen, whatever they might be called) were of high worth, so that it has become difficult to pay for things, the government considered solutions and ways to stop this disaster. Thus a value was fixed upon everything by an honorable councilor at Ulm, everyone to his worth. But this helped little, for solutions come from God only when it pleases Him and when He thinks it good. This happened on the seventh day of April. . . .

1640

In the beginning of this year, since we have a little quiet and peace from the war, practically our greatest work this winter is hunting wolves. For during the warfare many wolves came to our land. For, as punishment, God sent us evil animals into the land to devour our sheep and cattle.

Before the war, it was a wonder if one saw a wolf; but now and in these years, it is not unusual for us to have seen many together, for they run everywhere, young and old. They run among the livestock, even when two or three men are with the livestock, and take from the herd nanny goats and sheep. And they do not allow themselves to be taken, even if one goes after them with full force. Yes, they even come into the villages and in front of the houses and take cats and dogs away, so that one can no longer have any dogs in the villages. . . .

1642

The 29th of December the cavalry of Mercy[141] moved out of the land and took with them as prisoner the squire of Langenau.[142] We then had to ransom this same squire with a sum of money. For everything gets put onto the peasantry. It benefits all of them that we are only peasants.

1643

In the year 1643 . . . the Swedes went to Kinzigtal[143] and sat there. The Bavarians, however, went again to their military quarters in Tübingen. By

141. Franz von Mercy, Bavarian field marshal. He had brought two regiments of troops to Ulm to try to find winter quarters, but since the entire territory of Ulm was already filled with other Bavarian troops, he was forced to leave again.

142. Carl Ludwig Besserer, the mayor of Langenau.

143. A valley in the Black Forest that the Swedish army was using as its winter military quarters.

this march, the duchy of Württemberg and the domain of Ulm suffered as much damage as had ever happened during the entire war. Whereby not only the people made great complaints, but also the cities, villages, towns, houses, open country, fields, trees, and vineyards. Yes, the livestock themselves, if they could speak of it, would have witnessed, told, and complained of it, which the miraculous signs alone sufficiently indicated to me.

The 20th of February it rained blood various times near Stuttgart in the village of Vaihingen an der Enz. But also in the city of Stuttgart itself clumps of blood were found in a porridge and were seen by many people and spoken about in public sermons. . . .

1646

Every day many wagons of military provisioners come to Ulm, as well as several thousand riders. They have bought out all types of bread, meat, and beer, as well as grain and other things, so that it has become quite expensive. Then they supply it to the Swedish and French armies who are in the upper area of Ulm, and there are very many troops.[144] . . .

Because so many stolen goods now come into the city of Ulm by way of soldiers, military provisioners, and troops, and are bought by the burghers and the peasants, the ministers have forcefully preached against it and have made an outcry from the pulpit. It has also been forbidden several times by the government, but this has helped little and it has not been stopped; rather everything is still being bought. . . .

1648

The fourteenth day of October the noble, golden, and long-desired imperial peace was concluded at Münster, where the potentates had been together for more than four years negotiating the peace.[145] . . .

The twelfth day of November, a Sunday, although the peace was now concluded and the troops were now supposed to be disbanded, we retreated again to the city of Ulm with wives and children, horses and livestock.[146] And at this very time, the countryside was instructed by an official from Ulm that on Monday, that is to say the thirteenth day of November, one should hold a festival of celebration and thanksgiving, and joyfully observe it with

144. In 1646 the city of Ulm became a popular trading center where the French and Swedish armies bought military provisions.

145. Heberle is using the old Julian calendar. By the modern Gregorian calendar, the Peace of Westphalia was concluded at the two cities of Münster and Osnabrück on October 24, 1648. It took weeks for the news to reach Ulm. See Document 36.

146. They were fleeing the passage of French troops through the countryside.

sermons, communions, and diligent prayers, which we did diligently and with great joy at Ulm during our flight. We celebrated the festival as formally and with such a will as ever we had Christmas Day, and God be praised and thanked, this time we even fled happily, since it was the last flight—the twenty-ninth or even the thirtieth or more—all of which one would have difficulty describing. We did these and even more, going time and again to each other in other towns. For often one village and hamlet fled to another. There were also many flights into the woods and forests, all of which one could not possibly write down.

In sum, it was such a miserable business that even a stone would have been moved to pity, not to mention a human heart. For we were hunted like wild animals in the forests. One was caught and beaten badly, a second clobbered and stabbed, a third even shot dead, and from another were stripped and taken his little piece of bread and clothing. Because of this we cannot sufficiently praise and laud God for the noble peace that we have lived to see. For what have we endured in those thirty flights that occurred to the city of Ulm alone! One occurred during the dark of night and a great storm, a second in snow and great cold, a third occurred in danger from soldiers, so that we often lost our poor belongings on the way, yes, even our life and limbs.

The twenty-eighth day of November, we, the entire countryside, returned home with every joy and moved back home and to our houses, which we tidied up and put back together, for they were, in part, badly smashed, and the windows, ovens, and doors were destroyed. . . .

FOR FURTHER READING

Albrecht, Dieter. *Maximilian I. von Bayern 1573–1651.* Munich: Oldenbourg Verlag, 1998.

Asch, Ronald. *The Thirty Years War: The Holy Roman Empire and Europe, 1618–48.* New York: St. Martin's Press, 1997.

Asche, Matthias, and Anton Schindling, eds. *Das Strafgericht Gottes: Kriegserfahrungen und Religion im Heiligen Römischen Reich Deutscher Nation im Zeitalter des Dreissigjährigen Krieges.* Münster: Aschendorff, 2001.

Barudio, Günter. *Der Teutsche Krieg, 1618–1648.* Frankfurt am Main: Fischer, 1985.

Bély, Lucien, and Isabelle Richefort, eds. *L'Europe des Traités de Westphalie: Esprit de la Diplomatie et Diplomatie de L'esprit.* Paris: Presses universitaires de France, 2000.

Benecke, Gerhard. *Society and Politics in Germany, 1500–1750.* London: Routledge & Kegan Paul, 1974.

Bireley, Robert. *The Jesuits and the Thirty Years War: Kings, Courts, and Confessors.* Cambridge: Cambridge University Press, 2003.

Black, Jeremy. *European Warfare, 1494–1660.* London: Routledge, 2002.

Burkhardt, Johannes. *Der Dreissigjährige Krieg.* Frankfurt am Main: Suhrkamp, 1992.

Bussmann, Klaus, and Heinz Schilling, eds. *1648, War and Peace in Europe.* 3 vols. Münster: Veranstaltungsgesellschaft 350 Jahre Westfälischer Friede, 1998.

Croxton, Derek. *Peacemaking in Early Modern Europe: Cardinal Mazarin and the Congress of Westphalia, 1643–1648.* London: Associated University Presses, 1999.

Dickmann, Fritz. *Der Westfälische Frieden.* 7th ed. Münster: Aschendorff Verlag, 1998.

Duchhardt, Heinz, ed. *Der Westfälische Friede: Diplomatie, politische Zäsur, kulturelles Umfeld, Rezeptionsgeschichte.* München: R. Oldenbourg Verlag, 1998.

Holborn, Hajo. *A History of Modern Germany.* New York: A. A. Knopf, 1959.

Hughes, Michael. *Early Modern Germany, 1477–1806.* Philadelphia: University of Pennsylvania Press, 1992.

Ingrao, Charles W. *The Habsburg Monarchy, 1618–1815.* 2nd ed. Cambridge: Cambridge University Press, 2000.

Krusenstjern, Benigna von, Hans Medick, and Patrice Veit, eds. *Zwischen Alltag und Katastrophe: Der dreissigjährige Krieg aus der Nähe.* Göttingen: Vandenhoeck & Ruprecht, 1999.

Langer, Herbert. *Kulturgeschichte des 30jährigen Krieges.* Stuttgart: Kohlhammer, 1978.

———. *Thirty Years' War.* New York: Hippocrene Books, 1980.

Lee, Stephen J. *The Thirty Years War.* London: Routledge, 1991.

Limm, Peter. *The Thirty Years War.* London: Longman, 1984.

Livet, Georges. *La Guerre de Trente ans.* Paris: Presses universitaires de France, 1994.

Lockhart, Paul Douglas. *Denmark in the Thirty Years' War, 1618–1648: King Christian IV and the Decline of the Oldenburg State.* Selinsgrove: Susquehanna University Press, 1996.

Maland, David. *Europe at War 1600–1650.* London: Macmillan, 1980.

Mortimer, Geoff. *Eyewitness Accounts of the Thirty Years War, 1618–48.* Houndmills, Basingstoke, Hampshire: Palgrave, 2002.

Pagès, Georges. *The Thirty Years War, 1618–1648.* New York: Harper, 1970.

Parker, Geoffrey. *The Military Revolution: Military Innovation and the Rise of the West, 1500–1800.* Cambridge: Cambridge University Press, 1988.

Parker, Geoffrey, and Simon Adams, eds. *The Thirty Years' War.* 2nd ed. London: Routledge, 1997.

Parrott, David. *Richelieu's Army: War, Government and Society in France, 1624–1642.* Cambridge Studies in Early Modern History. Cambridge: Cambridge University Press, 2001.

Polišenský, Josef V. *War and Society in Europe, 1618–1648.* Cambridge: Cambridge University Press, 1978.

Porshnev, B. F. *Muscovy and Sweden in the Thirty Years' War, 1630–1635.* Cambridge: Cambridge University Press, 1995.

Pursell, Brennan C. *The Winter King: Frederick V of the Palatinate and the Coming of the Thirty Years' War.* Aldershot, Hants, England: Ashgate, 2003.

Rabb, Theodore K. *The Thirty Years' War.* 2nd ed. Lexington, MA: Heath, 1972.

Repgen, Konrad, and Elisabeth Müller-Luckner, eds. *Krieg und Politik, 1618–1648: Europäische Probleme und Perspektiven.* München: R. Oldenbourg, 1988.

Ritter, Moritz. *Deutsche Geschichte im Zeitalter der Gegenreformation und des dreissigjährigen Krieges (1555–1648).* Darmstadt: Wissenschaftliche Buchgesellschaft, 1962.

Roberts, Michael. *Gustavus Adolphus.* 2nd ed. London: Longman, 1992.

Schilling, Heinz. *Aufbruch und Krise: Deutschland, 1517–1648.* Das Reich und die Deutschen. Berlin: Siedler, 1988.

Schmidt, Georg. *Der Dreissigjährige Krieg.* München: Beck, 2002.

Sonnino, Paul. *Mazarin's Quest: The Congress of Westphalia and the Coming of the Fronde.* Cambridge, MA: Harvard University Press, 2009.

Sreenivasan, Govind P. *The Peasants of Ottobeuren, 1487–1726: A Rural Society in Early Modern Europe.* Cambridge: Cambridge University Press, 2004.

Steinberg, S. H. *The Thirty Years' War and the Conflict for European Hegemony 1600–1660.* New York: Norton, 1966.

Theibault, John. *German Villages in Crisis: Rural Life in Hesse-Kassel and the Thirty Years' War, 1580–1720.* Atlantic Highlands, NJ: Humanities Press, 1995.

Trevor-Roper, H. R. *The Crisis of the Seventeenth Century: Religion, the Reformation, and Social Change.* New York: Harper, 1968.

Wedgwood, C. V. *The Thirty Years War.* Gloucester, MA: P. Smith, 1967.

Wilson, Peter H. *From Reich to Revolution: German History, 1558–1806.* New York: Palgrave Macmillan, 2004.

Worthington, David. *Scots in the Habsburg Service, 1618–1648.* Leiden: Brill, 2004.

INDEX

Alsace, xvii, 3, 12, 91, 161, 162, 164,
238, 239, 242, 253, 273, 290, 292
Amalia Elisabeth of Hesse-Cassel, xiii,
xxi, 157–9, 161, 162, 190, 191,
198–200, 202, 203, 213, 215–27,
235, 243, 253, 269
Angoulême, Charles de Valois,
duke d', 8, 47
Anne of Austria, 161, 218, 219, 222,
224, 225
Arnim-Boitzenburg, Hans Georg
von, 76, 115, 138, 145, 148
Augsburg, 163, 178, 179, 207, 254,
258–60, 286, 288, 311; 1555
Peace of, xiv, xv, 45, 47, 69, 91–8,
119, 123, 142, 144, 154, 167–9,
235, 254, 258, 260, 261, 265;
Confession, xiv, xv, 2, 20, 66, 70,
91, 93–8, 108, 119, 123, 166–74,
258–65, 311 (see also Luther,
Martin; Lutherans)
Austria, Upper and Lower, ix, 3, 5, 9,
11, 16, 42, 68, 82–6, 146, 169,
215, 219, 233, 234, 238, 256,
262, 277, 283, 303, 305; estates
of, xii, 5, 35, 82; rebellious
peasants of, 68, 82–6
Avaux, Claude de Mesmes, count d',
218, 241, 271

Baden-Baden, 280, 294
Baden-Durlach, 12, 289, 294;
margraves of, 12, 154, 174, 176
Bailleul, Nicolas de, 217
Baltic Sea, xvii, 101–3, 155, 268,
276; coastal cities and territories
of, 69, 71, 75, 86, 101–3, 105,
155, 237, 281; trade and control
of, 67, 69, 70, 101–3 (see also
Pomerania; Stralsund)
Banér, Johan, 114, 159, 160, 205–7,
296

Barwälde, Treaty of, 71
Basel, 265, 273 (see also Switzerland)
Bavaria and Bavarians, ix, 11, 13, 49,
51–4, 68, 73, 76, 77, 82, 84, 86,
160–63, 171, 187, 190, 194,
204–12, 249–52, 280, 284–6,
288, 289, 291, 292, 296, 300,
301, 314, 322 (see also Maximilian
I of Bavaria)
Bernard of Saxe-Weimar, 52, 76,
145–9, 154, 155, 157, 158, 174,
176, 203, 208, 288, 289, 294,
299, 314, 315
Bohemia and Bohemians, xi, xii, xvii,
1–12, 20–46, 48–58, 60, 67, 68,
73, 75, 76, 78, 79, 120, 145, 147,
157, 162, 169, 171, 172, 174, 178,
207, 219, 234, 237, 257, 264, 297,
303, 305; Bohemian Confession, 2,
20, 21; king of (see Ferdinand II;
Ferdinand of Hungary; Frederick
V; Maximilian I, Holy Roman
Emperor); Letter of Majesty of, 2,
3, 9, 17, 18, 21–30, 33, 36, 40, 45;
queen of (see Elizabeth Stuart);
rebellious estates of, xiii, xvi, xvii,
1–11, 14–30, 34–44, 50–55, 82,
88, 92, 178, 228
Brandenburg, 6, 91, 105, 121, 135,
141, 142, 156, 159, 257; elector
of (see Frederick William; John
George)
Brandenburg-Ansbach, 268, 295,
304 (see also Joachim Ernst)
Breisach, 157, 162, 238, 272, 273, 299
Breitenfeld, 73, 113, 118, 160, 209, 284
Bremen, 67, 91, 101, 105, 153, 169,
237, 238, 268, 270
Brunswick-Lüneburg, 105, 112,
262, 280, 303 (see also Christian of
Brunswick; George of Brunswick-
Lüneburg)

Bucquoy, Charles Bonaventure de
Longueval, count of, 5, 9, 49, 50,
51, 52
Burgundy, 78, 241, 242, 248

Calvin, John, and Calvinism, xv, xvi,
xxii, 1, 2, 20, 70, 91, 104, 118,
119, 123, 138, 142, 143, 154,
158, 164, 169, 191, 193, 195,
196, 198, 200, 235, 254, 265, 272
Catalonia, xi, 158, 228, 239, 241,
242, 244, 245, 247, 248
Catholic League, 7–9, 46–9, 56, 71,
108, 118, 123, 139, 143, 275–6,
278, 280, 304, 313
Charles IV, duke of Lorraine, 172,
173, 220, 284, 291, 298
Charles V, Holy Roman Emperor, xiv,
1, 2, 97, 220, 243, 311
Chemnitz, Bogislav Philipp von, xii,
193
Christian von Anhalt-Bernburg, 9,
49, 51–3
Christian of Brunswick, 12, 13, 61,
62, 68, 79
Christian IV of Denmark-Norway,
xiii, 6, 13, 67–70, 77–82, 86, 90,
99, 161, 162, 169, 178, 204, 219,
228, 307
Christina of Sweden, 219, 237, 254,
255, 263, 267, 270, 272
Cologne, archbishopric of, 183, 186,
219, 257, 269; archbishop of, xi,
121 (see also Ferdinand of Bavaria)
Croatia and Croatians, 39, 85, 91,
108, 114, 115, 147, 184, 189, 321

Danube River, 43, 82, 85, 159, 189,
205, 206, 275, 279, 285, 286,
288, 295, 304, 305, 314, 320
Denmark and Danes, x, xvi, 67, 69,
80, 81, 86, 90, 153, 161, 217, 219
Donauwörth, 76, 209, 285, 288,
295, 296, 313
Dutch Republic and the Dutch,
ix–xi, xiv, 2, 3, 9, 12, 13, 63, 67,
69, 77, 81, 117, 124, 163,

180–82, 217–21, 223, 224,
241–4, 278

East Frisia, 157, 193, 198, 199, 203
Eberhard III of Württemberg, 154,
174, 176, 178, 310–12
Ecclesiastical Reservation, xiv, xv, 91,
95, 96, 144, 235, 254, 260
Edict of Restitution, xv, 69, 72,
91–8, 118, 119, 138, 144, 153,
158, 165, 178, 254, 310, 311
Elbe River, xx, 80, 105, 107, 108,
111, 283
Elizabeth Stuart, 37, 180, 181, 188
England, x, 243, 244; king of (see
James I)

Ferdinand, cardinal-infante of Spain,
76, 149
Ferdinand II, xv, xvi, 2–9, 11, 13, 35,
39–46, 67–72, 75–82, 87–99, 101,
104, 107, 119, 121, 123, 139,
144–6, 148, 151, 153–5, 157,
165–80, 189–95, 227, 254, 271,
303–5, 307, 308, 310, 311, 319
Ferdinand of Bavaria, elector of
Cologne, 6, 60–63, 78, 160, 221
Ferdinand of Hungary, later
Ferdinand III, Holy Roman
Emperor, 76, 145, 149, 154,
157–65, 175, 189, 198, 201–3,
205–7, 212–15, 218–21, 227–30,
233–41, 244, 245, 247–9, 254–7,
262, 263, 265, 267–9, 271, 272,
314, 316
Flanders, 9, 49, 243, 244, 245, 246,
293
France and French, ix, x, xi, xvi, xviii,
67, 75, 77, 108, 150–55, 160, 164,
198, 203, 208, 212, 213, 215–26,
233, 237–9, 241–9, 253, 254,
271–3, 276, 290, 292–4, 299, 304,
323; king of (see Louis XIII; Louis
XIV); relations and alliance with
Sweden, 71, 73, 75, 155, 157, 210,
211, 137, 198, 203, 213, 249, 323
(see also Hamburg, 1638 Treaty of;

Wismar, 1636 Treaty of); queen of (*see* Anne of Austria); rivalry with Habsburgs, x, 67, 70, 77, 151, 152, 155, 163, 244–9

Franconia, 75, 77, 91, 137, 163, 249, 269, 270, 284

Frankfurt am Main, 186, 270, 280, 281; 1619 electoral diet of, 6, 42; 1643–1645 deputations diet of, 159–62, 212–16, 265

Frederick V of the Palatinate, 5–9, 11–13, 31–9, 43, 44, 46, 48, 49, 53, 60, 61, 63, 65, 67, 68, 70, 79–81, 121, 154, 165, 170, 171, 174, 176, 180, 186, 188, 253, 256

Frederick Henry, 181, 223, 243, 244

Frederick William of Brandenburg, 159, 161, 181, 213, 237, 253, 268, 269, 280, 281, 303

Friedrich V of Baden-Durlach, 154, 174, 176

Gábor, Bethlen, 6–8, 43, 68, 86, 88, 227

Gallas, Matthias, 145, 157, 161–63, 219, 291

George II of Hesse-Darmstadt, xvi, 118, 123, 138, 142, 149, 156, 191, 193–5

George of Brunswick-Lüneburg, 158, 205, 262

George William of Brandenburg, xi, xv, 31, 71, 72, 75, 105, 154, 159, 173

Götz, Johann, count of, 157, 162, 295

Graubünden, 276–8

Guébriant, Jean-Baptiste Budes, 205, 211

Gustavus Adolphus, xiii, 67, 70–76, 98–108, 110, 112, 113, 115, 117–19, 124–37, 144, 149, 150, 160, 172, 174, 186, 188, 192, 228, 254, 284, 285

Habsburgs, ix, x, xiv, xv, 2, 67, 70, 138, 151, 155, 163, 244, 279; Austrian, x, xvi, 2, 6, 7, 43, 48, 63, 77, 88, 104, 151, 159, 161, 165, 208, 215, 227, 229, 236, 239, 244, 248, 255, 257, 263, 272, 273 (*see also* Ferdinand II; Ferdinand of Bavaria; Matthias); hereditary lands of, 2, 3, 5, 8, 9, 11, 39, 41–4, 46, 48, 60, 68, 76, 82, 84, 87, 104, 105, 155, 160–62, 165, 169, 171, 219, 233, 234, 238, 253, 254 (*see also* Austria; Bohemia; Croatia; Hungary; Silesia); rivalry with French (*see* France, rivalry with Habsburgs); Spanish, x, xv, 2, 6, 63, 67, 124, 163, 239, 244 (*see also* Ferdinand, cardinal-infante of Spain; Philip III; Philip IV; Spain)

Hague, The, 180, 203, 217, 218, 220, 224, 227; 1625 Hague Alliance, 67, 81

Halberstadt, 12, 61, 67–9, 91, 153, 169, 207, 237, 268, 269, 283, 284

Hamburg, 1638 Treaty of, 157

Hatzfeld, Melchior, 218, 221, 223, 225

Heidelberg, x, 13, 31, 257, 289, 303

Heilbronn League, 75, 76, 119, 137

Hesse-Cassel and Hessians, xv, xxii, 157, 158, 162, 163, 186, 190–203, 216–27, 235, 236, 253, 278; landgrave of (*see* Moritz; Wilhelm V); landgravine of (*see* Amalia Elisabeth)

Hesse-Darmstadt, 149, 150, 236, 300; landgrave of (*see* George II)

Hoë von Hoënegg, Matthias, xxi, 137–44

Horn, Gustav Karlsson, 76, 105, 114, 115, 117, 148, 208, 289, 314, 315

Hungary and Hungarians, ix, 3, 7, 8, 34, 43, 46, 50, 52, 86, 88, 89, 98, 108, 161, 227–30, 234 (*see also* Ferdinand II; Ferdinand of Hungary)

Hus, Jan, and Hussites and Utraquists, 1, 2, 4, 14, 15, 20, 23

Imperial court system, 123, 153, 154, 160; Aulic Council, xvi, 87, 121, 123, 168, 170, 171, 235, 255; Chamber Court, xvi, 96, 121, 123, 168, 170, 235, 264, 265

Ingolstadt, 160, 205, 206, 209, 249, 285, 296, 297

Italy and Italians, ix, 3, 9, 84, 108, 244, 245, 275–9

James I of England, 6, 8, 37, 82, 105, 178, 180, 236, 246

Joachim Ernst of Brandenburg-Ansbach, 8, 46–9, 188, 304

John George of Saxony, xi, xv, 6–9, 31, 63–7, 71, 72, 75–7, 105, 113–17, 137–44, 151, 153, 155, 160, 165, 166, 169–79, 216, 253, 305, 319

Karl Ludwig, 253, 256, 257

Kipper and Wipper period, 12, 58–60, 68, 190, 304–7, 319

Krosigk, Adolf Wilhelm von, 212, 213, 217, 218, 220, 224, 227

Langenau, 275, 276, 288, 295, 306, 308, 309, 313, 314, 321, 322

Leipzig, 73, 75, 113, 116, 160, 209, 270, 284, 285, 311; 1631 colloquy of, 71, 72, 119

Leopold Wilhelm, archduke of Austria, 160, 169, 206, 233, 240, 290

Linz, 83–5, 146, 233, 240

Longueville, Prince Henri d'Orleans, duke de, 241, 271

Lorraine, 155, 242, 290, 292

Louis XIII, xiii, 47, 82, 137, 151, 291

Louis XIV, 218, 243, 244, 246, 248, 255, 271–3

Lusatia, Upper and Lower, 1, 8, 9, 28, 31, 35, 153, 170, 219

Luther, Martin, xiv, 1, 83, 195

Lutherans and Lutheranism, xiv–xvi, xxii, 2, 8, 20, 66, 67, 70–73, 77, 82, 84, 90, 91, 96, 99, 108, 118, 119, 137, 138, 143, 158, 164, 166, 167, 169, 170, 176, 178,

186, 191, 193, 195, 235, 258, 274, 301, 305, 310, 311 (see also Augsburg, Confession)

Magdeburg, 68, 69, 91, 105, 168, 169, 238, 268, 269, 276, 284; sack of, xx, 72, 73, 107–13, 282, 283

Mainz, archbishopric of, 73, 118, 149, 156, 183, 185, 186, 201, 203, 236, 269; elector of, xi, 6, 63, 78, 121, 158, 160, 198, 199, 201, 202, 216, 235, 257

Mansfeld, Ernst, count von, 5, 7, 12, 13, 56, 68, 79, 82, 284

Marburg, 118, 123, 157, 162, 190, 198, 199, 201, 202, 212, 236

Maria Anna of Austria, 207, 211

Martinitz, Jaroslav Borsita von, 4, 14, 15, 17–19, 29

Matthias, Holy Roman Emperor, 2–6, 15, 16, 21, 23, 24, 26–8, 35, 40, 41, 84, 137, 145, 157, 219, 291

Maximilian I, duke, later elector, of Bavaria, xiii, xv, xviii, 7–9, 13, 46–56, 61, 63, 67, 68, 78, 80, 82–5, 118, 121, 153, 155, 160, 163, 165, 171, 205–7, 209–11, 220, 221, 236, 238, 247, 249, 253, 256, 257, 304, 308; Wilhelmine line, 117, 256, 257

Maximilian I, Holy Roman Emperor, 34, 93

Mazarin, Jules, 161–3, 217, 218, 220, 224, 227, 241–9

Mecklenburg, 69, 71, 101, 106, 107, 155, 177, 238, 303

Melander, Peter, count of Holzappel, 115, 163, 202, 278

Moravia and Moravians, 1, 5, 28, 31, 35, 42, 43, 68, 73, 86–8, 234, 303, 305

Moritz of Hesse-Cassel, 123, 192, 194, 195

Munich, 73, 160, 206–9, 211, 249, 285, 286, 302; Treaty of, 8, 13

Münster, bishopric and city of, 61,

160, 269, 270, 273; Peace of, 163; as site of Westphalian negotiations, 164, 212, 213, 215, 216, 233, 241, 247, 252, 255, 256, 271, 323

Neuburg, 285; count of, 77, 78, 183
Nördlingen, battle of, 76, 77, 148, 149, 151, 155, 178, 208, 288, 289, 315, 316; city of, 296, 300; second battle of, 162
Nuremberg, 71, 188, 249, 270, 288

Oñate Treaty, 2
Osnabrück, as site of Westphalian negotiations, 160, 164, 212, 215, 233, 252, 253, 255, 256, 271, 323
Ottoman Empire and Turks, xi, 34, 43, 44, 62, 76, 80, 86–8, 92, 106, 150, 195, 210
Oxenstierna, Axel Gustafsson, 75, 99, 103, 105, 151, 161, 177, 255

Palatinate, 8, 9, 12, 48, 67, 68, 234, 236, 295; Rhenish or Electoral or Lower, xi, xv, 5, 9, 11–13, 31, 46, 61, 73–5, 121, 137, 162, 165, 171, 173, 185, 218, 236, 257, 269, 270, 289, 292; Upper, 5, 12, 31, 37, 73, 165, 171, 188, 205, 206, 236, 253, 256, 269, 270, 297 (*see also* Frederick V; Karl Ludwig; Wolfgang Wilhelm)
Pappenheim, Gottfried Heinrich, count zu, 68, 83, 108–10, 117, 275, 278, 280, 281, 284, 299, 306
Passau, 1552 Peace of, xiv, 91, 93, 94, 96, 97, 119, 120, 167, 169, 258, 260
Philip II, 2
Philip III, 2, 8, 76
Philip IV, 63, 81, 90, 158, 239, 241, 245, 248, 255, 257, 278, 279
Piccolomini, Prince Octavio, 148, 160, 163, 206, 321
Pilsen, 56, 57, 147, 148
Poland-Lithuania, x, 70, 100; conflict with Sweden (*see* Sweden); king of (*see* Sigismund III)

Pomerania, xviii, 70, 71, 75, 101, 106, 107, 136, 154, 155, 164, 173, 237, 253, 268, 276, 281, 303
Portugal, xi, 158, 228, 239, 248
Prague, xvii, 2, 4, 6, 9, 14, 20, 21, 23–7, 29–31, 37, 38, 41, 49–51, 53–5, 68, 73, 162, 176, 180, 220; 1635 Peace of, xi, 153–5, 158, 159, 162, 165–77, 198, 205, 216, 234, 319; Defenestration of, xvii, 4, 5, 14–20, 27, 29, 303
Protestant Union, 6, 8, 9, 12, 46–9, 304

Rákóczi, György, xiii, 161, 162, 220, 227–32
Rantzau, Josias, 161, 211, 212
Regensburg, 76, 145, 285, 287, 288, 314; imperial diets at, 13, 63, 71, 158, 159, 188, 189, 204–7
Rhine River, xvi, 9, 67, 73, 76, 150, 155–7, 161, 162, 164, 181–6, 212, 216, 221, 238, 242, 244, 249, 276–8, 280, 292, 294, 295
Richelieu, Armand du Plessis, cardinal de, xvi, 70, 151, 161, 244, 246
Rottweil, 295, 299; 1643 battle of, 161, 211, 212, 298

Salvius, Johan Adler, 99, 105, 255
Saxony and Saxons, xii, 11, 57, 73, 75–7, 91, 113, 117, 145, 155, 156, 160, 162, 237, 269, 284; Lower Saxon Circle, 8, 13, 67, 68, 77–9, 204, 269, 270; Upper Saxon Circle, 270 (*see also* Bernard; John George)
Scotland and Scots, 6, 37, 75, 105, 113, 135, 146, 314
Servien, Abel, 218, 241, 272
Sigismund III, 69, 87, 89, 90, 100, 101, 219
Silesia and Silesians, 1, 5, 9, 28, 35, 53, 68, 76, 105, 157, 170, 172, 178, 179, 234, 262, 263, 303
Slawata, Wilhelm, 4, 15, 17–19, 29

Spain and Spanish, xiv, 2, 9, 12, 13,
     50, 61, 69, 76, 77, 108, 124, 149,
     151, 153, 155, 160, 161, 163, 164,
     179, 181, 182, 185, 217, 220, 223,
     228, 239, 241–9, 278, 288, 289,
     292–4, 319; Spanish Netherlands,
     xvi, 2, 61, 163, 239, 241–8, 278
Spinola, Ambrogio, 9, 12
Stralsund, 69, 99–103, 177, 237, 281
Strassburg, 273, 280, 289, 298
Stuttgart, 289, 290, 302, 323
Swabia, 75, 77, 91, 137, 210, 211,
     216, 238, 269, 270, 301
Sweden and Swedes, xvi, xviii, 69–73,
     75, 76, 90, 98, 99, 101–6, 110,
     113, 117, 124–7, 134–7, 145,
     148–51, 153–7, 159–64, 173,
     176–9, 181, 187, 189, 198, 203,
     204, 206, 209, 213–21, 249,
     253–5, 267–9, 270, 272, 275,
     283–9, 296, 314–16, 322, 323;
     conflict with Poland, x, 70, 89, 90,
     100–102; relations with Denmark,
     x, 67, 161, 216, 217, 219, 221,
     223, 228, 233, 237, 238; relations
     with France (see France); "The
     Swedish Drink," 150
Switzerland and Swiss, ix, 164, 253,
     265, 275, 277, 279, 295

Thurn, Heinrich Matthias, count
     von, 4, 7, 16–18, 27, 52, 53
Tilly, Johann Tserclaes, count of, 9,
     12, 13, 49–51, 53, 56, 67–9,
     71–3, 77, 79, 80, 107, 108,
     110–13, 117, 160, 284, 285, 313
Torstensson, Lennart, 160–63, 209,
     219
Translyvania, xi, 43, 86, 227–32;
     prince of (see Gábor, Bethlen;
     Rákóczi, György)
Trauttmansdorff, Maximilian, count
     von and zu, 162, 233, 235,
     238–40, 247, 248, 255, 271
Trier, archbishopric of, 184; elector,
     xi, 6, 78, 121, 155, 257

Tübingen, 290, 295, 299, 306, 322
Turenne, Henri de la Tour
     d'Auvergne, viscount de, 163,
     249, 299
Tuttlingen, 161, 162, 204, 211, 212,
     216, 217, 220
Tyrol, 3, 84, 238

Ulm, ix, xviii, xix, 46–8, 70, 73, 75,
     85, 154, 207, 270, 274, 275, 279,
     280, 288, 295, 302–24; 1620
     Treaty of, 9, 12, 46–9, 304; 1647
     Treaty of, 163
Usedom, 70, 98, 268

Verden, bishopric of, 67, 91, 219, 268
Vienna, 5, 17, 26, 27, 42, 43, 46, 98,
     146, 157, 160, 162

Wallenstein, Albrecht von, 11, 16,
     50, 60, 68–71, 73, 75–7, 80,
     86–9, 101, 118, 137, 144–8, 175
Wallonia and Walloon, 49, 52, 53, 108
Weidenstetten, 275, 276, 307–10,
     313, 315–17, 319–21
Werth, Johann von, 155, 157, 208,
     211, 212, 289, 291, 292, 294
Weser River, 105, 117, 173, 221, 223
Westphalia, 12, 61, 157, 160, 173,
     218, 222, 225, 233, 269, 270,
     280, 282; Congress of, xiv, xix,
     161–3, 212–16, 218, 233–40,
     252; Peace of, xiv, xvii, xix,
     252–73, 323, 324
Wilhelm V of Hesse-Cassel, xvi, 70,
     107, 118, 119, 123, 124, 142,
     154, 156, 157, 174, 176, 191–8
Wismar, 237, 268; 1636 Treaty of,
     155, 157
Witches and witchcraft, 126, 190,
     282
Wrangel, Karl Gustav, 163, 249
Württemberg, duchy of, 77, 210,
     211, 289, 290, 295, 296, 306,
     310, 311, 314, 316, 318, 323;
     duke of (see Eberhard III)
Würzburg, 73, 187, 284